The Early  of Frances Burney, 1868–1871
Volume I

The Early Diary of Frances Burney, 1868–1871
Volume I

WITH A SELECTION FROM HER CORRESPONDENCE AND FROM THE JOURNALS OF HER SISTERS SUSAN AND CHARLOTTE BURNEY

FRANCES BURNEY

COSIMO CLASSICS

NEW YORK

The Early Diary of Frances Burney, 1868–1871, Volume I: With a Selection from Her Correspondence and from the Journals of Her Sisters Susan and Charlotte Burney.
Originally published in 1889 by George Bell and Sons, London.
This edition published by Cosimo Classics in 2021.

Cover copyright © 2021 by Cosimo, Inc.
Cover image, portrait of Fanny Burney by Edward Francis Burney, 1785. Sourced from Wikimedia Commons, *https://commons.wikimedia.org/wiki/File:Frances_d%27Arblay_(%27Fanny_Burney%27)_by_Edward_Francisco_Burney.jpg*
Cover design by www.heatherkern.com.

ISBN: 978-1-64679-416-4

This edition is a replica of a rare classic. As such, it is possible that some of the text might be blurred or of reduced print quality. Thank you for your understanding, and we wish you a pleasant reading experience.

Cosimo aims to publish books that inspire, inform, and engage readers worldwide. We use innovative print-on-demand technology that enables books to be printed based on specific customer needs. This approach eliminates an artificial scarcity of publications and allows us to distribute books in the most efficient and environmentally sustainable manner.

Ordering Information:
Cosimo publications are available at online bookstores. They may also be purchased for educational, business, or promotional use:
Bulk orders: Special discounts are available on bulk orders for reading groups, organizations, businesses, and others.
Custom-label orders: We offer selected books with your customized cover or logo of choice.

For more information, contact us at www.cosimobooks.com.

A PREFACE

BY THE EDITOR.

This is believed to be the only published, perhaps the only existing, record of the life of an English girl, written by herself, in a century before that which is now in its wane. Such a portrayal of a young Englishwoman, and her times, would be interesting even if the girl had not been (as was this one) a born author, who lived among men and women more or less distinguished, herself became famous, and was admired by the admired, as well as praised by the common voice; whose brilliant reputation as a novelist was revived, some fifty years ago, by her fresh and still greater renown as a chronicler of English social and court-life, during many and marked years of the long reign of George the Third.

The novelist and the chronicler are shown in these still earlier diaries which are now for the first time published, as developing from year to year. Sketches revealing the future "character-monger"[1] alternate here with innocent, tender, and generous thoughts, and feelings of affection to kinsfolk and friends, more than commonly lasting, as well as warm; with traits of a disposition very mobile, but singularly steady; very lively, but very sweet; discreet, and considerate almost to moral precocity. The character of Frances Burney shows itself on every leaf of these journals, even as the story of her first youth tells itself as we turn them. They were the offspring of that real pleasure in writing, even in the mechani-

---
[1] Dr. Johnson.

cal part of it, which Richardson attributes to his heroine, "Clarissa," which he had felt himself; for it is not to be divined, but known. These journals gave Frances in old age, the delight which she had looked forward to receiving from them in her youth. No stronger proof of a clear conscience and a healthy mind could well be shown. In them there are erasures, there are long passages removed, and destroyed, but the context shows that the feelings of others, not her own, were to be considered and spared.

Two there were whose names prevail in these pages—her father, and her adopted father, Mr. Crisp, concerning whom she has left all standing which she wrote, early or late; nay, has added little ejaculations in their praise and honour.

It is following her, when we write first of them, who were first with her; of whom when she began to write she could not dream that one would live wholly, and the other mainly, through her writings.

"I love Burney: my heart goes out to meet him. . . . . Dr. Burney is a man for all the world to love. . . . It is but natural to love him. . . . I much question if there is, in the world, such another man as Dr. Burney." When Dr. Burney is named, such words as these of Dr. Johnson recur to us rather than the music which he composed, or the books that he wrote. We recall, too, the names of Admiral Burney, of the second Dr. Charles, and, above all, of Frances. If his reputation once gave lustre to theirs, his celebrity now ascends from that of his children. No list of his musical compositions is known to exist. His daughter admits that they were out of date even in her own day. No list of his many articles in the "Monthly Review," and the Cyclopædia of Abraham Rees, has ever been compiled; his "Tours" are less read than they might well be, and his "History of Music" has, in the very course and progress of Music, been superseded. The repute of his reputation survives. The concurrence of his contemporaries is on record that he was, "indeed, a most extraordinary man, . . . at home upon all subjects, and upon all so agreeable!—a wonderful man!"[1] His place in social life was unique, being due to what Dr. Johnson implied to be an almost unique blending of a happy temper of mind, an affectionate disposition, gentle and attractive manners (having dignity in reserve should it be needed), with a very active and versatile intellect, and considerable acquirements. The charm of character and of manners, the "vivacity and readiness of wit," which made him the man of the eighteenth century who gained and *kept* the greatest number of friends, can now be brought before us only by the warmth of the praise of those friends; and of the love (rising to enthusiasm) of his children, to which the diaries that follow bear continuous testimony. It is possible that his Memoirs of his own life and times would have interested many who would not even open one of the four quarto volumes of his "History of Music," or who would shun the technical (which is much the greater) part of his Tours of inquiry into the state of Music in the France, Italy, and Germany of 1770 and 1772.

It was his full purpose to leave such an account of his own long and varied life as might give a picture of nearly a century. He justly thought himself well fitted to write a book which might (as he said) "be read with avidity at the distance of some centuries, by antiquaries and lovers of anecdotes," although it would then have lost the poignancy of personality, which might "mortify and offend a few persons" of his own time. He justly wrote that "perhaps few have been better enabled to describe, from an actual survey, the manners and customs of the age in which they lived than myself; ascending from those of the most humble cottagers and lowest mechanics, to the first nobility and most elevated personages, with whom

---

[1] Arthur Murphy.

circumstances, situation, and accident, at different periods of my life, have rendered me familiar. Oppressed and laborious husbandmen; insolent and illiberal yeomanry; overgrown farmers; generous and hospitable merchants; men of business and men of pleasure; men of letters; men of science; artists; sportsmen and country 'squires; dissipated and extravagant voluptuaries; gamesters; ambassadors, statesmen, and even sovereign princes, I have had opportunities of examining in almost every point of view: all these it is my intention to display in their respective situations; and to delineate their virtues, vices, and apparent degrees of happiness and misery."

This was indeed a great promise made to future time, as Dr. Burney was born while George the First was not firm upon his throne, and lived until Buonaparte was a prisoner on board the "Bellerophon."[1] What might he not have told us had he been able to fulfil his plan, unchecked by engagements with pupils, and societies, musical, literary, and benevolent; by innumerable friends, and multitudinous invitations; by an old pledge to complete his "History of Music,"[2] and by an agreement made when he was seventy-five years old to furnish the musical articles for a new edition of the Cyclopædia of Chambers—" the shortest calculation for the termination of this work being" (as he wrote in 1801) "still ten years."[3] To fulfil this contract, he gave up writing for the "Monthly

---

[1] He was born in Raven Street, Shrewsbury, on the 12th of April, 1726, O.S., and died at Chelsea on the 12th of April, 1814, N.S., on the night of the general illumination after the first downfall of the first Napoleon.

[2] The prospectus of the "History of Music" was issued in 1770; the first volume was published in 1776; the second in 1782; and the third and fourth in 1789.

[3] We use Dr. Burney's own words when we speak of the first English Cyclopædia as the work of Chambers. "Ephraim Chambers,

Review," and laid aside his autobiography. The fragment which we have quoted, was written in 1782, and stood, without a page to follow it, until 1807, when Dr. Burney began to write his own life in earnest, at the age of eighty-one. At little less than the same age, his daughter Frances published that compilation from his twelve volumes of manuscript memoirs, his " countless, fathomless " mass of papers, and her own journals and letters,[1] which is known as the " Memoirs of Dr. Burney." In it she has indicated her reasons for suppressing his own narrative. They are more fully given in " quite a pamphlet" of a letter to her sister Esther, which was written in November, 1820.

It would fatigue the reader's fancy to follow her details of toil and disappointment. Of the twelve volumes, some were mere repetitions of others. " The dear, indefatigable author wrote frequently the whole of every *cahier* three times over himself," in small writing, with many abbreviations; and Frances (nervous in her turn) read some of the manuscript volumes in even four different copies lest her collation should

---

miscellaneous writer, b. at Kendal, probably about 1680; F.R.S., 6 Nov. 1729; d. at Islington, 15 May, 1740; *Cyclopædia*, 1728."—WOODWARD AND CATES' *Encyclopædia of Chronology*. According to the same authorities, Abraham Rees, a well-known Presbyterian pastor, successively tutor at Hoxton and Hackney, " edits Chambers' *Cyclopædia*, 1786," but in the edition to which Dr. Burney began to contribute in 1801, the name of Chambers was omitted. The Cyclopædia, which was published in parts, was not completed until 1820, five years before the death of Rees, who was born in 1743.

[1] The " Memoirs of Dr. Burney, arranged from his own Manuscripts, from Family Papers, and from Personal Recollections, by his daughter, Madame D'Arblay," were published in 1832, by Edward Moxon, in three 8vo. volumes. In 1820 it had been her intention to publish three 8vo. volumes of his Correspondence, after the Memoirs had appeared in print; but by 1832, this plan shrunk into that of adding a fourth volume of Letters to the three of Memoirs, and even this was never carried out.

be imperfect. She found the Memoirs to be the work, not of the father who wrote the "Tours," or the "History of Music," not even of the father whose spirits afterwards rallied so that he wrote "occasional essays" of better texture than the Memoirs, and very entertaining letters, some of which she has printed in his "Memoirs," but of a man dejected by the loss of his wife, of his "gentle Susan," and of many of his oldest friends; by the experience of one paralytic stroke, and the apprehension of another. Beginning with the thought that she "had nothing to do but to revise, and somewhat abridge," his narrative, her ultimate decision was to suppress all that he had written which would not maintain his literary "credit and fair fame."

She shrank "from a storm of disapprobation, if not invective, upon the editor[1] who, for a fortnight's quick profit from his former celebrity, had exhibited her faded father's faded talents." In the full conviction that he would have been his own expurgator had he not written in ill-health and seclusion, she at once destroyed all his manuscripts and papers which "could not have been spread, even in a general family review, without causing pain or mischief."[2] From the remainder, she chose such portions as resembled his manner of writing "when his memory was full and gay; ... *when he lived in the world.*" These amount to very few pages in the "Memoirs of Dr. Burney." After this long winnowing of his "voluminous piles of papers" and pocket-books, the rest of the book

---

[1] "His designed, wished, and bespoken editor."—*Mme. D'Arblay to her sister Esther*, Nov., 1820. Other quotations in the text are from the same unpublished letter.

[2] When a widower with six children, Dr. Burney married a widow with three, and two children were born of his second marriage; thus, it would have been marvellous had there not occurred some (however slight or gentle) friction, or conflict, of ways of thinking, feeling, and acting.

Preface.

appears to have been chiefly constructed from her own diaries, letters, and memory. She felt herself to be the guardian of her father's fame, and no more tender guardian could have been found, or fancied.

According to the bent of our readers, her decision to suppress, if not destroy, her father's autobiography, will be received with satisfied submission, or questioned, disapproved, nay, deplored.[1] "Invective" she did not escape at the time. Croker was lying in wait, and among his points of attack was that she had not suffered her father to tell his own tale, but had published her autobiography under the title of his Memoirs.

Her labour to prepare the book, none but herself could know. At the end of 1820 she had not even finished reading the correspondence of Dr. Burney, nor does she appear to have begun that looking through all her own diaries and letters which took place within the next ten years. In November, 1820, her anticipation was that "about three years' hard reading for myself will finally produce about three quarters of an hour's reading for my Lecturers."[2] Justification of the suppression of the mass of her father's papers she has left in abundance in that letter to her sister of sixteen quarto pages; at less length, but with even more strength, in her "Memoirs of Dr. Burney,"[3] she has pleaded justification. "All the juvenile voluminous MSS. (she writes to Esther) are filled with *literal* nurses' tales,—such as narrated by himself were truly

---

[1] Her words are, "All that I thought utterly irrelevant, or any way mischievous, I have committed to the flames; whatever admits of any doubt, or demands any enquiry, I have set apart;" but as she states that what she thought of value for biographical purposes was of "so little volume, compared with what" was "hopeless," there seems reason to think that not much was preserved.

[2] Here she thought first of the French word "*lecteurs*," then turned it into *lecturers*, instead of *readers*.

[3] See pages 382-3-4, 420-21, vol. iii., of the "Memoirs of Dr. Burney."

amusing, but on paper, and *read*, not *recited*, they are trivial to poverty, and dull to sleepiness." When he described his early life in London, she found him "giving his whole paper . . . to enormous long paragraphs, and endless folio pages, upon the city electioneering for organs, and concerts, and Stanley's rivalry, and Frasi, and local interests of the day." In " the various *cahiers* upon Norfolk and Lynn " there was " some more agreeable style of writing, but still upon people not generally known." " At last comes London; and then the great names begin to occur." . . . [Those of his correspondents, (most of whom where his friends), " Garrick, Diderot, Rousseau, Dr. Warton, Dr. JOHNSON,[1] Mr. Mason, Horace Walpole, Lord Mornington, Mr. Crisp, Mr. Greville, Lady Crewe, Mr. Bewley, Mr. Griffith, Mr. Cutler, Mrs. Le Noir, Lord Macartney, Lord Lonsdale, Duke of Portland, Mr. Canning, Mr. Windham, Mr. Wesley, Mr. La Trobe, Mr. Walker, Mr. Burke, Mr. Malone, Sir J. Reynolds, Mr. Seward, Kit Smart, Mrs. Piozzi."]—"Here I had the full expectation of detail, anecdote, description, and conversation, such as to manifest these characters in the brilliant light of their own fame, and to show our dear father the caressed, sought, honoured and admired friend of such a constellation; for such he was, and as much loved and esteemed as if he had been the universal patron of them all." Again she felt sore disappointment. For many years Dr. Burney had been too busy to do more than register in his pocket-books the first day of meeting each particular star of this constellation. He had trusted the rest (all besides the where, and the when) to a future time of leisure, which came only when his memory was impaired.

For his kind intentions towards them, antiquaries, at least,

---

[1] It was Madame D'Arblay's custom to write Dr. Johnson's name in large letters. "The brilliant light of their own fame" no longer manifests "the whole of this constellation." Some of the stars now need notes to explain their manner and degree of brightness.

Preface. xiii

will give Dr. Burney their gratitude. We believe that, in the end, Madame D'Arblay put it out of the power of any one to affirm, contest, or revise her judgement. Without blaming her, we incline to regret it. Even with the piteous picture before us of an aged Frances bending over boxes after boxes, and bags after bags, of papers, "wading, painfully, laboriously wading," through every note of appointment, or invitation, which her father had ever received, every pocket-book in which he had made entries,[1] and the twelve folio volumes of his autobiography, our provoked fancy teases us, by repeating that the aspect of the second fifty years of this century towards such records as lay before her is far from being that of the first fifty. Those "nursery-tales" might now be called Folk-lore; those accounts of obscure people in Lynn and Norfolk, materials for a narrative of the manners and customs of a town and county which, not long ago, had strongly marked ways of their own; and the trivial, or tedious, details of Dr. Burney's early days in the City of London, facts precious to those for whom he meant them,—that is, to lovers of anecdote, antiquaries, and even historians. The Memoirs of Dr. Burney are now rather consulted than read; but as the book is in the London Library, as well as in all permanent subscription-libraries and in many private libraries of its time, we need not draw much from it. Rather we would add to it a little

---

[1] The first leaf of what appears to have been Dr. Burney's pocket-book for 1791, has been preserved, owing to his daughter's having written some of her own Memoranda upon it.

Under "MEMORANDUMS, OBSERVATIONS, and *appointments*, in *January*, 1791," January 1, Saturday, Dr. Burney has entered—

"Miss Dillon Decr 14th 1790.   dine at
Lady Banks   14   Robson's.
Acct   begun June 5 of last year."

Under "Sunday 2—
Seward & fam^{ly} party,
Haydn arrives in England."

xiv ♦ *Preface.*

by quoting a few anecdotes from his own writings which his daughter overlooked, or did not copy because it could never have occurred to her how little his works would be read now, as compared with her own.

The Burney family waits for a genealogist and bibliographer. One ought to appear within it. Meantime, a family tradition brings it, with James I., from Scotland, in 1600. This might easily be the case with Dr. Burney's great-great-grandfather, as his grandfather, James Macburney, was born about 1653. He had an estate at Great Hanwood in Shropshire, and a house in Whitehall. He married a daughter of his Shropshire rector, Mr. Evance [Evans]. His eldest son, James (born at Hanwood in 1678), was a pupil of Dr. Busby at Westminster School, and of Dahl in painting.[1] When nineteen he married Rebecca Ellis, a girl of sixteen, who is said to have acted at Goodman's Fields Theatre.[2] Thereupon his father disinherited him, and himself married his own cook, whose son, Joseph, ran through the property.

James is said by Mme. D'Arblay to have possessed "neg-

---

[1] "Dahl, Michael, *painter*, b. at Stockholm, 1656. Visits England, 1678; Paris, 1679; Italy, 1680-3. Settles in England, 1688. D. in London, 1743."—WOODWARD AND CATES' *Encyclopædia of Chronology*, 1872. Dahl was a painter of portraits only. His own sovereigns, Christina, and Charles XI., of Sweden, sat to him, as did Queen Anne, Prince George of Denmark, and numbers of Englishmen and women of rank. Many of his portraits have been engraved. As he was of high repute, it would appear that James Burney (who afterwards became a portrait-painter) studied *seriously* with Dahl. That he was Dahl's pupil the Editor learned from some notes on the Burney family communicated to her by the owner of these manuscript diaries.

[2] This cannot be literally correct, as Goodman's Fields Theatre was not opened until 1728, long after the death of the first Mrs. Burney; but it may be explained if we suppose that the boy Burney married an actress in the company of Giffard, who, long afterwards (in 1729), succeeded Odell as manager of Goodman's Fields. Giffard was then an experienced manager, and became famous by bringing out Garrick.

ligent facility and dissipated ease." Her words bore a softer meaning in the last century than in this. James Macburney might now be called "clever all round," that is, he was agreeable, witty, an admirable dancer, and as good a player on the violin as a painter, but with much of that want of perseverance, and concentration of mind, that being "everything by turns, and nothing long," about him, which was the older meaning of the word "*dissipation.*" We know not when his wife died, leaving several children. Next he married Ann Cooper, a Shropshire young lady, not without money. Having nine children living out of fifteen (of the two marriages), he was at last forced to stick to some one way of earning money, and chose portrait-painting. He settled at Chester, leaving his last-born child, Charles (who was twin with a girl, Susannah), at nurse in the village of Condover, four miles from Shrewsbury. There, the boy was left for twelve or thirteen years. This was by no means an injury to him, his foster-mother, Dame Ball, being a simple, kind creature, who loved him, and whom he quitted "in an agony of grief." It was, perhaps, to his (apparent) abandonment in a village that he owed the vigourous health which enabled him afterwards to give lessons in music from eight in the morning until eleven at night, then write until four in the morning, and rise at seven,[1]—yet live to be eighty-eight. Such a brain as his could scarcely have been idle anywhere, or at any age, and such a rector as that of Condover, during the whole time of Burney's stay in it, was the very man to quicken its activity.

The Reverend George Lluellyn, who had in his youth been a page to Charles II.,[2] was "a lively Welshman, active in all

---

[1] This is taking his lessons at their greatest number, *i.e.*, during the London season, which ended after the King's birthday (the 4th of June); but it came to the same thing all the year round, as Dr. Burney was at work in his study when not teaching.

[2] This transition from the ante-room, or even the back-stairs, to the

his pursuits, a man of wit, and taste in the fine arts, fond of music, who had fitted his house with great taste, and had many good pictures, but spent more time in gardening than he did in anything else." Mr. Lluellyn liked "the Dutch manner of laying out gardens," with yew-trees cut into shapes; he liked not William of Orange, but was hand-in-glove with the Shropshire Jacobite leader (Kynaston Corbett, M.P.), and in 1715 sheltered rebels in his rectory. "The Whigs called him a Jacobitical, musical, mad Welsh parson."[1]

He had known Henry Purcell well enough to be able to supply Dr. Blow with more than thirty of Purcell's settings of music to words, when Blow brought out the "Orpheus Britannicus,"[2] so that between him and the eldest half-brother of little Charles (James Burney, organist then, and for many a year afterwards, of St. Margaret's, Shrewsbury), the child was little likely to lack music. We assume that some one must have minded his learning, as he got on very quickly at Chester Grammar School, and cannot have been there more than from three to four years,[3] which, of course, was not

---

church seems to have been not uncommon. In the Wentworth Papers, a lady in Queen Anne's reign is "most concerned at *those things called pages* ... they are what she has never been used to. ... When they have done with them, she'll make them all parsons." Mr. Luellyn was perhaps a relation of "Luellin," a Clerk of the Council in 1659-60, and a comrade of Samuel Pepys, whom we find dining with Pepys at a cook-shop, and also at "Heaven, a place of entertainment in Old Palace Yard."

[1] The quotations are from Dr. Burney.

[2] The first volume of Purcell's "vocal compositions" appeared in 1698; a new edition of it and a second volume were published in 1702, which Mr. Luellyn aided with his help; and a third volume in 1705.

[3] Writing to Fanny in August, 1797, Dr. Burney says, "I ran about Chester, the rows, walls, cathedral, and castle, as familiarly as I could have done fifty years ago; visited the Free School, where I *hic, hæc, hoc'd* it three or four years; and the Cathedral, where I saw and heard the first organ *I ever touched.*"

long enough for scholarship, but was long enough to give him some clue to it. At Chester School, he was only once punished: it was for prompting a friend. When about fourteen, the Cathedral organist, who was a pupil of Dr. Blow, had a fit of the gout. In a few days, he taught the musical school-boy, Burney, to play chants enough "to keep the organ going."

The following extract shows young Burney on his first approach to Handel: "When Handel went through Chester, on his way to Ireland, this year, 1741,[1] I was at the Public-School in that city, and very well remember seeing him smoke a pipe, over a dish of coffee, at the Exchange Coffee-house, for being extremely curious to see so extraordinary a man, I watched him narrowly so long as he remained in Chester; which on account of the wind being unfavourable for his embarking at Parkgate, was several days. During this time, he applied to Mr. Baker, the organist, my first music-master, to know whether there were any choirmen in the cathedral who could sing *at sight*, as he wished to prove some books that had been hastily transcribed, by trying the choruses which he intended to perform in Ireland. Mr. Baker mentioned some of the most likely singers then in Chester, and among the rest, a printer of the name of Janson, who had a good base voice, and was one of the best musicians in the choir. At this time, Harry Alcock, a good player, was the first violin at Chester, which was then a very musical place; for besides public performances, Mr. Prebendary Prescott had a weekly concert, at which he was able to muster eighteen or twenty performers, gentlemen and professors. A time was fixed for this private rehearsal at the *Golden Falcon*, where

---

[1] This was after the bad reception of "The Messiah," upon its first performance, owing to a cabal against him among "many great personages whom he had offended" in London. "Dulness," says the Dunciad, "drove him to the Hibernian shore."

Handel was quartered; but, alas! on trial of the chorus in the Messiah, '*And with his stripes we are healed,*'—poor Janson, after repeated attempts, failed so egregiously, that Handel let loose his great bear upon him;[1] and after swearing in four or five languages, cried out in broken English: 'You shcauntrel! tit not you dell me dat you could sing at soite?' 'Yes, sir,' says the printer, 'and so I can; but not at *first sight.*'"

Soon afterwards Charles Burney is found at Shrewsbury as a pupil in music of his half-brother, the organist; learning French, and to play upon the violin, from "little Matteis," who (in Burney's mature opinion) played Corelli's solos better than any one whom he ever heard afterwards. At sixteen, Charles was the future Doctor in little; learning every thing that any one would teach him, and "helping himself" to what he was not taught. He wrote, taught, tuned instruments, and copied "a prodigious quantity of music" for his brother. He says that he tried to "keep up the little Latin he had learned," to improve his hand-writing, and to compose. He does not tell us what he composed, but it seems to have been prose, verse, and music. He read much; and though angling with fervour, it was with a book in his pocket.

He heard Mr. Felton and Dr. William Hayes play on his brother's organ. He admired them, and they encouraged him.[2] "Thenceforward, he went to work with an ambition and fury that would hardly allow him to eat or sleep."

---

[1] His "great bear" of a temper.
> "Handel, as famed for *manners* as a pig,
> Enraged, upon a time, pull'd off his wig,
> And flung it plump in poor Cuzzoni's face,
> Because the little Syren missed a grace."
>   PETER PINDAR, *Ode upon Ode.*

See p. xxiii, for another instance of Handel's letting "loose his great bear."

[2] "The Rev. William Felton .... was a performer of considerable merit on the organ, and published a set of concertos for that instrument.

In the autumn of 1744, Arne, who is still a well-known English composer of music, was, after a stay of two years in Ireland, on his way to London to take his post at Drury Lane, as conductor of the orchestra and composer of music for that Royal theatre. He met young Burney, who was again at Chester, was pleased with him, and took him to London as his apprentice in music.[1]

If Charles Burney had suffered from what Madame D'Arblay calls "the parsimonious authority and exactions" of his half-brother, James, he was left far too much to himself by Arne, who cared not what was his conduct, and taught him very little : exacting only that he should copy a great quantity of music and make himself useful. His elder own brother, Richard, was then living in London. His seems to have been the only guidance given to Charles. It is described by Madame D'Arblay as "lordly tyranny." She wrote with the warmth of a daughter, whose imagination kindled at inattention, rigour, or show of superiority to such a father as hers, who, although the youngest born, was the ornament of his family and its chief; but Dr. Burney seems to have taken some neglect, some harshness, and much hard work in his early days very little to heart; and wrote gaily of what moved his daughter to pity, akin to indignation, long after all had passed into " honour, obedience, love, and troops of friends."

The Burneys of the generation before her own had been able enough, but with the exception of her father and his sister Rebecca, Mme. D'Arblay describes them as having been much

---

Dr. William Hayes . . . a good solo singer and organist; distinguished himself by his compositions of Church Music and several much admired catches, glees, and canons; was chosen professor of music at Oxford, and was for many years called upon to preside as a conductor of orchestras in different parts of the kingdom."—LYSONS's *History of the Meeting of the Three Choirs.*

[1] As the 1744-5 season at the theatre began on the 15th of September, this meeting was probably in August, 1744.

less amiable and united by affection than his children and their cousins. But then there were so many of them, that life was a struggle to live. There could not have been much amiss in his early life, as the enthusiasm of Dr. Burney for "old Shrewsbury" was a subject of pleasantry among those who knew him, and to dwell on Condover, and sing the songs of his dear old nurse, with an imitation of her tones, and the expression of her face, his delight even to his old age.

In 1819, Mrs. Piozzi writes to Sir James Fellowes, that Sir Baldwin Leighton is "a true Salopian, who, though well acquainted with both hemispheres, delights in talking only of Shrewsbury. He will now end his life where he began, a mile from his favourite spot;—a pretty spot enough, but its power over a soldier of fortune like General Leighton, or a full-minded man like my friend, the first Dr. Burney, is really to its credit.[1] When the last-named friend had occasion to kiss his majesty's hand two or three times within two or three years, I remember the wags saying, 'Why, Burney takes the King's hand, sure, for Shrewsbury-brawn; he puts it so often to his lips.'" The jest sounds like one of Mrs. Thrale's own, but Dr. Burney does really seem to have translated an Italian word, "*mostacciolo*," as "simnel," in order to have the pleasure of bringing Shrewsbury into a note in his "Life of Metastasio." This note explains that "mostacciolo is a cake made at Naples, of flour, sugar, eggs, and sweet wine, ... which is very different from a Shrewsbury simnel, which is a rich plum-cake, inclosed in an impenetrable case, or crust, made of flour and water, and coloured with saffron, which preserves it from injury and decay in the longest voyages to the most remote parts of the globe."

He did not see Shrewsbury again for fifty-three years. In 1797, Mrs. Crewe, to raise his spirits after the death

---

[1] In the life of Charles Darwin we may observe Shrewsbury as retaining the same power of attraction.

of Burke, insisted upon his accompanying her to Crewe Hall, in Cheshire, and went forty miles out of her way to show him Shrewsbury. Then he wrote to Fanny, "I ran away from Mrs. Crewe, who was too tired to walk about, and played the Cicerone myself to Miss Crewe, ... and M. de Frontiville, to whom I undertook to show off old Shrewsbury, of which I knew all the streets, lanes, and parishes, as well as I did sixty years ago." .... "The next morning .... I walked in that most beautiful of all public walks, as I still believe, in the world, called the Quarry; formed in verdant, and flower-enamelled fields, by the Severn side, with the boldest and most lovely opposite shore imaginable." .... "In a most violent rain, nearly a storm, we left my dear old Shrewsbury; and without being able, in such weather, to get to my dearer old Condover."[1]

"The walk by the Severn-side" is the scene of lovers' meetings in Farquhar's "Recruiting Officer." The "noble Serjeant Kite," speaking in "the street, Shrewsbury," bids all who desire to enlist, "repair" to him "at the sign of the Raven" (doubtless in Raven Street, where Dr. Burney was born); and Captain Plume censures "the March beer at the Raven."

Burney was in the orchestra at Drury Lane, under Arne. If he was a drudge, his work seems to have been relieved by plays and operas, as well as by concerts, in which latter he most likely took some part. The kindness of Arne's sister, Mrs. Cibber, "the most enchanting actress of her day," more than made up for her brother's negligence. Her house in Scotland

---

[1] At Condover, there is now a little railway-station on the line between Hereford and Shrewsbury. Condover is four miles, or ten minutes, by railway from Shrewsbury. On "the boldest and most lovely opposite shore imaginable," the new schools now rise. The ancient Raven Inn is near the old schools; some part of them are now used as a Free Library.

Yard, was the resort of "wits, poets, and men of letters." She made Burney welcome to it, and known to them. The rest was done by his modest and pleasing manners, great liveliness, and quick intelligence. At her house he gained the friendliness of Thomson and Garrick. There he again met Handel. Burney pauses in his volume on the Handel Commemoration of 1784, to tell us, that "after my first arrival in London, 1744, he" [Handel] "was seldom absent from the benefit for Decayed Musicians and their Families; and I have sometimes seen him at the Playhouses, the Opera, and at St. Martin's church, when Mr. Kelway played the organ. . . . . Besides seeing Handel, myself, at his own house, in Brook-Street, and at Carlton-House, where he had rehearsals of his Oratorios; by meeting him at Mrs. Cibber's, and at Frasi's, who was then my scholar,[1] I acquired considerable knowledge of his private character, and turn for humour. He was very fond of Mrs. Cibber, whose voice and manner had softened his severity for her want of musical knowledge. At her house, of a Sunday evening, he used to meet Quin, who, in spite of native roughness, was very fond of music. Yet the first time Mrs. Cibber prevailed on Handel to sit down while he was present (on which occasion I remember the great musician played the overture in *Siroe*, and delighted us all with the marvellous neatness with which he played the jig, at the end of it), Quin, after Handel was gone, being asked by Mrs. Cibber, whether he did not think Mr. Handel had a charming hand? replied, '*A hand*, Madam! you mistake, its a *foot*.' 'Poh! poh!' says she, 'has he not a fine finger?' '*Toes*, by G———, Madam!' Indeed, his hand was then so fat, that the knuckles, which usually appear convex, were like those of a

---

[1] Signora Giulia Frasi appeared in London in 1743. She chiefly sang Handel's compositions. Yet, though Dr. Burney writes as if Frasi was his scholar in 1744, when he was himself in pupilage, it is more likely that it was later on, when he was his own master.

child, dinted or dimpled in, so as to be rendered concave; however, his touch was so smooth, and the tone of the instrument so much cherished, that his fingers seemed to grow to the keys. They were so curved and compact, when he played, that no motion, and scarcely the fingers themselves, could be discerned."

Once, at a later time, Handel's temper broke loose on Burney. "At Frasi's, I remember, in the year 1748, he brought in his pocket the duet of *Judas Macchabæus*, 'From these dread Scenes,' in which she had not sung when that Oratorio was first performed in 1746. At the time he sat down to the harpsichord, to give her and me the time of it, while he sung her part, I hummed, at sight, the second, over his shoulder; in which he encouraged me, by desiring that I would sing out—but, unfortunately, something went wrong, and Handel, with his usual impetuosity, grew violent: a circumstance very terrific to a young musician. At length, however, recovering from my fright, I ventured to say, that I fancied there was a mistake in the writing; which, upon examining, Handel discovered to be the case: and then, instantly, with the greatest good humour and humility, said, 'I pec your barton—I am a very odd tog—Maishter Schmitt is to blame.'"

Burney was parted from Arne by Fulk Greville, a young man of rank, fashion, and fortune, who coveted all kinds of distinction, from eminence in metaphysics (in which he fancied himself strong) to pre-eminence on the race-course and in the hunting-field, in "all the fashionable exercises" of riding, fencing, shooting at a mark, dancing, and tennis, down, or up, to music and drawing, writing verses, and laying out gardens and plantations. Mr. Greville wished for the continual company of a good musician, who would give him lessons, and who was also fit for "the society of a gentleman." He doubted if there *were* such an one, but after hearing young

Burney (who was ignorant of his object) talk, as well as play upon the harpsichord, he was so much taken with him as to pay Arne three hundred pounds to cancel Burney's articles. Burney was even too much his companion, as Greville took him to the race-course and the gambling clubs —to Newmarket, to White's, and to Boodle's. He might do anything he chose, so long as Mr. Greville did not think it "*fogrum.*" Burney gave away the bride with whom Greville pretended to elope, because it was "*fogrum*" to be married like other people. Burney stood as proxy for a duke when Greville's baby was baptised.[1] He was to have gone to Italy with that "pair of our beauties," Mr. and Mrs. Greville (who are commemorated in the letters of Horace Walpole, and of Lady Mary Wortley Montagu), but just at that time he himself fell in love, and Mr. Greville graciously cancelled the unwritten articles which bound Burney to him by the words, "Why don't you marry her?" "*May I?*" cried Burney, and the deed was done. "*She*" (Esther Sleepe) "was a very lovely and intelligent girl, who made him as happy as a man could be made. But, before speaking of his married life, we must tell of a friendship which began three or four years before he met his wife, lasted two-and-twenty years after her death, and was shared with him by all his children. This was with Samuel Crisp, a man whose praise runs through all the Burney papers; whom Frances, from her earliest journal to her latest annotations on her letters and papers, never names but with expressions of love, honour, and reverence.

As he has hitherto been commemorated only by sundry misdescriptions in divers books, by a few lines in "The Gentleman's Magazine," an epitaph in Chesington Church, and some over-coloured paragraphs in Macaulay's review of Mme. D'Arblay's Diaries, let such amends as can, be made by

---

[1] Afterwards the well-known Whig beauty, Lady Crewe.

telling what may be learned of him from the Burney papers, and of his family from the volumes (in their thoroughness in all ways a pleasure to eye and mind) which the courteous kindness of Mr. Crisp, of Denmark Hill, has put at the service of the Editor.

For some time it was far from easy to affiliate Mr. Crisp; so many were the Samuels in his ancient and wide-spread family. To add to the puzzle, Mr. Crisp had a double in another Samuel Crisp, who was born three years before him, and died about eight months after him;[1] was, like himself, a bachelor, had some of his characteristics, and did things which "Daddy" might have done if his bent had been towards philanthropy instead of towards what is called "culture." This pseudo Samuel Crisp has slipped into the same line of the index to "The Gentleman's Magazine" with our Samuel, so that a reference to an article upon "his character" was, for a moment, thought to concern our dear and "honoured Daddy."

The Crisps had much originality, fervour, and force. Many of them were men of mark. Mr. Crisp's double was so well known in London, that it is surprising that Fanny should never have heard of him until she went to Bath in 1780. There she met a Miss Leigh, a cousin of her "Daddy," and very likely a cousin of Jane Austen also. While telling Miss Leigh how happy she was to see a relation of Mr. Crisp, Fanny was heard by Mrs. Bowdler, the mother of the Tunbridge Wells doctor who unintentionally enriched the English

---

[1] "Suddenly, at Macclesfield Street, Soho, aged 73, Samuel Crisp, Esq.: a relation of the celebrated Sir Nicholas Crisp." This is the notice of the death of the *double* in "The Gentleman's Magazine" for January, 1784. It would seem that it was his library which was sold in 1784, as our Samuel Crisp, who died in April, 1783, had sold his "books, prints, pictures, and musical instruments," and other works of art, before retiring to Chesington.

language with a new verb. Mrs. Bowdler, who (according to Fanny) was "a very clever woman," but "not a very delicate one," "cried out 'What Mr. Crisp is it? Is it Sam?' 'Yes, ma'am,' said I, staring at her familiarity. 'What,' cried she again, 'do you know little Sam Crisp?' 'I don't know for *little*,' returned I, much surprised; 'but he is the most intimate friend I have in the world, and the dearest. Do *you* know him then?' 'Do I? yes, very well; I have known little Sam Crisp this long while.' 'I can't imagine,' cried I, half affronted at her manner of naming him, 'why you should so *little* him; I know not any one thing in the world in which he is *little*,—neither in head nor heart,—neither in understanding, person, talents, nor mind.' 'I fancy, ma'am,' said Miss Leigh, 'you hardly mean the Mr. Crisp Miss Burney does.' 'I mean Sam Crisp,' said she, '*The Greenwich Traveller*.' This appeased me, and we cleared up the mistake." But not *wholly* was Fanny appeased, as on the next day, when she first saw Mr. Bowdler, the "very worthy" husband of this inelegant person, she describes Mr. Bowdler as being "an extremely little man, much less than Sam Crisp, I assure you, Mrs. Bowdler."!

"Little Sam Crisp," who had withdrawn from business for the last fourteen years of his life, paid the owners of the Greenwich stage-coach £27 yearly, for what "The Gentleman's Magazine" calls his "daily amusement of riding in the coach from London to Greenwich, and returning in it immediately."[1] He acted on "his favourite motto, *pro bono publico*, and with the least ostentation performed many generous and charitable actions, which would have dignified a more ample fortune.

---

[1] He may have had some early association with Greenwich, as Edward Crisp, who died in 1690, had "lands, messuages, and tenements, scituate in East-Greenwich," was the Master of the Trinity House at Greenwich, and in the commission of the peace for Middlesex, Surrey, and Kent.

He was the institutor of the *Lactarium* in St. George's Fields, and selected the Latin mottoes for the facetious Mrs. Henniver, who got a little fortune there. He projected the mile and half stones near London, and teased the printers of news-papers into the plan of letter-boxes. . . . . He was a good-humoured, obliging, and facetious companion, always paying a particular attention and a profusion of compliments to the ladies, especially to those who were agreeable."[1]

If he was a relation of the celebrated Sir Nicholas Crisp, it must have been collaterally, as was the case with our Mr. Crisp, who was a great-grand-nephew of Sir Nicholas, the direct line of whose heirs ended in 1740, in Sir Charles Crisp, of Dornford, in Oxfordshire. Sir Nicholas was a maker of history. What he did is to be seen in the State Papers and the Commons' Journals, in Clarendon and Rushworth, in Pepys and Evelyn. His younger brother Tobias, the great-grandfather of our Mr. Crisp, made still more noise than Sir Nicholas in his time, and even after it, but it was among polemical Puritans. He has shrunk into a small space in dictionaries of biography and in histories of controversy.[2]

These brothers sprang from a Leicestershire family, which in the sixteenth century had a Gloucestershire offshoot, if it were not rather the main stock transplanted. Towards the end of that century two cadets of the Crisps of Marshfield, near Bristol, became citizens of London. Ellis, the younger of the two, had a large house in Bread Street, a seat at Ham-

---

[1] These extracts are from "The Gentleman's Magazine."

[2] Granger counts four engraved portraits of Tobias to one of Sir Nicholas. Clarendon describes Sir Nicholas as being "a citizen of good wealth, great trade; an active-spirited man; a very popular man in the City, where he had been a commander of the train'd bands, till the Ordinance of the Militia removed him; which rather improv'd than lessen'd his credit."

mersmith, house-property in London and in Bristol, with land both in southern counties and in Yorkshire. He made the old kindly will of a prosperous, godly man, remembering all his kinsfolk, all his wife's kinsfolk, his city company, and the "poore people of the towne of Marshefielde," in which he was born, and where, with his brother, he had founded almshouses. He died in 1625, the year of his shrievalty, that year in which Charles I. dissolved his first Parliament.

Would that we had ample room to tell of his eldest son, "Capitaine Nicholas Crisp, Esquier," Charles I.'s "faithful farmer" of the Customs, and raiser of money; that adventurous merchant who "opened and settled the Guinea-trade, and built there the Castle of Coromandine"; that gallant Cavalier; that daring "Admiral of Sea-Pirats," who raised a squadron of ships as well as a regiment for his King;[1] who pawned for the King his collar of rubies,[2] trafficked for him, plotted and was in exile for him; whose spirit and whose fortune no fines or plundering by Parliament could sensibly daunt or diminish. In words[3] which his son, Sir Thomas,

---

[1] This is from the title of a party-pamphlet against Sir Nicholas, in the Bodleian Library. "Carolus I. Rex Angliæ, a copie of the King's Commission to Sir Nicholas Crispe, making him Admiral of the Sea-Pirats, May 6." 4to, London, 1645. Crisp had a commission to equip not less than fifteen ships of war, to which the King gave power to make prizes. This squadron kept the King's communications with the Continent open, and exchanged the King's tin and wool for arms and ammunition.

[2] The very "carcanet of large balas rubies, with a great diamond," which King James took from his dusty old grey hat, which it "encircled," in order to "opignorate, pledge, or lay in wad," for two hundred pounds, to George Heriot, saying, "Here—here—ye have had these in pledge for a larger sum, ye auld Levite that ye are. Keep them in gage, till I gie ye back the siller out of the next subsidy." The very "cimelia" which are restored to the King by Richie Moniplies, in the third volume of "The Fortunes of Nigel."

[3] In his own epitaph in the church of St. Mildred, Bread Street, of

wrote with pride, Sir Nicholas was an "ould ffaithfull servant to King Charles the ffirst, and King Charles the second, for whom he suffered very much, and lost one hundred thousand pounds in their services, but was repaired in a great measure by King Charles the second his justice, and bounty, and is here mentioned by his executor as a gratefull acknowledgement." This repayment will appear not the least notable fact in the life of Sir Nicholas. After the Restoration he was made a baronet, his ceaseless energy was then turned to improving brick-making, paper-mills, powder-mills, water-mills, etc. His desires "*pro bono publico*" were on a grander scale than those of Samuel Crisp, "the Greenwich traveller." He troubled the mind of Sir Richard Browne, sometime English Minister in Paris, by planning a wet-dock at Deptford, to hold "two hundred sail of ships." He treated with Browne's son-in-law, Mr. Evelyn, at Sayes Court, and brought him up to London "about a vast design of a mole to be made for ships in part of his grounds at Sayes Court."[1] To complete the multiform

---

which the Crisp family held the advowson. Sir Thomas was a first cousin of our Mr. Crisp's grandfather.

[1] "The vast design" of Sir Nicholas was baffled. The Admiralty was "talked over." The Duke of York visited Mr. Evelyn's "poor habitation, and viewed such things as" [he] "had to entertain his curiosity"; caused Mr. Evelyn to dine with him, at the Treasurer of the Navy's house, with the Duke of Ormond, and several lords; then they viewed some of Mr. Evelyn's grounds, and "laid aside the project of a receptacle for ships as a fancy of Sir Nicholas Crisp's." Crisp's design was to use some crown lands which it was found afterwards had been granted to Sir Richard Browne, (whose only child was Evelyn's wife, and brought the Deptford property to that family,) for his "mole" and "wet dock," or "sasse," which were parts of the same plan. We are told that the Evelyn family still hold the ground concerning which Sir Nicholas had "*a fancy*," as Mr. Evelyn wrote; or as Clarendon would have written, one of "*his own sprightly inclinations and resolutions.*" The loyalty of Sir Richard Browne was but that of a convert; the loyalty of Mr. Evelyn had been inactive in time of need; so that they may well have been perturbed.

xxx *Preface.*

Sir Nicholas, he was met, with the other Farmers of the Customs, by Mr. Pepys at Woolwich in 1662: when Pepys found them to be "very grave, fine gentlemen";—"very good company";—whom he was "very glad to know."

Samuel Crisp, next brother to Sir Nicholas, was probably concerned with him in what the King and Sir Nicholas called "a Commission of Array"; the Parliament named it a plot to seize the City of London. Samuel's estate was sequestered. Tobias, the third surviving son of Ellis, was, like his brothers, born in Milton's Bread Street, in 1602, a few years before Milton. He was of Eton, of Cambridge, and of Oxford, and rector of Brinkworth, in Hampshire, when the Civil War began. He had married Mary, daughter, and, in the end, heiress, of Rowland Wilson, citizen of London, and vintner, who seems to have been in Sir Nicholas Crisp's Guinea Company, but was the reverse of him in politics, being a member of the Long Parliament, and (in the fatal year 1648-9) one of the Council of State. This connexion may have sometimes saved the person of Sir Nicholas at the cost of his purse. In the same month of the same year[1] that the King raised his standard at Nottingham, Tobias (who was "Puritannically affected"), "to avoid the insolencies of the soldiers, especially of the Cavaliers, for whom he had but little affection, retired to London."[2]

Tobias had little "luck" alive, or dead. Shunning frays in Hampshire, he preached himself into worse in London, where he was "baited by *fifty-two* opponents in a grand dispute concerning freeness of grace." "By which encounter, which was eagerly managed on his part, he contracted a disease which brought him to his grave." That is to say, in the heat and the crowd, he was infected by the small-pox, of which he died on the 27th of February, 1642. The controversy raged long

---

[1] August, 1642.   [2] Anthony à Wood.

Preface. xxxi

after his demise. On the publication of a volume of his sermons after his death, the Westminster Assembly of Divines proposed that they should be publicly burned as heretical. His son Samuel, who was about ten when Tobias died, grew up a biblical student and a lay theologian. In 1689 he republished his father's works, and brought upon himself a seven years' strife. He provoked it by prefixing to the book the names of twelve Presbyterian and twelve Anabaptist ministers as approving the sermons. Samuel was denounced for reprinting sermons which should never have been preached, or published, at all. He defended himself in two volumes. The whole controversy rests undisturbed on the shelves of College-libraries, but John Gill, a Baptist minister, reprinted Toby in 1791.[1] In the latest book that gives a sketch of him, we find him as "Tobias Crisp, Antinomian"; but what one of his foemen called him, *i.e.* "*Crispinian,*" seems nearer the fact. A contemporary describes him as being "innocent, and harmless, of all evil; . . . zealous and fervent of all good."

His children were left to the care of their mother, and her father—Rowland Wilson. Tobias was rich, and their grandfather increased the wealth of the children. He left among them, the church lands of Merton Abbey, in the parish of Malden, in Surrey.[2] Among other property, he bequeathed

---

[1] We saw several volumes of it in *Merton* College Library. Some will remember that Walter de Merton first founded his college in the parish of Malden, (in which lies Chesington,) in 1264, but transferred it to Oxford ten years later.

[2] Ellis Crispe, sometime High Sheriff of Surrey, the eldest surviving son of Dr. Tobias, did not long retain his share of the Merton property, on which stood the remains of the priory. In 1668, he conveyed it to Thomas Pepys, Esquire, of Hatcham Barnes, Master of the Jewel Office to Charles II. and James II. It was an estate of importance, as may be seen by the following entry in the diary of Samuel Pepys: "May 21st, 1668. To the office, where meets me Sir Richard Ford; who among other things congratulates me, as one or two did yesterday, on my great

to his grandchildren his bad debts, namely, what " the Crowne of Portugall" and King Charles II. owed him. When his grandson, Samuel Crisp, died, in 1703, they were still unpaid. The first Samuel (1) describes himself in his will, made in 1701, as being then in his "sixty-nynth yeare," and "the last survyving son of Dr. Tobias Crisp." He had lived at Clapham in a pious and wealthy way, much as they who were called "the Clapham Sect" (or Set) did after him. His second son, Samuel (2), seems to have received more than the rest. His eldest, Pheasaunt, a merchant, who died at Bombay, had provision made for him, but was reminded that he "married Mr. Dolins' daughter" without his father's consent, or even his knowledge; that his father had lent him money "in his straits," which he had promised to repay to his younger brothers when he was worth four thousand pounds; and that he had borrowed a picture of "the Madona," which his father bequeathed to him, seemingly because Pheasaunt showed no signs of returning it. His father also leaves him his own "pocket-bible of forty-four yeares vse, hopeinge that he will make a good vse of it." Samuel, the second son, has the bible of Dr. Tobias. "My ffather's bible, printed, 1631, in the margent of which from 1675, to 1680, I made annotations from 1st Corinthians to the end." Four younger sons and a daughter are left more less curious bibles, some of them annotated. To one of them, Stephen, "to furnish him somewhat

---

purchase; and he advises me rather to forbear, if it be not done, as a thing that the world will envy me in: and what is it but my cosen Tom Pepys' [of Deptford] buying of Martin Abbey, in Surry!" Ellis was the only child of Tobias, who received a legacy from his uncle, Sir Nicholas: this silence concerning the rest, with other circumstances, persuades us that the other children of Tobias were dissenters. Samuel Crisp's share of the Merton estate was, in the end, sold by his grandson, our "Daddy." It may be noted, that although the land came to the Crisps from Rowland Wilson, there had been Crisps settled in the neighbourhood from the time of Henry VIII.

in the blessed worke of the ministery," the testator says, " I give all my manuscripts of Hebrew and Greek in my three times writing out the Bible in Hebrew and Greek letters, and rendring the whole into proper English. My booke of the list of 7000 and od sermons from 1648 to 1701, and all the sermon-books about 300, I give to my said sonne Stephen."

Samuel (2) survived his father Samuel fourteen years, dying in 1717. He had married into a family living not far from the old home of the Crisps at Marshfield. He left five daughters and an only son, our Mr. Crisp, the third and last Samuel of this line of the Crisps. His mother, Mrs. Florence Crisp, did not live two years after her husband, so that "Daddy" was brought up by his sisters, three of whom appear to have been older than himself. When just in his "teens," he became owner of his father's share in the Merton property, and of his mother's shares in land at Tockington in Gloucestershire, and at Camerton in Somersetshire. That he was well-taught we are assured; but there is a gap in his history between his father's death in 1717, and his meeting young Burney at the house of Fulk Greville, near Andover, which can only be filled by fancy.[1] All we know is that Mr. Crisp was a man of fashion, as well as of "taste"; that he was tall, handsome, of fine bearing, agreeable, and intelligent, excelling both as a musician and a painter when young, and that he did not let his accomplishments slip from him in

---

[1] Madame D'Arblay tells us that her father was "but seventeen years of age, when first he had this incalculable advantage." But Burney was some months past eighteen when he went to London in 1744, and time must be allowed for his stay as the pupil of Arne, before he met Mr. Greville. He probably met Mr. Crisp between, *at earliest*, 1745 and 1747, when he *may* have married, or 1748, when he must, at any rate, have married, as he had three children born to him by the middle of 1751—that is, by a couple of months after he was five-and-twenty.

middle-age. There are traces after he was seventy, of his accompanying Susan Burney on the harpsichord, and of his needing paint-brushes.[1] Even when his fingers were swollen by gout, his handwriting is remarkable for its delicacy. The Puritanism of Tobias, and the Nonconformity of his son Samuel, had become feeble in the second Samuel; there was no sign of it in " Daddy." He heard Farinelli, Senesino, and Cuzzoni with rapture, and dwelt on their praise in the time of Agujari, Gabrielli, and Pacchieroti. He loved Shakespeare and Molière, admired Fielding and Smollett, thought little of Richardson, considered Dr. Johnson a better talker than writer, and set Mrs. Montagu at naught.[2] As be-

---

[1] Half-a-dozen lines begging Susan to go to a colour shop in Newport Street, and buy " two ermine points, the shortest and stiffest " she can get, lie before us. They end thus:
"I'll pay Fannikin in money, and you in love——
"Your honoured daddy,
" S. CRISP.
" Chesington, July 6, 1778."
Below this, Fanny runs on to Susy, "'Honoured, quotha?' says I. 'Why, an't I?' says he. 'Suppose you are,' says I, 'it don't become you to say it.' 'Oh yes, it does,—and to think it too!'"

[2] Mr. Crisp writes thus to Fanny in 1778: " I have read Evelina over again, and if there is not more true sterling Genius in 3 pages of that work than in all Richardson's nineteen volumes put together I do hereby in form acknowledge myself to be the most tasteless of courteous or uncourteous Readers. However such an authority as Dr. Johnson's is not to be slighted; for which reason, I don't care if I do throw away a little in tumbling him over now and then, and try if I can find any thing to alter my opinion of so many years standing. I think there were 4 vol. of Pamela—the two first, and then 2 more of Pamela in high life—such high life!—8 of Clarissa, and 7 of Sir C. Grandison." Elsewhere, he speaks of " Pamela " as " poor stuff,—as it is, to my mind, at least." Of Mrs. Montagu, he writes to Fanny, in 1780, " I believe I have told you of several letters the Duchess of Portland showed me of hers formerly, (for I had no acquaintance with herself,) so full of affectation, refinement, attempts

came a man of wit, he supped with Quin, and had been intimate with Garrick. As a man of fashion, he knew the "*virtuosa*" Duchess of Portland, and Mrs. Delany, her friend, and the friend of his eldest sister. He was intimate with the beautiful Maria Gunning and her husband, Lord Coventry. Among other men of letters he was friendly with Owen Cambridge, "a man of good estate, not unknown to the Muses,"[1] as well as with Fulk Greville and *his* set, who probably called some of the others, "*fogrum.*" Mr. Crisp, in the words of the last century, was a "*dilettante,*" and a "*virtuoso.*" Greville, and Greville's friends, teased, ridiculed, or chid him for lingering by young Burney's harpsichord when they would fain have had him go a-hunting. He guided the clever and interesting boy Burney by the experience of a kind-hearted man twenty years his elder.

His play "Virginia," which has been represented as the main thing in his life, was not acted until he was forty-eight, although begun some years earlier. Whether any less shadowy affection than his love for *it* warmed those years of which we know nothing, must be left to conjecture. He tells Fanny in 1778, that "Molly Chute (an intimate and most infinitely agreable old friend of mine, long since dead), when I us'd to desire her to love me a great deal, would say, '*Look ye Sam, I have this much stock of love by me,*' putting out her little finger, '*and I can afford you so much,*' measuring off perhaps half the length of her nail, '*and I think that's pretty fair.*' I thought so too, and was well content,—but what shall I do with *you* who have so many to content? . . . .

---

to philosophize, talking metaphysics—in all which particulars she so bewildered and puzzled herself and her readers, and showed herself so superficial, nay, really ignorant in the subjects she paraded on—that in my own private mind's pocket-book, I set her down for a vain, empty, conceited pretender, and little else."

[1] So writes George Colman, the younger, of Owen Cambridge.

Well, I must do as I may, and that is the very nuthook humour of it."[1]

Now, to be "well content" with the little love Molly could spare him, shows that it was her friendship that he desired. In one of Susan Burney's amusing letters we find Mr. Crisp, when above seventy, delaying his party on their walk in order to admire the beauty of a Gypsy girl, on whom he gazed as upon a picture.[2]

Only one of his five sisters married (Anne, the eldest, being of set purpose a spinster), and Mr. Crisp may have had no love-story at all to tell, even as he had none to tell of being "wronged or cruelly cheated."[3]

As we are expressly told that Mr. Crisp never saw the lovely Esther Sleepe, whom Charles Burney married about 1748, it is most likely that he did not meet her husband for about thirteen years, nine or ten of which Burney spent at Lynn, while Mr. Crisp passed some of them in Rome.[4] In 1749 Burney was appointed organist of St. Dionis Backchurch, Fenchurch Street. He had pupils; he composed music, to which, except in one instance, he did not put his name; and he "took the organ part at the new concert established at the King's Arms," on the west side of Cornhill.

---

[1] Mr. Crisp's quotations are more ready than exact. What Corporal Nym *does* say is—

"Be advis'd, sir, and pass good humours: I will say '*Marry strap*' with you if you run the nuthooks on me: that is the very note of it."
—*Merry Wives of Windsor*, Act I. Scene 1.

[2] See p. 265, Vol. II.

[3] See p. 265, Vol. II.

[4] It is possible that Burney may have met Mr. Crisp on some visit from Lynn to London, but we are told expressly that their friendship was in abeyance, through absence only, "for many years," and was renewed by a purely accidental meeting, some time after the death of Mrs. Burney in 1761.

We have not seen the register of the birth of his eldest child, Esther (Hetty), but James, and a Charles (who probably died an infant), were baptised at St. Dionis.[1] Burney soon became seriously ill from work, study, and city air, and happening to be offered the post of organist at Lynn Regis, accepted it at the end of 1750, or beginning of 1751, being advised to live in the country by Dr. Armstrong, the poet, who was his physician. Mrs. Burney was left in London for nursery reasons, and did not join him until some months before the birth of her daughter Frances, on the 13th of June, 1752.

Frances received the Christian name of her godmother, Mrs. Greville,[2] from the Reverend Thomas Pyle, perpetual curate of St. Nicholas, in Ann Street, Lynn, a chapel of ease to St. Margaret's Church, of which church in the end he became the something short of orthodox "minister." Between 1706 and 1718 he had preached six pamphlets in support of the succession of the House of Hanover, which he published under the name of sermons. He had "engaged" in the Bangorian controversy in aid of his friend Hoadley, who made him a residentiary prebendary of Salisbury. Owing to his merits and efforts, his three sons had an almost fabulous

---

[1] In the baptismal register of St. Dionis Backchurch, Mr. Gibbs found: "July 5, 1750, James, s. of Chas. and Esther Burney (organist of this parish), born June 13." "June 16, 1751, Charles Burney, s. of Chas. and Esther Burney (organist of this parish), born June 3." This infant is not named in any Burney paper that we have seen. It will be remarked that James and Frances were born on the same day of the same month. The coincidence is apparent but not real, as one was born under the Old Style, the other under the New. The same is the case with Dr. Burney's dying on his birthday. The change of style must be reckoned.

[2] Sheridan's "Critic" was dedicated to Mrs. Greville. She left a fragment of a novel, which her daughter, Lady Crewe, wished Fanny to complete. Fanny says, "It has much spirit, knowledge of human nature, and gaiety in most of its parts."

amount of church preferment. Thus that Fanny was to spend her life among people of more or less note, was foreshown even at her baptism.

The port of Bishop's Lynn (the name was changed to King's Lynn when Henry VIII. wrested it from the see of Norwich) has lost consequence since the growth of Grimsby and Kingston-upon-Hull. It was a town of merchants who imported wine, and of brewers who exported beer, chiefly to the Baltic; a town where the venturous settled, to rise if they could into the powerful corporation; a town of high living rather than high thinking.[1] Although made much of, Charles Burney was ill at ease when playing upon an "execrably bad organ" to "foggy aldermen" totally ignorant of music, with a patron and local "oracle of Apollo" (Sir John Turner, M.P.) who was "extremely shallow"; but he tells us in a

---

[1] Details of Lynn life may be found in "My Grandfather's Pocketbook," which was published by the Rev. Henry John Wale in 1883.

Thomas Wale (the "Grandfather") was born in 1701, and was "put out apprentice" at Lynn to one of the second Mrs. Burney's family (Mr. W. Allen, Russian merchant) between 1718 and 1724. He lived some time in Russia, where he traded. In 1777 he was at Norwich, where he visited Mr. Peter Finch, whose "Lady" (he writes) "is own sister to ... J. Bagge, gran-son of my old friend J. Bagge, who married Sally Allen of Lynn. ... Visited this day also a Parson Pyle, youngest brother of Parson Pyle, diseased." At another time Mr. Wale went to Lynn and "walked to the Keys and almost all over y⁵ town." At a brewer's he was shown "a prodigious quantity of beer and ale, and one large warehouse of brandy. Mr. Everard ... concluded ... to send fifty or more casks of his pale ale (like Burton ale), which seemed nicely good, and twenty-five casks of porter by a ship they are about to send to Riga, being very well pleased with the sale of what last year he sent to our house." Among rich brewers and wine merchants, importers of timber from America, exporters of beer and of "ventures" of divers goods, one or two Scotch physicians, some attorneys and clergymen and their wives, Fanny must have passed months for some years running, after her father's second marriage to a Lynn lady, without reckoning that the first eight years of her life were spent at Lynn.

Preface. xxxix

note to the second volume of his "History of Music" (1782), that before he left Lynn the corporation granted him a new organ, made by his advice by Snetzler, "in place of one with worm-eaten wooden pipes"; and he halts in his first foreign tour to record Snetzler's sarcasms upon his first organ[1] at Lynn. In like manner, in his German tour, he pauses on the way between Berlin and Potsdam to say that "the road . . . is through a deep running sand, like the worst parts of Norfolk and Suffolk, where there are no turnpikes." On such roads his mare Peggy picked her way, while her master studied Italian poetry on her back, with a dictionary of his own compiling in one pocket of his great coat, and his commonplace-book in another. If "looking around him in Lynn, he seemed to see a void," visits to Houghton, Holkham, Rainham, and Felbrig, with occasional letters from Mr. and Mrs. Greville and Mr. Crisp, new friendships with Mr. Hayes and Mr. Bewley, and an approach by letters to Dr. Johnson, much reading and many pupils, a happy home and returning health, made up for the loss of London. His children, Susan and Charles, were born in Lynn, which he did not leave before 1760.

Meanwhile, Mr. Crisp's tragedy of "Virginia" had been played at Drury Lane Theatre on the 25th of February, 1754.

It was with tenderness towards that play which had been so dear to Mr. Crisp, that the Editor untied his manuscript of "Virginia"; with regret that she found all that she could admire was the conspicuous beauty of the penmanship,—the delicacy of the text written in the Italian hand, the exquisite neatness of the writing of the foot-notes from Livy (printed

---

[1] "I remember M. Snetzler, being asked by some churchwardens what he thought an old organ which they wanted to have repaired was worth, and what would be the expense of mending it, honestly telling them, that after he had appraised the instrument at one hundred pounds, that if they would lay out another hundred upon it, perhaps then it would be worth fifty."

with the pen) with which Mr. Crisp had fortified the text. It put her in mind of Rousseau's care for the beauty of the manuscript of his "Nouvelle Heloïse," and of how he tied it with blue ribands. Lying on the dainty writing was a single small quarto leaf of another tragedy upon "Virginia," which had been printed exactly one hundred years before that of Mr. Crisp. Had he kept it before him as a warning, or as an example? If it had been the key which had given him the note, no voice of his century could sustain it. In three lines on that black old leaf was more force than in Mr. Crisp's five acts, for it was from the "Appius and Virginia" of the great poet of "Vittoria Corombona" and "The Duchess of Malfy."[1]

From a single scene of Mr. Crisp's "Virginia" as given in "The Gentleman's Magazine," Macaulay had divined that "the whole piece was one blemish." Not even Macaulay could exaggerate the flatness of the plot, the feeble conception of character, the weakness of diction. We feel almost as if criticising our own father; but truth is mighty and *must* prevail; yet we were bent upon admiring our "Daddy's" "Virginia," *if* it were possible. The pathos of the play, "the pity of it," lay in Mr. Crisp's having felt so warmly and strongly without having naturally, or by acquisition, a power to make others feel, adequate in any wise to his aim and end. His heart had burned within him when he read and wrote of the piteous story of Virginia, as it burned within him in his oldest days, when the combined fleets of France and Spain made a show of menace in the Channel, and he wished he were "under ground . . . rather than see the insolent Bourbon trampling under foot this once happy island." To

---

[1] "Appius and Virginia," by John Webster, was printed in 1654. "Virginia," by Samuel Crisp, acted and printed in 1754. Mr. Dyce was of opinion that Webster's tragedy had been played long before 1654; indeed that Webster was not alive in that year.

him his tragedy may have seemed as pathetic as that of Webster, without the overflow of force or archaic jocosities of the previous century; not as what it resembles, the dry framework of "a theme," filled by a schoolboy.

It was not below many eighteenth century tragedies; not duller, for instance, than the "Zobeide" of Mr. Cradock "of Leicestershire," or the "Orphan of China" of Arthur Murphy. Nor is it correct to say with Madame D'Arblay, that it had a "catastrophe of a yea and nay character," that it neither succeeded nor failed; or with Macaulay, that there was "a feeling that the attempt had failed." Nine nights then brought three authors' benefits, and not many plays ran much longer. In his Epilogue, Garrick asked for little more—

> "Our author hopes, this fickle goddess, *Mode*,
> With us, will make, at least, nine days abode;
> To present pleasure he contracts his view,
> And leaves his future fame to time and you." [1]

Nine were as many as were secured for Johnson's "Irene." Mr. Crisp's play "ran" at least eleven nights at Drury Lane; was reproduced at Covent Garden, as well as at Drury Lane, in his lifetime; was reprinted (in 1778 and in 1784), in collections of standard English plays, from his own edition of "Virginia" in 1754. This, for that time, was success. If Mr. Crisp complained, what he must have missed was that admiration from the admired, which would have been sweeter than the applause of the pit of Garrick's bearing as "Virginius," of the working of his countenance while silent, and of his manner of saying "*Thou traitor!*" Yet in all his letters which we have seen, there is only a single sentence (that seized by Macaulay) which touches "Virginia," and even that is indirect. It merely supports a counsel to Fanny by his own experience. We could never have inferred from his letters,

---

[1] Garrick himself wrote and spoke the Prologue to "Virginia"; he also wrote the Epilogue, which was spoken by Mrs. Cibber.

or the letters of others about him, that he had, or had had, any great trouble but the gout (which we believe to have been his main misery), if it were not for Fanny's narrative, upon which Macaulay founded his. To her, who had heard Mr. Crisp speak of "Virginia," we must defer, but with a conviction that she herself would have "toned down" her picture had she known how much Macaulay would strengthen her outline and heighten her colouring. His inferences from her words are not unfair; but a close examination (which the "Memoirs of Dr. Burney" require as to dates and the order of events) would have shown, that in her sketch of Mr. Crisp facts are so run together, that his withdrawal to Chesington appears as a result of the cold reception of a play acted in 1754, whereas it was due to considerations of income and health ten years or more later.[1] One single fragment of a letter from Mr. Crisp to her father is all of their correspondence that Fanny has published. It was written shortly before Mr. Crisp left England, to press Burney to return to London. This he was not able to do for some years afterwards.

Mrs. Burney being the grand-daughter of a Huguenot, French was almost as much her language as English. She shared with her husband the pleasure and profit to be gained

---

[1] Mr. Crisp to Mr. Burney. [Probably written in 1756, or 7.] . . . .
"I have no more to say, my dear Burney, about harpsichords, and if you remain amongst your foggy aldermen, I shall be the more indifferent whether I have one or not. But really, among friends, is not settling at Lynn planting your youth, genius, hopes, fortune, &c., against a north wall? Can you ever expect ripe, high-flavoured fruit, from such an aspect? . . . . Take then, your spare person, your pretty mate, and your brats, to that propitious mart," [London] " and
 'Seize the glorious, golden opportunity,'
while you have youth, spirits, and vigour to give fair play to your abilities, for placing them and yourself in a proper point of view. And so I give you my blessing.
"SAMUEL CRISP."

from books. She made a translation from Maupertuis, which her husband published, after her death, with his own "Essay towards a History of Comets."

Among the three ladies in Lynn who read, she was the chief. The other two were Dolly Young, whom Esther Burney wished Dr. Burney to marry after her own death,[1] and Mrs. Stephen Allen, whom he did marry in the end.

While Mrs. Burney was "reading the best authors" with Hetty, Fanny was learning by ear. She was so slow in learning to read, that her sister Susan, who was between two and three years the younger, could read before Fanny knew her letters; but in her own words to Hetty (1821), "Well I recollect your reading with our dear mother all Pope's works and Pitt's 'Æneid.' I recollect you also spouting passages from Pope, that I learned from hearing you recite them before—many years before, I knew them myself." Her dulness seems to have been as superficial as the quickness of many children. Her mother, who was never deceived by it, said she had no fear of Fanny, when friends called the child "the little dunce." Nor does it appear that, after the dreary days of the alphabet and the copybook, anyone near to her thought Fanny dull. She was looked upon as considerate, reflective, and wise above nature; as a Mentor rather than a dunce. Her diffidence had much share in her apparent dulness. Diffidence ran in the family. Dr. Burney's polished manners concealed it; Fanny suffered from it through life; it has made her cousin Edward less known as a painter than he well deserved to be; and the two apparent exceptions, Fanny's sister Charlotte and her cousin Richard, may have been,—one somewhat flippant, the other a coxcomb by design,—out of a well-known turn taken by excessive diffidence.

---

[1] She had a local reputation. Richards mentions her as "the intelligent Miss Young" in his "History of Lynn."

In 1760 the Burney family left Lynn for London, where the head of it soon became the music-master most in request; but his wife sickened in Poland Street, apparently after the birth of her fourth daughter, Charlotte. As was the custom in cases of consumption, she was sent to "Bristol Hot Wells," (now called Clifton,) where she rallied. This change for the better did not last long. She died, after a short, severe illness, on the 28th of September, 1761. We are told that during their mother's last days, Fanny and Susan were sent to Mrs. Shields, a friend of their family, who lived in Queen Square, to be out of the way; and it is added that, when told of the loss of her mother, " the agony of Frances's grief was so great, though she was not more than nine years old, that Mrs. Shields declared that she had never met with a child of such intense and acute feelings.

Dr. Burney's loss was great; so was his grief. Nothing is known of his next few years. His friends did their utmost to cheer him; the Garricks being conspicuously kind. Dr. Burney struggled with his grief. He sought some task difficult enough to compel his attention, and made, at this time, a prose translation of Dante's greatest poem, choosing it because it was not among the Italian poems which he had read with his Esther.

Among Fanny's papers, the following, from Dr. Burney, is the first:—

[Woodhay, Berkshire, N° 1, 1763.] [1]

" FOR FANNY.

" My Fanny shall find
That I have in mind
Her humble request and petition,

---

[1] Woodhay, near Newbury, a "most sweet place," was the summer-

Which said, if I'd write her
A line 'twould delight her
And quite happy make her condition.

" I'm not such a churl
To deny my dear girl
So small and so trifling a favour;
For I always shall try
With her wish to comply,
Though of nonsense it happen to savour.

" 'Tho' little I say,
I beg and I pray
That careful you'll put these lines rare by;
For well they'll succeed,
If my love they should plead—
So now you've a letter to swear by.
"C. B."

"*La rime n'est pas riche*," but it gave the pleasure it was meant to give. Fanny has numbered it, headed it, and endorsed it in childish round hand; then added, in old age, "from my dear father, when I was ten years old." Fanny's next two numbered papers are letters from her father when in Paris, for the first time, on the occasion of taking her sisters Esther and Susan to school. One begins thus: " I write to my dear Fanny to tell her grandmamas, to tell her aunts, to tell her uncles, to tell her cousins, to tell all friends, that we are now at Paris. 'Tis now Wednesday night the 13th of June.[1] I am just come from the Comick Opera,

---

dwelling of Dr. Burney's kind friend, Susannah Maria Arne, (Mrs. Cibber,) who lived but three years after 1763. On her death, Garrick said, "Barry and I still remain, but Tragedy is dead *on one side*."

[1] 1764, Fanny's twelfth birthday.

which is here called the *Comédie Italienne*, where I have been extremely well entertained, but am so tired with standing the whole time, which every one in the pit does, that I can hardly put a foot to the ground, or a hand to the pen." His journey had been slow on account of one of those severe feverish colds to which Susan was subject. She was, to all seeming, quite well when they left Calais about ten o'clock at noon on the previous Thursday, but so tired when they reached Boulogne at five, that they "did not get into the chaise till near twelve o'clock, and lay at Abbeville, fifty-four miles from Boulogne." Poor Susan was again indulged by rest in bed until near eleven, before posting to Amiens, thirty miles farther, to dine. They slept at Breteuil; next day, they dined at Clermont, and slept at that "very delightful place, Chantilly." On Monday night they reached the Hôtel de Hollande, in Paris.[1] When Dr. Burney wrote, Susan was a little better, but he had been "excessively wretched about her," as she had had paroxysms of coughing, and of bleeding of the nose. Indeed one reason for taking her to school in France was the hope that the air might strengthen her. Dr. Burney next says, that Lady de Clifford, who lived below him in the hotel, "hearing we were English, very kindly sent to desire to see us." To-morrow, or next day, he will "have some cloathes to appear among French people in." He has found out his friend, Mr. Strange, [the great engraver,] and has been with Sir James Macdonald, "not minding dress with my countrymen."

In the second letter, (which was written on the 17th and 18th of June,) Dr. Burney informs Fanny that her sister Susan is a great deal better, but that he has made no progress towards finding a proper school for her and Hetty. "It turns out far more difficult to find out a proper house for them than I had

---

[1] He desires to be addressed "*Rue du Colombier.*"

expected." The next day he has "*hopes* of placing them much to his satisfaction"; "it will cost a good deal more money" than he expected, but he is "now too far advanced to retreat." Then comes a glimpse of Paris under Louis XV. The morrow is "a great festival, when all the Streets and Churches will be hung with Tapestry, and the finest Pictures in the King's Collections will be exposed. There will be likewise Processions of the Clergy in all parts of the City. Hetty and Susey have been out but very little yet, not having had proper Cloathes: and indeed if they had been ever so much dressed Sukey was unable to stir at Home or Abroad. I was on Sunday at the English Ambassador's Chapel, (Lord Hertford,) and saw there a great many English People, among whom was Mr Coleman, author of 'the Deuce is in him,'[1] etc., Mr Vaillant the Bookseller,—Mr Wilks, etc,—Ld Beauchamp son to the Ambassador has been very civil and has showed me the House wch his Father Lord Hertford lives in, and for wch his Lordship gives £800 a year. It is called l'Hotel de Brancas, the name of a French Duke now living, and is the finest and best furnished and fitted up I ever saw. Mr Hume, Secretary to the Embassy, is likewise very civil and Friendly to me,[2] as is Lady Clifford who lives in the same House and is own sister to the Duchess of Norfolk, indeed she is uncommonly kind to your sisters, who w^d not know what to do about dress but for her Ladyship."

* * * * * *

"Oh if you were to see what a Beau they have made of me here!—but [I] sh^d in my present dress, figure at a Birth Day in England, yet here I am not near so fine as a Tradesman, who have all fine figured or [ ]³ silk Coats, and Laced

---

[1] George Colman, the elder.
[2] David Hume. He kept up this friendship towards Dr. Burney.
[3] The word has been torn away.

Ruffles,—while mine are only plain. Adieu, adieu, I shall present Hetty with this bit of paper to write down her dream upon, for she is now fast asleep at my Elbow."

"Dear Fanny,
"You must not expect anything *very clever now*, as you have *some*times, from me, because I am hardly awake yet. Papa talks of his being a Beau, I am sure if you were to see *me* you'd say I was an old woman, but shorter, for papa beg'd the favour of Lady Clifford to Buy for me and Susey a silk thing a-piece, and her Ladyship has Bought the silk for a Negligée for me, and a slip for Sukey. Mine was finish'd to night, and I have had it on. The Girls at nine and ten years old weare sacks and Coats here, and have seen severall about my size in Hoops, and if little Charley was here he might wear a Bag and Sword, for he wou'd be thought big enough.[1]

"I shall write often to you dear Fanny when we are plac'd, and am, in the most affec^{te} manner, your Loving sister and Friend,

"E. BURNEY."

Paris dispersed much of Dr. Burney's melancholy. He began to read and write without an effort. With the encouragement of Garrick he translated the words and adapted the music of Rousseau's little piece, "Le Devin du Village,"

---

[1] The future Greek scholar was then, according to the received accounts, seven years old at the utmost; Susan was between nine and ten, Hetty about fifteen. We are told that Fanny was left at home, because Dr. Burney feared that she had some predisposition to Romanism, her grandmother Sleepe, whom she much loved and revered, being (although the daughter of a Huguenot refugee, and the mother of an English Protestant daughter) herself a Roman Catholic. This shows a state of things in which Roman Catholic members of Protestant families migrated from France rather than be parted from their nearest relations.

Preface.

for the English stage, under the infelicitous title of "The Cunning Man." Hetty and Susan he left with Mme. St. Mart, who had some English pupils of rank. Little Susan, in her tenth year, began what so far as we know was the first of the many Burney diaries. None of it has been found, but a leaf exists which Susan, in a quaint, business-like manner, styles an "Appendix to follow April 19, 1767, in my journal written in this year of our Lord, 1770." As in it Susan mentions Hetty's marriage and her father's journey to France and Italy, this must have been written in the latter half of 1770. It is so delicately written that we could exclaim with Pacchieroti in later years—*Come scrive bene quella creatura!* As to the composition, even in the year before, 1769, Fanny very truly wrote, "that Susan's letters would not disgrace a woman of forty." It contains a summary of what had befallen her schoolfellows and the friends, French and English, whom she left in Paris, not without a note that two of her English schoolfellows did not return Hetty's call and her own when they came back, not merely to England, but to Poland Street, where they as well as the Burneys lived. The leaf ends thus, "I went to Chesington, Monday, April 20 (1767), and was conducted to the coach by my two elder sisters, and Cousin Dick. The company contained in the leather conveniency were an old lady, and a young man who entertained me very much by his ridiculous account of a passion which he had conceived for my sister Fanny, whom he saw at the inn. I found him to be a lieutenant—his name Williams—a whimsical, clever young man. I have never seen him since."[1]

---

[1] Since this was written, there has come into our hands M. Perey's "Histoire d'une Grande Dame au XVIIIe. Siècle." The great lady was the Princess Hélène Massalska, who afterwards married Prince Charles de Ligne. At nine years of age she was sent to the Convent of the Abbaye-aux-Bois, in Paris, to receive from nuns of noble birth, among girls with many quarterings, the training necessary for great

Preface.

Some time after the death of Mrs. Burney, Mr. Crisp and Charles Burney met by accident at the house of their common friend Mr. Vincent. The next day Mr. Crisp went to Poland Street, and at once made all the children his firm friends. Such was their fervour, that (as they did in after days to their dear Mr. Twining) Fanny and Susan used to follow Mr. Crisp "jointly" to the door, going "like supporters on each side, and never losing a quarter of an instant that we could spend with him—our most beloved Mr. Crisp!—who arrived in our hearts the first, and took the place of all!"[1]

Fanny's love for Dr. Burney was no ordinary filial love; it was a passion. Her loyalty, enthusiasm, and devotion extended from him to his friends, even to those least likely to please a girl. See how she writes, for instance, of two able but very ungainly men,—Christopher Smart and William Bewley; the latter of whom was even repulsive in appearance. Mr. Crisp, a handsome, agreeable, highly-bred bachelor of fifty-five, was at once taken into the heart of the shy and silent little girl of nine. But for the great difference of years, one can have no doubt that it would have been *love* on her part. Dr.

---

ladies who were to adorn the Court of France. This Polish child found her schoolfellows (some of whom were approaching the arrangement of their marriages) amusing themselves by writing the memoirs of their own lives before they entered the convent, and during their abode therein. She followed what she calls the fashion, and has left a series of *cahiers* like those of Fanny, showing her life in and out of the convent, up to her marriage at fourteen. Hélène yields to no girl in putting before us what happened. Her sketches of the Abbaye, that nursery and training-school of ladies of rank before the Revolution in France, are of great value. She entered it in 1773. In 1764, Susan Burney, who was between nine and ten years old, was placed in Madame St. Mart's school in Paris. Perhaps *she* also found the fashion of writing some account of their lives prevailing among her school-fellows. At any rate she is the first of the known journal-writers of the Burney family, and hers is the earliest fragment which has been found.

[1] Diary of Mme. D'Arblay, vol. iv., p. 55.

Burney hinted as much when, in the very beginning of these journals, he calls Mr. Crisp "*Fanny's flame.*" To visit Mr. Crisp, to please him, to be approved by him, to write to him, to receive his letters, was Fanny's chief aim, until on her list of his letters she notes the fatal year which deprived her of him, 1783.[1] As she read and revised her papers of fifty years ago, in handwriting cramped or tremulous through age she added to her old tender phrases fresh words of praise of Mr. Crisp. By her love she won his. For some years there is no sign that he distinguished her more than Hetty, who also wrote to him, but in the end she was "Fannikin, the dearest thing to me on earth." Though out of *date* here, the following touching letters written when Mr. Crisp was very ill, while Fanny was staying with the Thrales, are not out of *place*. No words of another can tell of the love between Mr. Crisp and Fanny like their own.

[MR. CRISP TO MISS BURNEY.]

" My dear Fannikin,

"My weak state of health can never destroy my sense of your kindness; or prevent, while I am able, my acknowledging it. Your sending over a Messenger on purpose to enquire after an old, sick, obscure Daddy, surrounded as you are, with every thing that is splendid, gay, bright, happy, shews a heart not of the common sort;—not to be chang'd by a change of Situation, and Circumstances; the favour & smiles of the World:—tho' I always esteem'd it, I did not perfectly know its full value till Now.—You are to be envied for the possession of such a warm Muscle;[2] for though it may occasion you

---

[1] "Letters from and to my honoured friend, and earliest counsellor, Mr. Crisp." The number which she had preserved in each year is noted opposite the year from 1773; against 1783 are ejaculations of grief.

[2] If this expression should seem odd, what say we to Prosper Mérimée's

some palpitations which other people escape, yet upon the whole, it is amply its own reward, and so I wish you joy of it."—He then gives some account of the weakness and infirmities of his "crazy constitution." He expects a visit from Dr. Lewis, "an excellent Physician," and adds that "Either Kate, or I, (if I am able,) shall, (since you seem really to be anxious for your old Daddy,) let you know how I go on—and if you will, in return, let me hear some of your proceedings when your time will permit it will be most acceptable to me; for weak as I am, both in Body & Mind, I still interest Myself in whatever regards a Fannikin, and shall so continue to do to my last hour. Such in those moments, as in all the past, your most affectionate Daddy,

"S. C.

"Chesington, Friday, May 15, 1779."

MISS BURNEY " to SAMUEL CRISP, Esq'., at Chesington, near Kingston, Surrey.

"Streatham, May 20/79, *credo*.[1]

"My dear Daddy! Your last sweet Letter was the most acceptable I almost ever received in my life,—your extreme kindness to me nearly equalled the joy I had from hearing you were getting better. I do *long* to see you most eagerly, and will, with my first power, contrive it—indeed, I have made everybody *here* long to see you too, but I would not for any bribery be as little likely to have *my* longing gratified as their's is. Your *exculpation* of me was like yourself, liberal and unsuspicious;—and indeed, my dear Daddy, my heart

---

telling his *inconnue*—" Entre nous, je ne crois pas que vous ayez encore la jouissance de ce *viscère* nommé cœur."

[1] The dates and the "*credo*" were added by Mme. D'Arblay many years afterwards. The letter was written in 1779. It is franked thus by Mr. Thrale, "H free Thrale."

was as unalterably and gratefully attached to you as it *could* be, and so it must ever remain,—for, for many, many years, you have been more dear to me than *any* other person out of my immediate family in the whole world;—and this, though I believe I never was so *gross* before as to say it to *you*, is a notorious fact to all others;—and Mrs. Thrale is *contented* to come next you, and *to know* she cannot get above you.[1]—I am half ashamed of this *un*delicacy,—but your Illness & kindness joined *put me off my guard*. However, I hope you will make no bad use of my confession, ... believe me, ever and ever yours, "F. B."

A later letter runs in the same strain,—

[MR. CRISP TO MISS BURNEY.]

"June 26, 1781.

"How could you have the face to say to Miss Gregory[2] what you did, about me?—it is well for Us both, that I live out of the way, and out of the knowledge of the World; otherwise, how could *I* hope to escape the disgrace of being *weigh'd in the balance & found wanting*, & *you* the imputation of a most partial and egregious Puffer of an old, worn-out, insignificant Daddy, that never was a quarter of what you pretend, & now less so than ever?—I am not only well content, but delighted,

---

[1] Although he was delighted at Fanny's success in society, Mr. Crisp had not been without pain on losing much of her company when Mrs. Thrale tried to engross it to herself, to the prejudice of both her friend at Chesington, and her family in St. Martin's Street. "It is in vain to repine," he writes; "I must say to myself *Caro me, ci vuol flemma!*"

[2] Miss Gregory, who at that time lived with Mrs. Montagu, was a daughter of the Scotch physician who wrote "A Father's Legacy to his Daughters." She married the Rev. Archibald Alison, author of "Essays on the Nature and Principles of Taste," &c., and was the mother of a more voluminous writer, Sir Archibald Alison.

that your Judgment should be warp'd in my favor by your kindness; but if the Report of an Evelina should bring on a scrutiny into the merits of the Cause, what must I do then?—Well!—love me on!—Continue in your blindness, & I will take my Chance for the rest, & depend upon my *Obscurity* for my *security*."

To go back; on Mr. Crisp's return from Rome, where he had lived some years, in order "to indulge his passion for music, painting, and sculpture," after living some time in London, he fitted up a house at Hampton with the objects of art which he had collected in Italy. As we write, we learn that among these there was probably the first pianoforte ever brought to England.[1] He had inherited the hospitable bent

---

[1] Dr. Burney's article "Harpsichord," in the Cyclopædia of Rees, seems to authorize this statement. "The first harpsichord with hammers brought to England was made by an English monk at Rome, Father Wood, for an English friend (the late Samuel Crisp, Esq., of Chesington, author of Virginia, a tragedy), and a man of learning and exquisite taste in all the fine arts." Mr. J. W. M. Gibbs, to whom we owe this, and much more information acquired in those "intelligent and persistent researches in the British Museum," and elsewhere, for which he has been thanked by Mr. Napier in his edition of Boswell's Johnson, proceeds to say: "The article adds that Fulke Greville purchased this harpsichord of Mr. Crisp for 100 guineas. Now, as I understand the matter, the main distinction between the harpsichord and the pianoforte was, originally, that the latter was made to do with 'hammers' what the former did with quills, &c. Therefore this harpsichord with hammers was virtually a pianoforte. In Dr. Burney's article on Harpsichords cited above, it is said that 'In the beginning of the last century, hammer-harpsichords were invented at Florence, of which there is a description in the "Giornale d'Italia," 1711,' and it is well known (continues Mr. Gibbs) that Cristofori of Florence, about 1709, was one of the earliest, if not the earliest, of the makers of the *hammer*-furnished instrument as we, in the main, now have it. The appearance of the pianoforte, as distinguished from the harpsichord, in England, is most generally dated back to about 1767, in which year there was an announcement in a Covent Garden play-bill that "a new instrument called

of his great-grandfather, Dr. Tobias, who entertained at his Wiltshire rectory all who came, "many more than a hundred persons at a time, and ample provision made for man and horse." [This was a solid basis to his great popularity as a preacher.] Our Mr. Crisp made his house so pleasant, that the number of his guests began to tell upon his income, which Fanny says was not more than "easy," nay, "*small*, but unincumbered." He lived with people who had the habits of high station, with means of living much greater than his own, and through such friends he next sought "an honourable place with a good salary," but he had not taken part enough

---

'Piano-Forte'" would be played; but the above introduction from Rome by Mr. Crisp would bear an earlier date." It is probable that it would, as so far as any dates can be made clear from the narrative in the Memoirs of Dr. Burney, Mr. Crisp's residence in Rome was between 1750, the year in which Dr. Burney went to Lynn, and 1754, the year in which his tragedy "Virginia" was acted. It may be, that Mr. Crisp brought the instrument into England before it had yet been given the fanciful name of piano-forte, or forte-piano.

In Fanny's first diary, we find Mr. Greville (who had not long returned from his Bavarian Embassy) supping in Poland Street in August or September 1768. He asks Dr. Burney "if he play'd much on piano-fortes?" The words seem to carry his thoughts back to Mr. Crisp: "'If I was to be in town this winter,' said he, 'I should cultivate my old acquaintance with old Crisp.' 'Ah,' said papa, 'he's truly worth it.' 'Ay, indeed is he,' answered Mr. Greville, 'he's a most superiour man.'" This acquaintance was never renewed, Mr. Crisp having particularly desired Dr. Burney not to disclose his dwelling-place to Mr. Greville. This appears to throw back the transfer of Mr. Crisp's harpsichord with hammers to Mr. Greville to a time, it may be, ten or twelve years earlier than 1767.

Although the Editor has in several of her notes acknowledged the aid of Mr. Gibbs, she wishes, in this appropriate place, more especially to thank him for the zeal and patience with which he has assisted her endeavours to clear not only chronological and other questions directly concerning the Burney family, but also many minute points of literary interest collateral to the subjects of these diaries.

in politics to have claims upon any faction. He abhorred the furious factions of his day, and had brought back from the continent of Europe opinions less in agreement with those of Dr. Tobias Crisp than with those of Sir Nicholas, as, for instance, that "an arbitrary government mildly administered (*as France is, and has been of late years* . . .), is, upon the whole, the most permanent and eligible of all forms."[1] Mr. Crisp got no place (not even one in the Custom House!), but was seized by a fit of the gout, after looking at his bills; and in great fear of debt, sold his collections, gave up housekeeping, and joined an old friend whose purse and health were in a worse plight than his own, in what Madame D'Arblay calls "some pic-nic plan of sharing expenses." This friend, Mr. Christopher Hamilton, was the owner of Chesington Hall, in Surrey, a house much too spacious for his income. It was by no means Mr. Crisp's first stay at Chesington, so it may be that he withdrew to the old house, and shunned his old associates, not merely as a means of keeping within his income, but of improving his health, since Dr. Burney (who knew him well for nearly forty years) wrote in his epitaph on Samuel Crisp how great a part he might have played—

> "Had he through life been blest by Nature kind,
> With health robust of body, as of mind."

After the death of Mr. Hamilton (who was the last male of his branch of the Hamilton family), Mr. Crisp still clung to the old Hall, partly perhaps out of kindness, and even charity, to Mr. Hamilton's spinster-sister, and her niece Miss Cooke. By becoming her first boarder, he helped Mrs. Hamilton to maintain herself. He read, he rode on horseback, he kept up his accomplishments by practice; he went to London for some time every spring, but when past sixty, by degrees it

---

[1] See pages 262-3, Vol. II., for the greater part of this letter, which bears the date of 1779.

became his habit to go less and less to London, and (as Fanny put it to him), "to shun new, and shirk most of his old, acquaintances." This is what Macaulay describes as "losing his temper and his spirits; becoming a cynic and a hater of mankind," and "hiding himself like a wild beast in his den." Chesington was no den, but a kind of sanatorium, without doctors; a country boarding-house for the convalescent, a "Liberty Hall" for the young and healthy. It stood (it now stands only in a drawing by Edward Burney) in pure air, on high ground rising gradually from a wide common. It had many and spacious rooms, large gardens, wide "prospects" over a charming country, ample supplies of milk and chickens, eggs and fruit.[1] "Dear, ever dear Chesington," cries Fanny, "whereat passed the scenes of the greatest ease, gaiety, and native mirth that have fallen to my lot."[2]

It was to many more than Fanny "a place of peace, ease, freedom, and cheerfulness." Thither went Dr. Burney to arrange the notes of his French and Italian tour, under the eye of Mr. Crisp, to whom he played upon the harpsichord, or with whom he played at whist, or backgammon.[3] There the future Admiral threw down his cards, and sang and laughed

---

[1] Nor must we omit Mr. Crisp's cucumbers. When Fanny went with Mr. and Mrs. Thrale to Chesington, towards the end of September, 1781, their interest was great in seeing that antique hall of the Hattons. Fanny wrote afterwards to Mr. Crisp: "Pray tell Kitty" [Cooke] "that Mr. Thrale, when he talked of his prowling all over the Chesington house, said,—'Pray what does Mr. Crisp do with all those cucumbers in his room?'"—What Dr. Johnson did with the orange-peel that he dried, may be found in his letters to Miss Boothby, although he refused to tell it to Boswell; but Mr. Crisp may have stuffed his cucumbers with pearls (like those in the "Arabian Nights") for anything we know.

[2] This was written in 1786. See p. 124, Vol. I. Fanny adds, "All its inhabitants are good-humoured and obliging, and my dear Mr. Crisp alone would make it, to us, a Paradise."

[3] A sketch of Mr. Crisp at cards is preserved in Fanny's diary for

for joy, whirling Kitty Cooke about the room in a frenzied dance, when an express brought the news of his appointment to the "Latona" frigate of eight and thirty guns;[1] there Hetty took her babies and herself for change of air, and, with her husband, made music to Mr. Crisp; there Edward Burney took Fanny in a post-chaise "loaded with painting materials."[2] There Fanny and Maria Allen, with Jenny Barsanti, played Cibber's "Careless Husband," amid "outrageous mirth"; there Mr. Crisp and Hetty danced a minuet, as Madame Duval and Mr. Smith in Fanny's novel. This we *must* extract from Susan's diary; to show "the gloom" in which Mr. Crisp ended his life, "the same gloom in which, during more than a quarter of a century, it had been passed":[3] "Monday night after supper we were all made very merry by Mr. Crisp's suffering his wig to be turn'd the hind part before, and my cap put over it—Hetty's cloak—and Mrs. Gast's apron and ruffles—in this ridiculous trim he danced a minuet with Hetty, personifying *Madame Duval*, while she acted *Mr. Smith* at the Long Room, Hampstead![4]—The maids

---

1778. She blames a lady "famed for tonishness" for dressing in such a manner as "to obtain notice, and excite remark," and adds, "I always long to treat" [such people] "as Daddy Crisp does bad players (when his own partners, at whist), and call to them with a nod of contempt 'Bless you! Bless you!'"

[1] This was but a temporary appointment.

[2] "August 12, 1782.—We came in a chaise, which was well loaded with canvasses, pencils, and painting materials, for Mr. Crisp was to be three times painted, and Mrs. Gast once. My sweet father came down Gascoign Lane to meet us, in very good spirits, and very good health. Next came dear Daddy Crisp, looking vastly well, and, as usual, high in glee and kindness at the meeting. Then the affectionate Kitty, the good Mrs. Hamilton, the gentle Miss Young, the enthusiastic Mrs. Gast."—*Diary of Madame D'Arblay.*

[3] See Macaulay's review of the "Diary and Letters of Madame D'Arblay."

[4] See "Evelina," Letter L.

were call'd in to see this curious exhibition, and we all thought poor *Mutty* would have snigger'd away all her strength."

As a matter of fact, we commonly find Mr. Crisp laughing in these letters, and with a laugh quite his own. A gentleman whom Fanny met at Brighton in 1770, reminded her (she says) of Mr. Crisp. "He has not so good a face, but it is *that sort of face*, and his laugh is the very same: for it first puts every feature in comical motion, and then fairly shakes his whole frame, so that there are tokens of thorough enjoyment from head to foot."[1] Fun-making, with Fanny, was a frequent form of his melancholy. However, as he was well read in Molière, we do catch echoes of the "Misanthrope" in his letters and conversation, but rather of Philinte, than of Alceste himself. Look at that letter to Fanny on young ladies being, as it were, "*feræ naturæ*," and men "animals of prey," and then read Philinte's answer to the Misanthrope, Alceste:

> "Oui, je vois ces défauts dont votre âme murmure,
> Comme vices unis à l'humaine nature,
> Et mon esprit enfin n'est pas plus offensé,
> De voir un homme fourbe, injuste, interessé,
> Que de voir des vautours affamés de carnage,
> Des singes mal faisants, et des loups plein de rage."

As Philinte spoke to Alceste, so Mr. Crisp wrote to Fanny. He saw, and divined, that her youthful enthusiasm was far beyond even the enthusiasm natural to generous youth. The century of Molière had had good reason to distrust and dread enthusiasm. With the century of Mr. Crisp, it had, wrongfully, yet naturally, become a synonym with fanaticism. Mr. Crisp desired only that Fanny should learn to restrain her warmth of feeling before the movement of her life drew her among circumstances in which its exaltation might have en-

---

[1] "Diary of Madame D'Arblay," vol. i., p. 425.

dangered her happiness. She was so young, and even with him so timid, that he could not duly calculate the general justness of her perceptions, and clearness of her judgement.

Allowance must be made beside for Mr. Crisp's own vein of humourous exaggeration, of which there are many instances in these volumes. His affection it will be found, often showed itself in railing at his friends, old or young, and giving them hard names of playful abuse. He made out the world to be worse than it was in order to lead Fanny into making the best of it by practising discreet control of her feelings as a duty, not as a hateful self-suppression forced upon her by suffering from the results of too great openness of heart. To Mr. Crisp, Chesington was a contracted, and too often monotonous little world, but we see no token that he was ever gloomy unless he had the gout, or despondent except about the safety of England in the troubled years of the American War.

Mr. Crisp far too well knew himself beloved by a few ever to be morbid as he has been pictured. He smiles at the warmth of his young admirers towards a man of seventy. He tells the Burney girls that they are his "virtuous seraglio." Once, when he is writing on Susan's engagement, or approaching engagement, which was, perhaps, not yet made known to the elders, he says to Fanny, "when I *do* put her [Susan] to the cost of a Penny, . . . it will be directed . . . to Hetty's house, because of becauses—besides it looks so like an intrigue, and consequently I must be an *Homme à bonne fortune* with a young girl." [1]

Chesington was not dull except in winter. Often very droll people were to be met among Mrs. Hamilton's boarders; such as the odd group of foreigners, and Mrs. Simmons, and her sister, in 1774, who, with Kitty Cooke, were treasures of quaintness of speech. The "den" had strange animals in it,

---

[1] This is dated 15 Nov. 1780.

of the very kind Fanny loved, as she said, "for sport." That Chesington could not be reached by any carriage-road; that there was only one tolerable track across the common for Dr. Burney's occasional post-chaises; that Hook Lane and Gascoign Lane lay deep in mud all winter; that Mr. Thrale *must* use four horses when he drove to Chesington, from which his own Streatham could be seen with a telescope, as Chesington could be from Epsom when Fanny used her glass; that there was no regular delivery of letters except by the baker, that "The Parson"[1] brought them, or anyone else who came from Kingston, were grievances not peculiar to Chesington: Streatham, with its wits and its men of wealth, had what Mr. Crisp calls an "odious post." A letter which he wrote to Fanny on the 28th of March did not reach Streatham until the 2nd of April. Yet they came to Mr. Crisp somehow, those letters and journals of the girls: he knew more of their joys and their troubles than did Dr. Burney, who was either "passing from scholar to scholar," and dining in his coach on the road or writing in his study,—a "chaos" which his daughters felt to be peculiarly inaccessible to suitors for their hands. Their inclination or disinclination to this or that wooer seems to have been made known to Mr. Crisp, before it was timidly hinted to the busy Dr. Burney. We find Hetty desirous that Mr. Crisp should persuade Fanny to accept a very good offer of marriage; we find Fanny praying him not to press her to marry a man whom she could not love. Susan's engagement with her brother's comrade, Captain Phillips, is a subject of other letters, in which the lover is given a fictitious name. They were but anticipating their father, for on all points, as to books, or music, the education of his sons and the establishment of his daughters, Dr. Burney likewise con-

---

[1] "My patience" (writes Mr. Crisp to Fanny in 1778) "was almost exhausted, when lo! in comes your letter, brought by the parson."

sulted Mr. Crisp. The adopted father of eight Burneys could lack no interest in his life. It ended in severe suffering, but in no other gloom. He was almost worshipped by his kind nurses, Mrs. Hamilton and Kitty Cooke. Fanny, and Susan watched his bed, and it was with difficulty that Hetty and Charlotte were prevailed upon to keep away.[1] His sister, too, was there, a woman of the old Crisp fervour of character, who was devoted to her only brother, from whom circumstances had parted her early and long.

From the order of names in a will, she seems to have been Mr. Crisp's fourth sister. In 1725 she was still unmarried. She married a Mr. Gast, whose name has a French look. When a widow she joined her sister, Mrs. Anne Crisp,[2] in living at Burford in Oxfordshire, a place to which Mrs. Anne had probably been drawn by its being within reach of two other branches of the Crisp family, those of "Mr. Crisp, the

---

[1] Five years after his death, Fanny writes thus of Mr. Crisp to Susan: "Our most beloved Mr. Crisp!—who arrived in our hearts the first, and took the place of all! Ah, my dearest Susan, what a blank is to me the reflection that he is no more! Even to this moment I can scarce forbear, at times, considering how I shall relate to him my affairs, and what will be his opinion when he hears them! Yet the remembrance grows less bitter; for now, as you find, I can bear to name it. Till very, very lately, I was always forced to fly from the subject wholly; so poignant, so overwhelming I found it."

[2] The acquaintance between Anne Crisp and Mary Granville (Mrs. Delany) may have begun in those early days when the Granvilles lived in retired poverty at Buckland, near Campden, in Gloucestershire. The great friend of Mrs. Gast, at Burford, who shared her delight in Fanny's letters to Mr. Crisp, was "Molly Lenthall," a descendant of Speaker Lenthall, whose house Horace Walpole went to see in 1753, and Mrs. Boscawen in 1783. Walpole writes to Mr. Bentley: "At Burford, I saw the house of Mr. Lenthal, the descendant of the Speaker .... except a portrait of Sir T. More's family, by Holbein, the portraits are rubbish, though celebrated. I am told that the Speaker who really had a fine collection, made his peace" (after the Restora-

eminent lawyer of Chipping Norton," [1] and Sir Charles, the great-grandson of Sir Nicholas, and last baronet of his name, who lived at Dornford, in the parish of Wootton, in Oxfordshire.

Unless Mr. Crisp had another sister a widow, whose name was Gough, (of which we find no sign,) the following extract from a letter of Mrs. Delany's to her sister, Mrs. Dewes, gives us a glimpse of Mrs. Gast:—

"I must tell you a story of our old friend Nanny Crisp, though it cost me half a sheet more of paper. She has a sister Gough, younger by several years than herself, who has been abroad, and is a widow in very bad circumstances.[2] Mrs. Bernard, who told me the story, says she is very ordinary in her appearance, but an excellent creature, and far superior to our old acquaintance in understanding. A sister of Mrs. Bernard's was asked by a gentleman of a very good estate, who has one only daughter (a child), if she could recommend a wife to him who was qualified to make him a good companion,

---

tion,) "by presenting them to Cornbury, where they were well known, until the Duke of Marlborough bought that seat." "Lightly come, lightly go," if Lenthall paid Lord Chancellor Clarendon for his peace, as it is said, with what he himself had plundered from the houses of Royalists, or bought from those who stole. Many of his pictures are reported to be at "The Grove," in Hertfordshire. Mrs. Boscawen, who describes the mansion of the Lenthalls as "forlorn," says of the pictures, "*how* they *have* been neglected and spoilt!"

[1] His daughter was the first wife of Bishop Butler's patron, Bishop Talbot. Sir Charles Crisp married his father's first cousin, Anne Crisp, heiress of Sir Thomas Crisp, Knight, of Dornford, the youngest son of "old Sir Nicholas."

[2] Compare this with Mrs. Gast's statement to Fanny, that her "very long absences, even from her childhood," made it more than probable that she knew less of her brother's mind than was known by Fanny, adopted child. See Appendix, p. 329, Vol. II. The "Nanny Crisp" of this letter was certainly Mr. Crisp's sister, and Gough is probably a misreading or misprint for Gast.

and to educate his daughter; she immediately thought of Mrs. Gough; as he neither insisted on *youth, beauty,* nor *fortune.* She told him she could recommend just such a person who would make him a happy man. (They were at this time at Oxford, Nanny Crisp and her sister at Burford): it was agreed that Mrs. Price should carry him there to breakfast, she did accordingly, and what do you think happened? *He falls in love with Crisp,* and will not hear of Mrs. Gough! but Crisp has vowed to live and die a virgin, and will not admit of any addresses."[1]

Mrs. Gast took her brother's "Fannikin" upon trust from his descriptions, and her own journals, until she met her at Chesington in 1776. In 1777 we find her calling with her brother at "Newton House," in St. Martin's Street.

The first visit of Fanny to Chesington that is mentioned, was in the first half of the year 1766.[2] Soon afterwards Fanny, with little Charlotte under her care, was to have had her turn of two years' schooling, under Madame St. Mart, in Paris. This plan was delayed, and, in the end, dropped; owing to Mrs. Stephen Allen's coming, when a widow, to London, that her daughter Maria might have better teaching than she could obtain at Lynn. Mrs. Allen had lamented the death of Dr. Burney's first wife with him. He soon found the society of so handsome, well-read, intelligent a woman, consolatory. She, who had been married by her family to her cousin, (whom she merely esteemed,) found in Dr. Burney the husband of her choice. Some opposition from her family appears to have been avoided by a private marriage, in October, 1767. Mr. Crisp was in the secret, and himself hired rooms for the wedded couple in a farm-house near Chesington. It

---

[1] "Life and Correspondence of Mrs Delany," vol. iii., p. 52, First Series.

[2] This may possibly indicate the time when the Hall became a boarding-house.

was a stolen honeymoon. In accordance with the rules of the novel writer, the secret was made known through the misdelivery of a letter. The young Burneys and Maria Allen looked upon that marriage as a happy event which joined them all in one merry party in the same house.

Dr. Burney describes his second wife as being of a "cultivated mind, intellects above the general level of her sex, and with a curiosity after knowledge, insatiable to the last." Her "extensive reading, and the assistance of a tenacious and happy memory," enabled "her to converse with persons of learning and talents on all subjects to which female studies are commonly allowed to extend; and, through a coincidence of taste and principles in all matters of which the discussion is apt to ruffle the temper, and alienate affection, our conversation and intercourse was sincere, cordial, and cheering." There are hints in these papers, that some of her step-daughters thought she loved what *they* called "*argumentation*, better than any other thing in the world," and that those visitors who shared her love of discussion and controversy, were her favourites. As Mrs. Stephen Allen, she had held a sort of *bas-bleu* meeting once a week; as Mrs. Burney, she received men of letters, or art, almost daily, in an informal way. She was of a critical bent, and, eleven years later, Mrs. Burney was "the quarter from which" [Fanny] "most dreaded satire," should she discover the authorship of "Evelina." Under the influence of some hints from this new step-mother, who saw, and heard of, some scribbling, that girls who wrote lost their time, and risked their good repute, and some doubts of her own to the same effect, Fanny made that "great renunciation," that piteous bonfire of her works in prose and verse, in the paved court in Poland Street, while Susan looked on in tears.[1] Mrs. Burney not

---

[1] Among Fanny's tragedies and epic poems, she burned a novel

lxvi *Preface.*

merely meant well, but set a great and judicious value upon Fanny's head and heart. A singular proof of this remains in a letter which Fanny endorsed many years afterwards, "The Recommendation of Richard to F. B., when the latter was sixteen, from her mother-in-law." This letter was written after Fanny's return to London in the autumn of 1768, while Mrs. Burney was left at Lynn, awaiting the birth of her son Richard, to whom Fanny had written, in advance, a letter of welcome into the world; sending with it a baby's cap of her own embroidery.

"Thursday, y° 13th Octo^{r.}

"My dear Fanny,

"I've but a bad excuse to make for not acknowledging your two letters—as well as generous present to *the Unborn*—I've not been Well, and what was worse woefully out o' spirits —so much that I wanted resolution to take pen in hand, to any one but you know who—and I ought not even there—but I am better both as to health and chearfullness—so will try to thank you for all you say to *me* and *mine* indeed I comfort

---

called "The History of Caroline Evelyn." This name may have rung in her ears, echoed from a one volume tale by Colley Cibber's youngest daughter, Mrs. Charlotte Charke, "The History of Henry Dumont, Esquire, and Miss Charlotte Evelyn," which was in its third edition in 1756. Mr. Gibbs kindly tells us that he has also observed in various book lists "The Morning Ramble, or the History of Miss Evelyn," 2 vols, 12mo, 1775; and "Evelina, a poem," 1773. There was also Mason's heroine, "Evelina." Thus "Evelyn" and "Evelina" were names in stock for novels and verse in Fanny's young time. There was also a novel of that period called "The History of Miss Charlotte Villars." Villars is the name of the good clergyman in "Evelina," a novel which shows little research in names, as that of Dubois was the maiden-name of Fanny's grandmother, Mrs. Sleepe, and Macartney the maiden-name of her godmother, Mrs. Greville. She would not have taken names so near to her, had she ever expected to be known as an author.

Preface. lxvii

myself often, when I think how *doubtfull* the continuance of my Life is, by considering and reflecting on the goodness of your heart and disposition that they will expand in Acts of Kindness and Affection towards even the *half* of sweet Charlotte's relationship to you. Allow me my dear Fanny to take this moment (if there proves occasion) to recommend a helpless infant to your pity and protection, you will ev'ry day become more and more capable of the task—and you will, I *do* trust you will, for your *same* dear Father's sake, cherish and support *His* innocent child, tho' but *half* allied to you.—My weak heart speaks in tears to you my love, Let it be the Voice of nature, which is always heard, where the heart is not harden'd to its dictates. I'm sure yours is not. There—somehow I am easier now, I think you've heard and will *listen* to me—so I'll dry my eyes and seek a more chearfull subject. As for your letter, I shall lay it by, and it shall be ye first letter ever read by those it is addressed to,—as your cap shall be its first covering." [1]

This surely is a letter which does credit to her who wrote, and to her who received it. Fanny was never called upon to be more than a kind sister to the child, but she many times nursed his mother in illness with great attention. Allowing

---

[1] Richard Burney was born on the 20th of November, 1768. On his birth, Fanny's step-sister (Maria Allen) wrote a comical note in his name to Fanny, thanking her for the kind letter she had written, which was delivered to him the minute he was born, and for "*de joli bonnet*" of her working, "de first he dfd *port* on his *tête*." She puts into his baby-mouth a jargon which was much used by these girls, made up of the oddest of the phrases of broken English which they heard from the foreign musicians and singers who frequented Dr. Burney's house. The babe begins his note as "Master Newcome," and ends it by "hoping she will excuse de long lettre from him, her affectionate
"Broter,
"BERNAI."

for what Maria Allen called "the little rubs" of life, Mrs. Burney's affection for, and confidence in Fanny, was never lessened, and hers was a hearty letter of congratulation to Fanny when she learnt the authorship of "Evelina."

We may suppose this great burning of manuscripts to have happened just before these early diaries begin, as it is obvious that such an instinct for writing as Fanny's could not have been resisted for any length of time.

There was living while these journals were being written a young lady some part of whose early life ran singularly parallel with part of the early life of Fanny Burney. This was Lætitia Hawkins, only daughter of Sir John. The father of each girl wrote a "History of Music." The whole book of Sir John Hawkins, and part of that of Dr. Burney, were published in the same year, 1776. Each father employed his daughter as his amanuensis. Each daughter was secretly occupied in writing a novel, which the youngest brother of each aided her in getting published without her name. In Fanny's case, Dr. Burney's consent was asked, but so far as we see, Sir John Hawkins died in ignorance that his "*girl*" had published several novels anonymously. "I was," (wrote Miss Hawkins,) "I will not say *educated*, but *broke*, to the drudgery of my father's pursuits. I had no time but what I could *purloin* from my incessant task of copying, or writing from dictation—"writing six hours in the day for my father, and reading nearly as long to my mother." Fanny nowhere mentions how much time *she* spent daily in copying for her father, until at last she feared that her hand-writing had become so well known among compositors that she was fain to disguise it when transcribing her own "Evelina" for the press. *She* never complains; once only she speaks of "stealing time to write"; but the letters of Mr. Crisp and Mrs. Rishton show how seldom she was spared to visit her friends.

Preface. lxix

These two clever girls knew more or less of the same people of note;—from Johnson, Hawkesworth, Garrick, and Horace Walpole, down to Nollekens and Jenny Barsanti; but there is no sign that they ever were acquainted with each other. A decorous reserve prevails in Fanny's early diaries towards the works and deeds of the rival historian of Music, Peter Pindar's "fiddling knight," Sir John Hawkins. His book is merely named, without praise or blame.[1] Each of these girls followed her father in his opinions; but what a difference there was between the fathers! To borrow Mr. Crisp's phrase, Lætitia had been "planted against a north wall," Fanny against a southern. Sir John was a pragmatical person: "stiff in opinions," often "in the wrong"; a Puritan by birth and in grain, notwithstanding his love of music: Lady Hawkins, a severe disciplinarian towards her children and servants. All about Lætitia was what Peter Pindar calls "*magistratial;*"— all was intended to "awe the vicious, and encourage the deserving." Lætitia's "Reminiscences" and her novels bristle with moral opinions, magisterially given forth.[2] They

---

[1] There is a sentence not unlike a hit at Dr. Burney in the amusing, inexact, and censorious volumes of "Reminiscences" of Lætitia Hawkins. It is this, "Those who, in giving out that they write a history of what is deep in its own essence, make it their principal aim to amuse"—that is, to be clear and pleasant to readers. Once only she names a Burney; then it is Dr. Charles, the Greek scholar.

[2] There is now and then a droll likeness between the phraseology of Lætitia and that of Fanny. It is when they shun "poor language," which was in much discredit in their pseudo-classic days. "*Be elegant*" was a first precept for authors, years beyond 1800. Bishop Porteous even writes, as in commendation, of "the elegant brevity of"— St. John the Divine. Miss Hawkins tells us that *her* father, when young, was "the victim of variegated tyranny"; Mme. D'Arblay writes of *hers* as being under "the parsimonious authority" of an elder brother. With one, Twickenham is "our lovely situated and elegantly inhabited village"; with the other St. Martin's is "our vulgarly-peopled street." Such queerly formed phrases were not peculiar to these two young

leave on the mind how much better it was to have been born a Burney than a daughter of Sir John Hawkins. Those nearest to Fanny's "observant eye and attentive ear" were all gifted with good hearts, good brains, good tempers, and good spirits. The same may be said of her cousins, the children of Dr. Burney's elder brother, Richard of Worcester, who was himself a man of some distinction. Dr. Burney was a man not worldly, but endowed with great natural and acquired tact as his safeguard against an impulsive disposition, and a very open and tender heart. His character was simple, his intellect many-sided. When naming his chief works, we passed for the moment over his by-play (which might have been the life's labour of many an author); by-play, such as his quarto volume upon the commemoration of Handel in 1784; his three octavo volumes of the Memoirs of Metastasio, meant as a supplement to his "History of Music"; his poem (which he, perhaps wisely, burned) on Astronomy, in twelve books or cantos, each of from four to eight hundred lines; his projects for "balloon-voyages"; his Essay on Comets; and his collections for a Dictionary of Music; his many occasional pieces in prose, verse, or music; his benevolent plans and efforts; among which was one for founding a School of Music, a "*Conservatorio*" (like those he had seen at Naples and Vienna), "in the bosom of the Foundling Hospital," by choosing from the boys and girls those who had good ears for music and promising voices.

The many things which he did, or tried to do, were, perhaps, less extraordinary than the sweetness of temper

---

ladies. You can find the like if you turn over books of the eighteenth century. One such phrase occurs to us as we write, "novel-studied." It is used by Abraham Tucker for an habitual reader of novels. Fanny, however, grew worse as she grew older, and increased her elegant periphrases, until her style became what it is in the memoirs of her father.

Preface. lxxi

which he maintained in working and in suffering. There was nothing of "the enraged musician" about him, although Reynolds has depicted him with a more restless countenance than our fancy could have foreseen.[1]

He was born at the close of a classic period. His young enthusiasm had been roused by the brilliant writings of the band of Queen Anne's men. When with Mr. Greville, at Bath, he had watched and waited for hours to gain glimpses of Bolingbroke. It pleased him to think that Swift might have entered his house in Queen Square as the guest of Lord Mayor Barber, and it was suspected that he removed to a house in St. Martin's Street chiefly because it had been the dwelling of Sir Isaac Newton. This fine enthusiasm, with his natural gifts and graces, and acquired knowledge and accomplishments, carried him, with little effort of his own, into social and friendly relations with many of the foreign, as well as with most of the English, men of note throughout his long life. His friendships and acquaintanceships were an inheritance and an education for his children. They inherited also from him, and gave to, and took from, each other, pleasing manners and kindly ways. Family tradition ascribes to his eldest child, Esther ("Hetty"), great loveliness, great sweetness of temper, much good sense, and a strong "love of fun." The "Gentleman's Magazine" records that when eight years old she "gained great notice among musical people by her astonishing performances on the harpsichord at her father's parties."[2] Fanny describes her, at

---

[1] We judge only from the engraving in the 7th volume of Madame D'Arblay's Diary. In 1778, Mr. Richard Twining writes from Göttingen to his brother Thomas (Dr. Burney's friend), that "Heyne's manner is extremely animated. He seems to be all *esprit*. He frequently folded his arms, and nodded his head in a way which put me much in mind of Dr. Burney."

[2] If the Poland Street parties are meant, Hetty must have been about eleven years old when they were given; but she may have begun to play at her father's parties at Lynn.

sixty-eight, as being "all spirit and vivacity,"—"the spring and spirit of her family;—happily, foreseeing neither sickness nor *ennui*." Yet Hetty, and her cousin and husband, Charles Burney of Worcester, must have shared the weight of many burdens of sickness and toil, as well as played many a duet together to the delight of all their hearers. Charles had been a pupil of Dr. Burney, whom he sometimes assisted. He had pupils of his own; he gave concerts, was player on the harpsichord at Drury Lane Theatre, and composed music. After "long toils," he withdrew to Bath, where he passed "serene days, in the tranquil enjoyment of peace, rest, books, music, and drawing."[1] As Charles drew, so his brother Edward was in some measure a musician; a certain readiness, facility, and aptitude for many things being shared among the Burney family. Edward was a portrait-painter, but he is better known as a designer of illustrations for books. Good judges who have seen his drawings speak of their delicacy of outline with admiration. His diffidence, which his cousin Fanny thought was almost without parallel, withheld him from taking the place which was thought to be his due by contemporary critics. Readers will find another son of Richard of Worcester, the humorous and fantastic "Cousin Dick, the genius of of the family," giving gaiety to many pages of these diaries.

Of Dr. Burney's own sons, the Admiral appears to have

---

[1] The words between commas are those of Madame D'Arblay. The following dates of events were copied by Dr. Burney, or Dr. Charles the younger, from "The Public Advertiser" into that wonderful collection of theirs in several hundred volumes, of play-bills, cuttings from newspapers, &c. &c., which is now in the British Museum: "In December, 1765, Charles Rousseau Burney was engaged at Drury-Lane Theatre. He played, for the second time, on the 3rd of that month, which was the benefit-night of Dr. Burney as arranger of Rousseau's 'Devin du Village' for an English stage. On the 4th, C. R. Burney played a concerto before the King and Queen, who went to see Garrick as 'Bayes.'"

been the most original in his ability. His wit and humour made him welcome among wits and men of letters who have preserved his name. He was so great a favourite with Mr. Crisp that Fanny often writes of him at a time when his better-known brother, the learned Dr. Charles that was to be, is only named as being "the sweetest-tempered boy in the Charter-house School," and Richard, Dr. Burney's youngest son, praised only for his boyish beauty.[1] Mr. Crisp's interest in James Burney was an earnest of his merit.

Susan told Mr. Crisp, "You know you do not love to throw away praise." And how well worth having was his regard and approbation may be seen throughout these volumes. In a letter with no date but "October," to which Fanny added many a year later, "1779, credo," she wrote to Mr. Crisp, "Our Jem is at last come,—and I have quitted Streatham to visit him,—so now all our long anxieties and fears are over,

---

[1] Martin, the only son of Admiral Burney, was a barrister, who is chiefly remembered as having been from his childhood one of Charles Lamb's "dearest objects," and returning warmly his affection, and that of Mary Lamb; "refusing to be comforted" when, on the 20th of May, 1847, he saw her laid beside her brother. His sister, Sarah, who married her cousin, John Payne, was a brilliant personage, of whom Hazlitt speaks as "a young lady very much like her aunt" (Madame D'Arblay), "and as the latter I conceived might have been at her time of life." She is described to the Editor as having been "full of fun and spirits," given to "madcap doings." After she had (as her aunt said) " sowed her wild oats," she "lived much on the Continent, but chiefly at Rome with her husband." Her wit and ability were shown in conversation, and in very interesting and amusing letters to her kindred describing the best Roman society. It seems fitting that a grand-daughter of Sir Robert Strange should have met this grand-daughter of Dr. Burney in Rome. "I wish," writes Mrs. Edmund Ffoulkes, "that my old friend Mrs. Payne's letters could be published. She and her husband had most interesting society at their house in Rome;—foreigners who were met nowhere else among the English. Cardinal Antonelli received the Paynes specially."

and we are all, thank Heaven, happy, and at peace. He has brought us home an admirable journal, of which I have only read one year, but I have found it full of entertainment and matters of curiosity, and really very well-written, concise, pertinent, and rational. You will be quite delighted with it, and he means to lend it to you of *his own accord.*"

Susan, the next in order of birth, although two years and a half younger than Fanny, was so early mature in mind as to influence, as well as feel with, her elder sister. In these papers, no character discloses itself more delightfully than that of Susan. It is with regret that we give but few extracts from what has been preserved of her excellent "journal-letters" to Fanny, the bulk of them belonging to a time later than 1778. Susan rated her own ability far too low. She was amazed when her stepmother, Mrs. Burney, paid the compliment of supposing her to be the joint author of " Evelina." In a letter, which Fanny has most justly described as being " of incomparable sweetness,"[1] Susan apologizes for occupying the precious time of such a person as Fanny with her own poor letters. All owned Susan to be a " gracious creature." Count Louis de Narbonne said that she was "all that is '*douce*,' with all that is '*spirituelle*'"; Owen Cambridge exclaimed to Fanny, "What a charm is that of your sister! What a peculiar felicity she has in her manner! She cannot even move, —she cannot get up, or sit down, but there is something in her manner that is sure to give pleasure!"

The " *dolcissima voce*" of Susan was praised by Baretti; her critical knowledge of music was such that Pacchierotti declared her to be " *capable de juger en professeur.*" The same celebrated singer said to her, " *You* are attached to Miss Fanny, and *she* to *you,* more than [to] the rest. There seem *but one soul*—but *one mind between you;*—you are *two* in *one.*"

See p. 268, Vol. II.

Preface.

To write Fanny charming letters, full of finely-touched sketches of things and people, and of happy turns of expression; to bring London before Fanny's eyes when she was at Chesington or with the Thrales, satisfied Susan. Perhaps she was not, like Fanny, *compelled* to write. We know not if she could have *found*—we were about to write "*invented*," but "Evelina" was more of a "*trouvaille*" than of an invention—such a book as "Evelina," or constructed such a book as "Cecilia." Perhaps *she* had not the intense pleasure in perceiving, the delight in giving to paper, words and traits from which characters may be inferred, which is manifest throughout the following diaries; or the power of imagining circumstances from which tragic or comic consequences must ensue, which was shown by her sister in her early novels. We know only that she could put before Fanny all that she knew Fanny wished to know, in a manner which was her own, not that of Fanny. Hetty, James, and Susan were, writing strictly, all of her family who were of ages to influence Fanny. Others are brought in simply to show how considerable was the amount of ability in those of her own blood. Her own younger brother, the second Dr. Charles, was (as we have said) a school-boy when these diaries begin; her own youngest sister, Charlotte, a lively and affectionate girl, was in 1777 just beginning to show her pretty face at parties, and to write of them with a glee and a sense of what was absurd, which can amuse readers of whom she never thought. She had been in certain ways left much to herself, and there are some who think that because of that "her state was the more gracious."[1] Fanny's half-brother, Richard, had not been long at school when these early journals end. Sarah Harriett, her half-

---

[1] Southey, writing of his mother, (who was born in Fanny's year, 1752,) says, "My mother, I believe, never went to any but a dancing-school, and *her state was the* more gracious."

sister, who grew up to write several successful novels, was a droll and clever child, but scarcely out of the nursery.[1] As Pacchierotti said, "All! *all! very clever girls!* Sense and witta (*sic*) inhabit *here*. *Sensibility has taken up its abode in this house.* . . . . . All I meet with at Dr. Burney's house are superior to other people. I am myself the only *Bestia* that enters the house. I am indeed, *a truly Beast!*"[2]

If to be of such a family, in such a household, among such friends and acquaintances as those of her father, was *not* education, we hardly know to what to give that name. There were many more educated ladies in the last century than it is customary to think there were, but it would be difficult to overstate the poorness of teaching in the schools for girls. Fanny might have left no book behind her had she been sent to a boarding-school. That she never had any regular teacher was no dire misfortune, if it were some loss.[3] By bringing

---

[1] Dr. Burney describes this daughter as having "native spirits of the highest order, and distinguished ability."

[2] The poor man meant only that he felt himself to be a stupid person among so many who were clever. The French word *bête* expresses his meaning.

[3] When we remember that Macaulay had nothing but the Memoirs of Dr. Burney, and that short "Introductory Memoir" of Mme. D'Arblay, which is prefixed to her Diary, to guide him as to the circumstances and events of the first four and twenty years of Fanny's life, it is more remarkable that he has divined or comprehended so much, than that here and there some details should be inexact, or incomplete. In the main, the following paragraph from his review is correct, but it requires some qualification.

"It was not, however, by reading that her intellect was formed. Indeed, when her best novels were produced her knowledge of books was very small. When at the height of her fame, she was unacquainted with the most celebrated works of Voltaire and Molière; and what seems still more extraordinary, had never heard or seen a line of Churchill, who, when she was a girl, was the most popular of living poets."

It will be found that, at any rate, she had read Voltaire's "Henriade."

her father the books he needed while writing for the press, she earned the name of his "Librarian," and learned to find on his shelves others which suited her fancy, or fitted into her schemes for self-improvement. She was throughout her life a masterly listener to others, and had her reward. Not a word or gesture escaped the observation of the shy, silent, demure little girl. Her early progress in the study of character is very perceptible in these diaries. Putting aside

---

Molière seems to be brought in because Fanny says that she had not read his "Femmes Savantes." This is the stranger thing, because she must often have heard Molière quoted by Mr. Crisp, while it is not probable that Dr. Burney favoured the works of Churchill. Macaulay overlooks her not having read Akenside's "Pleasures of the Imagination," and Falconer's "Shipwreck," until 1788; and (strangest of all) Goldsmith's "Poems," until 1790. In an unpublished passage in her diary for 1778, Mr. Seward puts into her hands the poems of Collins, of whom she does not seem to have heard before she visited Streatham.

Macaulay continues: "It is particularly deserving of observation that she appears to have been by no means a novel reader. Her father's library was large, . . . but in the whole collection there was only a single novel, Fielding's 'Amelia.'" Mrs. Burney, however, was a great and general reader; strong in religious controversy, critical of new books. Novels were brought into the house if they did not abide in it. That Fanny was not a reader of novels *only*, is all that can be granted. It is obvious from letters, that Fanny could catch Maria Allen's allusions to some rather poor novels.

Through Fielding's novels she did but "pick her way," but she reminds Susan of their early love of Richardson's novels. Augusta Byron (aunt of the poet) has (she writes) just such an enthusiasm for her, as Susan and herself used to have for Richardson. On the whole, if we cannot say with Mrs. Thrale, that Fanny was "a good English classic," we find her with a fair amount of reading for one so constantly employed in one or other kind of writing. Her love of reading abode with her. She was not set in her eighteenth century classicism, like Mrs. Thrale, who was averse from Scott, or Lætitia Hawkins, who cavilled at his novels. Among the later letters written by Mme. D'Arblay, was one, long and warm, congratulating the young D'Israeli upon his "Contarini Fleming," nor was her praise disdained.

some hasty opinions at first sight, her judgements of the people whom she met are often correct, and could not have been bettered when her mind was mature. In fact, there is nothing more remarkable in Fanny than the continuity of her way of thinking from sixteen to eighty-eight. In 1768, when these early diaries begin, she was at an age most susceptible of impressions, but was endowed with a steadiness of character, marred by no taint of obstinacy, which gave unity to all she said and did throughout a long life. This is the more remarkable as she shared, in no mean degree, the power of her family for acting, which, in many cases, implies more mobility than that of countenance, gesture, bearing, and utterance.

The superficial form of acting, mimicry ("imitations" was the name she gave it), was also a gift of hers, but she never *displayed* it. It was spontaneous when she was with those she loved and thoroughly at ease.[1]

A singular proof of unity of character is given in her finding at seventy the pleasure which she had anticipated in reading her old diaries when she began to write in them at sixteen, the very age of dreams. No greater proof of purity of heart could be shown. She had many for whom to mourn;—nothing on her own part to lament, her days having been "bound, each to each, by natural piety." Herself endowed with a very warm heart, she was much beloved by her warm-hearted family,

---

[1] An officer of whom she had seen much when with the Thrales at Brighton, pressed her "to make amends" for his showing her his powers of "imitation" by a display of her own, at the expense of a lady known to both. "I was on the point of trying fifty times, for he was so earnest that I was ashamed of refusing; but I have really no command of my voice when I am not quite easy, and though I had run on in Mrs. ——'s way to Mrs. Thrale for half an hour together, it had been *accidentally*, and when some of her *cackle* just occurred to me, not *deliberately*, and by *way* of exhibition." (From an unpublished passage in the Diary for 1770.)

Preface.

who were very far from being unconscious of her gifts of mind. Even in her backward childhood, there is no sign that Fanny was ever thought a dunce by any one who knew her well.[1] Her early writings had an audience, if it were but of one sister. In 1767, Susan bewailed the burning of Fanny's papers. Next year, in the very first letter addressed to Fanny by Maria Allen (her correspondent for fifty years afterwards), Fanny is taxed with pedantry, rather than with backwardness; with a love of hard words and fine phrases, not with "poor language," or "inelegance" of diction. "I have no doubt," says Maria, "of your letters being so very much above our comprehension, that we shall adore you for a Divinity, for you know people

---

[1] We are told that her mother's friends called her "the little dunce," but that Mrs. Burney said she "was not uneasy about Fanny." Dr. Burney, in a memorandum written in 1808, puts her true case so clearly, that it is well to quote a part of what he says: "She was wholly unnoticed in the nursery for any talents, or quickness of study: indeed, at eight years old she did not know her letters; and her brother, the tar, who in his boyhood had a natural genius for hoaxing, used to pretend to teach her to read; and gave her a book topsy-turvy, which he said she never found out! She had, however, a great deal of invention and humour in her childish sports; and used, after having seen a play in Mrs. Garrick's box, to take the actors off, and compose speeches for their characters; for she could not read them. But in company or before strangers, she was silent, backward, and timid, even to sheepishness: and, from her shyness, had such profound gravity and composure of features, that those of my friends who came often to my house, and entered into the different humours of the children, never called Fanny by any other name, from the time she had reached her eleventh year, than The Old Lady." In this account of Fanny, her backwardness in learning to read, and her precocity in composing speeches for characters, are in strong contrast. The vivacity of her perceptions of life was probably a cause of her slowness in other ways; even of her bashfulness, and want of presence of mind. She saw and felt so much so early, that she was receiving and arranging her impressions when other children were "writing their copies," or "doing their sums."

almost always have a much greater opinion of a thing they don't understand, than what is as plain and simple as the nose in their faces. Now Hetty's letters and your Papa's—why they are common entertaining lively witty letters, such as Dr. Swift might write or People who prefer the beautiful to the sublime, but *you now* why I dare say will talk of *Corporeal* Machines, *Negation* fluid, *matter* and *motion* and all those pretty things—Well well, *Fanny's* letters for my money."[1]

In 1769, Dr. Burney was proud enough of his daughter's playful verses on his doctor's degree at Oxford, to show them to at least one of his friends. Not long afterwards she drew Mr. Crisp into that correspondence by letters which became the chief pleasure of his later years. In 1773, her Teignmouth journal was passed by Susan to Mr. Crisp, who not only delayed to return it that he might (as the girls said) "*browse* on its contents," but pressed Fanny to allow him to lend it to his sister in Oxfordshire. After the close of 1774, there seems to have been a continuous passing by Mr. Crisp to Mrs. Gast of Fanny's less private letters. In, and after 1778, Mr. Crisp copied Fanny's letters to Susan (which are now called "The Diary of Mme. D'Arblay"), with his own hand, that he might enjoy them often at his leisure, and Fanny

---

[1] The only letter of Fanny written before 1770, of which we know, is addressed from Lynn, in August 1768, to one of her aunts:—

"To Mrs. Gregg,
at her House,
York Street,
Covent Garden,
London."

It is in doggrel verse, and too slight in substance to be printed, but there is a dramatic effort to represent what will be said of it by her cousin Charles, her Aunts Gregg, Ann, and Rebecca, and her grandmother Burney, who is made to cry out—

Preface. lxxxi

found that Mrs. Gast was rather too willing to share the pleasure she took in them with her Oxfordshire friends.[1] The good Aunts Rebecca and Ann craved also for their dear girl's journals. Thus Fanny may be said to have had, from a very early age, a little public audience of few but fond admirers, which extended, in and after 1778, to the great public of three kingdoms, and, through translations, to France, Italy, and Germany.

> "Why Fanny!—child!
> My dear! you're frantic—mad—quite wild!
> I'm lost in wonder and amaze;
> Ah! Things were different in my days!
> When *I* was young, to hem and sow (*sic*)
> Was almost all I wish'd to know:
> But as to writing *verse* and *rhimes*—
> O dear! Oh (*sic*) dear! How changed the times!"

This is the only mention found of Mrs. Gregg, but Mrs. Burney the elder lived in York Street up to her death in 1775. She and Aunts Ann and Becky made their house a home for her son Richard of Worcester and his children when they came to London. His sons Charles and Edward appear even to have lived with their grandmother when youths. The publishers of these volumes occupy two houses in the short street to which this letter was addressed, so that in 1768, and in 1888, it has been delivered, in the same street, if not at the same house.

[1] When Fanny became an inmate of Streatham, she demurred to Mr. Crisp's copying her journal of the sayings and doings of the Streatham set. He replied, "In very many of the former letters of our ancient correspondence, there were a hundred particulars that would never bear the light, any more than *Streathamism*." .... He signed this letter, "Your loving untrusted

"DADDY."

After that letter Fanny once more permitted Mr. Crisp, not merely to copy her journals, but to send them to his sister, "as the strongest mark in my power to give her of my affectionate esteem;" adding, "I entreat you will enjoin her to read them quite alone, or, not to be cruel, to poor sick Mrs. Lenthnall (*sic*), under an oath of secresy and silence."

f

It is according to rule that a heroine should be described before she begins to narrate her own adventures, as Fanny is about to do. Was Fanny beautiful,—lovely,—or, at least, *pretty*? Neither pretty nor plain, we incline to think, but capable of looking charming from variety and force of expression rather than from beauty of complexion and regularity of features. There are proofs in these diaries that, when a girl, Fanny was attractive, and she looked like a girl long after she was a woman. Mrs. Piozzi, when an unfriendly witness, tells us that she was much admired at Bath when eight-and-twenty; and Miss Berry (who does not seem to have met her until she was Madame D'Arblay, and not far from fifty years of age) says, that at sixty, after her absence in France, she had "wonderfully improved in good looks in ten years, which have usually a very different effect at an age when people begin to fall off. Her face has acquired expression, and a charm which it never had before. She has gained an *embonpoint* very advantageous to her face." It was the *restoration*, rather than the *acquisition* of a charm, as we have ample proof that Fanny's earlier, as well as later, power of pleasing lay in her variability of expression. Her countenance reflected her feelings, or (as her father said), "poor Fanny's face tells us what she thinks, whether she will or no."[1] Mr. Thrale repeatedly pressed her to read a tragedy to him, because she had what he termed "such a *marking* face." She herself wrote, "Nobody, I believe, has so *very* little command of countenance as myself—I could feel my whole face on fire."[2] When, in

---

[1] Elsewhere he calls it "her *honest* face." It was faithful to her rapid perceptions, and pure feelings. Those who knew Fanny best, trusted her most. The dull, uncouth, absurd Kitty Cooke is an instance. Mr. Crisp writes in 1778: "Honest Kate, my only Housemate at present, says, 'I love Fanny, because she is sincere.'" "Good as gold," said Queen Charlotte, with whom Fanny had felt to the full in the dreadful time of the King's disorder of reason.

[2] This, however, was on an occasion when "the whole face" of any

Preface. lxxxiii

1802, she went to live in Paris among what was left unguillotined of the best French Society, it was said by Mme. de Tessé that "Mme. D'Arblay's looks filled up what her words left short," in her efforts to speak French.[1] Fanny was short in stature, and slightly made. Once Mr. Crisp cries out, "Why, what a small cargo for the Chesington coach!" At another time, "What a slight piece of machinery is the terrestrial part of thee, our Fannikin!—a mere nothing; a blast, a vapour disorders the spring of thy watch; and the mechanism is so fine that it requires no common hand to set it a going again." He often warns her against a habit which was due to her shortness of sight, "that murtherous stooping,

---

other young lady might have well been "on fire." Mr. Selwyn, who had been English banker in Paris, showed Fanny signs of a "distinguishing preference" (the language is that of the time); Mrs. Thrale thought him too elderly for a match, and more than hinted so to him in Fanny's presence, in dwelling on the evil and absurdity of marriage between the old and the young; in spite of Mr. Thrale's endeavours "to look her silent."

[1] Adrienne de Noailles, Marquise de Tessé, is described by Fanny as being "one of the most *spirituelle*, *instruite*, and charming of women." She was aunt of Mme. Lafayette, whose famous husband was a great friend of M. D'Arblay. It is a pity that it was dangerous to write journals between 1802 and 1815, the term of Fanny's residence in France. We lose her skilled observation of the best French society, tempered by literature, in the *salons* of the Princesse d' Hénin, Mme. de Tessé, and Dr. Burney's friends, the Abbé Morellet, and M. Suard, perpetual secretary of the French Academy. This society is sketched by M. Guizot, who was twenty when received in it in 1807. Through it, he found his future wife, Pauline de Meulan, (an *aristocrate* by birth, who gained her living by her pen), with whose brother, General de Meulan, Fanny was acquainted. To the pages of "M. GUIZOT DANS SA FAMILLE," we refer our readers for a brief notice of "les restes de la Société des Constituants, telle qu'elle se réunissait chez Mme. de Tessé et chez la Princesse d'Hénin, avec ses traditions de leur temps, ses habitudes élégantes, son estime de lettres, et ses principes politiques." [GUIZOT.]

which will one day be your bane." Her mother had been consumptive, and Fanny, like her sister Susan, was liable to very severe colds and coughs; some of which may be attributed to their practice of stealing away from warm parlours to write their long letters in fireless chambers. But like her father, Fanny was wiry; her "slight piece of machinery" withstood rude shocks. What blistering, bleeding, and lowering of diet it resisted!

In 1781, she says, "Sir Richard Jebb ordered me to be blooded again—a thing I mortally dislike,—asses' milk, also, he forbids, as holding it too nourishing! and even potatoes are too solid food for me! He has ordered me to live wholly on *turnips*, with a very little dry bread, and what fruit I like: but nothing else of any sort—I drink barley-water and rennet-whey." Mrs. Piozzi wrote to her in 1821: "A slight frame escapes many evils that beset a robust one; water-gruel and spinach were all *you* ever wanted." It may be said for the doctors, that while two of her brothers died long before her of apoplexy, Fanny, surviving all her sisters except the youngest, who was nearly twenty years her junior, lived, like her father, to eighty-eight years of age. What she called her "easy temperature as to food" (meaning her indifference as to what she ate, and how it was cooked), is not uncommon with those born to live longer than their brethren. Her "temperature" as to dress was no less "easy," or indifferent.[1] Twice only in these volumes does she tell us what she wore. It is only when she plays *a part* that she thinks it worth while to mention her gowns. One is the "pink Persian" worn at the masque-

---

[1] This "easy temperature" as to how she fared, was dressed, or lodged, appears to have been part of the Burney inheritance. Writing in 1781 of the means of marrying possessed by Susan and Captain Phillips, Fanny says, "I know there is *not any part of our family* that cannot live upon very little, very gaily; as cheerfully as most folks upon very much."

rade in 1770; the other, her "green and grey" dress as Mrs. Lovemore in "The Way to Keep Him." "Quels habits," cries Mme. de Sevigné from Brittany to her beautiful daughter in Provence, "quels habits aviez-vous à Lyon, à Arles, à Aix? Je ne vous vois que cet habit bleu!" In another place, she completes the sense of these words by saying "*Qui n'a qu'un habit, n'en a pas du tout.*" The cares and toils of dress were not the least part of Fanny's sufferings at court. It was with joy that she laid by her sacque, court-hoop, and long ruffles. She records, as if she shared it, Mr. Batt's pleasure in seeing her "no more dressed than other people." We have somewhere seen her described in later life as "changing her lodgings oftener than her gown." That is quite beyond the mark, but it is certain that she was much more indifferent to her apparel than were many of the *bas bleus* with whom she shrank from being classed. Their Queen, Mrs. Montagu, crowned her *toupet*, and circled her neck with diamonds, when she received an assembly of foreigners, literati, and maccaronis, in her dressing-room, the walls of which were newly painted with "bowers of roses and jessamines, entirely inhabited by little Cupids."

"I long" (wrote Mr. Crisp to Fanny in 1778) "to see your *Abord* with Mrs. Montagu, and Sir Joshua Reynolds. I hope he will take your picture;—who knows, but the time may come when your image may appear,

'*Fair as before your works you stand confest,*'

not

'*In Flowers and Pearls, by bounteous Kirkall drest,*' [1]

---

[1]   "Fair as before her works she stands confess'd,
    In flowers and pearls by bounteous Kirkall dress'd."
            The Dunciad, lines 159-60, book ii.
This was written sarcastically of Mrs. Haywood, "the libellous novelist, whom he stileth Eliza."—MARTINUS SCRIBLERUS.
Mrs. Haywood, who was no credit to novelists, has been said, far

like Garrick with the Comic and Tragic Muse, contending for you?" Fanny never sat to Sir Joshua, who had had two strokes of paralysis before she knew him. Höppner painted a portrait of her, and her cousin Edward two. In an engraving of one of them she "stands confess'd" before "The Diary of Mme. D'Arblay." It is said that Edward saw her by the light of love, and in this picture somewhat flattered her. In his first raptures over "Evelina," Dr. Burney wrote to her: "I never yet heard of a novel-writer's statue;—yet who knows?" Who knew indeed? The man whose name was given to the Brissotin party, Brissot de Warville, urged Dr. Burney to permit a portrait, or bust, or statue of his celebrated daughter to be set up in that desecrated church in Paris, which is still called the Pantheon, but was as firmly refused by Dr. Burney, at the entreaty of Fanny, as common sense and propriety dictated that he should be.

The toil needed to bring these early diaries into order of time cannot be guessed even by the few who have seen the original manuscripts with their mutilations and defacements, but the wearisome labour has been lightened by living in such pleasant company for so long. By degrees we have grown not only familiar with the Burney family, but with the ways of the house, and the way about their different houses; first, with that in Poland Street, and the wig-maker's next door, and Mrs. Pringle's close by, where Hetty and Fanny were made so welcome and happy for a while. We know Maria Allen's room, in which the girls "browsed" by the fire upon dainties brought out of "Allen's" cupboard; and Fanny's "pretty little neat cabinet, that is in the bed-chamber,—where I keep all my affairs,—whenever yet was there a heroine without one?"[1]

---

from correctly, to have given Fanny the hint for "Evelina" in her novel of "Betsy Thoughtless."

[1] The Chesington "little Gallery Cabinet," or, as Mr. Crisp called it,

Preface.

We know "the children's play-room," a closet up two flights of stairs, in which the younger children kept their toys, and Fanny wrote plays and novels, and the paved court below, in which she burned them all at fifteen. We see Lord Mayor Barber's house in Queen Square, which Pope, Swift, and Bolingbroke may have frequented, and in which Carte, the Jacobite, was put into a damp bed, to the sore damage of his health and the great hindrance of the publication of his "Life of the Duke of Ormonde." We see the pompous painted ceilings of Newton's house in St. Martin's Street, which, Dr. Burney explained, that he himself was not "such a coxcomb" as to have commissioned any painter to execute; nor, perhaps, was Sir Isaac such a coxcomb,—he who sneered at my Lord Arundel's famous "Marbles," as so many "stone dolls."

We know the three parlours, and the cabinets and *commodes* in the dining-parlour, with Mrs. Burney's *bureau*, and that of the Doctor, into which he thrust his private papers and his fees, until both *bureaux* were broken open by a former footman of theirs, who knowing far too well the ways of the house, was able to rob his old master and mistress of three hundred pounds. We know what music was lying upon the harpsichord one day in August, 1779, when Susan sent from Chesington for "a set of Motezuma, a set of Aprile's duets in M.S. given me by Lady Clarges, the set of Didone which contains ' *Son' regina*,' the second number of Sacchini's

---

"the Doctor's Conjuring Closet," in which Dr. Burney wrote when staying with Mr. Crisp, and which was given to the use of Fanny, when she was an acknowledged author, is another instance. "Dressing-rooms" were then in England, as in France, rooms of reception, in which ladies of fashion received their friends (*after* they had been dressed in another room), while the *friseur* gave the last touches to the curls, *toupet*, and *chignon*. A lady's *dressing-room* was a *show*-room, with silver "dressing-plate" and elaborate furniture.

'Tamerlano,' and of his duets."[1] All these were to be played to, or with Mr. Crisp.

Mr. Boone breaks his sword in going up the steep stairs, and wonders that he did not break his neck. "I am afraid," replies Dr. Burney, not without complacency, "that speaks ill for my stairs!—but they were constructed by *Sir Isaac Newton*, not by *me*." Looking over London, Fanny writes a novel in the Observatory of a man who we may be pretty sure never read a romance.[2] When Fanny, as Baretti said with a sneer, was "exalted to the Thralic Majesty," Susan sent to her at Streatham, or Brighton, or Bath, delightful (as yet unpublished) chronicles of all that went on at home.[3] We see Aunt Ann come in from York Street to tea, "in hopes that she should *meet with no foreigner*, as I had told her that we had seen Merlin, Piozzi, and Baretti, all so lately. However, our tea-things were not removed, when we were alarmed by a rap at our door, and who should enter but *l'imperatore del canto*" (Pacchierotti) "and his treasurer" (Bertoni). "I leave you to guess who was charmed, and who looked blank. They stayed with us full three hours." Susan corrects Pacchierotti's English exercises, and stops his sending that letter to "*the object of his particular despise*," Sheridan, in which he had

---

[1] At another time, Susan writes that "Mr. Crisp is fond of my father's third duet of the second set, which we play like anything." She also asks that [Dean] "Tucker's pamphelet, and the first set of [Dr. Burney's] duets," may be sent to Chesington.

[2] We are told that some time ago this Observatory was bought by an American, who removed it to his own country, forgetful that it lost its interest when not in its right place. What he acquired was, however, almost entirely a re-construction of this Observatory by Dr. Burney. In "the fearful hurricane of 1778 . . . its glass sides were utterly demolished; and its leaden roof . . . was swept wholly away."—*Memoirs of Dr. Burney*, vol. i. p. 291.

[3] The details in these last pages are chiefly gathered from these unpublished letters from Susan to Fanny.

drawn that slippery manager as swinging on a gallows for not paying the money due to Pacchierotti as his first singer at the opera.

Or we see Piozzi arrive, " in excellent spirits and humour," from a country-house where he has been spending two months. He plays " two or three of his new lessons," which Susan does not like, but he sings " some songs divinely." At another time Susan is very glad that Piozzi just misses Pacchierotti, of whom he is so jealous that " he walked off from me at a concert on seeing him approaching,—which, indeed, I was not sorry for." Piozzi, that almost historical character, appears on Susan's pages as touchy, and jealous of his betters in song. To be told that any one was not at home when *he* knocked at the door, he took as an insult. " *Not à tom !* " he cried to the Burneys, complaining that at the door of some great house he had again had " *la cattiva sorte del not à tom!*" But if Dr. Burney were in his study, or "abroad," (as they said then,) Mrs. Burney and the three girls made English and foreign friends welcome in St. Martin's Street. Mrs. Burney, who was not unconscious of her reading and power of speech, had favourites who shared her love of a thorough discussion of subjects. These were not always acceptable to her step-daughters. Mrs. Burney loved to see Baretti, or Mr. Penneck of the British Museum, or James Barry, R.A., enter the parlour. Fanny and Susan had favourites of another kind, from " Aristotle Twining " to Pacchierotti.[1] It must be owned that their raptures concerning Pacchierotti's manners and voice were only surpassed by the downright ravings of some girls,

---

[1] As we have here and there quoted Pacchierotti's opinions, it is well to copy what Mr. Richard Twining wrote of him to his admirable brother, " Aristotle Twining," in the year 1781 : " There were some musical people at Spa, and, in the first place, Signor Pacchierotti. He is not only an admirable singer, but also a sensible, modest, and agreeable man."

as recorded by Susan. Her journals abound in traits of the time and its noted people. Dr. Johnson brings blind Mrs. Williams to tea in St. Martin's Street. In his vast presence, that lively American, Mrs. Paradise, makes Barry dance a minuet with herself—Barry, whose politeness was as " rare as a bit of Peg Woffington's writing "! Barry provokes Susan by insisting on bringing her home from a tea-party, although her father's man-servant has been sent for her, and by staying in St. Martin's Street (she " verily believes") till midnight. Uninvited guests leave the house about eleven; after which there is supper, "an excuse with us, as you know," (says Fanny,) "for chatting over baked apples." Hetty, her husband, and his brother Edward, now and then "drop in " to supper; Dr. Burney appears, perchance with sword and bag, on his way from the King's brother's music party to his own "Chaos." He says a few kind and pleasant words; then bids all good night, and "outwatches the Bear," pondering over the little which has been spared to tell us of the manner of the music made by the "godlike Greek."

PERSONS OF THE DRAMA.

A LIST OF THOSE MEMBERS OF THE BURNEY FAMILY WHO APPEAR IN THESE PAGES.

MRS. ANN BURNEY (born Cooper), widow of James Burney (or Mac Burney), Esq.; a Shropshire lady, of advanced age, as she is said to have refused Wycherley, the dramatist, who died in 1715.

[She was the second wife of James Burney; his first having been Rebecca Ellis. James had fifteen children, of whom nine lived; but in some cases it is not clear of which marriage they came].

1. RICHARD, of Barborne Lodge, Worcester, elder son of James and Ann Burney; of whom more hereafter.
2. ANN, a daughter of James and Ann Burney.
3. CHARLES (known as Dr. Burney), their second son and youngest child. He was born in 1726, and married first, Esther Sleepe, who died September 28, 1761. Doctor of Music (Oxford, 1769); F.R.S., 1773; Member of the French Institute, Classe des Beaux Arts, 1811.

The children of Charles and Esther Burney were :—

1. ESTHER, married her Cousin, Charles Rousseau Burney.
2. JAMES (the Admiral), born June 5, 1750, married Sarah, daughter of Thomas Payne.
3. FRANCES, born at Lynn Regis, on the 13th of June, 1752, married Lieutenant-General Comte D'Arblay, an officer of the (Noble) "Corps de Gardes du Roi," and sometime commandant of Longwy; a Knight of the Orders of St. Louis, the Legion of Honour, and the "Lys."
4. SUSANNA ELIZABETH, married Molesworth Phillips, Lieut. Colonel of Marines.
5. CHARLES, married a daughter of Dr. Rose, of the "Monthly Review."[1]
6. CHARLOTTE ANN, married, first, Clement Francis, Esq., of Aylsham, Norfolk, secondly, Ralph Broome, Esq., of the Bengal Army.

---

[1] Another Charles, a son of Charles and Esther Burney, is found in the register of St. Dionis Backchurch, of which church Dr. Burney was chosen organist in 1749. He was born and baptized in June, 1751. He probably died young. Dr. Charles, the Greek scholar, is commonly said to have been born at Lynn, in 1757, or 1758.

Persons of the Drama.

DR. BURNEY married secondly (in October, 1767), Elizabeth, widow of Stephen Allen of Lynn-Regis, who appears to have been her cousin, as she was born an Allen.

The children of Charles and Elizabeth Burney were:—
1. RICHARD THOMAS, in the Indian Civil Service.
2. SARAH HARRIET, a novelist.

REBECCA BURNEY, who was living with Mrs. Burney the elder, was, most likely, a half-sister of Dr. Burney. There was also a sister, or half-sister, Mrs. Gregg, and a half-sister, Mrs. Mancer.

RICHARD BURNEY, of Worcester, had five sons, and three daughters, but as we do not know their precise order of birth, we put first (as he is always called " Mr. Burney "):—

CHARLES ROUSSEAU, who, in 1770, married his cousin Esther.
[Their eldest child, the only one named in these journals, was Anna Maria, who married M. Bourdois, an early friend of General D'Arblay. He was aide-de-camp to General Dumourier, and distinguished himself in the battle of Jemappes.
2. RICHARD.
3. EDWARD FRANCIS, the painter.
4. THOMAS.
5. JAMES.
6. ELIZABETH.
7. REBECCA (Mrs. Sandford).
8. ANNE (or Hannah), called " Nancy " (Mrs. Hawkins.)

The step-children of Dr. Burney were the Rev. Stephen Allen and his sisters, Maria (Mrs. Rishton) and " Bessy " (Mrs. Meeke). The other connexions mentioned are Mr. Sleepe of Watford (some kinsman of Dr. Burney's first wife); Mr. Thomas Burney, who had taken the name of Holt, "a cousin of ours"; Mrs. Allen, mother of the second Mrs. Burney; Mrs. Arthur Young (Patty Allen), Mrs. Burney's sister; and her husband, the well-known writer on agriculture.

We have no baptismal registers to quote for the ages of Hetty, Susan, or Maria Allen, but it is near the truth if we assume that when these diaries begin, Hetty was in her nineteenth year, Susan in her fourteenth, and Maria Allen about seventeen.

EARLY DIARY OF FRANCES BURNEY.

1768.

EDITOR'S NOTE FOR THE YEAR.

The first of these journals is wrapped in soft, old fashioned, blue paper, to which it has once been stitched. Madame D'Arblay has written on the cover, " Juvenile Journal, No. 1.—Curtailed and erased of what might be mischievous from friendly or Family Considerations." Within the cover, some figures, which seem to be hers, are hard to make out. There are also these words—" Original old Juvenile Private Journal, No. 1.—Begun at 15—total 66." If "total 66" refers to the number of leaves, or of pages, no such number is left, nor can any part of it have been written at the age of fifteen, unless it be the fanciful address to Nobody, which is upon a loose leaf, of a yellower and more worn look than the yellow and worn leaves which follow, it is also in slightly different handwriting. Upon this prefatory leaf we find again, " This strange Medley of Thoughts and Facts was written at the age of fifteen, for my genuine and most private Amusement." Below this, in a girlish round hand, is written " Fanny Burney."

More than fifty years, it is probable, lie between the writing of the Diary, and the writing of the notes on, and within, the cover; and in those years many of the "changes and chances of this mortal life" had befallen their writer; enough to blur a memory even so excellent as hers. Fame, and much life in public; a court life; a married life, involving a residence in a foreign country for ten years at a stretch; a stolen visit to England, a return to Paris, a flight to Brussels before Waterloo, England again, the death of a father, of a husband, changes of dwelling from London to Bath, from Bath to London; the burden of examining Dr. Burney's piles of manuscript, a toil which we have proof was not ended in 1820. What marvel, if looking over her own papers, from which she had been parted while living abroad, and which she seems not to have read and revised until she needed them to recall incidents essential to a memoir of her father, what marvel that she erred in her dates? The mistake of a year (be it for more or for less), in the life of any one, man or woman, is so common, in youth or in age, that it need not be mentioned unless other facts depend upon it. Miss Edgeworth (one of the least likely of women to be suspected of making herself out to be younger than she was), wrote, and published, in the memoirs of her father, that she was twelve years old when she first went to Ireland, whereas it is indubitable that she was fifteen; but she believed it, and that her first impressions of Ireland were taken at twelve years old, and not at the far more sensitive age of fifteen. So Miss Burney believed herself to have been fifteen in 1768; but that is disproved by the register of the Chapelry of St. Nicholas, in the parish of St. Margaret's, King's Lynn, which gives her baptism upon the 7th of July, 1752, by the Rev. Thomas Pyle—about three weeks after her birth on the 13th of June.

As the date of Dr. Burney's second marriage was uncertain, the register of St. James's, Westminster, has been examined for the sake of complete accuracy. Under the marriages was found in "1767, No. 7, 294. Charles Burney, of this parish, to Elizabeth Allen, of Lynn Regis, Norfolk, by Licence of the Archbishop of Canterbury, 2nd October, M. Pugh, Curate." The witnesses were Isabella Strange, and Richard Fuller.[1]

This completely tallies with the entry on "Monday night, May 30th," in this Diary, that "last night, Hetty, Susey, Charlotte, and I were at tea, mama and Miss Allen not being returned from Harrow," when the "charming" Arthur Young "entered the room." This second marriage was a secret from all the friends of Dr. Burney, except Mr. Crisp and Miss Dolly Young, for reasons which concerned the lady. Her mother, who seems to have had much control over her, and the brothers of her first husband (who was an Allen also and most likely her cousin), would apparently have opposed the match. The Allen family was rich, her husband's brothers were the guardians of her three children, and she had lately lost all the money which she could herself control by trusting its investment to an imprudent speculator.

Dr. Burney's income was a good one, but it depended upon his health, which had once before failed, and driven him for years from London to Lynn. Then he had six children, the eldest old enough to give trouble to a stepmother, had she not been so sweet-tempered as was Hetty; the youngest, Charlotte, about seven years old. "Since 1724," (according to an historian of Lynn), "when Stephen Allen was made a freeman of Lynn, on the payment of twenty nobles," the Allens had "figured among the first families in the town." The loss of Mrs.

---

[1] We shall meet Isabella, afterwards Lady Strange, in the year 1770. Richard Fuller, Esq., was one among five subscribers to Johnson's Dictionary, whose names were sent to Johnson from Lynn, in 1757, by the future Dr. Burney. Mr. Fuller was probably of a banker's family, as the Fullers and Hankeys are mentioned by Mme. D'Arblay as among the great city houses, that helped Dr. Burney to secure the organist's place at St. Dionis Backchurch, Fenchurch Street.

Allen's own fortune proved to her that Dr. Burney took little interest in her money ; and it was agreed between them that a secret marriage was the best way to avoid opposition to an open engagement. After a honeymoon spent near Chesington, the lady came to live for a while in Poland Street, but still as Mrs. Allen, and in a house of her own. In the end all came out through the wrong delivery of some letter. Things had been smoothed by the 30th of May, 1768. The two families were then living together, in Poland Street. Most likely before this journal begins, Fanny had made that famous bonfire of her writings in the paved court of her father's house (which his children used as a playground), while he was at Chesington, and her step-mother at Lynn.

To Lynn Mrs. Burney was drawn every year by her mother; perhaps, too, by the uncles of her children, and others of their Allen kinsfolk. Besides, she had a house settled upon her, and some one must live in it. Later on, we find Hetty or Fanny going to take her place at Lynn when she went to London. To that house the delicate Susan was sent for change of air, and Charlotte (during her holidays, and after she was taken from school), spent most of her time at Lynn, with little Bessy Allen. In the November of this year, Richard, Dr. Burney's son by the second marriage, was born at Lynn. With a stepmother so much in Norfolk, and with Dr. Burney giving lessons from eight, and in one case from seven, in the morning ; often dining in his coach, and coming home mainly to sit up the night through, writing in his study, Hetty, Fanny, and Susan were often almost entirely thrown upon their own guidance when in London. It will be seen that they ran some risks, but their innocent steadiness of character preserved their hearts from harm. Sweeter and purer girls it would be hard to find in any century ; nor did Susan lack aught but the health which was never granted her for long, to give her distinction as an author—scarcely second to that of her sister Fanny.

FRANCES BURNEY.

JUVENILE JOURNAL

ADDRESSED TO A CERTAIN MISS NOBODY.

Poland Street, London, March 27.

To have some account of my thoughts, manners, acquaintance and actions, when the hour arrives in which time is more nimble than memory, is the reason which induces me to keep a Journal. A Journal in which I must confess my *every* thought, must open my whole heart! But a thing of this kind ought to be addressed to somebody—I must imagion (*sic*) myself to be talking—talking to the most intimate of friends—to one in whom I should take delight in confiding, and remorse in concealment:—but who must this friend be? to make choice of one in whom I can but *half* rely, would be to frustrate entirely the intention of my plan. The only one I could wholly, totally confide in, lives in the same house with me, and not only never *has*, but never *will*, leave me one secret to tell her. To *whom*, then, *must* I dedicate my wonderful, surprising and interesting Adventures? —to *whom* dare I reveal my private opinion of my nearest relations? my secret thoughts of my dearest friends? my own hopes, fears, reflections, and dislikes?——Nobody!

To Nobody, then, will I write my Journal! since to Nobody can I be wholly unreserved—to Nobody can I reveal every thought, every wish of my heart, with the most unlimited confidence, the most unremitting sincerity to the end of my life! For what chance, what accident can end my connections with Nobody? No secret can I conceal from

Nobody, and to Nobody can I be *ever* unreserved. Disagreement cannot stop our affection, Time itself has no power to end our friendship. The love, the esteem I entertain for Nobody, Nobody's self has not power to destroy. From Nobody I have nothing to fear, the secrets sacred to friendship Nobody will not reveal when the affair is doubtful, Nobody will not look towards the side least favourable.

I will suppose you, then, to be my best friend, (tho' Heaven forbid you ever should!) my dearest companion—and a romantick girl, for mere oddity may perhaps be more sincere —more tender—than if you were a friend in propria persona— in as much as imagionation (*sic*) often exceeds reality. In your breast my errors may create pity without exciting contempt; may raise your compassion, without eradicating your love. From this moment, then, my dear girl—but why, permit me to ask, must a *female* be made Nobody? Ah! my dear, what were this world good for, *were* Nobody a female? And now I have done with preambulation.[1]

Monday Night, May 30.

O my dear—such a charming day! and then last night— well, you shall have it all in order—as well as I can recollect.

Last night, while Hetty, Susey,—Charlotte and myself were at tea, mama and Miss Allen not being returned from Harrow, and Papa in his study busy as usual, that lively, charming, spirited Mr. Young[2] enter'd the room. O how glad we were

---

[1] When, in 1760, Dr. Burney left Lynn for a house in Poland Street, he had there (in succession) as neighbours, The Duke of Chandos, Lady Augusta Bridges, Sir Willoughby Aston (with whose daughters Hetty and Susan Burney were at school in Paris) and other great people.

[2] Arthur Young was son of the Rev. Arthur Young, of Bradfield Hall in Suffolk, who had been chaplain to Speaker Onslow, and was made a Prebendary of Canterbury in 1749. Arthur, his son, was apprenticed to Mr. Robinson, one of the wine merchants of Lynn Regis. When about four and twenty, he married Martha Allen, sister of Mrs. Stephen Allen, who afterwards became the second wife of Dr. Burney. When he married he was in charge of his mother's farm at Bradfield. He was six or seven and twenty when Fanny first speaks of him, but had already published his "Farmer's Letters to the people of England," which went through a second edition in 1768.

to see him. He was in extreme good spirits. Hetty sat down to the harpsichord and sung to him—mama soon returned, and then they left it. *Well, and so*—upon the entrance of fathers and mothers—we departed this life of anguish and misery, and rested our weary souls in the Elysian fields—my Papa's study —there freed from the noise and bustle of the world, enjoy'd the * * *harmony* of chattering, and the melody of musick!— there, burying each gloomy thought, each sad reflection, in the hearse[?] of dissipation, lost the remembrance of our woes, our cruel misfortunes, our agonizing sorrows—and graciously permitted them to glide along the stream of reviving comfort, blown by the gentle gale of new-born hope, till they reposed in the bosom of oblivion—then—No 'tis impossible! this style is too great, too noble to be supported with proper dignity— the sublime and beautiful how charmingly blended! yes! I *will* desist—I *will* lay down my pen while I can with . . . . It would be miraculous had I power to maintain the same glowing enthusiasm—the same—on my word I can *not* go on, my imagination is rais'd *too* high, it soars above this little dirty sphere, it transports me beyond mortality—it conveys me to the Elysian fields—but my ideas grow confused—I fear you cannot comprehend my meaning—all I shall add, is to beg you would please to attribute your not understanding the sublimity of my sentiments to your own stupidity and dullness of apprehension, and not to my want of meaning—which is only too fine to be clear.

After this beautiful flow of expression, refinement of sentiment and exaltation of ideas, can I meanly descend to common life? can I basely stoop to relate the particulars of common life? can I condescendingly deign to recapitulate vulgar conversation? I can!

O what a falling off is here!—what a chatter there was!— however *I* was not engaged in it . . . . and therefore, on a little consideration, a due sense of my own superlative merit convinces me that to mention anything more of the matter would be nonsense. Adieu, then, most amiable—who? Nobody!

Not so fast, good girl! not so fast—'tis true, I have done with last night—but I have all to-day—a charming one it is, too—to relate. Last night, to my great satisfaction, Mama prevail'd on Mr. Y—— to promise to be of our party to-day to Greenwich. Well, he slept here. For my part, I could not sleep all night, I was up before five o'clock—Hetty and Susette were before six,—and Miss Allen soon after—while we were all adorning our sweet persons,—each at a looking-glass—admiring the enchanting object it presented to our view, who should rap at the chamber door but—(my cheeks are crimsoned with the blush of indignation while I write it)—Mr. Young! I ran into a closet, and lock'd myself up—however he did not pollute *my* chamber with his unhallow'd feet, but poor Miss Allen was in a miserable condition—her Journal, which he wanted to see, in full sight—on her open bureau. He said he had a right to it as her uncle. She called Hetty into her room and they were a long time ere they could turn him out of it.

Well but, now for the Greenwich party. We set out at about ten or eleven—the company was, mama, Mr. Young, Miss Allen, Stephen, and your most obsequious slave.—The Conversation as we went was such as I would wish to remember—I will *try* if I can, for I think it even worthy the perusal of *Nobody!*—*what* an honour!

Well, I have rack'd my brains half-an-hour—in vain—and if you imagine I shall trouble myself with racking the dear creatures any longer you are under a mistake. One thing, however, which related to myself, I shall mention, as *that* struck me too forcibly to be now, or perhaps *ever*, forgot: besides, it has been the occasion of my receiving so much raillery, &c., that it is requisite for you to hear it, in order to observe the decorum due to the Drama. Talking of happiness and misery, sensibility and a total want of feeling, my mama said, turning to me. "Here's a girl will *never* be happy! *Never* while she lives!—for she possesses perhaps as feeling a heart as ever girl had!" Some time after, when we were near the end of our journey, "and so," said Mr. Young—"my friend Fanny possesses a very feeling heart?" He harp'd on this some little time till at last he said he would call me *feeling Fanny*, it was *characteristick*, he said, and a great deal more such nonsense, that put me out of all patience, which same virtue I have not yet sufficiently recovered to recount any more of our conversation, charming as part of it was, *which* part you may be sure *I* had my share in, how else *could* it be charming ? ....

[All at once, Poland Street is left, and Frances writes from her stepmother's dowry-house, in the churchyard of St. Margaret, Lynn Regis; that fine church of which Dr. Burney had been organist for about ten years.]

From Lynn Regis.

I am reading the "Letters of Henry and Frances" and like them prodigiously. I have just finished Mrs. Rowe's Letters from the Dead to the Living—and moral and entertaining,[1]—I had heard a great deal of them before I saw them, and am sorry to tell you I was much disappointed with them: they are so very enthusiastick, that the religion she preaches rather disgusts and cloys than charms and elevates—and so romantick, that every word betrays improbability, instead of disguising fiction, and displays the Author, instead of human nature. For my own part, I cannot be much pleased without an appearance of truth; at least of possibility—I wish the story to be natural tho' the sentiments are refined; and the characters to be probable tho' their behaviour is excelling. Well, I am going to bed—Sweet dreams attend me —and may you sympathize with me. Heigh ho ! I wonder when I shall return to London !—Not that we are very dull here—no, really—tolerably happy—I wish Kitty Cooke[2] would write to me—I long to hear how my dear, dear, beloved Mr. Crisp does. My papa always mentions him by the name of my *Flame*. Indeed he is not mistaken—himself is the *only* man on earth I prefer to him. Well—I must write a word

---

[1] Elizabeth Rowe. 1674-1737. The book is "Friendship in Death, in twenty letters from the Dead to the Living," etc. She was a Calvinist, whose life was written by Toplady. Southey seems to concur with Fanny when he says, although with praise of Mrs. Rowe's poems, that "they are at times a little more enthusiastic than is allowable even for poetry."

[2] Kitty Cooke, who was about double Fanny's age, was the niece of Mrs. Hamilton, with whom Mr. Crisp lodged.

more—only to end my paper—so!—that's done—and now good night to you. . . . . .

[Here are erasures, and also misplacements of the original diary, which it is impossible now to remedy. Among these have been found a broken passage or two, worth preserving:

"Saturday.

"Oh my dear I have received the *finest* letter! . . . . . while we were at dinner a packet came from London. Papa opened it, and among other epistles was the following to me——"

Four lines of verse follow the address, "To MISS FRANCES BURNEY." These words only are quite legible—

"When first I saw thee . . . ."
"Incognitus."

Fanny then appears to tax whosoever wrote the epistle with taking the hint of his verses "from an old song I have often [heard] which runs thus,"

"When first I saw that . . . . .
Ah me" . . . .

Only a few detached words of what follows can be read. This fragment is merely given to show that Fanny was not without her share of the current compliments in verse which it was almost the duty of a gentleman to pay, and even a slight for a young lady not to receive. Another mutilated passage shows Hetty and A. (Maria Allen) as, for some time, amusing themselves with railing against Lynn, every thing, every body in it, and praising to adulation—London. "*I offered some few words* in favour of my poor old abused town—the land of *my* nativity—of the world's happiness! We disputed a little time, and Hetty suddenly cried, 'Hush, hush—Mama's in the next room—If she hears us—we two shall be whipt, and Fanny will have a sugar-plumb.' 'Ay,' cried A., ''tis her defending Lynn which makes mama and my grandmama so fond of her.' 'Fond of me!' cried I, 'what makes you imagine Mrs. Allen fond of me?' 'What she said of you—' . . . . . 'I am now writing in the pleasantest place belonging to this house. It is called sometimes 'the *Look Out*'—as ships are observed from hence, and at other times, the Cabin... . . . . . It is [at the] end of a long garden that runs along the house." . . . . .]

I am going to tell you something concerning myself, which, (if I have not chanced to mention it before) will, I believe, a little surprise you—it is, that I scarce wish for anything so truly, really, and greatly, as to be *in love*—upon my word I am serious—and very gravely and sedately, assure you it is a *real* and *true* wish. I cannot help thinking it is a great happiness to have a strong and particular attachment to some one person, independent of duty, interest, relationship or pleasure; but I carry not my wish so far as for a *mutual tendresse*. No, I should be contented to love *Sola*—and let *Dueto* be reserved for those who have a proper sense of their superiority. For my own part, I vow and declare that the mere pleasure of having a great affection for some one person to which I was neither guided by fear, hope of profit, gratitude, respect, or any motive but mere *fancy*, would sufficiently satisfy me, and I should not at all wish a return. Bless me—how I run on! foolish and ill-judged! how despicable a picture have I drawn of an object of Love! mere giddiness, not inclination, I am sure, penn'd it—Love without respect or gratitude!—that could only be felt for a person wholly undeserving—but indeed I write so much at random, that it is much more a chance if I know what I am saying than if I do not.

I have just finish'd " Henry and Frances "—They have left me in a very serious, very grave mood—almost melancholy—a bell is now tolling, most dreadfully loud and solemn, for the death of some person of this town, which contributes not a little to add to my seriousness—indeed I never heard anything so dismal—this bell is sufficient to lower the highest spirits —and more than sufficient to quite subdue those which are already low.

The greatest part of the last volume of "Henry and Frances," is wrote by Henry—and on the gravest of grave subjects, and that which is most dreadful to our thoughts— Eternal Misery. Religion in general is the subject to all the latter part of these Letters, and this is particularly treated on. I don't know that I ever read finer sentiments on piety and Christianity, than the second vol. abounds with—indeed, most of the Letters might be call'd with very little alteration— Essays on Religion. I own I differ from him in many of his thoughts, but in far many more I am delighted with him. His sentiments shew him to be a man possessed of all the humanity which dignifies his sex; his observations, of all the penetration and judgment which improves it, and his expressions, of all the ability, capacity and power which adorn it.[1] I cannot express how infinitely more I am charmed with him at the conclusion than beginning. Some of his opinions—I might say many of them—on divine subjects, I think, would be worthy a sermon—and an excellent one too.

It is a sweet, mild evening, I will take a turn in the garden, and re-peruse in my thoughts these genuine, interesting Letters. This garden is very small, but very, very prettily laid out—the greatest part is quite a grove, and three people might be wholly concealed from each other with ease in it. I scarce ever walk in it, without becoming grave, for it has the most private, lonely, shady, *melancholy* look in the world.

[Let us look into "the Cabin," with the eyes of Maria Allen, afterwards Mrs. Rishton. In 1778, writing from Lynn, she gives Fanny an account of her own new house in that town, and thus contrasts her Belvedere or "Look Out," (as they said in Lynn), with the "Cabin."

"Lynn, 3rd Sept. — You are very well acquainted with the house we now Inhabit which is Charles Turner's—and which is quite a palace in point of conveniences to the one we left. The rooms are large and handsome—and it is quite big enough for us—and Rishton has excellent stables and dog kennel down the yard—but what is most comfortable to us, the yard and premises are quite private, it leads to no granaries etc.—Consequently We are troubled with neither corn-waggons or porters—but we have every thing within ourselves—and a very large *Look-out*, as they are called here, which overlooks the river that I pass many hours in and which often brings back past scenes to my view when I think of the hours we used to spend in that little cabbin of my mother's—but this overlooks a much pleasanter part of the river, as we never have any

---

[1] This book is said to have been mainly written by Elizabeth, wife of Richard Griffith, of Millicent, in the County of Kildare. Mr. Griffith had some share in it, and in two more of her novels. She wrote, besides, other novels, poems, and comedies. He had written a novel before his marriage, which is said to have done anything but "dignify his sex." "Henry and Frances" was brought out anonymously, in six volumes, between 1766 and 1780. One of this couple's novels bore the good title of "The Gordian Knot," which has been used again, in our own time, by Shirley Brooks. This Mr. and Mrs. Griffith are by no means to be confounded with Ralph Griffiths, who brought out the "Monthly Review," with, as the legend goes, Mrs. Griffiths to correct "the copy" of the poor hack whom her husband boarded and lodged, Oliver Goldsmith.

ships laying against our watergate, at least very seldom, to what we had there, by which means we escape the oaths and ribaldry of the sailors and porters which used often to drive us from thence——."]

Tuesday, Cabin.

I have this very moment finish'd reading a novel call'd the Vicar of Wakefield. It was wrote by Dr. Goldsmith, His style is rational and sensible and I knew it again immediately. This book is of a very singular kind—I own I began it with distaste and disrelish, having just read the elegant Letters of Henry,—the beginning of it, even disgusted me—he mentions his wife with such indifference—such contempt—the contrast of Henry's treatment of Frances struck me—the more so, as it is real—while this tale is fictitious—and then the style of the latter is so elegantly natural, so tenderly manly, so unassumingly rational,—I own I was tempted to thro' (*sic*) the book aside—but there was something in the situation of his family, which if it did not interest me, at least drew me on—and as I proceeded, I was better pleased.—The description of his rural felicity, his simple, unaffected contentment—and family domestic happiness, gave me much pleasure—but still, I was not satisfied, a *something* was wanting to make the book satisfy me—to make me *feel* for the Vicar in every line he writes, nevertheless, before I was half thro' the first volume, I was, as I may truly express myself, *surprised into tears*—and in the second volume, I really sobb'd. It appears to me, to be impossible any person could read this book thro' with a dry eye at the same time the best part of it is that which turns one's grief out of doors, to open them to laughter. He advances many very bold and singular opinions—for example, he avers that murder is the sole crime for which death ought to be the punishment,[1] he goes even farther, and ventures to affirm that our laws in regard to penalties and punishments

---

[1] The pith of the passage upon which Fanny comments is in chap. xxvii. Dr. Primrose, "the great Monogamist," here speaks some of the language of his Master, William Whiston, who held it absolutely unscriptural to take human life except for murder : but " social combinations," " compacts " and " natural laws " never entered into Whiston's brain—See his very diverting autobiography.

are *all* too severe. This doctrine might be contradicted from the very essence of our religion—Scripture for [erasure] in the Bible—in Exodus particularly, death is commanded by God himself, for many crimes besides murder. But this author shews in all his works a love of peculiarity and of making [*sic*, but probably *marking*] originality of character in others; and therefore I am not surprised he possesses it himself. This Vicar is a very venerable old man—his distresses *must* move you. There is but very little story, the plot is thin, the incidents very rare, the sentiments uncommon, the vicar is contented, humble, pious, virtuous, quite a darling character.[1] How far more was I pleased with the genuine productions of Mr. Griffith's pen—for that is the real name of Henry,—I hear that more volumes are lately published. I wish I could get them, I have read but two—the elegance and delicacy of the manner—expressions—style of that book are so superiour!—How much I should like to be acquainted with the writers of it!—Those Letters are doubly pleasing, charming to me, for being genuine—they have encreased my relish for *minute, heartfelt* writing, and encouraged me in my attempt to give an opinion of the books I read.

Cabin, Wednesday Afternoon.

I always spend the evening, sometimes all the afternoon, in this sweet Cabin—except sometimes, when unusually thoughtful, I prefer the garden. . . . I cannot express the pleasure I have in writing down my thoughts, at the very moment—my opinion of people when I first see them, and how I alter, or how confirm myself in it—and I am much deceived in my *fore sight*, if I shall not have very great delight in reading this *living proof* of my manner of passing my time, my sentiments, my thoughts of people I know, and a thousand other things in future—there is something to me very unsatisfactory in passing year after year, without even a memorandum of what you did, &c. And then, all the happy hours I spend with particular friends and favourites would fade from my recollection. . . . .

---

[1] The "Vicar of Wakefield" had been published two years previously.

July 17.

Such a set of tittle tattle, prittle prattle visitants! Oh dear! I am so sick of the ceremony and fuss of these fall lall people! So much dressing—chit chat—complimentary nonsense—In short, a Country Town is my detestation—all the conversation is scandal, all the attention, dress, and *almost* all the heart, folly, envy, and censoriousness. A City or a village are the only places which I think, can be comfortable, for a Country Town, I think has all the bad qualities, without one of the good ones, of both.

We live here, generally speaking, in a very regular way—we breakfast always at 10, and rise as much before as we please—we dine precisely at 2, drink tea about 6—and sup exactly at 9. I make a kind of rule, never to indulge myself in my two *most* favourite pursuits, reading and writing, in the morning—no, like a very good girl I give that up wholly, accidental occasions and preventions excepted, to needle work, by which means my reading and writing in the afternoon is a pleasure I cannot be blamed for by my mother, as it does not take up the time I ought to spend otherwise. I never pretend to be so superior a being as to be above having and indulging a *Hobby Horse,* and while I keep mine within due bounds and limits, nobody, I flatter myself, would wish to deprive me of the poor animal: to be sure, he is not form'd for labour, and is rather lame and weak, but then the dear creature is faithful, constant, and loving, and tho' he sometimes prances, would not kick anyone into the mire, or hurt a single soul for the world—and I would not part with him for one who could win the greatest prize that ever *was* won at any Races.

Alas, alas! my poor Journal! how dull unentertaining, uninteresting thou art!—oh what would I give for some Adventure worthy reciting—for something which would surprise—astonish you! I have lately read the Prince of Abyssinia—I am almost equally charm'd and shocked at it—the style, the sentiments are inimitable—but the subject is dreadful—and handled as it is by Dr. Johnson, might make *any* young, perhaps old, person tremble. O, how dreadful, how terrible is it to be told by a man of his genius and knowledge, in so affectingly probable a manner, that true, real, happiness is ever unattainable in this world!—Thro' all the scenes, publick or private, domestick or solitary, that Nekaya or Rasselas pass, real felicity eludes their pursuit and mocks their solicitude. In high life, superiority, envy and haughtiness baffle the power of preferment, favour and greatness—and, with or without them, all is animosity, suspicion, apprehension, and misery!—in private families, disagreement jealousy and partiality, destroy all domestick felicities and all social cheerfulness, and all is peevishness, contradiction, ill-will, and wretchedness! And in solitude, imagination paints the world in a new light, every bliss which was wanting when in it, appears easily attained when away from it, but the loneliness of retirement seems unsocial, dreary, savouring of misanthropy and melancholy—and all is anxiety, doubt, fear and anguish! In this manner does Mr. Johnson proceed in his melancholy conviction of the impossibility of all human enjoyments and the impossibility of all earthly happiness.

. . . . . .

Wednesday, July, 10 in the morning.

We have just had a wedding—a *publick* wedding—and very fine it was I assure you. The bride is Miss Case; daughter of an alderman of Lynn, with a great fortune—the bridegroom, Mr. Bagg,—the affair has long been *in agitation* on account of Mr. Bagg's inferiority of fortune.[1] Our house is in the Church yard, and exactly opposite the great church

---

[1] In 1710 the names of Bagg, or Bagge, and of Case, occur in the list of the Corporation of Lynn. In 1763 Philip Case was Mayor for the second time. In 1832 a property which had been held by the Case family had passed to William Bagge, who was perhaps this bridegroom in his old age, or his heir. There was a double marriage between the Allens and the Bagges, Maxey Allen = Miss Bagge, J. Bagge = Sally Allen. In "My Grandfather's Pocket-Book," (edited by the Rev. Mr. Wale), are several notices of the Allens and Bagges. In 1792 Mr. Wale records that "one Mr. Case, an attorney of Lynn-Regis,—dyed there worth a deall, I think they say of money, £100,000." This was probably the bride's father.

door—so that we had a very good view of the *procession*. . . . . . The walk that leads up to the church was crowded almost incredibly a prodigious mob indeed!—I'm sure I trembled for the bride. O what a *gauntlet* for any woman of delicacy to run!—Mr. Bagg handed the bride and her company out of their coach, and then Mr. Case took her hand and led her to the church door, and the bridegroom follow'd handing Mrs. Case. O how short a time does it take to put an eternal end to a woman's liberty! I don't think they were a quarter of an hour in the Church altogether.—Bless me! it would not be time enough, I should think, for a poor creature to see where she was—I verily believe I should insist on sitting an hour or two to recover my spirits—I declare my heart ach'd to think how terrible the poor Bride's feelings must be to walk by such crowds of people, the occasion in itself so awful! How little does it need the addition of that frightful mob! In my conscience I fear that if it had been me, I should never have had courage to get out of the coach—Indeed, I feel I should behave very foolishly. When they had been in the Church about a quarter of an hour, the bells began to ring, so merrily—so loud—and the doors open'd—we saw them walk down the Isle—the bride and bridegroom first, hand in hand . . . . the bridegroom look'd *so gay, so* happy! Surely it must be grateful to her heart to see his joy! it would to *mine* I know. She looked grave, but not sad—and, in short, all was happy and charming. Well of all things in the world, I don't suppose any thing can be so dreadful as a publick wedding—my stars! I should never be able to support it! . . . .

Mr. Bewly, a great and particular friend of my papa's,— and a very ingenious, clever man, is now here. . . . . At breakfast time, we had, as you may imagine, a long conversation on Matrimony.—Every body spoke against a *publick* wedding,[1] as the most shocking thing in the world—papa said

---

[1] Compare this with a passage, or more, in Letter LXXII. of Goldsmith's "Citizen of the World" as, for instance, "I could submit to court my mistress herself upon reasonable terms; but to court her father, her mother, and a long tribe of cousins, aunts, and relations, and *then stand the butt of a whole country church*——"

he would not have gone thro' those people in such a manner for 5000 a year—and Mr. Bewly said that when *he* was married, his lady and self *stole* in to the Church, privately as possible, and ashamed of every step they took. . . . .

Cabin, Saturday, July.

And so I suppose you are staring at the torn paper and unconnected sentence—I don't much wonder—I'll tell you what happen'd. Last Monday I was in the little parlour, which room my papa generally dresses in—and writing a letter to my grandmama.[1] You must know I always have the last sheet of my Journal in my pocket, and when I have wrote it half full I join it to the rest, and take another sheet— and so on. Now I happen'd unluckily to take the last sheet out of my pocket with my letter—and laid it on the piano forte, and there, negligent fool!—I left it. . . . . Well, as ill fortune would have it, papa went into the room—took my poor Journal—read, and pocketted it. Mama came up to me and told me of it. O Dear! I was in a sad distress—I could not for the life of me ask for it—and so *dawdled* and fretted the time away till Tuesday evening. Then, gathering courage "Pray papa," I said, "have you got—any *papers* of mine?"

"Papers of yours?" said he—"how should *I* come by papers of yours?"

"I'm sure—I dont know—but"—

"Why do you leave your papers about the house?" asked he, gravely.

I could not say another word—he went on playing on the piano forte. Well, to be sure, thought I, these same

---

[1] Ann, widow of James Macburney, or Burney. In August, 1768 Fanny wrote a rhyming letter to her aunt, Mrs. Gregg, from "St. Margt's Church-yard, Lynn Regis."—We quote what concerns Mrs. Burney, her grandmother—

"And when my scrawl you read to Granny,
'Pure free and easy, Madam Fanny!
'And so you re'ly condescend
'To name *your Granny* at the end?'"

dear Journals are most shocking plaguing things—I've a good mind to resolve never to write a word more. However, I stayed still in the room, walking, and looking wistfully at him for about an hour and half. At last, he rose to dress— Again I look'd wistfully at him—He laughed—" What, Fanny," said he, kindly, " are you in sad distress ? " I half laugh'd. " Well,—I'll give it you, now I see you are in such distress—but take care, my dear, of leaving your writings about the house again—suppose any body else had found it —I declare I was going to read it loud—Here, take it—but if ever I find any more of your Journals, I vow I'll stick them up in the market place." And then he kiss'd me *so* kindly— never was parent so *properly*, so *well*-judgedly affectionate! I was so frightened that I have not had the heart to write since, till now, I should not but that—in short, but that I cannot help it! As to the *paper*, I destroy'd it the moment I got it. . . . .

We have had several little parties of pleasure since I wrote last, but they are not worth mentioning. My papa went on Thursday to Massingham, to Mr. Bewly's.[1] . . . .

I have been having a long conversation with Miss Young on journals. She has very seriously and earnestly advised me to give mine up—heigho-ho! Do you think I can bring myself to oblige her? What she says has great weight with me; but, indeed, I should be very loath to *quite* give my poor friend up. She says that it is the most dangerous employment young persons can have—that it makes them often record things which ought *not* to be recorded, but instantly forgot. I told her, that as *my* Journal was *solely* for my own perusal, nobody could in justice, or even in sense, be angry or displeased at my writing any thing.

---

[1] William Bewly, a country-surgeon at Massingham, a very little town in Norfolk, was called by his neighbours the " Philosopher of Massingham," from his attainments in electricity and chemistry, which brought him into communication with Dr. Priestley and other well-known men. Some years later he wrote the scientific articles in Griffiths' " Monthly Review." He was from the North of England, but has a notice among Norfolk worthies in the " History of Lynn," by W. Richards, 1812.

"But how can you answer," said she, "that it *is* only for your own perusal? That very circumstance of your papa's finding it, shows you are not so very careful as is necessary for such a work. And if you drop it, and any improper person finds it, you know not the uneasiness it may cost you."

"Well but, dear ma'am, this is an 'if' that may not happen once in a century."

"I beg your pardon; I know not how often it may happen; and even *once* might prove enough to give you more pain than you are aware of."

"Why, dear ma'am, papa never prohibited my writing, and he knows that I *do* write, and *what* I do write."

"I question that. However, 'tis impossible for you to answer for the curiosity of others. And suppose any body finds a part in which they are extremely censured."

"Why then, they must take it for their pains. It was not wrote for *them*, but *me*, and I cannot see any harm in writing to *myself*."

"It was very well whilst there were only your sisters with you to do any thing of this kind; but, depend upon it, when your connections are enlarged, your family increased, your acquaintance multiplied, young and old *so* apt to be curious—depend upon it, Fanny, 'tis the most dangerous employment you can have. Suppose now, for example, your favourite wish were granted, and you were *to fall in love*, and then the object of your passion were to get sight of some part which related to himself?"

"Why then, Miss Young, I must take a little trip to Rosamond's Pond."[1]

"Why, ay, I doubt it would be all you would have left."

---

[1] George Colman, the younger (writing in 1830), tells us of Rosamond's Pond, in St. James's Park. "This Pond is now fill'd up; it had some little islands upon it, forming part of the *Decoy*, upon one of which there was a summer-house, where the old Princess Amelia used to drink tea." From the days of Charles II. to those of George II. this pond had been rather the trysting-place of happy lovers or the *rendezvous* of the gay and giddy, than what Warburton said of it afterwards, "Consecrated to disastrous love, and elegiac poetry." It was filled up in 1770, perhaps to stop the suicides to which Fanny alludes in the text.

"Dear Miss Young!—But I'm sure, by your earnestness, that you think worse of my poor Journal than it deserves."

"I know very well the nature of these things. I know that in journals, thoughts, actions, looks, conversations—*all go down*; do they not?"

The conclusion of our debate was, that if I would show her some part of what I had wrote she should be a better judge, and would then give me her best advice whether to proceed or not. I believe I shall accept her condition; though I own I shall show it with shame and fear, for such nonsense is *so* unworthy her perusal.

I'm sure, besides, I know not what part to choose. Shall I take at random?[1]

Wednesday, August 10th.

. . . . Well, my [Nobody] I *have* read part of my Journal to Miss Young and what's more, let her choose the day herself, which was our Journey, the day in which I have mention'd our arrival, &c.[2] I assure you I quite triumph! prejudic'd as she was, she is pleas'd to give it her sanction,—*if it is equally harmless every where*—nay, says she even approves of it.[3] . . .

For some time past, I have taken a walk in the fields near Lynn of about an hour every morning before breakfast—I have never yet got out before six, and never after seven. The fields

---

[1] This conversation no longer exists in the original manuscript, but has been preserved in a transcript of selections from these diaries, made about forty years ago.

[2] This account of the journey to and arrival at Lynn which Miss Young thought so "harmless," is not to be found in this diary.

[3] This was the good and intelligent "Dolly Young," the dearest friend, at Lynn, of Esther, first wife of Dr. Burney. In 1832, Madame D'Arblay wrote that Miss Young "took charge of Mrs. Burney's little family upon every occasion of its increase during the nine or ten years of the Lynn residence," and "Miss Young's were the kind arms that first welcomed to this nether sphere the writer of these Memoirs" (of Dr. Burney). The first Mrs. Burney, on her death-bed, recommended her husband to marry Miss Young, as "the lady most capable to suit him as a companion," and the "most tenderly disposed" towards her six children, but Dr. Burney could not overlook her total want of grace and beauty.

are, in my eyes, particularly charming at that time in the morning—the sun is warm and not sultry—and there is scarce a soul to be seen. Near the capital I should not dare indulge myself in this delightful manner, for fear of robbers—but here, every body is known, and one has nothing to apprehend.

I am reading Plutarch's Lives—his own, wrote by Dryden has charm'd me beyond expression. I have just finish'd Lycurgus—and am as much *pleased* with all his publick Laws, as *dis*pleased with his private ones. There is scarce *one* of the former which is not noble and praiseworthy,—and as *I* think *very* few of the latter which are not the contrary—the custom of only preserving healthy children, and destroying weak *ones* how barbarous!—besides *all* his domestick family duties appear strange to me!—but you must consider how very, very, very bad a judge I am, as I read with nobody, and consequently have nobody to correct or guide my opinion: nevertheless, I cannot (forbear, sometimes) writing what it is . . . . I read Plutarch's Lives with more pleasure than I can express. I am charmed with them, and rejoice exceedingly that I did not read them ere now; as I every day, certainly, am more able to enjoy them. . . . .

[Here occur erasures and passages in disarray, from among which we rescue four lines of halting verse:—

"What beauties have met me!
"How often have I, sighing said
"Poor Hetty's charms are now quite dead
"Nor dare they vie with Fanny.
"MELIDORUS."

Fanny adds: "Your servant, Mr. Melidorus, I am much obliged to you. Who would not be proud to have such verses made on them?"]

Wednesday—August.

We had a large party to the Assembly on Monday, which was so-so-so—I danced but one country dance—the room was so hot, t'was really fatiguing. Don't you laugh to hear a girl of fifteen complain of the *fatigue* of dancing? Can't be helped! if you will laugh, you must.—My partner was a pretty youth enough—and *quite* a youth—younger than myself—poor dear creature, I really pitied him, for he seem'd to long for another caper—in vain—I was inexorable—not that he quite *knelt* for my hand—if he had *I might* have been *moved*—for I have an uncommonly soft heart—I am interrupted, or else I am in an excellent humour to scribble nonsense. . . . .

Poland Street.

Mr. Greville supped here, and talked of the *book fight* between Mr. Sharpe and Signor Baretti—concerning Italy, of which country the former has wrote an account; which the latter has absolutely confuted.[1] " I wish," said Mr. Greville, " men would not pretend to write of what they cannot be masters of, another country—It is impossible they can be judges ; and they ought not to aim at it—for they have different sensations, are used to different laws, manners and things, and consequently are habituated to different thoughts and ideas; 'tis the same as if a cow was to write of a horse—or a horse of a cow—why they would proceed on quite different principles, and therefore certainly could be no judge of one another." He asked papa if he play'd much on piano fortes.—" If I was to be in town this winter," said he, " I should cultivate my old acquaintance with old Crisp." " Ah," said papa, " he's truly worth it." " Ay, indeed is he," answered Mr. Greville,

---

[1] Samuel Sharp, surgeon to Guy's Hospital, an eminent writer on surgery, and a great friend and adviser of Garrick on theatrical matters, travelled for his health in 1765-6, and published his " Letters from Italy " in 1766. Baretti not only attacked him anonymously in a paper he was carrying on at Venice, but wrote two volumes in very good English to confute him in his own country. Both writers were able men. Both were praised by Johnson, who wrote in 1776, " I read Sharp's letters from Italy over again when I was at Bath. There is a great deal of matter in them." By the strange irony of circumstances Baretti, who had denied that any but *low* Italians, and those mainly *low* Romans, used their knives in sudden quarrels, as was averred by Sharp, himself stabbed a man in the Haymarket the very next year, and (if we are to believe Mrs. Thrale) long afterwards called attention to his pocket-knife, while using it at dessert, in her house, as being the knife with which he killed him.

"he's a most superiour man." This one speech has gain'd him my heart for ever. This man is exceeding fond of my father. Before he went to Germany[1] he used to sup with him perpetually, in the most familiar and comfortable style, and now again he resumes this freedom. His wife and daughter were and are the two greatest beautys in England, and Mrs. Greville is my godmother. Her Ode to Indifference is so excessively pretty that it almost puts me out of conceit with my desire to be favoured with a touch of the power of Cupid, when I happen to recollect it. How she would scorn me if she knew it—but I suppose she did not begin with a passion for Indifference herself—I should not like to be Mr. Greville if he converted her to that side.[2]

Sunday Night, Sept. 11.

. . . . . .

My sweet brother Charles is come home for the holidays, full of spirits, mirth, and good-humour. My aunt Nanny who

---

[1] Fulke Greville, only son of Algernon, second son of the fifth Lord Brooke, made believe to elope with Frances, third daughter and co-heiress of James Macartney, a gentleman of large fortune, and ancient Irish family. She was not of age, and the future Dr. Burney, who gave her away, in the presence of her two sisters, was the youngest of the party, being then about seventeen. When they played at asking pardon, Mr. Macartney drily said that "Mr. Greville had taken a wife out of the window, whom he might just as well have taken out of the door." Mr. Greville was grandfather of the Diarists Charles and Henry Greville. In Charles much of Fulke's superciliousness and fickleness may be traced. Dr. Burney suffered, as will be seen, from Greville's exacting and changeable temper. Mr. Crisp would not be "cultivated" any more. He forbade Dr. Burney to let Greville know where he lived. In a letter to Fanny, in 1779, Mr. Crisp writes of "the constitutional inconstancy of Greville . . . . who became my enemy for a time, though afterwards he became more attached than before." Later on Mr. Crisp adds, "through absence, whim, and various accidents, all Greville's friendship dwindled to nothing."

[2] Mr. Greville gave but too much cause for this ode, which was handed about by admiring copyists. Among others, General Fitzwilliam, in 1767, tells a lady that, from her copy of the poem he himself had taken and given forty copies.

went lately to see him at the Charter House, was assured there that he was the sweetest temper'd boy in the school.[1]

Papa is gone to supper with Mr. Greville. You must know this gentleman is the author of a book called *Characters, Maxims, and Reflections—Serious, Moral, and Entertaining.* I never read it thro', but what I have pleased me extremely.

Sept. 12.

Mr. Smart the poet was here yesterday. He is the author of the "Old Woman's Magazine" and of several poetical productions; some of which are sweetly elegant and pretty—for example: "Harriet's Birthday," "Care and Generosity,"—and many more. This ingenious writer is one of the most unfortunate of men—he has been twice confined in a mad-house—and but last year sent a most affecting epistle to papa, to entreat him to lend him half-a-guinea!—How great a pity so clever, so ingenious a man should be reduced to such shocking circumstances. He is extremely grave, and has still great wildness in his manner, looks, and voice; but 'tis impossible to *see* him and to *think* of his works, without feeling the utmost pity and concern[2] for him . . . . I am prodigiously surprised,

---

[1] Charles, second son of Dr. Burney, was placed by Lord Holdernesse in the Charter-House School in 1768.

[2] Any dictionary of biography will tell us that Christopher Smart gained the Seatonian prize five times, all but in succession; that his chief poem was "The Hop-Garden;" and that he scratched his "Song to David" on the wall of his cell with a key, during a fit of lunacy. The laurels of Smart were "sere and withered," until lately, when a great poet lit upon the "Song to David," and sung of it, "parleying" with Smart, as:

" Yourself who sang
A Song where flute-breath silvers trumpet-clang,
And stations you for once on either hand
With Milton and with Keats——"

—" Only out of throngs between
Milton and Keats that donned the singing-dress—
Smart, solely of such songmen pierced the screen
'Twixt thing and word, lit language straight from soul——"

Mr. Browning addresses those who may be startled——

"——Or blame, or praise my judgement, thus it fronts you full."
" *Parleyings with Certain People of Importance.*"

immensely astonish'd—indeed absolutely petrified with amazement—and what do you imagine the cause? You can never guess; I shall pity your ignorance and incapacity, and, generous, noble minded as I am, keep you no longer in suspense. Know then—Ha! this frightful old watchman how he has startled me—past eleven o'clock! bless you, friend, don't bawl so loud, —my nerves can't possibly bear it—no—I shall expire—this robust, gross creature will be the death of me—yes! I feel myself going—my spirits fail—my blood chills—I am gone! To my eternal astonishment, I am recovered!—I really am alive—I have actually and truly survived this bawling. Well, and now that I have in some measure *recollected my scattered spirits*, I will endeavour sufficiently to compose myself to relate the cause of wonder the first. Would you believe it—but, now I think of it, you can't well tell till you hear—well, have patience—all in good time—don't imagine I intend to cheat you—no—no—now attend. Miss Tilson, a young lady of fashion, fortune, education, birth, accomplishments, and beauty has fallen in love with my cousin Charles Burney. She is about seventeen, and she wrote her declaration to him on her glove, which she dropt for him to pick up. She is daughter to some Lady Kerry and has a portion in her own hands of several thousands, but this worthy Charles, not liking her, is above the temptation. Well, I'm so sleepy, I must . . . . you may hear more anon.

10 o'clock.

I left off with a little account of Miss Tilson—I shall only tell you that I heard of her passion and the amiable object by Hetty, who was told it by Miss Sheffield, and had it afterwards confirmed by the fair one's own mouth. An Amorosa so forward in Cupid's cause makes me almost revolt from my wishes for his darts, and really I think upon the whole, the most dignified thing for an exalted female must be to die an old maid. Her mother married Mr. Tilson on the death of the Earl of Kerry. She is very short but Hetty says very pretty.[1] . . . . .

---

[1] This is the first mention of Charles Rousseau, eldest son of Dr. Burney's elder (own) brother Richard Burney of Worcester. After

Wednesday Sept. 21.

I have not wrote you a line this age, my sweet Journal. Indeed I have no wonderful matters to scrawl, now—Is it not very perverse in Dame Fortune to deny me the least share in any of her so much talk'd of tricks? especially as I should, by means of my inimitable pen immortalize every favour she honour'd me with: but so it is, and so it seems likely to be; that I am to pass my days in the dullest of dull things, insipid, calm, uninterrupted quiet. This life is by many desired—so be it—But it surely was design'd to give happiness after (and not one ounce before) twenty *full* years are past, but till then —no matter what happens—the spirits—the health—the never dying *hope* are too strong to be *much* affected by whatever comes to pass—Supper bell, as I live!— . . . . .

I've finish'd the Iliad this age—I never was so charm'd with a poem in my life—I've read the Odyssey since— and Dr. Hawkesworth's Translation of Telemachus. I am going now to read Mr. Hume's History of England, which I shall begin to-morrow—well now adieu at once.

Hetty and I are going out to tea this afternoon to Mrs. Pringle's, a widow lady who lives in this street. She is a most sensible, entertaining, clever . . . .

Sunday, Noon.

We pass'd a very agreable evening at Mrs. Pringle's yesterday—Mr. Seaton, a very sensible and clever man, and a prodigious admirer of Hetty's . . . .[1]

---

his uncle became a doctor of music, he is commonly called "Mr. Burney" in these Diaries. As he is often named, and always with praise, this is preserved. On the 15th of July, 1750, Mrs. Delany writes :—" The present talk of Dublin is of Mr. Tilson's marriage with Lady Kerry last Thursday—nobody suspected it ; he is a very lively, gay man, and she rather of the insiped strain." " Lady Kerry," was Lady Gertrude Lambert, daughter of Richard, 4th Earl of Cavan, who married William, 2nd Earl of Kerry, in 1738, and afterwards Mr. James Tilson, of Pallice. Charles Burney appears to have given lessons for his uncle Charles in his occasional absence, and was thus perhaps thrown with Miss Tilson.

[1] Mr. Seaton appears to have been a younger son of Sir Henry Seton, or Seaton, Bart., who died in 1751.

Tuesday, Oct. 4th.

Dinner bell, I declare!—O dear, O dear, the kindest letter from Mr. Crisp. If my papa has not the most obdurate, barbarous and inhuman heart in the world, he *must* be moved by it to permit some of us to accept his invitation. We are all in agonies of fear and suspense—waiting with such impatience for papa's return. *If* he should refuse us!—I verily believe I shall play truant!—I wish he'd come home I shall be *so* happy to see that dearest of men again! and then Miss Cooke—the good Mrs. Hamilton, too—in *short*, Chesington is all in all. I am going to console myself with reading the Iliad till his return.

Achilles has just relented, and hastes to the assistance and succour of the Grecians—is it not a fortunate part?—if my dear papa would *just so* relent too, I could almost aver that he would give us equal joy, to that felt by the Greeks at the yielding of Achilles. . . . . .

Friday.

Mr. Crisp is come to town. . . . .

[Mrs. Colman][1] wife of the celebrated author who is also chief manager of that house, is extremely kind and friendly to us all—we are to dine at her house on Tuesday. Well, adieu for the present, if I pass an agreeable evening, I shall write again at night—or early to morrow—if not—your most obedient, very humble servant to command.

---

[1] Just here there is a group of mutilated passages of no interest. Out of them we save this, as it undoubtedly refers to Mrs. Colman, wife of George Colman the elder, who was a very old friend of Dr. Burney. In a fragment written by Susan Burney, in 1770, giving some account of her "acquaintance, in France in particular," that is, of those whom she had seen or known when at school in Paris, she says:—" Mr. and Mrs. Greville are mentioned in my journals from 67, as are Mr. and Mrs. Strange, and Mr. and Mrs. Colman, the latter never see me without reminding me of the *embarras* I was in to explain myself in English to them when I was at Paris." Here is an instance of Mrs. Strange's being with her husband in Paris, unknown to her chronicler, Mr. Dennistoun, who makes no mention of her joining him there until 1775.

Tuesday, Nov. 15th.

Monday morning, Mrs Pringle called here—to invite me to tea in the afternoon, to meet *the Emperor Tamerlane*,[1] however, I excused myself on the score of our having a little concert to night—"Well then," said she, "Shall he come here?" There was no saying No—so she agreed that he should be introduced by her son in the evening to papa—for mama is at Lynn. Cerveto,[2] who plays the base very finely, and his son, came in and, to grace the whole set, Mr. Crisp. We had a charming concert—Hetty play'd the piano forte, and Charles the violin, the two Cervetos the base, and papa the organ: and afterwards we had two solos on the violincello by young Cerveto, who plays delightfully—and Charles shone in a Lesson of papa's on the harpsichord. Mr. Pringle and Mr. Mackenzie (you must know he is grandson to the unfortunate Earl of Cromartie, who lost his estates, etc., in the Rebellion)[3] came in during the performance, drank a dish of tea—and away again. Well, now we come to Tuesday, that is—yesterday. At about five o'clock; Hetty and I went to Mrs. Pringle's, where we found to our great joy, Mr. Seaton was to be of the party—he is a charming man. We all went

---

[1] "Tamerlane," a play (1702-3) by Nicholas Rowe, which it was the custom to act in public on the 5th of November, as there was some shadowing of William III. in the Emperor Tamerlance (who was, for the nonce, represented as mild and merciful), and of Louis XIV. in the vanquished Bajazet.

[2] In his "History of Music," Dr. Burney tells us that the elder Cervetto, a player on the violoncello, came to England about 1739, and remained here until his death, at above a hundred years of age. His tone was "raw, crude, and uninteresting." "The younger Cervetto, when a child, and hardly acquainted with the gammut had a better tone, and played what he was able to execute, in a manner much more *chantant* than his father." It was the younger Cerveto whom Dr. Burney afterwards styled "the incomparable."

[3] The Earl of Cromartie was pardoned after being sentenced to death with Lords Lovat and Balmerino, but his title and estates were forfeited.

in our coach, Mrs. Pringle, her son, Mr. Seaton, and our Ladyships to see the play of Tamerlane acted by young gentlemen at an Academy in Soho Square. The play was much better perform'd than I expected, and the dresses were superb—made new for the purpose, by the members of the society, and proper for the characters and country—that is after the Turkish manner. The farce, too, was very well done. We were much entertain'd—Mr. Seaton was so very clever, droll, and entertaining, you can't imagine. When the performance was over, *Tamerlane* came to me, to open the Ball! But I was frighten'd to death, and beg'd and besought him not to begin—he said one of the members always did—however I prevail'd, after much fuss, to put Hetty and Andrew Pringle first, and we were second. I assure you I danced *like any thing*—and called the second dance . . . . . after which, I hopp'd about with the utmost ease and cheerfulness. . . . . . They were very perfect in the play, except in one speech; the young gentleman who perform'd Selima, suddenly stopp'd short, and forgot himself—it was in a love scene,—between her—him I mean—and Axalla, who was very tender. She—he—soon recovered tho' Andrew whisper'd us that when it was over—"He'd lick her!"—Stratocles, amused himself with no other action all the time but beating, with one hand, his breast, with the other he held his hat. I'm sure, I was ready to die with laughter at some of them. Arpasia and Moneses we all thought were the best perform'd. Tamerlane was *midling*; he seems to be about twenty—neither handsome, ugly, agreeable or disagreeable, and on the whole, very tolerable.

Thursday, Nov. 16th.

I have had to-day the first real conversation I ever had in my life, except with Mr. Crisp. . . . . . It was with Mr. Seaton. Hetty has seen him again and she is quite charm'd with him. He called with a message from Mrs. Pringle this morning and I had the pleasure of a delightful *Tête à Tête* with him—for Hetty, unluckily, was out, and Susette kept up stairs. I am really half in love with him, he is so sensible, clever, entertaining—His person is very far from recommending him to favour—he is very little, and *far* from handsome, but he has a sensible countenance, and appears quite an Adonis after half an hour's conversation. Do you know, he actually stay'd above three hours with me? I own to you that I am not a little flattered that a man of his superior sense and cleverness, should think me worth so much of his time, which is much more than ever I had reason to expect. He ask'd me, if my sister and self were engaged to Mrs. Pringle's this afternoon? "No—not that I know of, at least." "No? why Mrs. Pringle promis'd me I should meet Miss Burney and you there this evening. But she's a strange woman;—she has an excellent heart, and understanding, but she is not well versed in real delicacy and good breeding. But, however, I wish I could know if you ladies were to be there—because if I go at a venture, I may be disappointed, and then so much time is thrown away. I hope Miss Burney caught no cold last night, for she came away, just after a dance."

F. No Sir, I believe not. But you fared worse, I fear, it rain'd very hard, and Hetty says you could not get a chair or coach.

Mr. S. Why, I could have managed that better! There were but two chairs to be had. Miss Crawford, a young lady, who was with Mrs. Pringle, offered to go in the same chair as herself—and then Miss Burney could have taken me into her's. But she would not consent to it at all—and I see you laugh too!—I am afraid I made an improper proposal—

F. Improper! why surely you only laugh'd yourself.

Mr. S. No indeed. It is very common in Scotland, and in truth I know nothing of the English punctilios perhaps it was wrong. I feared so at the time, when Miss Burney refused me, and you can't imagine how much it chagrined me. But I see few young ladies, and often fear I make myself either particular or ridiculous.

F. Indeed, when my sister told me of it, I very naturally concluded you could only have made such a proposal in jest.

He caught up the words—*when my sister told me of it*—"O," said he, "how much I would give to hear some of your private conversations! I dare say they are very curious; and the remarks you each make, I am sure must be very clever. I dont doubt but you sometimes take me to task!"

F. I see you are now *fishing*, to draw out our sentiments: but I shall be on my guard!

Mr. S. O, When Mrs. Pringle trusted me with the message, I hesitated some time, to know whether I should call or not. For it is customary in my country to do so many things which appear singular here, that I am continually at a loss, and should esteem it a most particular favour, if you would have the goodness to tell me honestly, at once, when you see me making any of these gross mistakes.

F. I'm sure it would be highly vain and conceited in *us* to pretend to advise *you.*

Mr. S. Quite the contrary. And if I had the pleasure of hearing some of *your* private chats, I doubt not I should make myself quite another creature: for then, what you blamed, I would amend, and what you were pleased to be contented with, I would confirm myself in.

F. But *correction* should come from a superior—in character I mean—for merely to hear that *we* either approved or condemned does not make you either better or wose, as it may most likely, proceed from caprice, fancy, or want of judgment.

Mr. S. I beg your pardon—I doubt not your capacity to amend me at all. And as I am really a stranger to the manners of the English, it would be great goodness. I am so little in company with young ladies (I scarce know five) that I have not observed their little peculiarities, etc. The truth is, the young women here, are so mortally silly and insipid, that I cannot bear them.—Upon my word, except you and your sister, I have scarce met with one worthy being spoke to. Their chat is all on caps—balls—cards—dress—nonsense.

F. Upon *my* word, you are unmercifully severe.

Mr. S. Nay, it's truth. You *have* sensible women here, but then, they are very devils;—censorious, uncharitable, sarcastick.—The women in Scotland have twice—thrice their freedom, with *all* their virtue—and are very conversable and agreeable—their educations are more finish'd. In England, I was quite struck to see how forward the girls are made—A child of ten years old will chat and keep you company, while her parents are busy, or out, etc., with the ease of a woman of twenty-six—But then, how does this education go on? Not at all: it absolutely stops short. Perhaps, I have been very unfortunate in my acquaintance, but so it is, that you and your sister are almost the only girls I have met, who could keep up any conversation—and I vow, if I had gone into almost any other house, and talk'd at this rate to a young lady,—she would have been sound asleep by this time. Or at least, she would have amused me with gaping and yawning all the time, and certainly, she would not have understood a word I had uttered.

F. And so, this is your opinion of our sex?

Mr. S. Ay; and of *mine*, too.

F. Why you are absolutely a man hater, a misanthrope.

Mr. S. Quite the contrary. Nobody enjoys better spirits —or more happiness.

F. Then assuredly you have advanced most of these severe judgments, merely for argument, and not as your real thoughts. You know, we continually say things to support an opinion which we have given, that in reality we don't above half mean.

Mr. S. I grant you I may have exaggerated—but nothing more. Look at your ladies of quality—Are they not forever parting with their husbands—forfeiting their reputations —and is their life aught but dissipation? In common genteel life, indeed, you may now and then meet with very fine girls —who have politeness, sense, and conversation—but *these* are few. And then, look at your tradesmen's daughters—what are they?—poor creatures indeed! all pertness, imitation and folly.

I said a great deal in *defence* of our poor sex, and *all* I could say, but it sounds so poor compared to my *opponent*, that I dare not write it.

"And what are you studying here?" said he, "O ho, 'Marianne'! And did you ever read 'Le Paysan Parvenu'?"[1]

---

[1] "Marianne" and "Le Paysan Parvenu" have still a charm of their own. Mr. Seaton's comparison of these novels with Sir Charles Grandison is not very unfair; with "Clarissa," it is that of works of

They are the two best novels that ever were wrote, for they are pictures of nature, and therefore excell your Clarissas and Grandisons far away. Now, Sir Charles Grandison is all perfection, and consequently, the last character we find in real life. In truth there's no such thing."

F. Indeed! do you really think a Sir Charles Grandison *never* existed?

Mr. S. Certainly not. He's too perfect for human nature.

F. It quite hurts me to hear anybody declare a really and thoroughly good man never lived. It is so *much* to the disgrace of mankind.

Mr. S. Ay—you are too young to conceive its truth. I own to you, you are therefore more happy. I would give all I am worth to have the same innocence and credulity of heart I had some years since; and to be able to go through life with it.

F. But if, as you assert, nobody around you would be the same, would not *that* innocence rather expose you to danger, than increase your happiness?

Mr. S. Faith, I dont know, since you *must* be exposed to it at all events. Besides, when once—which *every* body must be—you are convinced of the wickedness and deceit of men, it is impossible to preserve untainted your *own* innocence of heart. Experience *will* prove the depravity of mankind, and the conviction of it only serves to create distrust, suspicion, caution, and sometimes causelessly.

F. But surely this experience has its advantages as well as its inconveniences, since without it you are liable to be ensnared in every trap, which, according to *your* account of mankind, they put in your way.

Mr. S. Assuredly—But, depend upon it, no one need fear missing this experience!

F. You seem to have a most shocking opinion of the world in general.

Mr. S. Because the world in general merits it. The

---

fancy with one of imagination, but there *is* a parallel between the lives of Pierre de Marivaux and Samuel Richardson. One was born in 1688, the other in 1689. Both wrote well-approved novels when of mature age; one died in 1763, the other in 1761.

most innocent time must be the rise of any state, when they are unacquainted with vice. Now Rome, in it's infancy——

F. O, *that* was not the most flourishing time of Rome, for in its infancy it was inhabited merely by villains and ruffians.

Mr. S. O but they soon forgot that, in forming their State: and established excellent Laws, and became models of morality, liberty, virtue.

F. Yes; and the first proof they gave of their virtue, was to murder their founder, to whom they were indebted for every thing—and farther to rob the neighbouring states of their wives and daughters, whom they forcibly detained. I can't say you have hit on the best country to shew the innocence of it's first state.

Mr. S. O you are too hard upon me! Well then the rise of the Grecian cities. They certainly were virtuous in their infancy. And so are all nations—in proportion to their poverty, for money is the source of the greatest vice, and that nation which is most rich, is most wicked.

F. But, Sir, this is saying, in reality, nothing for virtue; since if these people you mention were only virtuous thro' necessity, and *as* wicked as they *could* be, they are in fact full as vicious as *any* country whatever.

Mr. S. That's very true. In short I believe there was always the same degree of real (tho' there could not be of practical) vice in mankind, in all countrys, and all ages, as at present.

F. You must give me leave again to repeat that I fancy you inveigh thus violently against the world, *partly* at least in order to support your own side of the question; for surely any person who really and truly *thought* so like a misanthrope as you *talk*, must abhor mankind, and shut themselves up in a cave, away from them all. You absolutely appear to be the greatest satirist, and most severe judge of the world——

Mr. S. O, no. I assure you, nobody lives happier in it— or can have greater or more equal spirits, but I can see the faults of people nevertheless.

F. Permit me to say one thing, Sir: You tell me that you are a stranger, that you know not the manners of the ladies here; that you don't know *this*—are ignorant of *that* —(a lady's going home after a ball, for example!). Well,

Sir, give me leave to ask what you *have* observed? Why even all our faults! You have not been very blind to *them*, or taken much time to find them out! You seem to have taken the worst side of the question all the way.

Mr. S. O, Ma'am, your most obedient. . . . . . But, (looking at his watch) what a time have I detained you from your employments by my tongue! But it is so seldom I can find ladies who, like you and your sister, can keep up a conversation, that I am loath to lose them when I do, and I do protest, that to talk with a young lady who will answer me with the sense and reason that you do now, gives me far more pleasure than all the plays, operas or diversions in the world: for none of them can be compared to a sensible, spirited conversation!

I should be ashamed to write down these [much] undeserved, *outré* compliments, but that they are made, as you see, only when they are unavoidable, and consequently become no compliment at all. I am quite surprised to find how much of his conversation I have remembered, but as there was only him and myself, it was not very difficult.

[Below this eight lines are erased, which seem to begin with "Writing for papa." This is the only allusion throughout these Diaries to what was Fanny's constant work when with her father.]

Saturday, Nov. 18th.

[Eight scored out lines of a new paragraph end the last page left of this year's Journal. A few sentences may be made out]:—

We passed the most curious evening yesterday . . . . Never sure did any conversation seem more like a scene in a comedy . . . . I must tell you something of what pass'd.

[The names of Hetty and of Mrs. Pringle may be read. Fifty-three years afterwards, Fanny wrote to Hetty—"October 21, 1821. Though so sluggish to learn, I was always observant: do you remember Mr. Seaton's denominating me at fifteen, *the silent, observant Miss Fanny?*" Perhaps she broke her nearly total silence among strangers for the first time in this very long talk with Mr. Seaton. This passage is particularly interesting as giving the first example of her extraordinary power of retaining protracted conversations unmarked by any special brilliancy, or novelty of thought. She does not even appear to have seen that the wily Mr. Seaton was trying to please her as well as her lovely sister. Her innocent enjoyment was in the argument, and in repeating it in writing.]

1769.
Saturday, Jan⁷. 7th.

[Much has been cut from the Diary of this year, and it has many erasures. It appears to have been in two or three *cahiers*, which all lie now within one quarto sheet of paper, so much are they shrunk in size.]

O dear! O dear! how melancholy has been to us this last week, the first of this year! Never during my life have I suffer'd more severely in my mind, I do verily believe!—But God be praised! I hope it is now over! The poor Susette, who I told you was disappointed of her Lynn journey by a violent cold, was just put to Bed somewhat better when I wrote to you this day se'night—I soon after went to her, and found her considerably worse. She talk'd to me in a most affecting style, her voice and manner were peculiarly touching.

"My dear Fanny," cried she, "I love you dearly—my *dear* sister!—have I any *more* sisters?"—O how I was terrified—shock'd—surprised!—"O yes!" continued she, "I have sister Hetty—but I don't wish her to come to me now, because she'll want me to drink my barley water, and I can't—but I will if *you* want me—and where's papa?" For my life I could not speak a word, and almost choak'd myself to prevent my sobbing. "O dear! I shall die!" "My dear girl."[1] "O but I must though!—But I can't help it—it is not my fault you know!"—Tho' I almost suffocated myself with smothering my grief, I believe she perceived it, for she kiss'd me, and again said "How I love you! my *dear* Fanny!—I love you dearly!" "My sweet Girl!" cried I—"you—you *can't* love me so much as I do you!" "If I was Charly I should love you—indeed I should²——Oh!—I shall

---

[1] Here two or three words are torn away.
[2] This seems to be, not Charles, but little Charlotte, the youngest of the first family of Dr. Burney.

die!"—"But not yet, my dear love—not yet!" "Oh yes—I shall!—I should like to see papa first tho'."

In short, she talk'd in a manner *inconceivably* affecting—and how greatly I was shock'd, *no* words can express. My dear papa out of town too!—We sent immediately for Mr. Heckford, an excellent apothecary, who has attended our family many years. He bled her immediately, and said it would not be safe to omit it—She continued much the same some hours. Between 1 and 2 I went to bed, as she was sleeping, and Hetty and the maid sat up all night, for Hetty was very urgent that I should. She had a shocking night. At 7 o'clock Mr. Heckford was again call'd. She had a blister put on her back; he beg'd that a physician might be directly applied to, as she was in a very dangerous way!—O my good God! what did poor Hetty and myself suffer!—

Dr. Armstrong was sent for—and my good Aunt Nanny who is the best nurse in England, tender, careful, and affectionate, and but too well experienced in illness. We were much inclined to send an express after my dear papa to Lynn, but resolved to wait while we possibly could. Unfortunately Mr., Mrs. and Miss Molly Young all came very early to spend the day here—I never went *to* them, or *from* Susy, till dinner, and then I could eat none, nor speak a word. Never, I believe, shall I forget the shock I received that night. The fever increased—she could not swallow her medicines, and was quite delirious—Mr. Heckford said indeed she had a *very* poor chance of recovery! He endeavour'd himself to give her her physick, which he said was *absolutely* necessary, but in vain—she rambled—breathed short, and was terribly suffering—her disorder he pronounced an inflammation of the breast.[1]—"I am sorry to say it," said he, "but indeed at *best* she stands *a very* poor chance!" I felt my blood freeze—I ran out of the room in an anguish beyond *thought*—and all I could do was to almost rave—and *pray*, in such an agony! O what a night she had! We all sat up—She slept perpetually, without being at all refresh'd, and was *so* light-

---

[1] In modern phrase, of the *lungs*.

headed! I kept behind her pillow, and fed her with barley water in a tea-spoon the whole night, without her knowing of it at all—indeed she was dreadfully bad! On Monday however, the Dr. and apothecary thought her *somewhat* better, tho' in great danger. We all sat up again. We wrote to papa, not daring to conceal the news, while her life was thus uncertain—On Tuesday, they ventured to pronounce her out of danger—We made Hetty go to bed, and my aunt and I sat up again—and on Wednesday, we two went to bed, the dear girl continuing to mend, which she has, tho' very slowly, ever since. My beloved papa and mama have both wrote to us quite, kindly——

Jan⁷., Tuesday.

My sweet Susette is almost well. I think of nothing else but to thank God Almighty enough, which I am obliged to run out of the room to do twenty times a day, for else I cannot breathe—I feel as if I had an asthma except when I am doing that.

Wednesday.

Papa's come back, and we are all happier than ever we were in our lives.

Thursday, Jan. 19th.

Well, my dear creature, we have great hopes and expectations of happiness to-morrow. Susette is *quite* recovered. We are going to a great party at Mrs. Pringle's—When Susette is well enough, she is still to go to Lynn where mama and Charttie and Bessy and Miss Allen will pass the winter. Adieu—*pour le present*.

Saturday, Jan⁷. 21st.

There was a very great party at Mrs. Pringle's . . . . . We danced till 2 o'clock this morning. Mr. Crawford with Hetty, and a Mr. Armstrong with me—a young man with a fine person, and a handsome face, but who made me laugh to so immoderate a degree that I was quite ashamed; for he aim'd at being a wit, and yet kept so settled a solemn countenance, with such languishing eyes, that he made himself quite ridiculous.

N.B.—Pages 4 and 5 burnt. [This is in Mdme. D'Arblay's writing.]

Dr. Armstrong I see now, at last, with real pleasure, for I *have* seen him lately with a very contrary feeling. He asked Susette many questions concerning her health—" I can tell you," said he, " you have had a very narrow escape! you was just gone! the Gates of Heaven were in view—" " O," cried I, " they shut them on her—I fancy she was not good enough to enter!" " O yes," answered he, " they were very ready to receive her there—but I would not let her depart,— I thought she might as well stay here a little while longer."[1]

Monday, Feby. 13th.

The ever charming, engaging, beloved Mr. Crisp spent the whole day with us yesterday. I love him more than ever— every time I see him I cannot help saying so—never can there have been a more *truly* amiable man—he appears to take a *parental* interest in our affairs, and I do believe [loves] us all with a really fatherly affection. The frankness—the sin-

---

[1] Dr. Armstrong left strong impressions on the memory of Fanny. When she was eighty, she wrote that "the very sight of him was medicinal," and that "his prescriptions were unsparing, but well-poised." Dr. Burney and Dr. Armstrong were friendly before Dr. Armstrong was sent to Burney, when he had a fever, by another Scotchman (the Honble. and Revd. Mr. Home). Dr. Armstrong put blister after blister on Burney until he was (as his daughter says) almost covered with blisters, and almost flayed alive. He then ordered Burney to live out of London. Thus Armstrong was the indirect cause of Fanny's being born at Lynn. Dr. Armstrong was one of those who have been called "the unpoetical poets" of the last century. The "Art of Preserving Health" was published in 1744— the year in which Dr. Burney went to London. It is commonly to be found in the duodecimo poets of the last century, side by side of, or bound with, "The Union," and the poems of Allan Ramsay and Blair. It has been lifted bodily into several selections of poetry, such as "The Elegant Extracts," and Dr. Aikin's "British Poets." Dr. Armstrong is said to have written four stanzas (74-5-6-7) in the first canto of his friend Thomson's "Castle of Indolence." They are *medical* stanzas, showing the ill effects of indolence and "false luxury."

cerity with which he corrects and reproves us, is more grateful to me, than the most flattering professions could be, because it is far, far more seriously and really kind and friendly. His very smile is all benevolence as well as playfulness. He protests he will take no denial from papa for Hetty and me to go to Chesington this summer, and told papa to remember he had *bespoke* us: I fancy he is weary of asking almost, and I am sure my dear papa is tired of refusing —for what in the world can be more disagreeable, more painful to a mind generous and good as his?—I declare I am almost ashamed to hear Chesington mention'd before him, and cannot for my life join in intreaties to go, tho' my heart prompts me most *furiously*.

[The proceedings on "Valentine's" Day—Feb. 14—have been erased, but the date remains legible.]

[Poland Street], Feby. 16.

How delightful, how enviable a tranquility and content do I at present enjoy! I have scarce a wish, and am happy and easy as my heart can desire. All are at Lynn but us three, Papa, Hetty, and I, so that I am very much alone, but to that I have no objection. I pass my time in working, reading, and thrumming the harpsichord. . . . . I am now reading Stanyan's Grecian History. Tho' the *words* are not obsolete, the style and expressions are not at all familiar, and many of the latter what at present, I believe, would not be reckoned extremely elegant. But it is, nevertheless, a very clever book, which *I* need not say, since it is generally approved; but that's no matter.[1] Susy and I correspond constantly. Her letters would not disgrace a woman of 40 years of age. My dear papa is in charming health and good humour, tho' hurried to death—You will perhaps admire the consistency of my expressions, and allow most cordially that *I* have a right to criticize others—Prithee, my good friend, don't

---

[1] Temple Stanyan, the author of this Grecian History, was, for some time, British Minister at Constantinople. He had previously written "An Account of Switzerland." "The Swiss," said Dr. Johnson, in 1778, "admit that there is but one error in Stanyan."

trouble me with any impertinent remarks,—past twelve o'clock! and I must rise at seven to-morrow! I must to bed immediately—I write now from a pretty neat little closet of *mine* that is in the bed chamber, where I keep all *my* affairs—Tell me, my dear, what Heroine ever yet existed without her own closet?

Sunday Night.

My Grand-Daddy is here to night, to the *very* great satisfaction of us all. He gave us a great deal of excellent general advice, and told us very gravely this—" Experience is never good till 'tis *bought*." Hetty, in a very gay and flighty manner assented, and added that every body should have experience of their own, [and] not follow advice from other people's "—" Ay," returned he, " let them have it!—and it must be *paid* for too! yes, *well* paid for!"[1] . . . . . O, I must tell you that I have at last fallen in Love, and with a gentleman whom I have lately become acquainted with : he is about sixty or seventy—has the misfortune to be hump-back'd, crooked legged, and rather deform'd in his face—But, in sober sadness, I am delighted with the Dean of Coleraine, (whose picture this is,) and which I have very lately read. The piety, the zeal, the humanity, goodness and humility of this charming old man have won my heart—Ah! who will not envy him the invaluable treasure?[2]

Saturday.

If my dear Susette was here I should want nothing. We are still only us three together. 'I seldom quit home con-

---

[1] A passage in the "Memoirs of Dr. Burney" (p. 135 vol. iii) confirms the conjecture that "My Grand-Daddy" was Mr. Crisp. Dr. Burney, who was nearly twenty years younger than he was, used to call him "Daddy." Hence "Grand-Daddy." A little later on he is brought closer still to Hetty and Fanny by being called "Daddy." All Fanny's grand-parents, except Dr. Burney's mother, seem to have been dead when she wrote this.

[2] "The Dean of Coleraine" (1752) is a novel in three volumes, from the French of the Abbé Prévost, best known as the author of "Manon L'Escaut." The French title is "Le Doyen de Killérine, histoire morale," etc.

sidering my youth and opportunities. But why should I when I am so happy in it? following my own vagaries, which my papa never controls, I never can [want] employment, nor sigh for amusement. We have a library which is an everlasting resource when attack'd by the spleen—I have always a sufficiency of work to spend, if I pleased, my whole time at it—musick is a feast which can never grow insipid—and, in short, I have all the reason that ever mortal had to be contented with my lot—and I *am* contented with, I *am* grateful for it! If few people are more happy, few are more sensible *of* their happiness. But what of that?—is there any merit in paying the small tribute of gratitude, where blessings such as I have received *compel* it from me? How strongly, how forcibly do I feel to whom I owe all the earthly happiness I enjoy!—it is to my father! to this dearest, most amiable, this best beloved—most worthy of men!—it is his goodness to me which makes all appear so gay, it is his affection which makes *my* sun shine.

But if to this parent I owe all my comfort—it is to my God I owe *him*! and that God who hath given to me this treasure which no earthly one can equal, alone knows the value I set on it.—Yet what value can compare with [its] worth?—the *worth* of *such* a treasure? a parent who makes the happiness of his children! I am in a moralising humour.—How truly does this Journal contain my real and undisguised thoughts!—I always write in it according to the humour I am in, and if any stranger was accidentally reading it, how capricious—inconsistent and whimsical I must appear! One moment flighty and half mad,—the next sad and melancholy. No matter! it's truth and simplicity are it's sole recommendation, and I doubt not but I shall hereafter receive great pleasure from *reviewing* and almost *renewing* my youth, and my former sentiments, unless, indeed, the latter part of my life is doomed to be as miserable as the beginning is the reverse, and then indeed, every line here will rend my heart!—I sigh from the bottom of it at this dreadful idea, I think I am in a humour to write a funeral sermon— . . . . . Hetty is gone to Ranelagh, and I fancy does not *sympathize* with me! that is, not *just now*.

[Here, in whose writing is uncertain, are the words: "15 burnt to 21."]

* * * * *

Our party last evening was large and *brilliant*. Mr. Greville, the celebrated Dr. Hawkesworth, Mr. Crisp and my cousin dined with us. In the evening, Mrs. and Miss Turner of Lynn,[1] two gentlemen named Vincent, and Mr. Partridge made a very agreeable addition to our company.

Dr. Hawkesworth does not shine in conversation so much superior to others as from his writings might be expected. Papa calls his talking book language—for I never heard a man speak in a style which so much resembles writing. He has an amazing flow of choice words and expressions. 'Twould be nonsense to say he is extremely clever and sensible; while the *Adventurers* exist, that must be universally acknowledged,—but his talents seem to consist rather in the solid than in the brilliant. All he says is just, proper, and better expressed than most *written* language; but he does not appear to me to be at all what is called a wit, neither is his conversation sprightly or brilliant. He is *remarkably* well bred and attentive, considering how great an author he is; for without that consideration, he would be reckoned so.[2] He has a small tincture of affectation, I believe;—but I have quite forgot the wise resolution I so often make of never judging of people by first sight! Pity! that we have all the power of *making* resolutions so readily, and so properly, and that few or none are capable of *keeping*

---

[1] The Turners were of the family of Sir John Turner, who had, years before, procured the organist's place for Dr. Burney at Lynn Regis. A Mr. Partridge was, in 1755, Recorder of Lynn. A Mr. Vincent was a friend of both Mr. Crisp and Dr. Burney. At his house they accidentally met, after a separation of many years, during which Mr. Crisp had travelled, and Dr. Burney married and lost a wife whom Mr. Crisp had never seen, but whose children he was to treat as his own. Mr. Vincent *may* have been the same Vincent who was for thirty years the chief player on the haut-bois at Covent Garden Theatre and in the Queen's band.

[2] If by no means "a great author," Dr. John Hawkesworth was a pleasant and fluent writer, who could turn his pen to anything, and was agreeable to readers, and popular with publishers. He condensed the Parliamentary Debates for "Sylvanus Urban." For two years he

them! But here again am I judging of others' want of fortitude by my own weakness! O dear, I am always to be wrong! However, I think I may prevail on myself not to be my *own* judge rashly. Why should I think I am *always* to be wrong? I know not I am sure; certain it is I have hitherto never been otherwise; but *that* ought not to discourage me, since so inconsistent is human nature allowed to be, that for that very reason 'tis impossible I should be the same creature at the conclusion as at the beginning of my life. So who knows but I may turn out to be a wiseacre?

* * * * *

O! I am to go to a wedding to-morrow—the partys—one Mr. John Hatton, glass polisher,[1] and Mrs. Betty Langley, spinster, our old cook. Perhaps I may give you, Miss

---

brought out "The Adventurer," writing half the papers himself. Like Dr. Johnson, too, he wrote an Eastern tale. He edited "Swift," he translated "Telemachus," he even found words for the music of a fairy piece, nay, of an oratorio, or more. Like Dr. Johnson, too, he had the ill-will of Sir John Hawkins, who wrote of him mainly to run him down. Hawkesworth and Hawkins had begun life in the same manner, that is, as Presbyterians and lawyer's clerks, and seen much of each other as neighbours, if not friends. Kind Sir John tells us that Hawkesworth had but "a small stock of learning," that he was "ostensibly the governor of a school for the Education of young females," and became so unduly elevated by receiving a Lambeth degree of D.C.L., that he neglected his early friends, etc. Sir John's "derangement of Epitaphs" was such that he meant to praise "Rasselas," when he said that "'Rasselas' is a specimen of our language scarcely to be paralleled; it is written in a style refined to a degree of immaculate purity, and displays the whole force of *turgid* eloquence!" The best excuse which can be made for Hawkins, who has written so harshly of Dr. Johnson, and many other men of letters, is to be found in a letter from H. Walpole to Mason, in 1782.—"Why do you fall so foul of my friend, Sir John Hawkins, who is a most inoffensive, good being? Do not wound harmless simpletons, you who can gibbet convicts of magnitude." Therefore "*ostensibly*" may not mean aught of ill if "*turgid*" be laudatory. The rest of the meaning is that Mrs. Hawkesworth kept a girls' boarding-school at Bromley, Kent. As for neglect of early friends, here we find Hawkesworth with Burney, whose acquaintance he had made at the house of Fulk Greville in 1745, before he was "elated"—duly or unduly.

[1] This seems to be meant as a pleasantry upon Hatton's being a footman.

Nobody, an account of this affair to-morrow. I never had the honour of being at a wedding in my life—but tho' this will be the first, I fancy it will not be the last too.

I am vastly sorry Mr. Crisp is gone—I shall think of him every Sunday at least, all my life I believe.—I am now going to *charm* myself for the third time with poor Sterne's "Sentimental Journey." * * * * *

Monday Eve, May 15th.

Well, the wedding is over, the good folks are join'd for better for worse.—A shocking clause that!—'tis preparing one to lead a long journey, and to know the path is not altogether strew'd with roses.—This same marriage ceremony is so short, I really should have doubted its validity had *I* been the bride; though perhaps she may not find the road it leads her to very short; be that as it may, she must now trudge on, she can only return with her wishes, be she ever so wearied. We have spent an exceedingly agreeable day, I speak for myself and a few more at least, I will not answer for the bride and the groom's feelings, at least not for the latter—tho' they neither of them appeared miserable; but had *I* been that *latter*, I fear I could not have said so much for myself.—As to the bride, she is blythe as the month; if one can compare in any degree a weed of December, with the fragrance of May; for a weed in truth it is, and a weed not in its first prime. But I must give some account of the *wedding*. . . . . To begin with the Company, first, The Bride. A maiden of about fifty. . . . . She was dressed in a white linnen gown, and with all the elegance which *marks* her character and station, having the honour to be cook to Mr. Burney. The Bridegroom. A young man who had the appearance of being her son. A good, modest, sober, and decent youth. He was in blue trim'd with red. . . . The Father (of the day) Mr. Charles Burney, Junr. . . . Not merely her husband, but her father too was young enough to own her for a mother. . . . The Bride's maids, three. 1st, Miss Anne Burney, who may count years with the bride herself. . . . 2nd, Miss Esther Burney. . . . And 3rd, Miss Frances Burney. . . . . .

We went in papa's coach, as many as it would hold,—the *gentlemen* were obliged to walk—which condescension is not inconsiderable, for Mr. *Somebody*, and the bridegroom too, have the honour of being footmen to very *topping* people! The bride supported her spirits amazingly.[1] . . . .

[On or just after] Monday, May 22.

A droll mistake happened to me to day—We live commonly in a parlour which is forwards, and I saw a gentleman walking at the other side of the street who stopt before our house, and looked at the window some time—and then crossed the way and knocked at the door. Papa happened to be at home. —" Who is it? " said he.—I told him I did not know, but I believed some man who had a tolerable assurance by his staring.—The gentleman came immediately into the parlour, and after asking papa how he did, came up to me, and said —" I have called in ma'am, on purpose to pay my respects to you—and———." I stared, and could not recollect I had ever seen him before, nor imagine who it was, and, was quite at a loss what to do, but my papa relieved me by saying—

" O! *this* is not your acquaintance—this is her sister—"

" No! " cried he—" well, I never saw any thing so like! I really thought it was Miss Burney! "

Helas! what flattery! But still I was puzzled to think who it was, till by papa's conversation I discovered at last he was Lord Pigot, . . . who I had heard was of the party yesterday at Mrs. Pleydell's. But how fortunate it was for me that papa chanced to be at home—I should have been horridly confused at his mistake else, for nothing on earth is so disagreeable as to be obliged to tell any body *you don't know them;*—it is mortifying on both sides. His Lordship did papa the honour to invite him and us, he said to a concert, and to spend the evening at his house but as, I knew it could not be really meant for me, I begged not to go; and

---

[1] Eleven years afterwards, Susan, when writing to tell Fanny of their Sister Hetty's serious illness, caused by fright during the riots of 1780, says, " I am sure you will rejoice to hear that good creature Betty Hatton is with her."

papa thought the same, so they've gone without me . . . . Younger sisters are almost different beings from elder one's, but, thank God, it is quite and unaffectedly without repining or envy that I see *my* elder sister so continually gad about and visit, etc, when I rest at home. I fancy Lord Pigot is a very agreeable man—he is undoubtedly polite and lively. Charles and I sup alone. We are reading that satirical, entertaining poem the "New Bath Guide"—but I have read very little lately, tho' I doat on nothing equally; but I have had sufficient employment in working. . . . . In speaking of Lord Pigot's taking me for Hetty, my papa accounted for the mistake by saying—"You may have observed, my Lord, that people who live together, naturally catch the looks and air of one another, and, without having one feature alike, they contract a *something* in the whole of the countenance which strikes one as a resemblance. There are two ladies who your Lordship very likely has seen, Mrs. Greville and Mrs. Crewe, mother and daughter. In examining their faces, they are as different as one face can be from another; yet by living together, they have accustom'd themselves so much to the same habits and manners, that I never see one, without thinking of the other."

* * * * *

Thursday, June.

What an age since I last wrote! I have been wavering in my mind whether I should ever again touch this Journal, unless it were to commit it to the flames—for this same *mind* of mine would fain persuade me that this same *Journal* of mine is a very ridiculous—trifling, and useless affair; and as such, would wisely advise me to part with it for ever—but I felt at the same time a regret, a loss of some thing in forbearing to *here* unburthen myself the pleasure which (in imagination at least) awaits me in the perusal of these sheets hereafter, pleaded strongly in favour of continuing to encrease them—and now that I have once more taken courage to begin, I think and already feel twice the content I did while this dear little book was neglected.

I have much to write, and as I am to day entirely alone, why I have both time and opportunity, but as I am not at present much inclined to be particular—I shall only mention a few occurrences that are past.—

In the first place, my sister and self lately spent the evening at Mrs. Pringle's.—Her party was—Mr. Scot, who had been preceptor to the King when he was Prince of Wales [1]—Mr. Seton, and Mrs. and Mr. Debbieg, his sister, and brother in law, who are a very polite, sensible couple. The company divided into little partys immediately—Mr. Debbieg—his lady, Mrs. Pringle and Andrew went to cards—a *diversion* I always avoid—Mr. Seton and Hetty amused themselves very comfortably together . . . . in an uninterrupted tete-a-tete. If Mr. Scot had not been there, I should have made some excuse for coming home; but as he was, I was extremely well contented to stay, for he disliked cards as much as myself, and very good naturedly devoted the whole evening

---

[1] George Lewis Scott (named after George I., at whose Court of Hanover his father held an appointment) was, nevertheless, reputed to be a Jacobite. From the company in which he is found in these journals, it seems very likely that such was the case. He was recommended by Bolingbroke, through Lord Bathurst, as sub-preceptor to the Prince of Wales, in 1752. Then there was a turmoil—as it was thought he might give his pupil notions of the divine right of kings—nay, even persuade him of the justice of yielding his claims to those of the Stewarts. About the same time Scott married Sarah Robinson, younger sister of the better-known Mrs. Montague. Sarah was called "*The Pea*," because the sisters were "as like as two peas." Mr. and Mrs. Scott soon separated. Her friends said that he was a bad man, but did not say why. A rumour was spread that he had tried to poison her. His pupil, George III., who always remembered him with affection, said, long afterwards, that it was "a gross and wicked calumny," invented by an intriguing upper preceptor, Dr. Hayter, Bishop of Norwich, "against a man of the purest mind, and most innocent conduct." Scott was made a Commissioner of Excise as a reward for his services, and is found well spoken of, even by Walpole and Mason. He was a friend of Gibbon. In 1777, when Johnson was preparing his prefaces to "Lives of the Poets," Boswell wrote to him—"I believe George Lewis Scott and Dr. Armstrong are Thomson's only surviving companions while he lived in, or about London." He was talked of as "*George Lewis*," to mark him out from a less amiable and reputable Scott, who was, like him, a very tall man, and a writer—Mr. Scott, chaplain to Lord Sandwich.

—(till supper seperated *parties*) to me. That he is very clever, his office of Preceptor *ought* to make undoubted—and he is very sociable and facetious too, and entertained me extremely with droll anecdotes and storys among the Great and about the Court .... All the party was surprised to see that *he* would, and that *I* could be so sociable and intimate, but he was so good-natured and unassuming that I was quite at my ease with him.

Not long after, Mrs. Debbieg and Mr. Seton called here ... to invite Hetty and me to drink tea and spend the evening with the former.—Hetty joyfully accepted the invitation—it was not convenient for me to go, and so she made my excuses. She spent an exceeding agreeable evening—they all made very civil enquirys about me, and ... Mr. Seton offered to fetch me, so did Andrew—and Major Debbieg himself—but Hetty, who knew I should not be delighted to see them all here, made excuses for me.

* * * * * *

Miss Crawford called here lately—she is very earnest for us to visit her—but *we* are not very earnest about the matter:—however, the laws of custom make our spending one evening with her necessary. O! how I hate this vile custom which obliges us to make slaves of ourselves!—to sell the most precious property we boast, our time;—and to sacrifice it to every prattling impertinent who chooses to demand it!—Yet those who shall pretend to defy this irksome confinement of our happiness, must stand accused of incivility,—breach of manners—love of originality,—and ... what not. But, nevertheless, ... they who will nobly dare to be above submitting to chains their reason disapproves, them shall I always honour—if that will be of any service to them! For why should we not be permitted to be masters of our time?—Why may we not venture to love, and to dislike—and why, if we do, may we not give to those we love the richest jewel we own, our time?—What is it can stimulate us to bestow *that* on all alike?—'tis not affection—'tis not a desire of pleasing—or if it is, 'tis a very weak one;—no! 'tis indolence—'tis custom—custom—which is so woven around us—which so universally commands us—which we all blame—and all obey, without knowing why or wherefore—which keeps our better reason, that sometimes dares to show it's folly, in subjection—and which, in short, is a very ridiculous affair, more particularly as it hath kept me writing on it till I have forgot what introduced it—I feel myself in no excellent mood—I will walk out and give my spirits another turn, and then resume my pen.

Sunday afternoon. June.

Now don't imagine that because I have not wrote sooner since the walk I proposed taking in order to amend my spirits and temper, I have so ill succeeded as not to have gain'd the desired point till now—no, no, I have been in most *exceeding good humour* I assure you, tho' not at all inclined to write: nor indeed am I at present, but as I believe I shall not have time to employ myself in this *pretty manner* again soon, and as I have a most remarkable and very interesting affair to relate, I have resolved, neck or nothing, to take the pen once again in hand. This same affair is that—

My papa went last Monday to Oxford, in order to take a Doctor's Degree in Musick: Is not *that* a grand affair?— He composed an Anthem by way of exercise to be perform'd on the occasion, in which his pupil Miss Barsanti was to be the principal singer, and make her first appearance in publick. .... His Anthem was performed last Thursday, and gave much satisfaction—indeed the musick of it is delightful—Poor Barsanti was terrified to death, and her mother, who was among the audience, was so much affected, that she fainted away; but by immediate assistance soon revived.[1] However, notwithstanding her fears and apprehensions, Barsanti came off with flying colours and met with great applause . . . . . My dear, kind papa wrote us a short note to let us know all

---

[1] Miss Barsanti (we are told by Lætitia Hawkins), was the daughter of "a little old Lucchese," a humble musician, and of a Scotch woman; who, in later days, when her daughter Jenny acted in Dublin, was known by the Irish as "the big woman." Jenny suited herself to both the Hawkinses and the Burneys—that is, to the two Historians of Music, and their families, and was helped by both to make way as a singer, and afterwards as an actress.

was well over the moment the performance was finished—The very great kindness of his thinking of us at so busy a time, I shall remember with the most grateful pleasure all my life . . . . . As Hetty keeps the letter, I will copy it here, for I shall always love to read it: . . . . .

"Oxford, Thursday June 22nd,
"past 2 o'clock.

"My dear Girls,

"I know it will please you much to hear that the performance of my Anthem is just very well over, not one mistake of consequence—Barsanti did extremely well, and all was much applauded — I shall to-morrow have both my Degrees (for I must first take that of Batchelor of Musick) with great unanimity and reputation—Dr. Hayes is very civil; and lends me his robe with a very good grace[1]—Adieu —I know not when I shall get home."— . . . . .

This made us extremely happy. We have pass'd this week quite alone, but very comfortably and cheerfully. And now for something concerning myself, at which I am a little uneasy.

As I found Friday was to be the *Day of Days* that my father took his degrees, as soon as we had read this letter, I ran upstairs and wrote one to him in verse—which I am horridly afraid he will think impertinent—I read it to Hetty before I sent it, and she persuaded me it would merely have the effect I intended, namely to make him laugh—I wish it may, but I shan't be happy till he comes home . . . . . I will copy from memory the foolish thing I sent, 'tis an attempt at Cranbo—and a poor one enough.—

---

[1] Dr. William Hayes was Heather Professor of Music in the University of Oxford, from 1741 to 1777; University Organist at St. Mary's, etc., etc. Dr. Burney has written, in a memorandum which refers to a time before he was eighteen, "The celebrated Felton, and after him, the first Dr. Hayes, came from Oxford to Shrewsbury on a tour, while I was studying hard, without instruction or example; and they amazed and stimulated me so forcibly by their performance on the organ, as well as by their encouragement, that I thenceforward went to work with an ambition and fury that would hardly allow me to eat or sleep."

TO DOCTOR LAST.[1]

1.

O aid me, ye Muses of ev'ry degree,
O give me the standish[2] of Mulberry Tree
  Which was cut for the Author of " Ferney ; "
O give me a quill to the stump worn by Gray,
And paper which cut was on Milton's birth-day,
  To write to the great Doctor Burney.

2.

O Doctor, of Doctors, the Last and the Best,
By Fortune most honoured, distinguished and blest,

---

[1] A pun, alluding to the character in the " Devil on Two Sticks."—(*Author's Note*.)

" The Devil upon Two Sticks," a most diverting satire in three acts (called by Foote a comedy), brought him above three thousand pounds during the acting season of 1768. It was directed mainly against doctors of all degrees, up to the President of the College of Physicians, Sir William Browne,—a very odd, clever man, who was then at war with the Licentiates of Medicine. In this piece, an Irishman and a Scot, a Jew, and a Quaker, all doctors, are against Dr. Hellebore (Browne). He is preparing to repulse their attack upon his College in Warwick Lane, when Last, a shoemaker, enters, seeking his way to the College, to obtain a doctor's license, because, though "bred-up" a shoemaker, he was "born a doctor, being the seventh son of a seventh son." The Devil upon Two Sticks directs him to the College, and assumes the form of Doctor Hellebore, with his "large wig and superior importance." Foote, who acted this part, closely copied the dress of Sir William Browne, who had wit and good-humour enough, although then past eighty, to send him his own muff, to make what (as he said) was so good a personation as to his coat, sword, wig, and eyeglass, complete. Last is licensed, after a very droll examination, by the supposed Hellebore ; who then proceeds to lecture upon " some notable discoveries of his own " (which amount to a theory of germs), of which much mirth is made by Foote. We meet Sir William for a few minutes hereafter. " Dr. Last's Examination " was, shortly afterwards, extracted from the comedy, and played occasionally as an interlude of one act, although the whole piece still held the stage.

[2] An ink standish cut out of a mulberry tree, planted by Shakespeare, for Mr. Keate, author of "Ferney—An Epistle to Voltaire." (*Author's Note*.)

Of " Ferney—an Epistle, etc.," H. Walpole writes, with a sneer, that it " gives M. de Voltaire an account of his own tragedies."

And may you for ever be her nigh!
O smile (if a Doctor's permitted to smile),
Your new acquir'd[1] gravity lessen awhile
To read this, O dread Doctor Burney.

3.

For the letter most kind we to day did receive
With grateful affection our bosoms do heave;
And to see you, O grave Sir! how yearn I!
'Tis true the time's short since you last was in town,
Yet both fatter and taller you doubtless are grown,
Or you'll make but a poor Doctor Burney.

4.

For I never can think of a Doctor, not big
As a Falstaff, and not with a full bottom'd wig,
And the sly air Fame gives an atterney;
Not more at the bag did the citizen's stare
Of Harley, when Harley was made a Lord Mayor,
Than I at the thin Doctor Burney.[2]

5.

O! may Wisdom, which still to Good Humour gives birth,
May fatness with dignity, goodness with mirth,
Still attend you, and speed your town journey!
And O! till the hour that Death us shall part
May Fanny a corner possess of the heart
Of the owner of her's, Doctor Burney!

---

[1] "Natural" was first written.

[2] In 1761 Foote makes Smirk, who is suddenly called upon by Prig ("the greatest man in the world in his way that ever was, or ever will be,") to take his place as an auctioneer, consult his wife as to what manner of wig he is to wear at the sale. She tells him that "a bag is too boyish, deficient in dignity for the solemn occasion." In 1778, Boswell writes—"There is a general levity in the age. We leave *physicians* now with bag-wigs." Full-bottomed wigs were worn by physicians and others who would not appear light-minded. The Aldermen of London wore such wigs when waiting upon the King and Queen in 1761, with an address after their marriage. So, probably, they did in Harley's procession as Lord Mayor, in 1768. *Perhaps* he ought to have worn a "large flowing wig of many tiers,"—"a *nine-storey* wig, highly-

Mersh, June 29th.
Thursday Night.

We are arrived thus far on our journey to Lynn. . . . .

Papa came home from Oxford on Sunday night, as we expected—We ran to meet him with as much joy as if instead of a week's, we had groan'd at a year's absence—I had frighten'd myself not a little before he came, lest he should be angry at my pert verses—but the moment he arrived, I forgot everything but the pleasure of seeing him. He was more kind—more affectionate than ever ; if possible—tho' he two or three times called me " Saucy Girl ! " of which however, I wisely chose to take no notice, rather preferring to drop the subject. Notwithstanding his extreme hurry and business, he had thought of us when at Woodstock, and most kindly brought us both presents from that place—but the best thing he showed us was the *Oxford Journal*, in which his affair was mentioned. Who wrote it we know not, but I will copy the paragraph.—

[From the] *Oxford Journal*, June 23rd.

" On Thursday last was performed in the Musick School an Anthem composed by Mr. Charles Burney, of Poland Street, London, as an Exercise for the Degree of Doctor of Musick: which was received with universal applause, and allowed by the judges of musical merit to be the most elegant and ingenious performance that was ever exhibited here on the like occasion. The vocal parts were performed by Miss Barsanti (being the first time of her appearance in publick) Messrs. Norris, Mathews, Price, Millar, etc.; the instrumental by Mr. Burney, the composer—Messrs. Malchair, Charles Burney Junr., Richard Burney, Park, Pasquali, Lates etc., And yesterday Mr. Burney was admitted to his Degree, to which he was introduced *ex officio* by the Rev. Mr. Hornsby, Savilian

---

powdered, with long curls, such as was worn by Saunders Welsh, the friend of Dr. Johnson, when he rode as High Constable of Westminster. Thomas Harley (who thus broke through custom) was, although a wine-merchant in the City who had married a daughter of his father's steward, a son of the third Earl of Oxford, and grand-nephew of Queen Anne's Earl Robert.

Professor of Astronomy. The whole of the Musical Performance was conducted by our Professor, Dr. Hayes.[1] Miss Barsanti's voice and manner of singing were greatly admired, both in the above performance, and in the Musick room on Thursday and Friday nights: and the young lady, who is a scholar of Dr. Burney, will, if we mistake not, in time amply repay the publick any indulgence with which they may be disposed to encourage the becoming diffidence of modest merit."

There's for you!—"think of that Master Brooke." Well, when papa had been returned a short time, unfortunately a play called "Dr. Last in his Chariot" was mentioned by Charles.[2] . . . .

Papa looked at me—I looked any other way—"Oh! you saucy girl," cried he. Charles appeared curious, I was horridly ashamed. "What do you think," continued papa, "do you know this abominable girl calls *me* Dr. Last?"—Charles and Hetty both laughed, and papa took up the letter, and holding it out to me said—"Come, do me the favour of reading this!"—I would fain have torn it, but papa drew it back, and was going to read it—I beg'd him not—but *in vain*, and so I ran out of the room. But, to own the truth, my curiosity prevailed so far that I could not forbear running downstairs again with more speed than I ran up, and into the next room, where I found . . . . by papa's voice and manner that he did not appear displeased—though he half

---

[1] By the Statutes of Oxford, a candidate for the degree of Doctor of Music "shall compose a song in six, or eight parts, and shall publicly perform the same, 'tam Vocibus, quam Instrumentis etiam Musicis,' in presence of Dr. Heather's Professor of Music. This being done, he shall supplicate for his grace in the Convocation House, which being granted by both the Savilian Professors, he shall be presented to his degree." Dr. Burney's exercise was performed three years running at Choral Meetings in Oxford. In 1770 the lovely Linley (Mrs. Sheridan) sang instead of Jenny Barsanti, and turned the heads of more than undergraduates.

[2] In 1769 Isaac Bickerstaffe, with some help from Foote, continued the character of Dr. Last (who was the shoemaker-doctor in the "Devil upon Two Sticks"), in a piece adapted from Molière's "Malade Imaginaire," Foote playing Ailwou'd, the fanciful patient, but the play had little success.

affected to be so—he read it loud—. . . . "I assure you" said papa, "'tis very *good stuff!* I read it to Mrs. Playdel, and she was much pleased—particularly with the last stanza—and to one or two of my new Oxford friends at breakfast, and we had a very hearty laugh—"

This was enough—I ran once more upstairs, and lighter than a feather felt my heart!

* * * * * *

O—but one thing has very much vexed me—my papa has read my nonsense to Mrs. Skinner, an intimate acquaintance and a very clever woman, and she insisted on having a copy which papa desired me to write—I was horrid mad, and beg'd most earnestly to be excused, for such trash, however it may serve to read at the moment, must be shocking a second time; but papa would take no denial—"It's very sufficient," said he, "for the occasion, and for your age." However, I am as much mortified at doing this, as if my first fear had been verified, for I cannot at all relish being thus exposed to a *deliberate* examination. . . . .

Lynn Regis,
St. Margts Church Yard, July.

Once more I take up a pen to write to my Journal, which I thought I never again should do. . . . .

We find every body here well. My mama is in better health than ever . . . . Miss Allen is the same generous, unaffected, lively girl as ever—Susette much improved in every particular—Charlotte mighty pretty and . . . . also improved, indeed she is a sweet good girl; . . . . Bessy is more graceful and more handsome than ever. * * * *

But I am extremely uneasy at present on the account of my elder brother—so are we all. He told us in his last letter, which we had above half a year ago, that he expected to be home this last Spring—we have long been impatient for his arrival—and we find by the newspaper that the Aquillon, his ship, was paid off last week: what can be the meaning of his not writing to us then?—We know not how to enquire for him, nor where to direct to him—dear, dear fellow! how much do I wish to see him—My papa I perceive is very anxious: he has written to town with directions for his journey hither in case of his going there. I think of him from morning to night from fear of some accident.[1]

We have nothing but visiting here, and this perpetual round of constrained civilities, to persons quite indifferent to us, is the most provoking and tiresome thing in the world; but it is unavoidable in a country town, where everybody is known, as here. Its a most unworthy way of spending our precious and irrecoverable time, to devote it to those who know not it's value—why are we not permitted to *decline* as well as *accept* visits and acquaintance? It is not that we are ignorant of means to better employ ourselves, but that we dare not pursue them. However, restraint of this kind is much, much less practised or necessary in London than else where—Excuses there are no sooner made than admitted—acquaintance as easily dropped as courted—company chosen or rejected at pleasure—undoubtedly the same plan *might* be pursued here, but how? with breaking the customs of the place, disobliging the inhabitants, and incurring the censure of the town in general, as unsociable, proud, or impertinent innovators. Seeing therefore what must be submitted to, 'tis best to assume a good grace, only its horrid hard . . . . .

Saturday Morn. Aug.

* * * * *

It is with great satisfaction I observe Hetty (who some time before we left town grew melancholy and sad) has the

---

[1] This was her sailor brother, James Burney, who was a midshipman with Admiral Montagu at ten years of age. His short education had been partly given him by Eugene Aram, who was hanged at York in 1759, for a murder committed fourteen years before. Hood's poem, "The Dream of Eugene Aram," was founded upon Captain Burney's recollections of how the gentle usher paced the playground at Lynn, arm-in-arm with one of the elder boys, talking of strange murders, and how he himself had shuddered on seeing Aram taken to prison, with handcuffs on his wrists—or, as Hood wrote, "gyves." The date of his birth, and the place, as commonly given in books, are 1749, and Lynn Regis; but the Register of St. Dionis Backchurch contains this entry, under baptisms—"July 5, 1750, James, s. of Chas. and Esther Burney (organist of this Parish), born June 13."

same constant flow of spirits and gaiety she inherited from nature. Few things, I think, are more dispiriting than perceiving a disposition alter from liveliness to dejection,—nothing so much saddens me.

Would to God we could hear good news of my brother even now . . . . I never see a stormy night without shuddering, nor a letter without trembling.

* * * * *

Poland Street, London.
Sunday, Septr. 8th.

Papa, Hetty and I have been at this ever dear house, in charming London above a week,—I am now in my little closet, and intend writing the memoirs of the past ten days for the perusal of my *dear friend*, whose gratitude I doubt not will be as great as the obligation requires.

Mama, Miss Allen, Susette, Charlotte, Bessy and beautiful little Dick [1] remain at Lynn till we return there, I believe—and sorry we are all round at the separation. Mama, Allen, and Susette accompanied us as far as Thetford, where we saw the remains, which we visited carefully, of monasteries and abbeys, very curious and *antique*. Called to supper.—

12 o'clock.

There is something in the sight of the ruins of antiquity, which always inspires me with melancholy, and yet gives me a pleasure which compensates for the pain—'Tis dreadful to see the ravage of time and the fury of war, which are the joint causes of the destruction of cities, etc—and yet 'tis pleasing to discover the taste of former ages by the remains of their works, and to endeavour to trace the rise and progress we have made in improving or altering the fabricks, laws, and customs of our forefathers; and we can form no opinion, with equal certainty of truth, by any other means than by the *relicks* we have preserved—

---

[1] "Dick," afterwards called in letters "*Bengal Dick*," was the only son of Dr. Burney by his second marriage. He went to India, where he died in 1811.

Tuesday, Sept.

. . . .

At Thetford we slept, and the next morning separated. Miss Allen and sweet Susette looked weeping after us till the road turned. Our first stage was very gloomy—we spent it in regretting the absence of those who had so much contributed to enliven our first day's journey, which was really delightful—but we recovered our spirits afterwards, and were very comfortable—we slept at Hockrel that night and on Friday evening got to town—rather slow travelling, but the same horses with our heavy large coach could not go faster. We dined that day on Epping Forest—what a delightful spot! we almost always go different roads to Lynn, which makes a variety of prospect and novelty of view highly preferable to the high road sameness. Hetty was charmed even with the smoak of London. God bless it. . . . .

Poland Street, Tuesday.

* * * * *

Here we are again, and with as much happiness both in present possession, and in prospect for the future as can possibly fall to a mortal's lot:—if my dear James would write!—

* * * * * *

That sweet Mrs. Pleydell would win a heart of stone. . . . . There is a something, *je ne sais quoi* in the really amiable or agreeable which does not need intimacy or time to create esteem and admiration for them: for my own part, I love many people with sincere affection whom I have not seen above half an Hour—of this number is Mrs. Pleydell, who has something in her manners which engages the heart as effectually, immediately, as many thousand people would be able to do in years.[1] I hear she is now at Tunbridge. Besides her being so very beautiful. . . . .

---

[1] Mrs. Pleydell was daughter of Mr. Holwell, the first in rank among the hundred and forty-six British prisoners who were thrust into the "Black Hole of Calcutta" on the 21st of June, 1756. He was one of the three and twenty who survived that dreadful night.

Saturday.

.... it was my turn to sit up ... for papa made a late visit to Mr. Greville. When the door opened I heard him and some other talking very earnestly and loud and into the room together they both *bolted*—and then I knew the voice of Dr. Hawkesworth. He was engaged so deeply in conversation, with papa, that neither seemed to know what they were about. However, on coming into the parlour the Doctor made his compliments to me, and out of it they then stalked again, and ran up into the study where they stayed some time, and then flying down the Dr. wished me good night, and got into the coach again, and papa followed and talked with him at the door of it some time. There is an earnestness, a spirit in the conversation of very superior men which makes them absolutely forget every body and every thing about them, and which, when one knows not the subject which engages them, appears ridiculous to *spectators*; to *hearers* the appearance is different —I was only a *spectator*, and could not possibly help laughing heartily to see them capering about all the time they talked as if they were bewildered. I believe it was only to look for books, and authors, and authorities for what they said.

* * * * * *

Friday.

I pass unnoticed—for so the world did by me.

Poor Mr. Smart presented me this morning with a rose, blooming and sweet as if we were in the month of June.

"It was given me," said he "by a fair lady—though not so fair as *you!*" I always admired *poetical* licence!— . . . . . This, however, is nothing to what he afterwards amused himself with saying. The Critical Reviewers, ever eager to catch at every opportunity of lessening and degrading the merit of this unfortunate man (who has been twice confined in a mad house), would think all the most rancourous observations on his declining powers fully justified, and perhaps even pronounce him to be in a state of mind that rendered him a proper object to return a third time to Bedlam, if they heard that he had descended to flatter and praise *me*! even me, *F. B.*, or Q in a corner.[1]

* * * * * *

13th Nov.

Poor Mr. Hayes, an old, and intimate friend of papa's is below; he has lost his wife while we were in Lynn, and I dread meeting him.[2] I live in perpetual alarm—every rap at the door I think will bring me news—my rest is very much disturbed—I dream confused things of my brother for ever. But all that relates to *me* is nothing. My papa observes my low spirits, and asks the cause; 'tis impossible for me to answer. He is more kind, more affectionate to me than ever. Dearest, best of fathers!

* * * * * *

Decr. 20.

My dear brother has now been home these three weeks! . . . . and my beloved father daily appears more and more kind and affectionate to this dear brother, and we are now all happily settled. This affair never gave us more uneasiness, than, thank God, it does at last happiness. James's character appears the same as ever—honest, generous, sensible, unpolished; always unwilling to take

---

[1] Perhaps Fanny avenged the wrongs of Smart, and of Hawkesworth, so far as in her lay, by writing her sarcastic dedication of "Evelina" to the "Monthly and Critical Reviewers." Those Reviewers were then as terrible as ever were Jeffrey and Gifford; more so, perhaps, for about 1770, there were only two reviews—"The Monthly," and the "Critical." Smollett had been editor of the "Critical Review," and Goldsmith had written in it up to 1760, or thereabouts. Fanny was hereafter to be connected with Monthly Reviewers by the marriage of her brother Charles with the daughter of Dr. Rose of Chiswick. Nay, Dr. Burney himself, in his old age, wrote for the "Monthly Review" many articles of which no list has been found.

[2] Mr. Hayes was reputed to be a natural son of Sir Robert Walpole, whom he much resembled in face, and in the better parts of Sir Robert's character. In April, 1745, we find Stukeley, the antiquary, writing, "Mr. Hayes, governor of Landguard-Fort in Norfolk, visited me. He showed me a great number of Roman coins, found there, it having been a Roman castrum." He left his fine collection of coins to Dr. Burney.

offence, yet always eager to resent it; very careless, and possessed of an uncommon share of good nature; full of humour, mirth and jollity ; ever delighted at mirth in others, and happy in a peculiar talent of propagating it himself. His heart is full of love and affection for us—I sincerely believe he would perform the most difficult task which could possibly be imposed on him, to do us service. In short, he is a most worthy, deserving creature, and we are extremely happy in his company—tho' he complains that we use him very ill, in making engagements in which he cannot join from ignorance of the partys; but " 'twas unavoidable, Fate and Necessity," as Lord Ogleby says.[1]

Sunday.

We are going to lose our dear brother again; as he is going on a new voyage, and he is now on board his ship, and quite happy, and quite good and amiable. He has applied himself very much to the study of mathematicks lately, and will take a very good collection of books with him. God prosper him![2]

---

[1] We believe that no single play is so often quoted throughout the early, and later Diaries, and letters, of Fanny Burney, as that highly successful comedy of Garrick and George Colman (the elder), "The Clandestine Marriage." Doubtless, Fanny saw it many times, from the box of Mr. Garrick, or of Mr. Colman. "Lord Ogleby" is a decrepit *beau*, of a type which was dying out in 1766, and was quite distinct from that of the Maccaronies, who were coming on. He is, although a superannuated coxcomb, a *gentleman*, with a dash of French sentiment.

[2] This, and all praise of James Burney in this year's journal, or in others, is true, and not the mere statement of a partial sister. Captain Burney endured many hardships with but tardy recompense; yet, when on land, he led a delightful life—in youth, with Johnson and "The Club;" in age, with Charles Lamb, Hood, Hazlitt, Cary, Southey, and even with Wordsworth and Coleridge. It was to Wordsworth that Lamb wrote in 1822:—"Every departure destroys a class of sympathies. There's Captain Burney gone! What fun has whist now? What matters it what you lead if you can no longer fancy him looking over you?" Admiral Burney wrote a book on Whist, which went through several editions. "He was a fine old man," (writes H. C. Robinson), "a humourous old man—a character, a fine, noble creature, with a rough exterior, as became the associate of Captain Cook." It fits into Fanny's sketch of him that he dropped Hazlitt out of his whist-parties, because "Hazlitt affronted him by severe criticisms on the works " of his sister Fanny.

Dec. 26th.

I have spent this day alone, nevertheless, very comfortably. I have at present so many pursuits, that my whole time can be very well employed at home, and could if every hour doubled in length. I am now aiming at some knowledge of the Grecian History; I began Stanyan some time since, but never finished it, I am just beginning to read Smith's translation of Thucydides' history of the Peloponnesian War—I mention the *translator*, lest I should be suspected of reading the original Greek. . . . *I think the precaution necessary!*

* * * * *

1770.

Jan. 10th, 1770.

How very differently do I begin this year to what I did the last! O, how unhappy I then was—My poor Susan on the brink of the grave!—But I will not waste time in recollecting past misfortunes, when present happiness opens so fair a prospect to make me forget them. In truth, I have a most delightful subject to commence the present year with—such a one, as I fear I may never chance to meet with again. —Yet why should I look into futurity with a gloomy eye?— But let me waive all this nonsense, and tell you, my dear, faithful, ever attentive Nobody—that I was last Monday at a masquerade!

Has Nobody any curiosity to read an account of this frolic? I am sure Nobody has, and Nobody will I satisfy by writing one. I am so good natured as to prevent Nobody's wishes.

This Masquerade—how does that word grace my Journal! was, however, a very private one, and at the house of Mr. Laluze, a French dancing master. . . . .

Hetty had for three months thought of nothing but the masquerade—no more had I. She had long fixed upon her dress; my stupid head only set about one on Friday evening. I could think of no character I liked much, and could obtain; as to Nuns, Quakers, &c. (which I was much advised to) I cannot help thinking there is a gravity and extreme reserve required to support them well, which would have made me necessarily so dull and stupid, that I could not have met with much entertainment, and being unable to fix on a *character*, I resolved at length to go in a meer *fancy dress*. . . . .

One day—and who could do it less in?
The masqueraders spent in dressing.

It is really true that all Monday we passed in *preparationing* for the evening. . . . .

Oh, I must tell you, that speaking of my distress in regard to a dress one day to Mrs. Mancer, a very notable, talkative, good sort of old gentlewoman, and who is a half aunt to us—she said—" Why I'll tell you how Miss Fanny should go—as Flora, the *Goddess of Wisdom!*"

We had a *concourse* of people to see us and Hetty, who was dressed early, went down to receive them. They sent me up repeated messages to hasten; . . . . . and when I *was* ready, they had made so much fuss, that I was really ashamed to go down, and but for my *mask*, which I put on, I could scarce have had courage to appear . . . . . Hetty went as a Savoyard, with a *hurdy gurdy* fastened round her waist. Nothing could look more simple, innocent, or pretty. My dress was, a close pink Persian *vest*, ... covered with gauze, in loose pleats, and with flowers &c. &c . . . . . a little garland or wreath of flowers on the left side of my head . . . . . When I came down, I found assembled Captain Pringle,[1] Mr. Andrew, the three Miss Pascalls,[2] Mr. Lambe, their father-in-law, ... my aunt, James, Charles, and Hetty . . . . . so that our parlour was tolerably filled. Both our dresses met with approbation. Not one of the company could forbear repeatedly wishing themselves of our party. Nothing appears so gay, flattering and charming as a masquerade; and the sight of two who were going, and in very high spirits, was absolutely tantalising.

The Captain had a fine opportunity for gallantry—to say the truth, those whimsical dresses are not unbecoming. He made a story for me—"That I had been incarcerated by the Grand Seignor as a part of the Seraglio, and made prisoner

---

[1] Captain Pringle was an Engineer-Officer. The last time we hear of him is as going to Newfoundland in 1772, under the command of Captain (afterwards General) Debbieg.

[2] It is a mere conjecture that Fanny had much to do in after years with one of the Miss Pascalls. A Mr. Pascal was a page to the Dowager-Princess of Wales, and, on her death, was taken into the household of her son, George III. A sister of his married Mr. Thielky, or Thielcke, and was wardrobe-woman to Queen Charlotte under Mrs. Schwellenburg and Miss Burney.

by the Russians in the present war; and that the generosity of the commanding officer had prevailed with him to grant me my liberty, and that I had consequently thrown myself into the protection of the bravest and noblest people of Europe, and sought shelter from oppression in this Land of Freedom." We stayed with this company about half an hour, and then . . . . . the Captain handed us into the coach, and away we drove. We called for Mrs. and Miss Strange,[1] and then went to Mr. Lalause, who lives in Leicester Square.[2] Miss Strange had a white satin Domino trimmed with blue Mr. and Mrs. Lalause were neither of them in masquerade dresses . . . . .

The Room was large, and very well lighted, but, when we first went in, not half filled, so that every eye was turned on each new comer. I felt extremely awkward and abashed, notwithstanding my mask . . . . . Hetty went in playing on her *hurdy gurdy*, and the company flocked about her with much pleasure. I was soon found out by Miss Lalause, who is a fine girl, about sixteen . . . . . she had on a *fancy* dress . . . . . much in the style of mine. The first Mask who accosted me was an old Witch, tall, shrivelled, leaning on a broomstick, and, in short, a fear inspiring figure, apparently, by his walk, a man . . . . . "Thou thinkest, then, that that little bit of black silk is a mask?" cried he. I was absolutely confounded, for I thought directly that he meant to laugh at my mask, but on recollection I believe he was going on with some compliment, but I was so unable to rally, that with a silly half laugh, I turned on my heel, and walked away as far off as I could . . . . . I observed a Nun, dressed in black, who was speaking with great earnestness, and who I soon discovered by her voice to be a Miss Milne,[3] a pretty

---

[1] The wife and elder daughter of the famous engraver, Robert Strange. Mrs. Strange (Isabella Lumisden) had been one of the witnesses of Dr. Burney's second marriage.

[2] M. Lalauze performed with Rich in a pantomime at the great entertainment given in 1740 by Frederick, Prince of Wales, in the gardens of Cliefden, when the masque of "Alfred" was first produced.

[3] Probably Miss Milne, or rather Mylne, was related to Robert Mylne, surveyor of St. Paul's Cathedral, and builder of old Blackfriars Bridge. He was a friend of Sir Robert Strange.

Scotch nymph I have met at Mrs. Strange's. I stopt to listen to her. She turn'd about and took my hand, and led me into a corner of the room—" Beautiful creature " cried she, in a plaintive voice, "with what pain do I see you here, beset by this crowd of folly and deceit! O could I prevail on you to quit this wicked world, and all it's vices, and to follow my footsteps ! "

" But how am I to account," said I, " for the reason that one who so much despises the World, should choose to mix with the gayest part of it? What do you do here? "

" I come but," said she, " to see and to save such innocent, beautiful, young creatures as you from the snares of the wicked. Listen to me ! I was once such as you are, I mixed with the world; I was caressed by it, I loved it—I was deceived ! Surrounded by an artful set of flattering, designing men, I fell but too easily into the net they spread for me. I am now convinced of the vanity of life, and in this peaceful, tranquil state shall I pass the remainder of my days."

" It is so impossible," said I, " to listen to you without being benefitted by your conversation, that I shall to the utmost of my power *imitate you*, and always choose to despise the world, and hold it in contempt—at a *Masquerade !* "—

" Alas," said she, " I am here merely to contemplate the strange follies and vices of mankind—this scene affords me only a subject of joy to think I have quitted it."

We were here interrupted, and parted. After that I had several short conversations with different Masks. I will tell you the principal dresses as well as I can recollect them. They were a Punch who was indeed very completely dressed, and who very well supported his character ; the Witch whom I mentioned before was a very capital figure, and told many fortunes with great humour; a Shepherd, of all characters the last, were I a man, I should have wished to have assumed ; a Harliquin, who hopped and skipped about very lightly and gayly ; a Huntsman, who indeed seemed suited for nothing but the company of dogs ; a Gardener ; a Persian ; two or three Turks, and two Friars; an admirable Merlin, who spoke of spells, magick and charms with all the *mock heroick* and bombast manner which his character could require. There were also two most jolly looking Sailors, and many Dominos, besides some dresses which I have forgot. Among the females, two sweet little Nuns in white pleased me most, there was a very complete Shepherdess, with the gayest crook, the smartest little hat, and most trifling conversation one might desire; nevertheless full as clever as her choice of so hackneyed and insipid a dress led one to expect. You may imagine that she was immediately and unavoidably paired with the amiable Shepherd I mentioned before. There were two or three young pastoral nymphs to keep her in countenance : and I can recollect no other dresses, save an Indian Queen; and Dominos.

I seized the first opportunity that offered of again joining my sage monitor the fair Nun—who did not seem averse to honouring me with her conversation. She renewed her former subject, expatiated on the wickedness and degeneracy of the world, dwelt with great energy and warmth on the deceit and craft of man, and pressed me to join her holy order with the zeal of an enthusiast in religion . . . . . A pink Domino advanced, and charged her not to instill her preposterous sentiments into my mind; she answered him with so much contempt that he immediately quitted us.—We were then accosted by the Shepherd, who would fain have appeared of some consequence, and aimed at being gallant and agreeable—poor man! wofully was he the contrary. The Nun did not spare him. " Hence," cried she, "thou gaudy animal, with thy trifling and ridiculous trappings, away let not this fair creature be corrupted by thy company! O fly the pernicious impertinence of these shadows which surround thee!"——

" The—the lady"—stammered the poor swain—" the lady will be—will be more likely—to be hurt—by—by you than—than——"

" Yes—yes," cried she—" she would be safe enough were she followed only by such as thee!"

Hetty just then bid me observe a very droll old Dutchman, who soon after joined us. He accosted us in high Dutch—not that I would quarrel with any one who told me it was *low* Dutch! . . . . it might be Arabick for aught I could tell! He was very completely dressed, and had on an exceeding droll old man's mask, and was smoking a pipe. He presented me with a quid of tobacco, I accepted it very cordially. The Nun was not disposed to be pleased. She attacked poor Mynheer with much haughtiness—" Thou savage! hence to thy native land of brutes and barbarians; smoak thy pipe there, but pollute not us with thy dull and coarse attempts at wit and pleasantry ! " . . . . The Dutchman, however, heeded her not, he amused himself with talking Dutch and making signs of devotion to me, while the Nun railed and I laughed. At last she took my hand, and led me to another part of the room, where we renewed our former conversation.

" You see," she cried, " what a herd of danglers flutter around you; thus it was once with me; your form is elegant; your face, I doubt not, is beautiful; your sentiments are superior to both: regard these vipers then with a proper disdain; they will follow you, will admire, court, caress and flatter you—they will engage your affections—and then they will desert you ! It is not that you are less amiable, or that they cease to esteem you; but they are weary of you; novelty must atone in another for every loss they may regret in you: —it is not merit they seek, but variety. *I* speak from experience ! " I could almost have taken my Nun for Mr. Crisp in disguise.

" 'Tis rather surprising," said I, " that one who speaks with such rigour of the world, and professes having quitted it from *knowing* its degeneracy, and who talks of experience in the style of age, should have a voice which is a perpetual reminder of her own youth, and should in all *visible* respects, be so formed to grace and adorn the world she holds in such contempt."

" Hold ! " cried she, " remember my sacred order; and remember that we nuns can never admit to our conferences that baleful enemy of innocence, flattery ! Alas, you learn this from men ! Would you but renounce them ! what happiness would such a convert give me ! " . . . .

The Dutchman and the Shepherd soon joined us again. The former was very liberal of his tobacco, and supported his character with much drollery, speaking no English, and but a few

Dutch words, and making signs. The Shepherd seemed formed for all the stupidity of a Dutchman more than the man who assumed that dress; but *he* aimed at something superiour.— . . . . . The Nun, looking on her veil and habit as a sanction to the utmost liberty of speech. . . . . spoke to them both without the least ceremony. . . . . All she said to *me* did honour to the name she assumed—it was sensible and delicate, it was *probably* very true; it was *certainly* very well adapted to her apparent character: but when we were joined by men, her exhortations degenerated into railing; which though she might intend the better to support her part, by displaying her indignation against the sex, nevertheless seemed rather suited to the virulency and bitterness of a revengeful woman of the world, than the gentleness and dignity which were expected from the piety, patience, and forbearance of a cloister.

"And, what," said she to the Dutchman, "what can have induced such a savage to venture himself here? Go, seek thy fellow-brutes! the vulgar bestial society thou art used to, is such alone as thou ought to mix with." He *jabbered* something in his defence, and seemed inclined to make his court to me.

"Perhaps," said she, "it may be in the power of this fair creature to reform thee; she may civilize thy gross and barbarous manners."

The Dutchman bowed, said "*yaw*" and put his hand on his heart in token of approbation. "Ay," said the poor Shepherd, whose eyes had the most marked expression of stupidity (if stupidity can be said to have *any* expression) that I ever saw, and his words and manner so exactly coincided with his appearance, that he was merely an object for laughter—He served only for such to *me* at least; for indeed my spirits were not very low, and I knew there was nobody present but friends of the house.—Refreshments were then brought and everybody was engaged with a partner; Merlin,[1] a delightful Mask, secured Hetty, and the Dutchman my ladyship. Every body was then unmasked, and when I presently turned hastily round, I saw a young man so very like Mr. Young that

---

[1] "Merlin" was Henry Phipps,—the first Earl of Mulgrave.

at the first glance I thought it was him, but what was my surprise at seeing the Dutchman! I had no idea that he was under fifty, when behold he scarce looked three and twenty. I believe my surprise was very manifest, for Mynheer could not forbear laughing. On his part he paid me many compliments, repeatedly and with much civility congratulating himself on his choice. "I have been smoaking them all round," cried he, for he had always a tobaco pipe in his hand—"till at last a happy whiff blew away your mask, and fixed me so fortunately." . . . .

Nothing could be more droll than the first dance we had after unmasking; the pleasure which appeared in some countenances, and the disappointment pictured in others made the most singular contrast imaginable, and to see the old turned young, and the young old—in short, every face appeared different from what we expected. The old Witch in particular we found was a young officer. The Punch who had made himself as broad as long, was a very young and handsome man; but what most surprised me, was the Shepherd whose own face was so stupid that we could *scarcely* tell whether he had taken off his mask or *not*.[1] . . . .

[Tuesday.]

We have been engaged some time to a private dance at the Reverend Mr. Pugh's,[2] who I have mentioned in my Chronicles. Aunt Becky is to be our chaperon. But I was so ill with a cold this morning that I rose with a resolution of sending an excuse; but was prevented by Mr. Pugh's calling. He earnestly beg'd me not to disappoint him, and promised me I should rest as often as I pleased.—He protested he would not upon any account have me fail coming, as he has settled all the partners, and I should break his schemes.—"I should be

---

[1] This was a masquerade never to be forgotten by Hetty and Fanny. In 1779 Fanny tells how "a younger brother of the Harry Phipps that Hetty danced with at Mr. Lalauze's," was brought by Lady Ladd to visit Mrs. Thrale at Streatham.

[2] The Reverend Mr. Pugh, Curate of St. James's, was the old friend who married Dr. Burney to Mrs. Allen.

more particularly sorry at your absence, Ma'am," said he—as I have engaged you to the most elegant and agreeable man of my whole company—who would be extremely disappointed ; and who, I flatter myself, would make the evening very happy to you." I am never fond of being engaged unseen, as in those cases, two people are frequently disappointed. Mr. Pugh was too urgent to be refused. . . . .
How I have got this violent cold I cannot tell—it affects me in a cough, sore throat, and most dreadful headache, attended with a slight fever. I shall really be an amiable object, for I am pale as possible, and my eyes heavy as lead. How would a philosopher or moralist hold me in contempt! to have so many complaints—yet go to a ball! it appears ridiculous to me myself. . . . .

Feb. 7th.

Near a fortnight has elapsed since our Dance at Mr. Pugh's. . . . . I was infinitely better that evening than I had been, and when we set off for South Street, I was in much higher spirits than any of the party, though Hetty was very cheerfull, and also Aunt Rebecca.[1] . . . . Mr. Pugh welcomed us very joyfully—and introduced us to the company who were seated formally at tea. Hetty told me she was sure she had fixed her eye on my partner. . . . . "There he is," said she, "and I can read in his face everything that is clever and agreeable. I hope *I* shall dance a minuet with him." . . . . Tea being over, we marched into a larger room, and minuets were begun.
"Come, gentlemen," said Mr. Pugh—"choose hats—I won't let you choose partners!" . . . . After all I cannot approve this plan of settling partners unseen—the usual privilege the men have of pleasing themselves I think far preferable, as only one *can* be dissatisfied then. . . . . Mr. Pugh presented the ladies to the gentlemen—
"This lady," when he came to me, "is your partner,

---

[1] Aunt Rebecca, "an ancient and very amiable sister of Dr. Burney," died a spinster between 1802 and 1812, while Fanny was in France.

Captain Bloomfield." .... Indeed he was very unfortunate—for he did not himself tire the whole evening, and poor little I was fatigued to death after the second dance. .... I very much admired the lady who danced with Mr. Pugh, who was very pleasing. .... I had said many things in her praise occasionally to Captain Bloomfield, and I then asked if he knew her?

"I have the honour, Ma'am," said he, "to be her brother!—Don't you think," added he, laughing,—"we are very much like?"

There was another young lady there who addressed herself so frequently to the Captain, and *smiled* so *tenderly* at him, that I could not forbear observing to Hetty that Mr. Pugh was cruel to have given her any other partner;—but when the night was half over, I found this was another sister.

At two o'clock we returned to the parlour to sup. And here Mr. Pugh and Captain Bloomfield seemed to vie with each other which should have least ease and rest himself, or give most to others. I was now scarce able to move, I did however *force* my feet to go down two or three dances, but with great pain, ... for indeed I was very indifferent; .... yet the spirit which every body supported, as well as the extreme alacrity of Captain Bloomfield, made me ashamed to sit still. .... As to Captain Bloomfield, he could assuredly be no sufferer by an exchange, for Miss Kirk was very pretty and agreeable .... And after going down one more dance, which completely finished me, Captain Bloomfield, seeing me fatigued, considerately led me to a seat—just by me sat poor Miss Kirk. "How perverse this is," said I, to him, "here is a lady who is not at all tired, and there is a gentleman who is;—and here am *I* knocked up:—and you not at all!"—

"Well?" said he, with quickness, "and what do you imply by that!"

I then proposed an *exchange*.

"Do you want to get rid of me?" cried he.

I did not know what to say to this. .... Nevertheless, I was convinced that only his delicacy prevented his being in *raptures* at the proposal;—therefore, after a short pause I pressed him much to ask Miss Kirk to dance, declaring myself very sorry to deprive him of that pleasure,—

"But I would rather" said he, "*sit* with *you*, than *dance* with any other lady."

I cannot say I believed him:—but on my further urging him, he told me he was too sensible of his happiness to fling it away.—As to Miss Kirk, I had made my proposal to *her* first, never imagining that Captain Bloomfield would object; . . . . and she frankly and honestly agreed to it. But nothing I could say would induce him:—he certainly thought I should regard it as a reproach on my inactivity; and he chose rather to suffer himself, than make another ashamed.

"And how do you know," said he, "that the *gentleman* would agree to quit his partner?"

"O—if that is any objection" cried I, "*I* will undertake to speak to *him*—you see he is tired to death already—"

"O, that will pass off," replied he—"he might be as unwilling to relinquish *his* partner, as I am mine, for why should not he be contented and happy?—She is very pretty and agreeable; and, as you observed, looks all good humour.—"

"O leave him to me," said I, "I will readily manage him.—"

"Nothing" returned he, "shall prevail on me to dance without *you*, but your *really* desiring it, and unless it would do *you* a favour—"

I regarded this as a delicate *assent*—therefore I answered—"It *will* do me a favour;—a great one!—"

"But *how?*" said he: "because you think it will oblige *me?* or because you wish to get rid of me?"

There was no answering this—and so I made no further attempt: And then we only conversed, and very agreeably, for the rest of the evening. At 5 o'clock, or rather more, every one gave up. Late as it was we could not go home, as the carriage was not to be found. We therefore returned again to the parlour, where we were entertained with catches and glees by part of the company, namely Mr. Pugh, Captain Bloomfield, Mr. Porter, Mr. Burney, and my sister. Mr. Porter is a clergyman of Woolwich, whose lady I must mention. . . . . I committed a fault from inattention, (chiefly owing to my extreme fatigue) which was, seating myself, after having gone down a dance, without walking it up again:—and Captain Bloomfield either forgot this punctilio also, or did not choose to remind me of it: however this lady took great offence at it—for while we were seated, she came and addressed herself to Captain Bloomfield, keeping her back towards me, and affecting not to see me; and, not in the gentlest manner, she cried—

"And so *you* are sit down!—*you*, who are such a *young* man give out first:—and that after going *down* a dance, tho' you could not walk it up again!" This reproof I was conscious was meant for *me;*—the Captain, I believe was rather distressed: the gentle lady's volubility satisfied herself, however, for she did not wait for any answer. "Had you been really fatigued," continued she—"you might have shown it by sitting before you had gone down the dance—I must say it was very ill bred!—and I did not expect it from *you*, Captain Bloomfield! *you*, who are so *polite* a man!"

I was sensible the reproof was, to *me*, just; but nevertheless it was exceeding gross and illnatured to address this discourse to either of us.—Captain Bloomfield did not once look towards me; he did not even plead my indisposition, but taking the whole affair to himself, with the utmost good humour he said—"But I am sure you are too compassionate not to pity me, when you hear my disaster, for I was unable to dance longer, as I sprained my ancle,—and what then could a poor man do?" I believe she was somewhat calmed by his tranquility;—for she softened her voice, but said, as she left us—"Well, to be sure it might not be *your* fault—but it was very rude, and I am very sorry *you* had any share in it!" I was quite shocked and disconcerted at this unexpected lecture.—The Captain very delicately still looked another way, and did not turn towards me. . . . . However I spoke to *him*—"You were in the right," said I, "not to be angry, for not one word of this was meant for *you!*"

"And you," cried he, "have too much sweet[ness], I am sure, to think of it any more." Soon after we came home.

Mr. Pugh has since proposed bringing Captain Bloomfield to a music party at our house, and also has earnestly invited us to another dance at Woolwich with aunt Rebecca, where Captain Bloomfield, he said, would be very happy to *dance again with Miss Fanny.* But we did not go.

* * * * * *

About this time we received the following note from the Masquerade Dutchman.

"The Dutchman presents his compliments to the Miss Burneys, and takes the liberty to enclose three tickets for the Chelsea Assembly hoping the Miss Burneys will have the goodness to find a chaperon. The Dutchman will do himself the honour to wait upon the Miss Burneys this evening, with the Doctor's permission, to know whether he may exist again or not."

[This was a rather more serious case of love at first sight than would be inferred from what is left in the manuscript. The letter, answered with so much decision, was the second sent by "Mynheer Dutchman," as he is called in the notes of Mme. D'Arblay. Perhaps (as she loved euphony) she did not care to write that his name was *Tomkin.* So we gather from Maria Allen, who, writing to Fanny four years later, jests thus upon her presumed admirers of 1770 and 1772 : "And so Miss Fanny Burney has mounted her little *bay* nag *Grub,* and is riding away *tantivi*—upon my word ma'am, very pretty usage— pray let me know the meaning of all this at your peril or you may depend I shall dispatch a note to the *Tomkin,* the *Bloomfield;* nay, I don't know whether I shall not touch up the *poganpole* (M. Pogenpohl, in the Diary 4, 1772), and tell them what pretty freaks you have taken into your pretty noddle." Fanny had been long in writing to Maria, who at once suspects that she was writing a novel, as was the case about that time (1774). In a letter to Mr. Crisp (of the 10th of May, 1775), with reference to an offer of marriage which Dr. Burney and Mr. Crisp advised her to accept (the suitor being pressing, and having a good income), she writes : "Had marriage from prudence and convenience been my desire—I believe I have had it quite as much in my power two or three times as now—particularly there was a certain youth not *quite* so hasty to be sure, as Mr. Barlow, but not far otherwise, who took much pains for cultivating our acquaintance. I happened to dance with him at a private masquerade at Mr. Lalauze's, and he called two or three times afterwards, and wrote two notes, with most pressing requests, through a third person, that he might be introduced to my father, and know whether *he might exist again,* or not. However, after the answer received, written by myself to the second note, I heard of him no more."]

I never coloured so in my life, for papa was in the room,

and Hetty read the note out aloud, and then, laughing, flung it to me to answer, saying she knew she had nothing to do with it; and wishing me joy of my first serious conquest. I was so very much surprised I could not speak. Papa said it was coming to the point very quick indeed, and he must either be a very bold man, or a young man who knew nothing of the world. But he said I must return the tickets, but might let him come to tea, as he deserved civility, by naming him (papa), and then we might see more how to judge him. I was quite frightened at this—but very glad papa and Hetty both left me to answer the note for myself, for as they thought him serious I determined to be so too.[1] . . . .

I wrote the following answer, and sent it off without shewing it to papa, to put an end to the whole at once.

"Miss Burneys present their compliments to the Dutchman, and as they cannot go to the Chelsea Assembly, they beg leave to return the three tickets with many thanks.

"They are very sorry it will not be in their power to have the pleasure of seeing him this evening, having been some time pre-engaged. February 19th. Wed : Morn*."

This note will, I doubt not, be [the last] I shall have to answer from this gentleman—indeed it is the *first* also that I have *answered*: nevertheless, I [fa]ncy he will condescend to *exist* still. . . . .

My dear James has been gone [some] time—he went on board the Green[wich] East India man, he was in very [good] spirits, and we have all great hopes that he will have a happy and prosperous voyage.

The same evening that I sent the Dutchman's note, we spent at [Mrs.] Pringle's. Mr. Seaton, Mr. Crawford, Mrs. Mackintosh and her two sons made her party. Mr. Seaton was all assiduity and attention to my sister.—Mr. Crawford willingly would have been the same, but . . . . Mr. Seaton was so much more agreeable, that no one else could engage

---

[1] Some comparison with Captain Bloomfield is here crossed out. It looks as if Fanny had written that *the Captain* would not have been "so abrupt."

her for three minutes. As to the Captain, it would [be] difficult to decide to whom he [add]ressed his conversation most—[we were] rival Queens with him, but which [was the] Statira[1] is doubtful.

Mr. Mackintosh is a very stupid [youn]g man, who is, unhappily, possessed [of a] very great fortune, which could [hardly] be worse bestowed. He has per[sua]ded himself that he has a great regard for me, and, moreover, that he has a genius for poetry, and has made [an] Acrostick on my name which is very well worth pres[erving]. 'Tis the] most laughable stuff I ever saw.

> Fancy ne'er painted a more beauteous Mind,
> And a more pleasing Face you'll seldom find;
> None with her in Wit can vie,
> No, not even Pallas, may I die!
> You'll all know this to be Fanny!

> Beautiful, witty and young,
> Unskilled in all deceits of Tongue,
> Reflecting glory on her Sex,
> None can her in Compliments perplex
> Easy in her manners as in her Dress—
> You'll that this is Fanny all must guess.

To complete the elegance and brilliancy of this Acrostick, the paper on which it is wrote is cut out in the shape of a Fan. . . . .

After supper, Captain Pringle amused himself with writing ladies names on [the] glasses, beginning with our's, and [th]en wrote gentlemen's under them. Andrew wrote *his* under mine, Hetty [ch]ose Lord Pigot for one, and I Mr. Crisp for another. They had given up the dance [which] Mr. Seton hinted of to us, but [prop]osed having a farce, in which we [wer]e all to perform, and after some time [we]

---

[1] It may be needful to remind some readers of Dryden's play of "The Rival Queens" (Roxalana and Statira).

fixed on—" Miss in Her Teens." [1]—Mr. Crawford undertook Rodolpho, Andrew, Fribble (which parts had been much better reversed), the Captain, Capt. Flash, Mr. Seaton, the Man, Mrs. Pringle the Aunt, Hetty, Miss Biddy, and for me, Tag. They were all very eager about it, and fixed a day for a rehearsal;—but when I came home and read the farce, I found the part of Tag was quite shocking—indeed I would not have done it for the universe, and I we[nt] and told Mrs. Pringle so directly. She could not accuse me of affectation for the moment she read it attentively she said to her sons she was sure [I] should not do it; which was very kind of [her]. . . . .

Not long after this visit we received a note of invitation from Mrs. Debbieg. . . . . The Captain went with us in papa's coach. Poor Andrew was gone to the East Indies. I wish . . . . he may meet with my dear James. Mr. and Mrs. Debieg are a charming [coup]le;[2] and never was there more conjugal [ha]ppiness visible than in them. They have three children, whom they doat on. Mrs. Debieg is gentle, polite, sensible, engaging—Mr. Debieg is every thing that can render him deserving of such an amiable wife. Mr. Seton lives chiefly with them, and there appears the most affectionate and true harmony among them all. Mr. Se[ton] again

---

[1] A farce by Garrick, first acted in 1747, at Covent Garden. The chief characters were Captain Flash, a swaggering, but far from courageous, officer, and Fribble, a contemptible, effeminate dandy. Woodward acted Flash, and Garrick Fribble. Mrs. Pritchard played the part which was to have been given to Fanny—that of a serving-woman deserted by her husband, a soldier. In earlier days Dr. Burney had played Fribble (on a private stage) to Mrs. Greville's Miss Biddy Bellair, the heroine, and Greville's Captain Flash. In 1747, Mrs. Delany tells her sister, "*Nothing can be lower*, but the part Garrick acts himself, . . . he makes so very ridiculous that it is really entertaining. It is said he mimics *eleven* men of fashion—Lord Bateman, Lord Hervey, Felton Hervey, and our friend Dicky Bateman,—I must own the latter is a striking likeness."

[2] Hugh Debbieg, an officer of high character, took rank as a major of engineers from July 23, 1772, when he was sent to Newfoundland. Later on, when one of the six colonel commandants of the corps of engineers, he is brought into the Rolliad as disagreeing with the Duke

appeared to me in a more favourable light; his ch[arm]ing sister must reflect honour on all [her] relations. If the sincerity of this ma[n] equal'd his sense, wit, polite and ins[in]uating address, I would not wish Hetty a happier lot than to be his. . . . .

We went to Mr. Lalause' Benefit . . . . . though without the l[east] expectation of receiving pleasure, a[s the] play was an old revived one, and perfor[med] by a *set of Ladies and Gentlemen who never appeared on any Stage before*. We went [with] Mr. Mrs. and Miss Stra[nge] and some more company of their party, into the same box.[1]

---

of Richmond, Master-General of the Ordnance, and being "oppressed" by him:—

> "Learn, thoughtless Debbeige, now no more a youth,
> The woes unnumbered that encompass truth;
> Nor of experience, nor of knowledge vain,
> Mock the chimæras of a sea-sick brain.
> Oh, learn on happier terms with him to live,
> Who ne'er knew twice, the weakness to forgive!
>
> * * * * * *
>
> Thy skill, thy science, judgment to resign!
> With patient ear, the high-wrapt tale attend,
> Nor snarl at fancies which no skill can mend.
> So shall thy comforts with thy days increase,
> And all thy last, unlike thy first, be peace.
> No rude *courts-martial* shall thy fame decry."

[1] In 1763 this Mr. Lalauze was the subject of a rather warm set of letters to and from Mrs. Strange. Lalauze was "a very clever Frenchman, who had a connexion with one of the London theatres." He taught dancing to the children of Robert Strange, who was then at Bologna. Little Jamie Strange was his very best pupil, so Lalauze asked Mrs. Strange to permit her boy to dance upon the stage at his benefit, with his daughter Miss Lalauze. Now Jamie, or rather James Charles Stewart Strange, was godson of the old Chevalier; an honour which his mother had begged for him even before his birth, through her brother, Andrew Lumisden, who was secretary to that prince, and attainted for his share in the Rebellion of 1745. Robert Strange himself had served under Prince Charles, having been drawn into it by his Bella, who refused him her hand unless he fought for her king; so that he was under a cloud, and lived chiefly abroad. In her mother's pride, Mrs. Strange wrote to her "Robie" that "Jamie" was about to dance upon the stage. Strange wrote to Lumisden, in Rome, to beg him to use an influence which he knew to be greater

It was most wretchedly performed. It is called Themistocles and Aristides—never were heroes more barbarously murdered. Miss La Lause and her father danced a minuet à la cour between an act, after which she came into our box.
. . . . When the play was over Mr. Henry Phipps, Hetty's Masquerade partner came to speak to her. He is so very agreeable and well bred, that, young as he is, it is a pleasure to hear him converse.
The next morning Mr. Phipps called. He is more properly Mr. Henry Phipps,[1] being the second son of Lord Mul-

---

than his own, to prevent the boy from figuring on the boards of a theatre. Andrew took it heartily up, and sent his sister an over solemn warning against a theatrical style of dancing; backed by dreadful examples of young Englishmen who were laughed at in Italy for showing off as if they were stage-dancers. Bella replied with vigour, that "Jamie knows no more of a *theatrical carriage* than you do. He moves and dances *like a gentleman.* His master is as much unlike a dancing-master as *your Holy Father.*" This was not the Pope of Rome, but a certain Reverend Mr. Wagstaffe, who was chaplain to Lumisden and the faithful few of the English Church in the Pretender's household. Then Bella gave Andrew an ominous hint that "I shall vindicate myself *on the deafest side of your* head," adding that "I will not quit *my* knowledge of mankind to the best of you" [men-folk]. I have seen throw (*sic*) things you yourself have been blind to, as the foibles of men, or *wemon*" (*sic*); of which foibles, she will do herself the justice to say, she has "as few as any she that ever wore petticoats." She adds, that her husband and brother, both being in Italy, had much better "submite the care of the children" to her, as she hereby desires them to do. Indeed, she had half-a-dozen to mind while Strange lived abroad. As for Robie, all she has to say to *him* is, "My love to him when you write to him,—or, *you may send him this.*" Of course, "Robie" had "to *submite*" in 1763, and to go on "*submiting;*" as here, in 1772, we find Bella taking her own daughter, with Fanny and Hetty, both to the masquerade of Mr. Lalauze and to his benefit. As Jamie was only ten years old in 1763, Andrew and Robie might have spared themselves their trouble. Sir Lawrence Dundas, in due time, got Jamie a writership in India, and of poor Miss Lalauze we hear again in a later Diary.

[1] This is a mistake; Henry Phipps was the third son of the first Baron Mulgrave. In 1792 he succeeded his eldest brother, "The Polar Captain" in the Barony of Mulgrave, and in 1812 was created the first Earl of Mulgrave. He was the father of the first Marquis of Normanby, who wrote some novels, which were fashionable in his time. Constantine (sometimes called the "Polar Bear," or "Ursa Major,"

grave. He is really one of the most amiable, sensible, and well-bred youths I ever saw. It is impossible not to forget while he is talking that he is so young, for he is so very clever and sensible, that not a word escapes him which would not do credit to double his years. It is a question whether he is most polite or most entertaining. The Dutchman also joined us—a bold man he certainly is not, for he looked very, very dejected—but his note, and papa's and Hetty's opinion of his being so serious, made me think it right to answer nothing that he said beyond yes or no.—However he contrived to hand me to the coach.—

Lynn Regis, April 20th.

Is Nobody surprised at the date of this ?—Ah, my good and excellent friend, when I last addressed myself to you from fair London town, I very little imagined that my *next* address would be from Lynn ! I have now been here nearly a fortnight, but have not had time or inclination to write to my Journal, nor should I now but from the pleasure that I take in recollecting and relating what passed during the space of time between my last writing and my journey hither. . . . . . Sir Lionel Pilkington spent an evening with us. He is an old and intimate acquaintance of papa's, a man famous for wit and *dry* humour. He is also, which is rare with men of that sort, very well bred, for in general they affect a bluntness and

---

from his rough manners), sat in the House of Commons (being an Irish peer) at the same time as his brothers Charles, who also was in the Navy, and Harry, who was in the Army. In the once famous, and still most amusing, "Probationary Odes," they are all brought into an Amœbæan dialogue between Dr. Prettyman and Mr. Banks :—

> " PRETTYMAN. Sooner the ass in fields of air shall graze,
> Or WARTON's Odes with justice claim the bays ;
> Sooner shall mack'rel on the plains disport,
> Or *Mulgrave's* hearers think his speech too short ;
> Sooner shall sense escape the prattling lips
> Of Captain CHARLES, or Col'nel HENRY Phipps ;
> Sooner shall Campbell mend his phrase uncouth,
> Than Doctor Prettyman shall speak the truth ! "

conciseness which quite excludes the attention and respect necessary for a *polite* man.[1] . . . . .

On Wednesday evening, . . . we went to Mrs. Cornelys' with papa and Miss Nancy Pascall. The magnificence of the rooms, splendour of the illuminations and embellishments, and the brilliant appearance of company exceeded any thing I ever before saw. The apartments were so crowded we had scarce room to move, which was quite disagreeable, nevertheless, the flight of apartments both upstairs and on the ground floor seemed endless. . . . The first person that we saw and knew was Lord Pigot.[2] . . . He spoke to papa with his accustomed ease and pleasantness, and called Hetty his *little friend*: neither did he forget little *me*. He appeared to be of no particular party, and frequently joined us. He asked papa—" Dr. Burney, but when will you come to one of my Concerts, and dine with me, with the young ladies?" Papa did not fix any time, and to my great concern I have quitted town before he did, for I had great pleasure in the thought of being of the party. The Rooms were so full and so hot that nobody attempted to dance. . . . . . I must own this evening's entertainment more disappointed my expectations than any I ever spent; for I had imagined it would have been the most charming in the world—but papa was but half recovered, and went . . . . . . merely that we should not be disappointed of seeing the apartments. What other father . . . would have been so very indulgent . . . . . . and though he could not enjoy at all the evening's entertainment, yet was he all kindness

---

[1] A Yorkshire baronet, who was member of Parliament for Horsham from 1754 to 1768.

[2] This pleasant and musical Lord Pigot came to a sad end. In 1775 he was made Governor of Madras. In 1776 a majority of his own council "suspended" and imprisoned him, proclaiming their leader Governor in his place. He died on the first of May, 1777, in the Garden Fort, just after the East India Company had voted his restoration. Mason wrote to H. Walpole, " I shrewdly suspect some dark practice in this death of Lord Pigot; pray tell me what you think of it." Walpole answered, "I know no more than you see in the newspapers, and thence you may collect that there was more than meets the ear." The rebellious officials were tried, but not, it was considered, adequately punished.

and affection to us—he is one of the few who can be dejected without losing his sweetness of temper. Nevertheless our knowledge of his indisposition prevented our being comfortable . . . .

The next evening, rather late, Mrs Pringle sent an invitation to my sister and self, to drink tea, sending word she was quite alone. Hetty was out, but I went, and found Mrs. P. and Mr. Seton sitting together, with little Clement Debieg, the latter's nephew . . . . Soon after Captain and Mrs. Debieg came, full dressed and in *high* spirits, from some great dinner, I was obliged to make excuses for *my* appearance, which their cheerfulness and good humour soon made me forget. Mr. and Mrs. Debieg and Mrs. Pringle went to cards—Mr. Seton and myself declined playing—I never do but at *Pope Joan, Commerce*, or *My Sow's Pig'd!*[1]—We therefore entered into a very comfortable conversation: he enquired much after my sister—and regretted her absence. So did every body. Captain Pringle did not come home till supper. I spent a very agreeable evening; the party though small were *select*, and each in high good humour and spirits. Mr. Debieg appears at every meeting to more and more advantage; he is really a charming man, sensible, well bred, unaffected, and very droll. Mrs. Debeig is happy, very happy I am sure in the possession of the heart of such a man; and his affectionate, . . . and obliging behaviour to her, evidently declare her to have retained, *though a wife*, all the influence and power of a mistress. And this might perhaps be more universally the case, were women more universally such as Mrs. Debieg. She is indeed truly worthy her happy lot—with great *dis*advantage of person, for she is actually ugly; her many amiable qualities, the goodness and excellence of her mind, are so marked in her countenance, that she claims a place in the very heart immediately. I quite forget whether I mentioned that at the visit we made to this charming pair, there

---

[1] Mr. Gibbs kindly informs the Editor that "My Sow's Pig'd" is not in Hoyle; and that the only mention of it he has found is in "Notes and Queries" (5th Series, vol. v. p. 129), where it is named as one of several old card games in a list given in a MS. Diary, dated 1629.

were of their company two gentlemen of the name of Dundas ? —Major Dundas, the younger was much *smitten* with Hetty; Mr. Dundas the eldest was at that time .... engaged in contesting an election to be member of Parliament for ———. Mr. Debieg told me that he had gained his cause; and I found that, by way of rejoicing, they intended having a dance at their house; which they fixed to be the next Tuesday, because that was the aniversary of their marriage day, and they invited Mrs. and Captain Pringle, and my sister and self to it. I answered for *one*—I knew I *might* for the other, tho' I did not choose it..... A formal note followed next day to Miss Burney and Miss Fanny Burney with the invitation for Tuesday. Mrs. Pringle *chaperoned* us, and we were almost the first in the room; but I will mention the whole party by name, for indeed they well deserve it. To begin, *as I ought*, with the women. Mrs. Seaton, a very engaging woman, about twenty-three, widow of Major Seaton, an elder brother of our acquaintance— she is rather handsome, extremely elegant in her manners, and mild and sensible in her conversation. Mrs. Pringle, who was as gay, chatty and clever as usual. Mrs. Debieg herself, who is always charming. Miss Peggy Adams, *an old flame of Mr. Seaton's* she is called: she is about twenty-six or seven, ugly in person, and too reserved in manners to permit me to judge of her, but I will imagine she has some remarkable qualities to have engaged Mr. Seaton's attention, though I cannot wonder he has transfered it to another object, when I see how striking is the difference between them: nevertheless, I am concerned to find this additional proof of the fickleness of his disposition. Miss Stuart, she is about nineteen or twenty, has a fine face in spight of the small pocks, is modest, well-bred, and very silent. Miss Dalrymple, who we have frequently seen at Mrs. Pringle's. She too, is reported to be an old flame of Mr. Seaton's—she is about twenty-eight or nine, rather handsome, lisps affectedly, simpers designedly, and looks conceitedly. She is famed for never speaking ill to any one's face, or well behind their backs. An amiable character. Miss Burney and Miss Fanny Burney— sweet charming young creatures!—I need not describe. Now to the men. I must begin with Mr. Debieg, for whom I have conceived a great regard: he was all spirits and sweetness, and made, with his other half's assistance, all his company happy. Sir Harry Seaton, the eldest brother of Mr. Seaton and Mrs. Debieg: he is very unlike either; grave, reserved, silent, yet perfectly well-bred, and very attentive; and there is something in his manners *prévenant*. Mr. Dundas, to whose successful election we owe this meeting, almost the same words I have used for Sir Harry Seaton would suit him, save only he was less reserved, rather.[1] Major Dundas, his younger brother, very unlike him;—conceited, talkative, coxcombical. Mr. John Dundas, a Cousin to these gentlemen, a well-behaved man, nothing extraordinary. Mr. Adams, very sensible, very polite, and very agreeable,—the most so, Mr. Debieg excepted, of the whole party. Mr. ——— Adams, his younger brother, a well-behaved good sort of young man.[2] Mr. Farquar, he is . . . . . very droll and a favourite rather of Hetty's for his

---

[1] It was for the gain of an election upon petition that Mrs. Pringle's party was given. James Dundas, Esquire, contested Linlithgowshire at the general election of 1768, with John Hope, Esquire, a nephew of the Earl of Hopetoun. Dundas was beaten, but petitioned Parliament against the return of Hope in its first session, and renewed his petition in its second. On the 27th of March, 1770, he was reported to have been duly elected, and Mr. Hope was, accordingly unseated. He was of the Dundas family, of Castle Dundas, Linlithgowshire, but related to the Arniston family, and the famous "Harry," Pitt's friend (Lord Melville). Mrs. Strange was related to Sir Lawrence Dundas through his marriage with one of the Bruces of Kennet, and the Pringles of Whytbank were akin to her. Perhaps Fanny's Pringles were of that family. We never meet Mrs. Strange and Mrs. Pringle together in these Diaries, but Mr. Scott, the Jacobite ex-tutor of the King, is found at the houses of both.

[2] There were four brothers, John, Robert, James, and William Adam, who about this time began building "that noble pile, the Adelphi," upon a site which they had bought, as a heap of ruins, of what had been the town-house of the Bishops of Durham, on the Strand. We learn from a passage in Fanny's Diary for 1773, that Robert and James Adam were the brothers named in the text. Miss Peggy, one of Mr. Seaton's many "flames," was probably of the same family. They were, soon afterwards, in great repute as architects. Robert, who was born at Kircaldy, in 1728, was royal architect from 1763-4 to 1768, in which year he was chosen M.P. for Kinross. He was the chief of the brothers whose names are given to streets in the Adelphi Buildings quarter.

pleasantry.[1] Mr. Robinson, a very handsome young man, and also .... agreeable,—tolerably, at least. Captain Pringle, who has lately rather risen in my opinion, as he has forbore giving himself the airs he formerly did: he seems less conceited, and speaks less in a rhodomantide manner, and is also less liberal of flattery and compliments. Mr. Alexander Seaton, I need not give his character—indeed I could not—I once thought I knew it—I now am sure I am ignorant of it. I believe I have mentioned the whole party; and though my account may be very faulty, it is such as I think.

We .... began dancing about 9 o'clock:—then, when the company stood up, Mr. Seaton took my hand .... He was as entertaining and agreeable as ever: seemed in high spirits, and danced extremely well; though he was scarce a moment silent. I told him of my *frolick* for Friday; of going to Lynn—he seemed sorry. He very gravely, with an "*upon my honour,*" assured me that nobody throughout the town would more sincerely regret my absence than himself. I thanked him kindly for his opinion of my friends' affection! He is perpetually accusing me of *mauvaise honte*, tho' in civiller terms, he exaggerates compliments such as never were put together before. He often protested that he knows not any living creature who possesses so much modesty *with* MY *parts and talents!!* which, *for my years, exceed all his acquaintance's!!* he says that till that morning that he had that long conversation with me at our house ... he had no conception of my character, and that but for that circumstance, he might never have known *my abilities!!!* he very frequently and earnestly advises and presses me, *as a friend,* to join more generally in conversation, etc, etc, etc. Ha! Ha! Ha!

Mr. Seton is artful: I have seen that: he courts my good opinion, and I know why; he flatters me in a peculiar style, always affecting a serious air, and assuring me he speaks his real sentiments:—I some times think he does not know *how* to do that;—though there is an insinuating air of sincerity in his manner whenever he is serious, which often staggers me, in

---

[1] Afterwards Sir Walter Farquhar, a physician of note, who is called in 1808, by his patient, Dr. Burney, "our wise and good Æsculapius."

spight of the prejudice I have conceived against him for his unworthy trifling with so sweet, so amiable a girl as Hetty:—in short, I have no fixed opinion of him. I know he is agreeable to a superior degree; and I believe he is as artful as agreeable.[1]

"But for how long are you going?" said he: I told him for the whole summer.—

"Just now," said he, "that I have *begun* to be acquainted with you! I never knew your powers, I believe, quite completely till the last time I saw you at Mrs. Pringle's, when you ventured to open your mouth, while the rest were at cards, and was really so entertaining—"

I would not hear him on this subject, conscious as I am of my deficiency that way:—He admired the philosophy with which I bore this stroke of leaving town—I affected to need none for it.

"What would your sister say in a similar situation?"

"O there's very little to be *said*,—she would *go* as I do."

"I believe she would have hanged herself first!" He said this laughingly, but sarcastically.

Presently we sat down and joined her, when he said to her —"What do you think Miss Fanny says?—She tells me that if it had been *your* lot to be carried into the country, thus in the Spring you would have just taken your garters and hanged yourself!"

---

[1] It is in keeping with the character of Mr. Seton, or Seaton, that he should be as hard to *find* as he was to *hold*. We fancy that we can trace him to have been one of the four sons of Sir Henry Seaton, who also had a daughter; probably Mrs. Debieg. This Sir Henry died in 1751, and was succeeded by another Sir Henry. A Sir Henry Seaton served in the war of the conquest of Canada, and settled in New York. Perhaps he was the father of Alexander, who may have come from America, and returned to some part of it, as the last time he is named it is as being likely to obtain some appointment, although he had not gone with his brother-in-law, Debieg, to Newfoundland. Once again he is named, in Fanny's diary of the year 1780. She returns a letter which has been "sent me to peruse, from Mr. Bruce to Mr. H. Seton, not *Alexander*."—Her editor has omitted this return of memory to the fickle Seton of 1770.

I railed at him to no purpose, he absolutely insisted *I* had told him so!—Hetty did not know which to believe. He ran on with more stuff to the same purpose; Hetty looked at me; —I cleared myself, and insisted on *his* clearing me:—

"Well" said he, laughing, "I believe I added the garters!"

"Why, did I say any thing at all about hanging?" cried I—

"Nay" returned he, "when I had given the garters, I was obliged to give a use for them!"

At the end of two dances, ... Mrs. Debieg told us we were to change partners every two dances. Mr. Seaton then took out Hetty .... and Mr. John Dundas made his bow to me. .... These two dances over, Captain Pringle marched to me;—Mr. Farquar to Hetty. The Captain professed much concern at my approaching journey—though he so seldom saw me, he said, it was a pleasure to him to know he lived in the same neighbourhood—He rejoiced, however, that we did not both go—then he should have put his whole house in mourning,—now only half of it—etc—etc—

After that I went down two dances with Mr. Robinson. .... We then left off for supper. During the time of rest, I was happier than in dancing, for I was .... more pleased with the conversations I then had with Mr. Dundas, Mr. Adams and others, than with my partners, and they all in turn came to chat with me, with as much good humour as if I had been as good a talker as I am a listener. Mr. Dundas the elder and Mr. Adams are quite high conversers. I was never more pleased. ....

When supper was over, all who had voices worth hearing were made to sing—none shone more than Mr. Adams; though in truth he has little or no voice, ... yet he sung with so much taste and feeling, that few very *fine* voices could give equal pleasure: I cannot but much regret the probability there is of my never seeing him again. I may see many fools ere I see such a sensible man again. Mr. Robinson also sung and showed to advantage his fine teeth and face.—Miss Dalrymple also showed to *dis*-advantage her conceit and self approbation;—Hetty with *one* song only gave more pleasure than any other.

Poor Mrs. Pringle, who hates musick, unless it be Maggy Lauder, was on the rack of impatience and vexation all the time. She is seldom silent three minutes, yet seldom speaks without applause ; therefore this musical entertainment was absolute torture to her. For the life of me I could not forbear laughing. She gave as many hints against singing as she possibly could, but nobody would take them—between every song she cried ;—" Pray gentlemen and ladies take breath ! Upon my word you ought not to suffer for your complaisance—" Still they were not tired ;—more eagerly than before, she cried out—" Why, bless me ! you'll kill yourselves ! pray, Mr. Debieg, speak !—Mr. Adams and Miss Dalrymple are so very polite, that they won't consider themselves ; —but *we* ought !" Finding this also fail, quite out of patience she exclaimed—" Why ! good folks, this is all very fine, but you should not give us too much of it ! let us have a little conversation—Mr. Debieg, why won't you talk ?—Come, Sir Harry, I am sure, is of my side ; bless us, what's to become of our tongues ?" Mr. Seaton did not let *his* be idle ; his whole attention was confined to Hetty, and his conversation more *flattering* than ever ;—equally so at least. Well might he be proud of engaging her as he did, for she met with the most flattering and apparent approbation of every one present. . . . .

We took our leaves at about three in the morning, I mine with much concern, assured as I was of not seeing them again so long, if ever : for mama's not being acquainted with this family, may probably put an end to our intimacy when we are all in town again. Mr. Seaton handed Hetty to the carriage. —Mr. John Dundas very civilly *beg'd the favour of my hand*, which, just as I had held towards him, Major Dundas, impertinent coxcomb ! pushed himself between us, and very cavalierly took it. I can't say it made any difference to me, but I cannot bear the airs of that Major. Mr. John laughed it off very well, threatning to send him a challenge next day ; bidding him remember Montague House ;[1] and not imagine he would pocket such an affront.

---

[1] Duels were fought in the fields behind old Montague House, which stood on part of the site of the British Museum.

Captain and Mrs. Pringle came home with us: the former intimated his intention of calling to pay me a farewell visit ere I went;—fearing the consequences of his despair, I would not prohibit him. Poor Hetty passed an uneasy night, racked with uncertainty about this Seton, this eternal destroyer of her peace!—*Were* he sincere, she owned she could be happier in a union with him than with any man breathing:—indeed, he deserves her not;—but the next morning, when she had considered well of every thing, she declared were he to make her the most solemn offer of his hand, she would refuse him,— and half added—*accept of Charles!*

Wednesday.

At breakfast entered Captain Pringle;—pitied Hetty, pitied himself, for my intended absence—nor did he exclude *me* from his pity—in truth it was I most merited it. He hoped, however, that I did not carry my *heart* down with me! assured me I should find it very troublesome in the country, and vastly more entertaining to go without that, though not without a successor to it—he told me I was now at the most *susceptible age*, and hoped I made not a bad use of my time: —said the country was intolerably insipid without la belle passion. Having stayed about two hours, he made his compliments, and departed. Soon after Mr. Seaton called, on pretence of bringing Hetty a Poem, which she had expressed a wish to read, Goldsmith's *Deserter*.[1] I wonder he chose to bring it! How blind to our *own* failings are we! . . . .

---

[1] This passage offers a pleasant puzzle to those who care for minute literary details. Bishop Percy says that "The Deserted Village" was published in 1769. But Sir James Prior, another of Goldsmith's editors, quotes from the "Public Advertiser" of the 26th of May, 1770: "This day, at 12, will be published, price 2s., 'The Deserted Village,' a poem by Dr. Goldsmith, printed for W. Griffin," etc. Mr. Gibbs, who has recently edited Goldsmith's works for the Bohn's Standard Library of Messrs. Bell, has kindly furnished me with the facts of this note. He informs me that he has examined the early editions of this poem, and that "the dates, according to their titles, are, of editions one to five, 1770; of edition seven, 1772," thus confirming Prior's statement. Yet here, in Fanny Burney's Journal, at a date prior to April 20, in fact, at about April 8th, we have Mr. Seaton apparently making a present

I now come to Thursday, my *last* day ... in town.

In the morning Harry Phipps called—and stayed some time. Hetty and I wished to form a friendship with him, nor has he shewn any aversion to such a scheme;—there is something very engaging in him. Soon after, tat tat tat too .. ... Tat, tat, at the door—and enter Mr. Seton. I was quite amazed—he marched up to me, and presented me with a little parcel, which on opening I found to contain a dozen franks directed to Hetty. *Free, Dundas!* He had mentioned this to her before, tho', as she rather declin'd it, from our little acquaintance with Mr. Dundas, we did not expect them. Mr. Seaton said that my sister should have a dozen directed to me, if I would tell him my direction. Imagine my blushes etc. He stayed near two hours. I don't admire being obliged to him.—He says that Mrs. Debieg mentioned it to Mr. Dundas—but it's much the same. Really Mr. Dundas must wonder we should permit such a request after only seeing him twice! I should not like he should think ill of us, for we think very well of him. Mr. Seaton told me that he has a wife and daughter in Scotland, the latter married. Just after he was gone . . . . . Mr. Young whom we had not seen for an age called to-day. He was most absurdly dressed for a common visit, being in light blue, embroidered with silver, a bag and sword, and walking in the rain! He

---

of a copy of Goldsmith's poem. Mr. Gibbs conjectures that a solution of this problem must lie in the direction of one or other of the following possibilities:—(1) Mr. Seaton may have got hold of "an advance copy" to gratify a fair lady's wish, and Fanny Burney, may have mistaken the title for "The Deserter;" (2) there may have been a "Deserter" by somebody else, and Mme. D'Arblay, years after, forgot this, and wrongly attributed the work to Goldsmith, being at the same time oblivious of the real title of Goldsmith's poem; or (3) Goldsmith may have written a poem, "The Deserter," which is now lost, perhaps buried in some periodical work of the time. It will be observed that the words originally written were "called the *Deserter*." These, some fifty years after (for it is in her later handwriting) Mme. D'Arblay altered by crossing out "called the," and adding "Goldsmith's." She did not alter "*Deserter*," on which word her blame of Seaton hinges. "Strange" (as she says) "to tell," Fanny had not read Goldsmith's Poems up to 1790, when a copy was given to her by Mrs. De Luc.

looked extremely well, and looked tolerably *conscious* of it—Upon my word he is quite altered from what I thought him on our first acquaintance—he [is grown] all airs and affectation; —assumed a coxcombical assurance and indolence joined—yet I believe this was *put on*—for what purpose I cannot tell, unless it were to let us see what a power of transformation he possessed. He bowed to the ground at entering, then swinging his hat the full extent of his arm,—" This is the most unfortunate shower," cried he, " or, rather, I am most unfortunate in being caught in it. Pray how does Dr. Burney do? Where is he?" We, in return, enquired after Mrs. Young. " She's very well, in the environs of Soho, I believe." " At Mrs. Cornelys', I presume," said Hetty. " Ay sure," returned he—" just going to open a ball with Lord Carlisle.[1] But where is Dr. Burney?" Once again we answered, out, on business; and retorted a second enquiry after Mrs. Young. " We just now parted in a pet," said he, " but, I think, we were to meet here—"

Soon after she came in a chair. After common salutations —" Pray how came you to leave me so, Mr. Young?" cried she—" Only think," turning to us—" the fellow of a coachman drove the horses' heads towards a court in Soho Square, and pretended he could not move them; and Mr. Young was fool enough to get out, and let the man have his way,—when he deserved to be horse-whipped." " Instead of which," returned he, " I gave him a shilling! where's the difference?" " Who but you " cried she " would not have made the man come on with us? or else not have paid him?—and so I was forced to run into a toyshop, where he politely left me to my fate—and where I chanced to meet with a chair." O rare Matrimony![2] thought I.

---

[1] This seems to have been meant for a pleasantry. Mrs. Cornelys gave her subscription balls in Carlisle House (on the east side of Soho Square, at the corner of Sutton Street), a nobleman's mansion, which she altered and enlarged.

[2] This is a quotation from Garrick's farce of " The Irish Widow ": " *Bates*. The affair of marriage is, in this country, put upon the easiest footing; .... they are united at first for their mutual convenience, and separated ever after for their particular pleasure—O rare Matrimony!"

Mr. Young turned to Hetty—"Where is Dr. Burney?" "Why, dear," cried she, "I told you twenty times, out, on business." "O! ay, I believe you did—" "When will Miss Allen leave Bath," said Mrs. Young. "Why, is Miss Allen at Bath?" cried he. "Mr. Young," exclaimed she,—"how can you be so affected! why you knew she was there a month ago—" "Not I, faith! never heard a syllable of the matter —not a single syllable!" "I have no patience with such affectation—you knew it as well as I did" cried she. "Miss Burney" cried Mr. Young fixing his eyes earnestly on her face, "how does Mr.—what's his name?—Charles, I believe—ay, how does Mr. Charles Burney do?" "Very well, I believe" said she, half smiling in spight of a studied composure. "When does my sister come to town?" asked Mr. Young. "Next Tuesday" said I—"and I go to Lynn to-morrow." "To-morrow! is this magick? and why do you go?" said Mr. Young. "To take mama's place, and be very notable." "And for that do you go?—No reason besides?—" "Not one!" "I'll go too!—when is it?" "Next Tuesday." "I'll go too, I protest!" cried Mr. Young. "Pray do;" said I, "it will be very worth while!" "I will, upon my honour!"

He then insisted on Hetty's singing—which she did, and most sweetly. They went away about nine. My dear papa soon after came home. I told him of my franks, though in some fear that he should think me wrong in consenting to have them, though I don't know how I could have refused them. . . .

Lynn Regis.

My Susette and I are very comfortable here. . . . . . We work, read, walk, and play on the harpsichord—these are our employments, and we find them sufficient to fill up all our time without ever being tired.

I am reading again, the History of England, that of Smollet. . . . . . I have read to the reign of George the Second, and, in spight of the dislike I have to Smollet's language and style of writing, I am much entertained, for scarce a name is now mentioned that is not familiar to my ear, and I delight in thus *tracing* the *rise* and *progress* of the great characters of the age. . . . .

We meet with great civility and kindness in this town, and—— . . . . .

[To MISS BURNEY, Chesington.]

My dearest sister,

With a very short time to write, and a very great deal to say, I take up my pen to thank you most heartily for your comfortable letter. I had thought it very long on the road. We are now in daily expectation of the important letter from papa—and let me say one thing—it seems to me not unlikely that immediately that papa receives the last pacquet, he will write to my uncle. I hope therefore that you have ere now acquainted him with your affairs, or else that you directly will, as it would be shocking for him to hear of it first from abroad, and as he would then perhaps always believe that you intended to secret it from him.

How can it have got about, God knows, but every body here speaks of your marriage as a certain and speedy affair. So you will have it in town. I fear mama cannot go ;—as for me, I am ready to break my heart when I think of being absent from you. O that it were in my power to quit this place directly ! But I hope all for the best ; indeed I cannot bear to *suppose* that I shall be away from you. Miss Allen goes to Snettisham to-morrow—is too busy to write, but will from thence. Susette's best love attends you. I have had a sensible and affectionate letter from my cousin, which I beg you to thank him for in my name.

Sweet Chesington !—abominable Lynn !

My dear Hetty, I shall write myself into the vapours and then give them to you—so I will have done. But I must say how much I admire your plan of life. Certainly it would seem very strange for you to have gone to the Coffee House, for all his and your own acquaintance will be visiting you on the occasion. I will write to you the very instant we hear from Venice. My kindest and best love to my ever dear Mr. Crisp and to dear Kitty. Let us know about the Barbornes[1] when you can. Adieu, my dearest, dear sister. I am in much haste. My first wish is to be with you. God forbid I should not! Believe me ever with the utmost affection

Your

FRANCES BURNEY.[2]

Poland Street.

I have not written for an age—the reason is, my thoughts have been all drawn away from myself and given up to my dear Hetty—and to her I have been writing without end;— so that all my time besides was due to my dearest Suzette with whom I have been reading French : having taught myself that charming language for the sake of its bewitching authors—for I shall never want to speak it.

With this dear Suzette and my sweet little Charlotte, it is well I can be so happy : for Hetty, my dear Hetty, has given herself away from us. She has married at last her faithful Charles. God send her happy! He is one of the worthiest young men living.—I am come up to town to spend a little time with them. They are now in our house till they can find a dwelling to their taste.

Papa has bought a house in Queen Square. It is settled

---

[1] The family of Richard Burney, of Barborne-Lodge, Worcester, the "uncle" named in this letter.

[2] Arthur Young hinted, on a previous page, that there was some tie between Charles Rousseau Burney and his cousin Hetty, so that no wonder "it got about" in Lynn. On the back of this letter there is a date in pencil of "July, 1770," which may be in Fanny's writing. We do not know the exact date of the marriage. The reference to the "pacquet from Venice" shows that Dr. Burney was then on his first tour, and was not present at it, as he writes, in his "Present State of Music in France and Italy," "I left London in the beginning of June, 1770." He did not return until January, 1771, when he was welcomed by his family and Mr. Crisp to his new house in Queen Square, which was bought by Mrs. Burney in his absence, so that the communication which Fanny advises her sister to make was to her uncle, Richard Burney, father of the bridegroom, who was not to be shocked by hearing of it first from Dr. Burney on the Continent.

by Mr. Crisp to my very great grief that we are quite to drop Mrs. Pringle, that we may see no more of Mr. Seton.

For this reason I shall be glad to quit Poland Street,—that I may no more see Mrs. Pringle since I dare not visit or even speak to her, when it is not unavoidable, as it was a few days since, when Miss Allen and I were standing at the parlour window, and Mrs. Pringle passed, but seeing me turned back and made a motion for me to open the window, which I did, though I was terribly confused what to say to her, for it was not in my power to explain the reasons of my absence from her; yet, after so much kindness and civility as we have met with from her, I am sure excuses were very necessary. She asked me how I did, and immediately added —" Pray what have I done that you never come near me?" I was much at a loss what to say, but stammered something about the hurry of moving, want of time, etc.—She shook her head—" Want of time!—what only next door? . . . . I'll assure you I think it very ungrateful in you." Her bluntness confounded me, which I believe she saw, for she said in a softer manner—" Well, my dear, I am glad to see you so well—I wish you good morning"—and walked away. I am truly sorry to say I believe this is the last time I shall speak to Mrs. Pringle. I have a very strong sense of the favours we have received from her, and were it in my power, would convince her that I have—but it is not. Just before her eldest son, the Captain, went abroad last spring, he gave to my sister a Copy of Verses on her, and me, which I will write out.

[Four stanzas follow, professing to be French. Captain Pringle most likely copied them in part from a book, grafting upon them some conceits of " his own pure brain." " Belle Vénus," [1] and " Madame Minerve," took human forms one day, and made such mischief among hearts on earth, that the cry of men rose to Olympus. In his wrath, Jupiter banished the goddesses for ever,—(of all places in the world,) to Poland Street, Soho (" *la rue de Pologne* ") bidding them be women for *the rest of their lives!*

" Soit femmes pour le reste de la vie ! " (*sic.*)

---

[1] " 1. Miss Hester.
2. Miss Fanny Burney."
[Captain Pringle's own explanation of whom he meant.]

This line is a fair sample of the sense and grammar of these verses, which, after copying in her youth, Madame D'Arblay has noted in her age, as being " out of all metre, and not French." They are also " out of all" spelling, and right accents, but as we printed the not much wiser effusions of " Incognitus," " Melidorus," and Mr. Mackenzie, Captain Pringle's merit mention. As Lord Mulgrave wrote of a generation before theirs, " Without *his song* no fop is to be found."]

Can any thing be more galant ? My sister and myself propose in future signing no other names than those of Venus and Minerva.

Wednesday Oct. [1 ?]

.... our play, which I shall presently copy a bill of. There was just a week's interval from the proposing and the performing. But I will begin with a play bill, which I had the honour to draw up.

. . . the 29th
Will be presented,
By a Company of Comedians in Queen Square.[1]

* * * * * *

Queen Square, Nov. 16.

I have now changed my abode, and quitted dear Poland Street for ever. How well satisfied shall I be if after having lived as long in Queen Square, I can look back to equally happy days!

We have a charming house here. It is situated at the upper end of the square, and has a delightful prospect of Hamstead and Hygate, we have more than room for our family, large as it is, and all the rooms are well fitted up, convenient, and handsome.[2] ....

---

[1] This has been crossed out, but so much as is given above may be read; and it may be discerned that the parts were played by the Burneys, their cousins, and Maria Allen. It shows the family turn for acting.

[2] Dr. Burney liked this house because it had been that of John Barber, the " Johannes Tonsor " of the charming correspondence of Swift and his friends. Lord Mayor Barber, printer to Queen Anne and to the City of London, lived and died a hearty Jacobite, bequeath-

I left Mr. Burney and my sister with regret; I passed five happy weeks with them.

[The following fragment is in a proper place here, as winding up the record of the waverings of Mr. Seton.]

.... Though he never knew his own mind while she was single, ... and that his friends, and his party, knowing [his] disappointment, and not knowing how his behaviour incurred it, all look upon her marriage as if it was jilting him. I know, [that] they all thought much higher for her [than] Mr. Burney, who has nothing to offer but the fruits of his profession; and she is [so] pretty, and so accomplished, so agreeable and so active, that both in and out of her family [it] was imagined she would connect herself to far more worldly advantage. The extreme worth, however, [and] excellent though unpretending understanding [of] Mr. Burney and his goodness of heart, and regard from childhood will, I trust and hope, make her happy, and make ....

[Here ends a record of "such love as belongs to admiration, and leads to flirtation, and *ends in nothing at all.*"[1] But the strong measure of moving to Queen Square to be out of the close neighbourhood of so easy a *chaperon* as the good-natured, social, hospitable Mrs. Pringle, did no more than change the scene and the actors upon the stage. We shall soon see that it was also the proverbial change, "from the frying-pan into the fire"; for in Queen Square lived Sir Richard Bettenson, Mr. Rishton's uncle by marriage, and Sir William Browne, M.D., whose daughter was married to his great-uncle. Hence the square was a little Lynn Regis when the Burneys also entered it; and there were two young people who could easily renew the love-affair begun at Lynn. *Madame Minerve* (herself all fancy-free) was soon to watch and chronicle another inroad of the great god Cupid. Herself younger than Hetty and Maria, she observed their growing

---

ing £300, £200, and £100, respectively, to his friends Bolingbroke, Swift, and Pope. In a plan of London by J. Gibson, 1767, Queen Square has only two parallel blocks of houses, and is unfinished on the other sides. Upon the north it lies open to St. George's Fields and Lamb's Conduit; in fact, Fanny must have seen Highgate and Hampstead as villages on the heights, with clear fields between them and Bloomsbury.

[1] So wrote Fanny (many years afterwards), in "Camilla"; perhaps, not without memory of 1770.

attachments with tender and anxious care, with a sister's feelings, but also (how can nature be expelled?) with the eye of an unconscious artist. Hetty, the sweet and sensible, had scarcely settled into a very happy married life with her modest and constant Charles, than the stormier love-tale of Maria Allen and Martin Folkes Rishton began to occupy the mind of Fanny. She was not to lack a heroine, or (as in 1768) to complain of "insipid calm and uninterrupted quiet." Discreet she was; but the warnings of Dolly Young as to the danger of "all going down" in journals was not always heeded. Twelve pages at the end of this Diary have been cut out, perhaps by her own hand, perhaps by the hand of some one still more discreet. We learn from Fanny's own memoranda that they contained the names of Miss Allen and Mr. Rishton. Much of the Diary of 1771 has, in like manner, been sacrificed to prudence; but Fanny preserved, as long as she lived, a bundle of Maria's letters, which (though they have undergone some censorship) half show, half hide, a romance which stirred her fancy, and, it may be, turned back her thoughts to the story (which she had burnt) of "Caroline Evelyn." These letters have been elsewhere described by Fanny as being "flighty, ridiculous, uncommon, lively, comical, entertaining, frank, and undisguised." They are also not a little indiscreet; and, in one of them, Maria most justly describes herself as not being "near so squeamish as you [Fanny] are." In fact, nothing lying before the Editor gives a higher opinion of the natural refinement of Hetty, Fanny, and Susy, than the contrast between what they did and wrote, and the occasional doings and writing of this impulsive girl. The contrast in education is equally striking. Maria could spell tolerably, and her writing was neat, and even good when she chose to take pains; but she was commonly careless, and often left her readers to correct her grammar and spelling, and supply little words of connexion. Dateless for the most part are her letters; and, although they have been numbered in most cases by Mme. D'Arblay, the order of numbering cannot always be trusted.

Nothing could surpass the confidence felt in Fanny by Maria, and the affection between them was never altered. In a letter of 1780, or later, Maria writes: "My heart at this instant glows with the same love and friendship it ever felt towards you, and I love your father as I ever did, and never will be the ungrateful wretch I must feel myself ever to forget his paternal kindness to me when I lived under his roof."

As we have no cooking at all in these early Diaries, and our heroine does but twice describe her own apparel, we wish to show that the Burneys did more than drink tea, and can only find Maria (who was rather "*notable*") to fill the void. Here is part of a letter from Warham, then the abode of Sir John Turner.[1] It seems to have

---

[1] Mr. John Turner, who was said to have been a waiter at a Cambridge inn, was, in 1675, chosen a common councillor of Lynn Regis, and within two years' time became alderman, mayor, and member of

been written after Hetty's marriage, but whether in 1770 or 1771 it is hard to tell. She writes as if about to take the place of her mother as mistress in Dr. Burney's house. We introduce Maria by this fragment, and she begins to open her love-affairs in the lively letter which follows it.]

[From MARIA ALLEN to FANNY BURNEY.]

.... Oh as I come Along some *House keeping* thoughts enterd my noddle as follows—tell Jenny I have Alterd the dinner on Monday—and intend having at top fry'd smelts—at Bottom the Ham—on one side 2 boild Chickens—on the other a small pigion Pie with 3 pigions in it and let the Crust be made very *Rich* and eggs in it—in the Middle a Orleon plumb Pudding—and a Roast Loin of Mutton—after the fish. There must be french beans round the Chickens—and let her get some green gages and filberts—and a few good orleans for after dinner— —Oh and pray remember that the Window blind belonging to the Common parlour be put up and the door shut when the Ladies come in that there may not seem a fuss—and let the Carpet be Laid down in the Musick Room for I shall carry them up there till dinner is ready—and let the hair cloth on the Stairs be taken away—for you Susey, and the Children can go up by the Study all the time they are with us to prevent dirt. Excuse All these ORDERS but they accur'd to me as necessary things while on my journey.

[To MISS FANNY BURNEY.]

My dear Fan,

Prepare a good Stomach and good pair of Shoes for an agreable walk to Cornhill[1]—to eat your fill of Delicious

---

parliament for the borough. "From him sprang the family that afterwards bore great sway in this town for a whole century" (see "A History of Lynn," by W. Richards, 1812). This descendant, Sir John Turner, had the Walpole interest, and (with a Walpole) fought and won a violent election battle against William Folkes in 1747. Sir John contested Lynn for the last time in 1768.

[1] The advice to prepare a good appetite for cheesecakes at Cornhill, possibly means that Fanny was to go to an inn to receive some parcel from Norfolk, by "machine," or waggon, and to pay the inn the tribute of eating cheesecakes, those dainties being in readiness at most

Cheesecakes—(does not your mouth water at the bare Idea) I was at the Assembly forced to go entirely against my own Inclination. But I always have sacrificed my own Inclinations to the will of other people—could not resist the pressing Importunity of—Bet Dickens—to go—tho' it proved Horridly stupid. I drank tea at the—told old T[urner]—I was determined not to dance—he would not believe me—a wager ensued—half a Crown provided I followed my own Inclinations—agreed—Mr. Audley asked me. I refused—sat still—yet followed my own Inclinations. But four couple began—Martin was there—yet stupid—nimporte—quite Indifferent—on both sides——Who had I—to converse with the whole Evening—not a female friend—none there—not an acquaintance—All Dancing— —who then—I've forgot—nimporte—I broke my Earring—how—heaven knows—foolishly enough—one can't always keep on the Mask of Wisdom—well n'importe I danced a Minuet a quatre the latter end of the Eve—with a stupid Wretch—need I name him—They danced Cotillions almost the whole Night—two sets—yet I did not join them—Miss Jenny Hawkins danced—with who—can't you guess—well—n'importe— —

Some folks broke their promise of not Dancing. Well who could resist—the object was tempting—only half a Dance—the rest of time stupidly. Not a soul I know there of my own sex who are not too much engaged to speak to me—well nimporte—I drank tea with no one in no party—I was an Alien—quite save that poor bewitched solitary thing—not quite—got into the Chariot to come home. Young Mrs. Hogg's Coachman forgot to set me down at our own door—drove me in Chequer Street. I did not go in with her tho much askd—came home—was I alone—guess—well all is vanity and vexation of spirit—did I pass a happy eve—guess—did My going answer the expence of the cheesecakes—yes—Was I better pleased on Wednesday or Thursday morning—The Latter— . . . You remember saying to me

---

inns. In 1667, Mr. Pepys says that at the Red Lion, at Barnet Wells, he "did eat some of the best cheese-cakes that ever I did eat in my life." There may, however, be some playful double meaning in the word "cheesecakes."

. . . . . the night before you went these words—" Write me a full account of the Assembly you need not mind explanitions—I shall not need them as I know how affairs stand—I will explain them to Hetty—" I have obeyed your orders, though have been rather to explicit I think—Adieu continue to love me—and remember me to dear Hetty and her Charles—

I am yours sincerely
MARIA LUCIA ALLEN

[Lucius appears to have been one of the Christian names of Mr. Rishton. Maria has playfully written "Lucia," then blurred it with her finger. Susan adds this postscript:—]

" Susanna sends her love to all 3—has nothing to say, as is not able to write so much yet say so little as Miss A—"

1771.

[We cannot tell how much has been cut away from the diary of this year before the first date which remains in it, that of the 11th of April. Thereby we have lost all account of Dr. Burney's joyous return to his family in January, and of his speedy retreat to Chesington to arrange his notes, and the journals of his tour in France and Italy, for publication.

In her elder days, Mme. D'Arblay drew up a list of "*persons and things as occurring*" in her diaries from 1768 to 1779.

It seems probable that what she entered upon this list she meant to stand when her manuscripts were published. As the name of Miss Ford is the first upon her notes for this year (1771) she herself most likely cut out what went before it. We assume (we can do no more than *assume*) that when the names of people exist in her notes, and nothing about them is to be found in her journals, the pages are in many cases missing by accident, in many others through the varying measure of discretion, and sense of fitness, in those who handled them about 1847. Her own effacements, which are numerous, can almost always be known to be hers, by their extreme thoroughness; the lines being so closely scored through and through that scarcely one word can be made out. Those of later hands, have sometimes been read, and printed. Between the paragraph upon Christopher Smart at p. 127, and that on Signor Martinelli, p. 129, passages concerning her brothers, Charles and James, her sister Susan, Leoni, Signor Corri, and Signora Bicheli, were once in this journal; after Martinelli, and before Dr. Armstrong, p. 131, we have lost all that was written of Mr. Sleepe, Mr. James Sansom, and Mr. Francis Sansom; after Dr. Armstrong, p. 132, of Mrs. Barsanti, Miss Riddle, Mrs. Sansom, Mrs. Burney, senr., Miss Mainstone, Miss Const, Molly Stancliffe, and Mrs. Const.]

Queen's Square, Bloomsbury—
April 11.

*   *   *   *   *   *[1]

I have of late been led into many reflections from the strange and unexpected behaviour I have seen on several occasions: one happened this morning. Mrs. Colman,

---

[1] We have here omitted three pages of these moral reflections which

wife of the famous author Mr. Colman,[1] a sweet amiable woman, was taken ill and died suddenly rather more than a fortnight since. We were intimately acquainted with, and very sincerely regretted her. In point of understanding she was infinitely inferior to Mr. Colman; but she possessed an uncommon sweetness of temper, much sensibility, and a generous and restless desire of obliging, and of making her friends happy. So amiable a character must, I am sure, endear her infinitely to Mr. Colman, whom she, with the greatest reason, was beyond expression attached to. He is one of the best tempered (though I believe very passionate) of men, lively, agreeable, openhearted, and clever. Her daughter, Miss Ford, is about sixteen, very genteel in person, well bred, and very well educated. Her son, George Colman, is still younger. Poor Mrs. Colman was doatingly fond of both her children. I have heartily pitied them for the loss of such a mother, ever since I heard of it.

This morning it happened that only I was at home, when I heard a violent rap at the door, and John came in with Miss Ford's name. I felt myself almost shudder with the idea of

---

were not only acceptable, but obligatory, in a century so much less impatient than our own. In fact, they were part of the moral and mental costume of the period; but we have retained enough of them in the Diary of 1768 to preserve the historical colouring which would have been blurred had they been wholly left out.

[1] George Colman (the elder), born at Florence in 1732, was the only son of Francis Colman, British Resident in Tuscany, and of a sister of the wife of Pulteney, Earl of Bath. As a minister's child he had, by precedent, a claim that George II. should be his godfather, as Queen Caroline had been godmother to his sister. On his father's death in 1733 Pulteney became his guardian, educated him at Westminster School, and Christ-church, Oxford, and entered him at Lincoln's Inn. George would have been left even more of Pulteney's money than was the case, had he not alarmed his uncle by liking things theatrical. In 1767 he became one of the proprietors of Covent Garden Theatre. He managed the Haymarket after Foote gave it up in 1776. He wrote, or rather adapted, many pieces for the stage. He had a share in the most successful comedy of the time, "The Clandestine Marriage." His "Jealous Wife," and "The Heir-at-Law" of his son George, have kept the stage in our own time.

what she must suffer from entering a house in which her mother had been so intimate, and while her death was so recent; and, when she came in, I knew not what to do with my eyes, to prevent their meeting her's. I was equally distressed for words, not knowing how to address her on this melancholy occasion. But I soon found my apprehensions were needless; for she received my salute, and seated herself with great composure, and without manifesting any concern. I talked, as well as I was able, of indifferent matters, and she followed as I led, with the utmost ease and serenity; offered to call upon me any morning that would be agreeable to me, to go an airing, spoke just as usual of Mr. Colman and her brother, whom I enquired much after; and with the ready politeness of an old mistress of a family hoped soon to have the pleasure of seeing me in Queen Street! Then, said she was going to St. James' and so many places, that she could not possibly stay longer.

I held up my hands and eyes with astonishment, when she left me. Alas! thought I, is all the tenderness of the fondest of mothers so soon forgot? or, is it that, becoming the mistress of the house, for such Mr. Colman has made her, having his servants and equipage at her command,—is it in such things to compensate for the best of parents?[1]

April 20.

I went last night with mama and Miss Allen to Ranelagh.

---

[1] This girl, who shocked Fanny so greatly, is said to have been upon the stage at six years of age. She afterwards married a Mr. Wilkinson. Her half-brother (George Colman the younger) was but nine years old when his poor mother died. He tells a piteous little story in his "Random Recollections." On the night of Maundy Thursday, 1771, he was to be taken home from Marylebone School to enter Westminster after the holidays. He had been told that a servant should be sent for him. None came. He sobbed for some time, but was piqued at last. He *went to bed in his stockings*, making a vow that he would never pull them off again until he had seen his mother. Never again did he see her. That night she was dying, having taken a wrong medicine. On Good Friday (March 29, 1771), the little lad was taken home to a house with closed shutters, to begin his acquaintance with loss and grief.

... I saw few people that I knew, and none that I cared for.

[Here occurs a gap, which we find from Mme. D'Arblay's notes was once filled with the affairs of "Mrs. Doctor Burney," Miss Allen, and Mr. Rishton. As the second marriage of Dr. Burney, and the reaching the grave age of fifteen, moved Fanny to burn her elegies and odes; nay, her tragedies and epic poems, and to indulge only in writing journals, with some scruples even about that; so it would appear that the experience she had of other people's love-affairs stirred her mind to begin "Evelina" early in 1774. To tell a tale aright which, to our belief, had an influence over Fanny's imagination, we must begin with a pedigree.

Martin Folkes, an eminent barrister, was father of Martin Folkes, a bencher of Gray's Inn, who married Dorothy, one of the three coheiresses of Sir William Hovell, of Hillington Hall, in Norfolk, not far from Lynn. Martin (II.) had three sons, of whom only the eldest (Martin) and the second (William) need be named. Martin (III.) is the Martin Folkes whose name abounds in the memoirs, autobiographies, and journals of the men of letters or science of his period [1690-1754]. He was of Westminster School, and a pupil of the famous Dr. Laughton at Clare Hall, Cambridge, and had also studied at Saumur. He was named Vice-President of the Royal Society by Newton in 1722-3, and contested the Presidentship with Sir Hans Sloane, upon the death of Newton, in 1727. Failing to win, he travelled in Germany and Italy for two years. In the end he succeeded Sloane as P.R.S., Dr. Hartley as a foreign member of the Académie des Sciences, and the Duke of Somerset as President of the Society of Antiquaries. Oxford gave him his D.C.L. before his own University offered her own degree of doctor. He wrote many papers upon a great variety of subjects, for his fancy was kindled by all things interesting in art, science, or learning, though he is charged by a contemporary with "refusing constantly" (as P.R.S.) "all papers that treat of the Longitude." No wonder. The longitude was the "great *Boar*" (as they spelled it) of that time. The more serious charge of making "infidelity fashionable" in the Royal Society, by being himself "an errant infidel and loud scoffer," is made by several writers, as well as by his brother in the Royal Society and Society of Antiquaries, Stukeley, who also wrote himself M.D. and S.T.P. Stukeley was (as the poet Gray said) "a gossip in coffee-houses," as well as in his Common-place Book. Yet, as he had seen much of Martin Folkes from at least 1720, called him his "good friend," and given him a fibula, we may (after allowing for a few palpable errors) give some credence to the sad story he tells, which bears upon the fortunes of Martin's grandson, Martin Folkes Rishton. It tallies, besides, with the more generous account given by Nichols. "Before he was at age" Martin Folkes married from Drury Lane Theatre a beautiful, discreet, and even exemplary woman, who acted under the name of Lucretia Bradshaw. His mother, on hearing of his marriage, threw herself out of a window. She only broke her arm (which was less than she meant to do), but the fracture may not have been in vain as a useful warning to her youngest son William, who, in due time, married twice, and went where money was.[1] His second wife was the only child and rich heiress of that odd Norfolk man, Sir William Browne, President of the College of Physicians. To President Folkes a Martin (IV.) was born, of Westminster School, Clare Hall, and Saumur—a brilliant youth, who shared his father's likings, especially for coins and medals. He was in Rome with his father when poor Lucretia (once Bradshaw) went mad upon religion. She was brought home to a house for lunatics at Chelsea, where she remained, surviving her husband. Her son was killed by a fall from his horse, while ending his studies in France. Martin Folkes resigned the Presidentship of the Royal Society in 1751, after an attack of paralysis, but lingered in life until the middle of 1754. He was renowned for collecting curious and beautiful things, and giving generously to students. To his Society he left his portrait of Lord Verulam, and a ring for future Presidents, which he had himself worn as P.R.S. To his brother William he bequeathed their mother's estate of Hillington; to his two daughters, Dorothy and Lucretia,[2] twelve thousand pounds apiece. Dorothy (says Stukeley) had run away with "an indigent person," "a bookkeeper," of the name of Rishton, who "used her very ill." Certainly Dorothy was only left a couple of family portraits, while her younger sister was made her father's executrix, and heiress of what he loved best, his "great and well-chosen library," his fine collection of English coins, and vast gatherings of objects of *virtù* or curiosity. Two years after his death, Lucretia, his daughter (who was then four-and-thirty), married Richard Bettenson, who also is said by Stukeley to have been at that time an "indigent person." At any rate, the fine library and rich museum of Martin Folkes were sold the year Lucretia married; the sale lasting fifty-six days, of which the books consumed forty-one, and the prints and engravings eight. Lucretia died two years after her marriage. In 1773 we find Bettenson, who had succeeded to a baronetcy, living in Queen Square, with a large income, but in an over-frugal way. He was childless, and the baronetcy expired with him; so that he treated his wife's nephew and his own ward, Martin Folkes Rishton, as his heir, and sent him to travel for two years in the beginning of this year, 1771—partly, perhaps, to keep him out of harm's way in the form of Maria Allen, who may have been as beautiful as her mother had been

---

[1] William, from whom the present family descends, was a barrister, and agent for the Lancashire estates of the Duke of Montagu.

[2] Lucretia was also left his silver plate. Stukeley makes both Dorothy and Lucretia marry two years after their father's death; but, in the absence of other evidence, the will makes it likely that Dorothy had married in his lifetime.

and her sister then was. We have not found any reasons why Mrs. Burney was so very warm against Mr. Rishton, except that he had been extravagant at Oxford, and that she had heard some story that he had done something unworthy of a gentleman. Mr. Crisp, Hetty, Fanny, and Susan, were under the same belief that he was an unfit and unsafe lover for Maria, but Fanny and Susan (the *confidantes*) were much more pitiful than the "wifish Hetty," although they pleaded on the side of Discretion; with the usual result, as may be seen hereafter.]

May 8.

My father's book, '*The present state of Music*,'[1] made its appearance in the world the 3rd of this month, and we flatter ourselves it will be favourably received.—Last Sunday was the first day for some time past, that my father has favoured us with his company in a sociable style, having been so exceedingly occupied by writing in those few hours he spends at home, that he really seemed lost to his family; and the comfort of his society and conversation is almost as new as grateful to us. He prints this book for himself. He has sent a multitude of them to his particular friends as presents; among others, to the famous Dr. Hawkesworth, to that charming poet Mr. Mason,[2] to Mr. Garrick, and Mr. Crisp, who, all four, were consulted about it when a manuscript, and interested themselves much with it. Dr. Shepherd,[3] Mr. Colman, Dr. Armstrong, Mr. Strange, Dr. Bever,[4] Giardini,[5]

---

[1] The title of this book is: "The Present State of Music In France and Italy: or The Journal of a Tour Through Those Countries, Undertaken To Collect Materials For A General History of Music, By Charles Burney, Mus. D." There was a second edition in 1773. We give Dr. Burney's own account of his undertaking: "When I left England, I had two objects in view: the one was to get what information I could relative to the music of the ancients; and the other was to judge with my own eyes of the *present* state of modern music in the places through which I should pass, from the performance and conversation of the first musicians in Italy."

[2] Dr. Burney had made the acquaintance of Mason at the house of Lord Holdernesse, to whom the poet was chaplain.

[3] Dr. Shepherd was Plumian Professor of Astronomy and Experimental Philosophy in the University of Cambridge from 1760 to 1796.

[4] Thomas Bever, LL.D., Oxon., 1752, was a jurist. In 1781 he published a "History of the Legal Polity of the Roman State."

[5] Felice Giardini was the first violin player in Europe. "The

and many others had likewise books, before the publication. . . . .

We had a great deal of company last Sunday. Mrs. Sheeles and Mr. and Mrs. Mailing, her son and daughter, dined and spent the evening with us. Mrs. Mailing is a sweet woman, with whom we were intimate before her marriage, and who now, to our great regret, lives in the North of England.[1] After dinner Sir Thomas Clarges, a modest young baronet,[2] and Mr. Price, a young man of fashion, called and sat about two hours. The latter is lately returned from his travels and was eager to *compare notes* with my father. He is a very intelligent sensible and clever young man. He is a kinsman to Mr. Greville.[3] . . . .

Yesterday, after tea, we were cheered indeed; for *rap-tap-tap*, and entered Mr. and Mrs. Garrick with their two nieces. Mr. Garrick who has lately been very ill, is delightfully recovered, looks as handsome as ever I saw him, is in charming spirits, and was all animation and good humour.[4]

---

arrival of GIARDINI in London, in the spring of 1750, forms a memorable æra in the instrumental music of this kingdom." " Of his academy, scholars, manner of leading at the opera and oratorio, performance in private concerts, compositions vocal and instrumental, I shall say nothing here, lest my praise should be too much for others, and too little for himself."—DR. BURNEY.

[1] These names should be Shields and Maling. "Mrs. Sheeles" was the kind friend of the Burneys, who took Fanny, Susan, and Charles to her house in Queen Square, some days before the death of their mother. Of Mrs. Maling, Mme. D'Arblay tells that she had often said " Why did not Sir Joshua Reynolds paint Dr. Johnson when he was speaking to your father, or to you?" Mrs. Maling had observed that the sight of Dr. Burney or of Fanny seemed to light up Johnson's countenance. Mrs. Maling was the wife of Christopher Maling, Esquire, of West Herrington, in the County of Durham. Sophia, their daughter, afterwards married the Harry Phipps named in 1770.

[2] This Sir Thomas Clarges, whose name is preserved in that of Clarges Street, where his grandfather had his house, was a descendant of John Clarges, the farrier in the Savoy, whose daughter Anne married General Monk.

[3] For Mr. Price, see a note to the diary for 1772.

[4] " I see him now," wrote Letitia Hawkins, over forty years after his death, " I see him now in a dark blue coat, the button-holes bound with gold, a small cocked hat laced with gold, his waistcoat very open ;

Mrs. Garrick is the most attentively polite and perfectly well-bred woman in the world; her speech is all softness; her manners, all elegance; her smiles, all sweetness. There is something so peculiarly graceful in her motion, and pleasing in her address, that the most trifling words have weight and power, when spoken by her, to oblige and even delight.[1]

---

his countenance never at rest, and indeed seldom his person; for in the relaxation of the country [at Hampton] he gave way to all his natural volatility, and with my father was perfectly at ease, . . . sometimes sitting on a table, and then, if he saw my brothers at a distance on the lawn, shooting off like an arrow out of a bow, in a spirited chase of them round the garden." Miss Hawkins adds that she was much more afraid of Garrick than of Johnson, " whom I knew not to be, *nor could ever suppose he ever would be thought to be an extraordinary man.* Garrick had a frown, and spoke impetuously; Johnson was slow and kind in his way with children." The lithe and lively Gascon, who was connected with the Fermignacs, and claimed by French Garricks as a kinsman, was low of stature, but well shaped (*bien pris*), with brilliant, full, black eyes, and a dark complexion, alert and "alive in every muscle and every feature." It has been said that there was a resemblance between Garrick and the first Napoleon. A nephew of Garrick, who was exactly like his uncle, was arrested (under the belief that he was Buonaparte) in 1803, while travelling in Wales, but allowed to return to England by way of Tenby, under a pass from the Mayor of Haverfordwest.

[1] Eva Maria Veigel, or Weigel, a charming dancer, was born in Vienna. Her name which in Austrian-German, means *violet*, was changed into "*Violette*," or "*La Violetta*," by her patroness, the Empress Maria Theresa. She came to England in 1744, where she lived with the Countess of Burlington, (wife of the Earl who designed his own palace), while performing on the stage. Garrick married her in June, or July, 1749, after a courtship and a settlement carefully superintended by the Earl and Countess, who gave her a dower of £6,000—to which Garrick added £4,000, in her settlement. All agree as to the attractions and great good sense of Mrs. Garrick. Mrs. Piozzi wrote on the 17th of January, 1789: "That woman has lived a *very wise life*, regular and steady in her conduct, attentive to every word she speaks and every step she treads, decorous in her manners and graceful in her person. My fancy forms the Queen [Charlotte] just like Mrs. Garrick; they are countrywomen, and have, as the phrase is, had a hard card to play; yet . . . . they will rise from the table unhurt either by others or themselves . . . . having played a saving game." What Mrs. Piozzi meant was that Mrs. Garrick maintained her ordinary manner towards herself on her second marriage, with a singer,—(a calling akin to that of Garrick and of

The Miss Garricks resemble, the eldest her aunt, the youngest her uncle, in a striking manner. Softness, modesty, reserve and silence characterise Miss Garrick, while Kitty is all animation, spirit and openness. They are both very fine girls, but the youngest is most handsome, her face is the most expressive I almost ever saw of liveliness and sweetness.[1]

Dr. King, who has just taken the doctor's degree, came in and figured away to his own satisfaction before Mr. Garrick, whom he so engrossed, that I thought it quite effrontery in him. I wonder he had the courage to open his mouth; but men of half-understandings have generally (I believe) too little feeling to be overpowered with diffidence.[2] Besides

---

La Violetta), when other people shunned "Thrale's gay widow." Dr. Burney, to whom Mr. and Mrs. Garrick had shown the greatest kindness when he lost his first wife, writes emphatically that "Mrs. Garrick had every faculty of social judgment, good taste and steadiness of character, which he wanted. She was an excellent appreciator of the fine arts; and attended all the last rehearsals of new, or of revived plays, to give her opinion of effects, dresses, and machinery. She seemed to be his real other half." .... Mrs. Garrick survived her husband more than forty years, dying in 1822, at a great age.

[1] These young ladies were so much admired, that Miss Hawkins (who lived near them when in the country), says that she was "duly jealous of their re-echoed praises." They were Arabella and Catherine, daughters of George, the only brother of David who left children to keep up the name of Garrick. Miss Garrick married in his life-time, "Kitty," after his death. He gave each £6,000, the same sum that he had received with "La Violetta." By the way, the name originally was "*Garric*." The word *Garigue* is found in French dictionaries as meaning a piece of waste ground, a "*lande*," but in the south of France it takes the form of *Garric*, and is applied to stretches of ground in the "*landes*" which are overgrown by stunted oaks, and brushwood of oak—the *primary* meaning of the word being an oak. The word under the form of "*Garriga*" is found in Spain.

[2] Poor Dr. King, who actually had the impertinence to open his mouth before Garrick, was author of "The Rites and Ceremonies of the Greek Church," 1772, 4to, and of a pamphlet on the climate of Russia, where he had lived as chaplain to the English Factory at St. Petersburgh. His judgment may have been the less esteemed, as (being a Lynn man) he seems to have advised the second Mrs. Burney; and, being an "unfortunate but honourable speculator," lost her all the money she possessed absolutely. He was John Glen King, D.D., F.R.S.; born, 1731; chaplain in Russia, 1764; rector of Wormley, in Hertfordshire, 1786. He had a London chapel in 1786. He also wrote a paper in the

the man is wont to preach, and that has taught him to prose, which he does unmercifully.

Dr. Bever, a very civil, heavy-headed man of the Law, who had listened with attentive admiration, but quite dumb, to every word Mr. Garrick spoke; but, upon something being advanced relative to the Chancery, he ventured to offer some reply. I really pitied the poor man; for, when Mr. Garrick turned round to him, and every body was silent to hear him; his voice failed him; he hesitated, confounded his own meaning, and was in so much confusion, that he could not make himself understood.

I sat by the youngest Miss Garrick, and had some comfortable [conversation] with her. Mrs. Garrick with much kindness took my hand when she spoke to me, and Mr. Garrick enquired most particularly after every one of the family.

I never saw in my life such brilliant, piercing eyes as Mr. Garrick's are. In looking at him, when I have chanced to meet them, I have really not been able to bear their lustre. I remember three lines which I once heard Mrs. Pleydell repeat, (they were her own) upon Mr. Garrick, speaking of his face :

" That mouth that might Envy with passion inspire ;
Those eyes! fraught with genius, with sweetness, with fire,
And every thing else that the heart can desire—"

This sweet poetess, on the very Sunday that I am writing of, set out for the East Indies.[1]

" Archæologia " on the Barberini Vase, and began a history of Roman consular and imperial coins. Ninety-two folio engravings for this work were published after his death in 1787.

[1] In 1832 Mme. D'Arblay describes Mrs. Pleydell as having been rivalled only by Miss Linley for youthful beauty. " This lady, in taking leave of Dr. Burney," for whom she had a great regard, " presented to him a Chinese (?) painting on ivory, which she had inherited from her father," Governor Holwell, who "estimated it as a sort of treasure." It was a procession of the Great Mogul. Sir Joshua Reynolds and Sir Robert Strange said that the female heads in it were so highly finished that they might be set in rings.

June 3rd.

Alas! my poor forsaken Journal! how long have I neglected thee, faithful friend that thou hast been to me, I blush at my inconstancy; but I know not how it is, I have lost my goût for writing. I have known the time when I could enjoy nothing without relating it. Now, how many subjects of joy, how very many of sorrow have I met with of late, without the least wish of applying to my old friend for participation, or rather relief? Perhaps I am myself the only one who would not rather be amazed that a humour so particular should have lasted so long. Nevertheless, I shall not discourage the small remains of it which this night prompt me to resume my pen. My dear brother James has returned home in very good health and spirits, to mine and all his family's sincere satisfaction. As to merchandise, the few ventures he took out with him, he has brought back unchanged! Poor soul, he was never designed for trade—

My dear father has gained more honour by his book, than I dared flatter myself would have attended it. We hear daily of new readers and approvers. Mr. Mason has written him a very polite letter upon it, desiring to introduce him to Sir James Gray,[1] one of the most accomplished men of the age, who was so much pleased with my father's book, as to beg of Mr. Mason to make them acquainted.

Dr. Brookes, husband to the Mrs. Brookes who wrote "Lady Julia Mandeville" and many other books, has also written to praise it.

Mrs. Young has been on a visit to us for some days. She and her Caro Sposo . . . . . . are a very strange couple—she is grown so immoderately fat, that I believe she would at least weigh [ ] times more than her husband. I wonder he could ever marry her! They have however given over those violent disputes and quarrels with which they used to entertain their friends, not that Mrs. Young has any reason to congratulate herself upon it, quite the contrary, for the extreme violence of her overbearing temper has at length so

---

[1] Sir James Gray had been British Resident at Venice, was afterwards at Naples, and finally, Ambassador to the Court of Spain.

entirely wearied Mr. Young that he disdains any controversy with her, scarce ever contradicting her, and lives a life of calm, easy contempt.

I had the favour of a short tête-à-tête with him t'other day, mama, etc, being out or engaged. He had taken up Mr. Greville's "Characters, Maxims, and Reflections," and asked if it was written by *our* Mr. Greville. He opened it, and read aloud.[1] "There!" cried he, laughing, "that's his opinion of the sex! what do you think of that, Miss Fanny?"—"Oh! he gave the reins to his *wit* there; I am sure he has, nevertheless, a very high opinion of women." "Well! but what is there against a woman, that she yields to temptation? why, a woman who could resist all possible temptation, must be an animal out of nature! such a one never could exist." . . . . He then shook his head at me and asked me what made me say Mr. Greville had so high an opinion of women? "His conversation and his connexions. It would be very extraordinary if he had not."

"Why so, why so?"

"His wife is so very superior and amiable a woman, that——"

"That's nothing! that does not matter a straw. A sex ought not to be judged of by an individual." "But we are very apt to judge of others from those we are nearest connected with." "But man and wife can never judge fairly of each other; from the moment they are married, they are too prejudiced to know each other. The last character a man is acquainted with, is his wife's, because he is in extremes; he either loves, or hates her."—"Oh! I don't think that! I believe there are many more who neither love nor hate, than there are who do either."—"It's no such thing!" cried the impetuous creature, "you will find no such thing in life, as a medium; all is love or hatred!" I could have said, it is much oftener *indifference* than either; but I thought it would be too pointed, and dropped the argument. I recommended to him to read the characters of Mrs. Greville and Mrs. Garrick,

---

[1] Here Fanny left the space for a few lines blank in her diary, meaning to copy what Mr. Young had read, but, as in a few other cases, she never filled the blank.

which are written under the names of *Camilla* and *Flora*. He read the former in silence; when he came to the latter, he gave the involuntary preference of immediately reading aloud. Camilla he said was too celestial. He was perfectly enraptured with the description of *Flora*. . . . .[1]

The famous Philidor,[2] so much celebrated for his surprising

---

CAMILLA, [Mrs. Garrick.]

[1] From "Maxims, Characters, and Reflections," 2nd ed., 1757: "Camilla is really what writers have so often imagined; or rather she possesses a combination of delicacies, which they have seldom had minuteness of virtue and taste enough to conceive: to say she is beautiful, she is accomplished, she is generous, she is tender, is talking in general, and it is the particular I would describe. In her person she is almost tall, and almost thin; graceful, commanding, and inspiring a kind of tender respect; the tone of her voice is melodious, and she can neither look nor move without expressing something to her advantage. Possessed of almost every excellence she is unconscious of any, and thus heightens them all: she is modest and diffident of her own opinion, yet always perfectly comprehends the subject on which she gives it, and sees the question in its true light: she has neither pride, prejudice, nor precipitancy to misguide her; she is true, and therefore judges truly."

FLORA, [Mrs. Greville.]

"You see a character that you admire, and you think it perfect; do you therefore conclude that every different character is imperfect? What, will you allow a variety of beauty almost equally striking in the art of a Corregio, a Guido, a Raphael, and refuse it to the infinity of nature! How different from lovely Camilla is the beloved Flora! In Camilla, nature has displayed the beauty of exact regularity, and the elegant softness of female propriety: in Flora, she charms with a certain artless poignancy, a graceful negligence, and an uncontrolled yet blameless freedom. Flora has something original and peculiar about her a charm which is not easily defined; to know her and to love her is the same thing; but you cannot know her by description. Her person is rather touching than majestic, her features more expressive than regular, and her manner pleases rather because it is restrained by no rule, than because it is conformable to any that custom has established. Camilla puts you in mind of the most perfect music that can be composed; Flora of the wild sweetness which is sometimes produced by the irregular play of the breeze upon the Æolian harp."

[2] François André Philidor, who is still remembered as a writer on chess, as well as a great chess player, was, in the words of Dr. Burney, in 1771, a composer of music, who "drinks hard at the Italian fountain." "The French (Burney adds), are much indebted to

skill at the game of Chess, is just come to England; he brought my father a letter of recommendation from the celebrated M. Diderot.[1] He is going to have a new edition, with considerable amendments and additions, of a book upon Chess, which he wrote formerly in England. A plan of his work M. Diderot has drawn up for him; but he had got it so vilely translated, that my father had the patience, from the good-natured benevolence of his heart, to translate it for him himself. M. Philidor is a well-bred, obliging, and very sociable man; he in also a very good musician.

My father has been honoured with letters from the great Rousseau,[2] M. Diderot, and Padre Martini,[3] three as eminent men, as the age has produced, I believe, upon his book.

M. Philidor for being among the first to betray them into a toleration of Italian music, by adopting French words to it, and afterwards by imitating the Italian style in several comic operas, which have had great success."

[1] Diderot had, the year before, shown great courtesy to Dr. Burney. "He entered" (writes Burney) "so zealously into my views concerning the history of his favourite art," [of music] "that he presented me with a number of his own MSS., sufficient for a volume in folio, on the subject. These, from such a writer, I regard as invaluable. 'Here, take them,' says he, 'I know not what they contain: if any materials for your purpose, use them in the course of your work, as your own property; if not, throw them into the fire.'"

[2] In 1770, Dr. Burney says of Rousseau, whom he met in Paris: "I was so happy as to converse for a considerable time with him upon music, a subject which has received such embellishments from his pen, that the dryest parts are rendered interesting by his manner of treating them, both in the Encyclopédie, and in his Musical Dictionary. He read over my plan very attentively, and gave me his opinion of it, article by article." Elsewhere, Dr. Burney highly commends Rousseau's "Lettre sur la musique Françoise," for which Rousseau was burnt in effigy at the door of the Opera-House in Paris.

[3] Padre Martini was a Franciscan friar at Bologna, and "Maestro di Capella" in the church of his order. He was a composer of music, and author of a treatise upon it, which is often quoted by Dr. Burney with deference. He began a history of music upon a plan so vast that he did not live to finish it. Dr. Burney went to Bologna mainly to see him, and Farinelli; Martini "being regarded by all Europe as the deepest theorist" upon music. Martini had a fine library of books and MSS., in which Dr. Burney spent a great part of his time at Bologna. "Upon so short an acquaintance" (Burney writes of

I have lately spent several evenings in paying visits with mama and Miss Allen, and have been tolerably [tired of] it. I was at Ranelagh with them last week, but I had not the good fortune to see any body I wished. I went there again last Friday with my sister, my aunts, and Mr. Burney, and fortune was equally kind. However, we were very well pleased, the sense of my aunt Anne, the good nature of her sister Rebecca, the obliging disposition of Mr. Burney, and the lively, engaging sweetness of my beloved Hetty formed a party I could not but be happy with.

July 3rd.

We have had a visit from a bridegroom this afternoon. It would not be very easy to guess him—Mr. Hayes! That poor old man has suffered the severest grief from the great loss he sustained by the death of his first wife; he has never ceased to regret her, and nor ever will he. Contracted is that mind, which, from his second marriage immediately, doubts his sincerity. How could a man at his time of life, having no children or near relations, support himself alone, with the most sociable disposition in the universe? His beloved wife never could be restored to him, and he has therefore sought a companion, whose esteem and society may tranquilize the remainder of his days. For my own part, I applaud and honour every body who, having that lively and agonizing sensibility which is *tremblingly alive* to each emotion of sorrow, can so far subdue the too exquisite refinement of their feelings as to *permit* themselves to be consoled in affliction. Why should despair find entrance into the short life of man? It is praiseworthy to fly from it,—it is true philosophy as well as practical religion, says, often, my dear father, to *accomodate* ourselves, without murmuring, to our fortune.[1]

* * * * * *

Martini) "I never liked any man more; and I felt as little reserve with him after a few hours conversation, as with an old friend, or a beloved brother; it was impossible for confidence to be more cordial, especially between two persons whose pursuits were the same."

[1] Although Dr. Burney's "good and gay-hearted old friend," Mr.

I am just returned from Chesington, to which dear place Miss Allen took me. I had not been for almost five years. The country is extremely pleasant at Chesington. The house is situated on very high ground, and has only cottages about it for some miles. A sketch of our party : Mrs. Hamilton is the mistress of the house, which was her brother's, who, having lived too much at his ease, left her in such circumstances as obliged her to take boarders for her maintenance. She is a very good little old woman, hospitable and even-tempered.[1]

Hayes, lived more than twenty years after Fanny made this entry, we are told so little more of him that this seems the place to record that he left Dr. Burney his library, and made James Burney his general heir, thereby giving him the house No. 26, James Street, Buckingham Gate, wherein he entertained Charles Lamb and his compeers.—See Mr. W. C. Hazlitt's recent edition of the "Letters of Charles Lamb."

[1] Mrs. Sarah Hamilton, an ancient maiden-lady, on the death of her spendthrift brother Christopher succeeded to some property at Chesington, a chapelry in the parish of Malden, in Surrey, about eighteen miles from London, lying between Epsom and Kingston. After giving up his house at Hampton, Mr. Crisp had lived with her brother in the picturesque old house, which was built by the Hattons, and of the same date as Hampton Court. So fallen were Mr. Hamilton's fortunes, that it had lost even the name of The Hall. Mr. Crisp's kind advice helped the poor woman in her confused affairs. Half of the house, and what was left of its grounds, were let to a farmer. Mr. Crisp became Mrs. Hamilton's first boarder in the other half. He chose a suite of rooms, with a light and pleasant cabinet at the end of a corridor, which he gave up to Dr. Burney as his writing-room when he visited Chesington. This was called by Mr. Crisp "the Doctor's Conjuring Closet." Chesington (to abridge Mme. D'Arblay's account of it) was a house with nooks and corners—" quarters of staircases" leading to unused rooms ; garrets, or rather cells, in great number, and in all shapes, to fit the capricious forms of the leaded roof; windows in angles nigh the ceiling; carven cupboards and carven chimney-pieces, above blue and white tiles; "a tall canopied bed, tied up to the ceiling;" japan cabinets, with two or three hundred drawers; old pictures and tapestry presenting knights and damosels; before the windows, "straight old garden-paths," and across the leaden ridges of the roof a view of the country for sixteen miles round. Altogether an enchanting house, fit to form the fancy of the young. It is all gone; but, perhaps, in the little church there still remains the epitaph written by Dr. Burney on his beloved friend, Samuel Crisp. This church, which is of the thirteenth century, was restored in 1854. The living is in the gift of Merton College, Oxford. The name is more commonly written

Mademoiselle Rosat,—who boards with her; she is about forty, tall and elegant in person and dress, very sensible, extremely well-bred, and when in spirits, droll and humorous. But she has been very unhappy, and her misfortunes have left indelible traces on her mind; which subjects her to extreme low spirits. Yet I think her a great acquisition to Chesington. Miss Cooke,—who I believe is forty, too; but has so much good-nature and love of mirth in her, that she still appears a girl. My sister Burney,—than whom I know few prettier, more lively, or more agreeable. Miss Barsanti, who is a great favourite of my sister's, and was by her and Miss Allen invited to Chesington. She is extremely clever and entertaining, possesses amazing power of mimickry, and an uncommon share of humour. Miss Allen, and myself, and the females. Mr. Crisp, whose health is happily restored,—I think I need not give his character. Mr. Featherstone,—brother of Sir Matthew, a middle-aged gentleman, who, having broken his leg, walks upon crutches.[1] He is equally ugly and cross. Mr. Charles Burney brings up the rear.[1] I would my father did ! . . . .

Miss Barsanti has great theatrical talents; her voice is entirely lost, but from distressed circumstances her mother designs her for the stage, as she cannot be a concert or opera-singer; and very kindly my father, who, as she was his pupil, wishes to serve her, begged Mr. Crisp would hear her *spout*, while she was at Chesington. To make her acting less formidable to her, Miss Allen and myself proposed to perform with her, and accordingly we got by heart some scenes from ' *The Careless Husband,*'[2] in which she chose to be Edging,

---

Chessington. Once we read of Susan's going *towards* Chesington by coach; but there was only one " safe route across the wild common," and Dr. Burney's chaises were guided by " a clue " given to him, but concealed from others, by Mr. Crisp. Maria Allen, writing in 1773 of her journey from Tetsworth to Oxford, tells Fanny that the roads were more dreadful than can be conceived—literally worse and more dangerous than Hook Lane, or the Common leading to Chesington, in the winter.

[1] The Northumbrian name of Featherstonehaugh is commonly so shortened by its owners, and by others, in speech, but not in writing.

[2] A Comedy, by Colley Cibber, actor, dramatist, and Poet Laureate.

myself Lady Easy, and Miss Allen Sir Charles. That droll girl has so very great a love of sport and mirth, that there is nothing she will not do to contribute to it. We had no sooner fixed upon this scheme, than we were perplexed about the dressing Sir Charles. We all agreed that it would be ridiculous for that gallant man to appear in petticoats, and Maria had no idea of *spoiling sport;* she only determined not to exhibit before Mr. Featherstone; as to Mr. Crisp, as he was half author of the project, we knew it would be in vain to attempt excluding him, and Mr. Burney could not be avoided; besides, his cloathes she intended to borrow; but unluckily, we found upon enquiry, he had no wardrobe with him, the cloaths he wore were all his stock: this quite disconcerted us. Mr. Crisp was so tall and large, it was impossible Allen could wear any thing of his. We were long in great perplexity upon this account; but being unwilling to give up the frolic, she at length, though very mad at it, resolved upon the only expedient left,—to borrow cloathes of Mr. Featherstone. I never met a character so little damped by difficulties as her's; indeed, she seldom sees any, and, when she cannot help it, always surmounts them.

To ask this of him, made his being one of the audience inevitable; but it was the last resource. Accordingly, Allen and Barsanti watched one morning for his coming into the gallery upstairs, from which all the bed-chambers lead, and addressed themselves to him very gravely, to ask the favour of him to lend them a suite of cloathes. The man laughed monstrously, and assumed no small consequence, on their begging him to keep the affair secret, as they intended to surprise the company; for they were obliged to explain the motives of the request. This seemed something like confidence, and flattered him into better temper than we ever saw him in before. He led them to his ward-robe, and begged Allen to choose to her fancy. She fixed upon a suite of dark blue, uncut velvet. I was in a closet at the end of the gallery, not able to compose my countenance sufficiently to join them, till a loud laugh raised my curiosity. I found she had just been begging the favour of a wig; and he produced a most beautiful tie, which he told her his man should dress for her. She then asked for stock, shoes, buckles, ruffles, and stockings, and all with great gravity, assisted by Barsanti, who reminded her of so many things, I thought she would never have been satisfied. Mr. Featherstone enjoyed it prodigiously, sniggering and joking, and resting upon his crutches to laugh. For my own part, the torrent of their ridiculous requests made me every minute, march out of the room to laugh more freely. . . . . We settled Saturday evening for our performance. Meanwhile, Mr. Featherstone was observed, as he hobbled up and down the garden, to continually burst into horse-laughs, from the diversion of his own thoughts.

On Saturday morning, rehearsing our parts, we found them so short that we wished to add another scene; and, as there is a good deal of drollery in the quarelling scene between Sir Charles Easy and Lady Graveairs, we fixed upon that, Miss Allen to continue as Sir Charles, and Barsanti to change her cap or so, and appear as Lady Graveairs. . . . . While they studdied their parts, Kitty Cooke and myself, as we frequently did, walked out, visiting all the cottages within a mile of Chesington. Upon our return to dinner, Barsanti told us she found the *new scene* too long to get in time.

Miss Allen and I, being both sorry, after some deliberation, agreed to perform it ourselves, and accordingly we, after dinner, hurried up-stairs, and made all possible expedition in getting our parts, resolving not to act till after supper. While we were studdying ourselves with great diligence, Miss Barsanti ran upstairs, and told us that Mr. Crisp had informed all the company of our intention, and that they were very eager for our performance, and declared they would never forgive us, if we disappointed them. This flurried me violently, insomuch that my memory failed me, and I forgot my old part, without seeming to learn my new one. I can, in general, get by heart with the utmost facility; but I was really so much fidgetted, that my head seemed to turn round, and I scarse knew what I was about. They, too, were flurried; but my excessive worry seemed to lessen their's. I must own it was quite ridiculous; but I could not command myself, and would fain have been off . . . .; but my repentance came too late.

We three retired after supper, and I could not forbear being highly diverted at seeing Allen dress herself in Mr. Featherstone's clothes. They fitted her horribly; the back preposterously broad; the sleeves too wide; the cuffs hiding all her hand; yet the coat hardly long enough; neither was the wig large enough to hide her hair; and, in short, she appeared the most dapper, ill-shaped, ridiculous figure I ever saw; yet her face looked remarkably well. . . . .

My repentance every moment increased; but in vain; they insisted upon no further delay; and accordingly we descended. . . . . As we came down, the servants were all in the hall; and the first object that struck us, was Mr. Featherstone's man, staring in speechless astonishment at the young figure in his old master's clothes.

Unfortunately for me, I was to appear first, and alone. I was pushed on; they clapped violently. I was fool enough to run off quite overset, and unable to speak. I was really in an agony of fear and shame! and, when at last Allen and Barsanti persuaded me to go on again, the former in the lively warmth of her temper called to the audience *not to clap again; for it was very impertinent.* I had lost all power of speaking steadily, and almost of being understood; and as to action, I had not the presence of mind to attempt it. Surely only Mr. Crisp could excite such extreme terror! My soliloquy at length over, *Edging* entered with great spirit, and spoke very well. I was almost breathless the whole scene; and oh! how glad when it was over! Sir Charles's appearance raised outrageous mirth. She required all her resolution to stand it. Hetty was almost in convulsions. Mr. Crisp hollowed. Mr. Featherstone absolutely *wept* with excessive laughing; and even Mamselle Rosat leaned her elbows on her lap, and could not support herself upright. What rendered her appearance more ridiculous was that, being wholly unused to acting, she forgot her audience, and acted as often with her back to them as her face; and her back was really quite too absurd, the full breadth of her height!

I had soon after to make my appearance as Lady Graveairs. To be sure, I was in proper spirits for the part; however, a few exceptionable speeches I had insisted on omitting, and I was greatly recovered, compared to my former appearance. Barsanti, at a sudden thought, went on and made an apology, "that the *gentlewoman* who was to have performed Lady Graveairs, being taken ill, her place was to be supplied by the performer of Lady Easy. To be sure it was rather in the barn style.

I acquitted myself with rather a better grace now, and we were *much applauded*. Not having performers sufficient for a regular plan, we finished with such a short, unsatisfactory scene, that they all called out for *more*. Allen, intending to carry the affair off with *a joke*, took Barsanti and me each by the hand; and led us on; but whether from shame or what I know not, when *she* had bowed and *we* had curtsied, she was wholly at a loss, and could not think of a word to say. So, after keeping the company in a few minutes' suspense, "In short," cried she, "you know the rest," and ran off.

It is easy to suppose laughs were not spared for this ridiculous attempt.

We all left Chesington with regret; it is a place of peace, ease, freedom, and cheerfulness, and all its inhabitants are good humoured and obliging, and my dear Mr. Crisp alone would make it, to us, a Paradise.

* * * * * *

[There is no date or post-mark to a letter which is numbered 8, and addressed by Maria Allen, from Lynn, "to Miss Fan and Suk—." Sir Richard Bettenson had, as has been said, sent his ward to travel, about the end of January in this year, making him promise to remain abroad for two years. Maria writes: "Well girls—such a piece of news—if it does but astonish you equal to what it did me in hearing it you won't have recovered your surprise by the time I see you again—Rishton—my—yes the very identical Martin—Folkes—Lucious *(sic)* —etc.—Rishton is come over—and now in England—I can't write any more I must leave you to get over your exclamations and then proceed.——I must skip over all trumpery Lynn occurrences when such a subject as this demands my pen.—Well my journey into Norfolk has more than answer'd all my expence and trouble in hearing this intelligence." But after all, Maria knows no more than "*Rishton is in England!*" "Old Squire Rolfe."[1] had "on Friday (the day we came

---

[1] A Norfolk gentleman, who had married a first cousin of Mr. Rishton's mother.

home from Chessington) been at dinner at his son's in Welbeck Street —when the door open'd and in came [Mr. Rishton]." The Rolfes were "really terrify'd at seeing him as all the company concluded he was then at Thoulouse—he had never mentioned his returning, or even hinted at it—and they all sat in silent astonishment," for he *had* mentioned in his last letter liking the place extremely. Martin was looking very well—When asked what could have brought him over in such a hurry? "he smiled, but said nothing to the question." He had gone to Croome to see Mrs. Jessey "on Sunday, the day Dr. Hawkesworth dined with us." This is all that Maria can "pick up," but it is thought that he is in London. His letters are directed to the St. James's Coffee-house. He has come back at the end of five months; it cannot be with his uncle's consent. "I neither eat drink nor sleep for thinking of it—Whether I am glad or sorry, I shall leave for another opportunity,—or your own clever heads to find out." Maria wishes Susy, who (she knows) is *rich*, would pay her milliner's bill for her; and "you, Fanny, woud enquire what is the newest Parisian cut for the sleeve of a riding-habit."[1] Little Charlotte is with her at

---

[1] This does not *always*, or even *often*, mean a habit for riding on horseback. *That* was more commonly called a riding-*skirt*. The distinction between the two is shown in a diary kept by Mary Hamilton, (a niece of the well-known Sir William), in 1783, while paying a very quiet visit to the Dowager-Duchess of Portland at Bulstrode. "Dec. 3rd.—Got up a little after 8, had my hair dress'd for y⁰ day, though I put on as usual for y⁰ morning a riding-habit." After breakfast, she rode on horseback. On coming in, she writes, "I changed my riding-skirt, and put on my habit again." She appears to have dined in her habit. In 1782, Fanny went with the Thrales to the last ball of the season at Tunbridge-Wells. She says that some of the ladies were in riding-habits, and they made admirable *men*. "'Tis *tonnish* to be so much undressed at the last ball." Lady Eleanor Butler and Miss Ponsonby, ("the ladies of Llangollen,") appear in their portraits as walking, and sitting at dessert, in their riding-habits. The cut of their habits to the waist is that of men's clothes,—and altogether they look like respectable, well-beneficed clergymen. In Miss Austin's "Emma," which was published in 1816, Mr. Dixon saves the life of Jane Fairfax at a Weymouth water-party, when, "by the sudden whirling round of something or other amongst the sails, she would have been dashed into the sea at once, and was all but gone, if he had not, with the greatest presence of mind, caught hold of her habit." [Miss Bates *loquitur*.] In his second set of "Reminiscences," Mr. T. Mozley says, "'till, I should say, 1835, it was a very ordinary thing to meet with ladies who, to save the trouble and cost of following the fashion, never wore anything but a closely-fitting habit. It required a good figure and bearing." Mr. Mozley adds that it was "the usual travelling-dress for ladies," that is, even for ladies who did not wear it daily. We think

Lynn, but "the Governor"[1] is (happily for Maria) in London. In a postscript—" I *don't* desire my love to Hetty—'tho you may give it to her husband."]

* * * * * *

Queen Square, August.

Dr. Hawkesworth has this moment left us; he called on my father, who with mama is, at present, at Mrs. Allen's in Lynn; but he did us the favour to sit here some minutes nevertheless, only Susan and myself at home. .... The admiration I have of his works, has created great esteem for their author; though he is too precise to be really agreeable, that is, to be natural, like Mr. Crisp and my dear father. ....

But now I speak of authors, let me pay the small tribute of regret and concern due to the memory of poor Mr. Smart, who died lately in the King's Bench Prison; a man by nature endowed with talents, wit, and vivacity, in an eminent degree; and whose unhappy loss of his senses was a public as well as private misfortune. I never knew him in his glory, but ever respected him in his *decline,* from the fine proofs he had left of his better day, and from the account I have heard of his youth from my father, who was then his intimate companion; as, of late years, he has been his most active and generous friend, having raised a kind of fund for his relief, though he was ever in distress. His intellects, so cruelly impaired, I

---

that Mr. Mozley brings the custom down rather too late, and that it can only have continued in very out-of-the-way places as a daily dress. It is so obsolete that we have known ladies speak of their mothers, or grandmothers, being married in their riding-habits, as if it had been some exceptional, and distinguished thing to have done, of a rather "fast" nature, instead of a token of privacy, and of desire to spare expense. It was, in fact, being married in the gown in which you meant to travel, made of some solid material, with no furbelows, *(falbalas.)*

[1] Slang is of all centuries. Maria calls her mother "the Governor"; and Charlotte (with whom her stepmother was not in favour) has divers ways of writing of her, generally implying that Mrs. Burney the second was *masterful.* She was an Allen who had married an Allen, so that if the family temper was wilful and warm, Maria had a double share of it by inheritance.

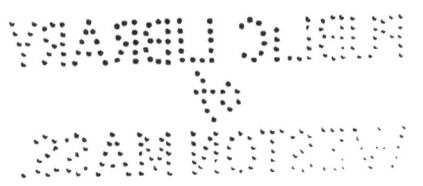

doubt not, affected his whole conduct. In a letter he sent my father not long before his death, to ask his assistance for a fellow sufferer and good offices for him in that charity over which he presides, he made use of an expression which pleased me much, "that he had himself assisted him, according to his *willing poverty*."[1]

*　*　*　*　*　*

Mr. Gray, too, the justly and greatly celebrated Gray is dead! How many centuries had he been spared, if Death had been as kind to him, as Fame will be to his works![2]

---

[1] In another letter to Dr. Burney poor Smart wrote, " I bless God for your good-nature, which please *take as a receipt.*"

Christopher Smart had, by collateral descent, the blood of Bernard Gilpin, "the Apostle of the North;" and, by direct descent, that of Peter Smart, a "peevish, froward and furious" puritan divine, and a writer of Latin and English libels in prose and verse. Peter was head-master of Durham Grammar School in 1598, and afterwards, a prebendary of the Cathedral of Durham, in which he preached an outrageous sermon in 1628, levelled against his brethren in that Cathedral, and above all against the learned and loyal John Cosin, afterwards one of the most munificent of Bishops. Smart also wrote and published 1,490 Latin verses mainly against Cosin. He was very severely punished for his sermon, but cropped up again during the rebellion, and appeared against Laud on his trial. His violence of language leads to a strong opinion that he was far from sane. Poor Christopher was born in Kent, but taught at Durham Grammar School, and sent to Cambridge by a Durham nobleman. He gained a fellowship at Pembroke College, which he resigned upon marrying the stepdaughter of Newbery, the publisher and bookseller, with whom he wrote "The Old Woman's Magazine." Dr. Burney, who had known Smart from the early days of his own apprenticeship to Dr. Arne, introduced Smart to Newbery, and Smart made the "Rambler" known to Burney while he was organist in unlettered Lynn. If Smart inherited his forefather Peter's heat of brain, his piety was much more amiable, and all were kind to poor Christopher. Johnson wrote to help him; in 1759, Garrick not only gave a play for his benefit, but finished his little piece, "The Guardian," in the utmost haste that it might be acted on that night. The "benefit" brought Smart a good sum of money. One of Smart's two daughters, Mrs. Le Noir, wrote a book called "Village Manners," which she dedicated to Dr. Burney.

[2] Gray died July 30, 1771.

August.

I am now devoting all my leisure to the study of Italian. O! what a language of sweetness and harmony!

Dr. King has been with me all this afternoon, amusing himself with spouting Shakespeare, Pope, and others. Though I say amusing himself I must, however, own that it was the only way he had any chance of amusing me; but his visit was unconscionably long, and as I happened to be alone, I had the whole weight of it. For the first time, however, I did not regret Miss Allen's absence, for she sees the ridiculous part of this man's character in so strong a light, that she cannot forbear showing that she despises him every moment. The strongest trait of her own character is sincerity, one of the most noble of virtues, and perhaps, without any exception, the most uncommon. But, if it is possible, she is too sincere: she pays too little regard to the world; and indulges herself with too much freedom of raillery and pride of disdain towards those whose vices and follies offend her. Were this a *general* rule of conduct what real benefit might it bring to society; but being *particular* it only hurts and provokes individuals. But yet I am unjust to my own opinion in censuring the first who shall venture, in a good cause, to break through the confinement of custom, and at least show the way to a new and open path. I mean but to blame severity to *harmless* folly, which claims pity and not scorn, though I cannot but acknowledge it to be infinitely tiresome, and for any length of time even almost disgustful.

Dr. King fancies himself a genius for the Theatre; he had the weakness to pretend to show me how Garrick performed a scene of Macbeth! "I generally," said he, "say to myself how *I* should perform such and such a part, before I see it; and when Garrick is on the stage, how *I* should speak such or such a speech; and I am generally so happy to find we agree; but the scene where he fancies he sees the dagger in 'Macbeth,' he surprised me in; he has a stroke in that quite new; *I* had never thought of it; if you will stand here, I will show you." Stand I did, as well as I could for laughter. Could anything be more absurd? He with his clumsy arms and vacant eyes imitate Mr. Garrick!

* * * * * *

We live very peaceably and quietly; I rise very early,—5, 6, or 7, my latest hour. I have just finished Middleton's History of Cicero,[1] which I read immediately after Hooke's Roman History. It is a delightful book; the style is manly and elegant; and, though he may be too partial to Cicero, the fine writings he occasionally translates of that great man, authorize and excuse his partiality.

Many of my father's Italian friends, and of the English ones he made in Italy, have been here lately; and among them . . . . Signor Martinelli. That original genius has been intimate in our family, from my infancy. He is the author of the *Lettere familiare e critiche,* and is now writing a history of our country in Italian. He has a most uncommon flow of wit, and with it the utmost bitterness of satire and raillery of ill nature. His vanity and self-conceit exceed every persons I ever saw; and, far from endeavouring to conceal this weakness, he glories in it, and thinks he but does himself justice in esteeming himself the head of whatever company he is in, and openly manifesting that he does so. He is not satisfied with priding himself that he speaks to the Great with *sincerity,* he piques himself upon treating them with *rudeness.* He was boasting to this effect in his broken English, and said—"I hear the nobleman talk—I give him great attention—I make him low bow—and I say, My Lord! you are a very great man,—but for all that,—a blockhead!"
. . . . He is an admirable *story-teller,* if he could forbear making himself the hero of all his tales; but the every purport of his speaking is, to acquaint the company with his consequence.[2]

---

[1] The title of this book is "History of the Life of M. Tullius Cicero," 1741.
[2] "On Thursday, April 15, 1773, I " [Boswell] " dined with him " [Johnson] " and Dr. Goldsmith at General Paoli's. We found here Signor Martinelli, of Florence, author of a History of England in Italian, printed at London."

[MARIA ALLEN to FANNY and SUSAN BURNEY.]

Dear Toads,

I have kept an exact Journal ever since I have been out—which is all addressed to the Two Divinities of Queen Square—but I have had no opportunity of remitting it to you, since I left home but propose myself the pleasure of reading it with a proper emphasis and delivery when we meet to browse over a pot of Castalian Porter and a Welsh Rabbit either in Charles Street[1] or Queen Square so I shall, keep you in perfect suspence till that time—which will Be next Saturday sen'night—pray let the morning be usher'd in with every public manifestation of Joy—. . . I am at present as happy as I can be deprived of Two of the greatest Blessings in life your company and the heart of [Rishton], tho' I am not quite certain of the latter—

To rouse your Curiosity, I have seen him—and danced Next Couple to him a whole Evening. I was at Lynn two or three times during which time my Mother received a letter from Madame Griffodière who informed her that she had received a letter from her Mother at Geneva who had not room for any more in her family nor coud not procure me Lodgings near her so that my boarding with her was renderd impracticable—which really distress'd me very much as I am determined at all events to spend the winter Abroad.[2]

[Maria then fears she shall "miss of travelling with Mrs. Combe," but has "another string to her Bow," which Fanny will find explained in her Journal.]

My Grandmother will not hear of my Mother's going

---

[1] Hetty's house.

[2] This letter is too long to be given in full; it is also quite disjointed. In another place in it Maria speaks of what would be her "terrible disappointment" should she not go to Geneva, "after I have been plagued so much already, . . . and now have leave to go by myself too, and have spoke of it publickly to every one that I met," but that "even setting out at an uncertainty, although very disagreeable" [would] "be better than what my future prospects are in England."

abroad, and I believe has absolutely forbid her—and I fancy she [my mother] will stay at Lynn some months this winter.

[After a commission to Hetty, "Allen" runs on thus :—]

You, Mrs. Fanny, I desire to dress neatly and properly—without a hole in either Apron or Ruffles—and go to Madame Griffodières in Wells Street—and ask if she has received any letter. . . . . I desire you all to be at home on Saturday morning to receive me—tho' as you are very Poor, I believe I shall dine with Hetty—so desire that I may have a boil'd *Orlean plomb* pudding for my dinner—that is for my own private eating—and some delicate toasted cheese for my supper—and let my bed be well aired. Mind what I say and dont be rude and neglect your visitor—or else I shall go to Chesington on Sunday—

My love to Jem—I am sorry to hear that he has been Ill—I hope my presence will revive him—pray get the skittle ground marked out—and every thing in order—

I am yours
Allen.

[This letter is addressed to—
"Miss Burney,
"Queen's Square,
"Frank John (*sic*)   "Bloomsbury,
"Turner.   "London."

It has a Thetford stamp, without any date, and a London post-mark of 7 S.E. It is endorsed (perhaps by Mme. D'Arblay) "Warham, 1771," and numbered No. 10, erroneously, as the letter numbered 9 was dated by Maria herself "Novembre le 21, 1771."]

* * * * * *

September 13th.

I had the pleasure to meet Dr. Armstrong yesterday; he is an amazing old man; I believe he is seventy, and he yet retains spirits and wit to a great degree; his memory is rather impaired, but his health seems perfect, and he says by *starts* most excellent things. The general of people at his time of life are confined by infirmities; but he walks out perpetually and always unattended; his conversation is, indeed, very unequal; but he has sallies of humour that are delightful. He has lately made a short tour of Italy; but was past the age of enjoying foreign countries or manners.[1]

* * * * * *

My father spent a few days lately at Hinchinbroke at Lord Sandwich's, to meet, Mr. Banks, Captain Cooke,[2] and Dr. Solander, who have just made the voyage round the world, and are going speedily to make another.[3] My father,

---

[1] Dr. Armstrong published in this year (1771) "A Short Ramble through France and Italy." He travelled with Fuseli in Italy. As is almost usual with travellers, they quarrelled, and parted at Genoa. The quarrel was about the right way to pronounce some English word, of which Fuseli said he, a Swiss, was quite as good a judge as a *Scotchman* could be. Their disagreement was made up when Dr. Armstrong was dying. Fuseli, by the advice of a friend, called upon him. The Doctor could not resist a sarcasm: "So you have come back?" FUSELI: "Yes, I have come home." ARMSTRONG: "Home? You mean to London?—'the needy villain's gen'ral home.' However, I *thank* you for your visit. I am glad to see you again." If not a Jacobite, he, at any rate, "lived near the [White] Rose." He was a cousin of Lady Strange, and made a visit to her brother and his cousin, Andrew Lumsden (who had been secretary to the Stewart Princes), in Paris, on his return from Italy. In 1773 he published "Medical Essays." He lived until 1779.

[2] Cook's first voyage round the world (July, 1768, to July, 1771) was mainly undertaken by the Government at the instance of the Royal Society, that the transit of Venus over the disc of the sun might be competently observed. Another object was to make discoveries in the South Pacific Ocean, and explore New Zealand. Mr. Banks gained permission to sail with Cook, and took with him Daniel Charles Solander, M.D., LL.D., a Swede, who had been a pupil of Linnæus, and brought letters of introduction from him to England. He got an appointment as Under Librarian at the British Museum, which was then in its early days. John Montagu, fourth Earl of Sandwich, thrice First Lord of the Admiralty, was one of Dr. Burney's musical patrons, and, in 1772, as the Doctor tells with gratitude, "was pleased to honour me with recommendatory letters, in his own hand, to every English nobleman and gentleman who resided in a public character in the several cities through which I passed" [on the German tour].

[3] Mr. (afterwards Sir Joseph) Banks, P.R.S., was a Lincolnshire landowner. On leaving Oxford in 1763 he visited the coasts of Newfoundland and Labrador. "That wild man, Banks, who is poaching

through his Lordship's means, made interest for James to go with them, and we have reason to hope he will have a prosperous and agreeable voyage.

* * * * * *

My father has had a happy opportunity of extremely obliging Dr. Hawkesworth. During his stay in Norfolk, he waited upon Lord Orford,[1] who has always been particularly friendly to him. He there, among others, met with Lord Sandwich. His Lordship was speaking of the late voyage round the world and mentioned his having the papers of it

---

in every ocean for the fry of little islands that escaped the drag-net of Spain," so sneers Horace Walpole at the rich amateur of science. Banks and Solander had had enough of the hardships of the first voyage. The Admiralty hired Dr. Förster and his son, a couple of Germans, in their place at ten days' notice. Banks had paid his expenses and those of his friend. Banks and Solander, instead of going again to the South Seas, went upon what Mrs. Delany calls a "summer's tour," namely, a cruise, in which she assures her niece they "made the discovery of an island on the Western coast of Scotland called Staffa," . . . with "a cave of a very particular form." . . . " From thence they went to Iceland, which is 65 degrees north latitude, not far from Greenland: there *they met with a mountain* called Hecla, which had been a volcano—and ' boyled ' a partridge in seven minutes ' in a fountain called Geyser.'" We read of Banks in Mme. D'Arblay's later journals and memoirs as entertaining her father and brother James at his London parties—or, as Horace Walpole called them, his " Saturnalia." As Cook put his papers, so Banks gave his journals of the first voyage in the " Endeavour " into Hawkesworth's hands, and, at the request of Banks, James Burney helped in compiling the narrative of the last, when the pen had dropped from Hawkesworth and from Cook.

As for Dr. Solander, he was given the charge of the Natural History department in the British Museum, but Fanny never met him until about 1780, when she found him " very sociable, full of talk, information, and entertainment. My father has very exactly named him, in calling him a philosophical gossip." This was at Mr. Thrale's house in the Borough, just as the news of the death of Cook had reached England.

[1] This was Horace Walpole's " mad nephew," of whom a kinder account is given in the "Memoirs" of Dr. Burney, than in the letters of his uncle.

in his possession; for he is First Lord of the Admiralty; and said that they were not arranged, but mere rough draughts, and that he should be much obliged to any one who could recommend a proper person to *write the Voyage*. My father directly named Dr. Hawkesworth, and his Lordship did him the honour to accept his recommendation. The Doctor waited upon Lord Sandwich, and they both returned my father particular thanks for their meeting.[1] Yet I cannot but be amazed, that a man of Lord Sandwich's power, &c., should be so ignorant of men of learning and merit, as to apply to an almost stranger for a recommendation. Pity! pity! that those should be most sensible of talents, who cannot reward worth!

* * * * * *

My father is at present most diligently studying German. He has an unquenchable thirst for knowledge; and would, if he had time, I believe, be the first linguist in England.

---

[1] This will be found to have been a fatal kindness to poor Hawkesworth. The six or seven thousand pounds paid him for his labour, and the notice taken of him at the Admiralty, stirred up all the envious scribblers to run him down. Even Garrick quarrelled with him, because he did not give Becket, the bookseller, the option of publishing his book. Rumour had made so much of it that Mrs. Delany tells her niece it was to be in at least fourteen volumes folio! When Hawkesworth touched mathematics or astronomy Cambridge men pointed out his blunders; others blamed his morality; and, to crown all, Cook did not support the accuracy of the narrative. Cook excused his own part in the account of his second voyage as being "the production of a man who has not had the advantage of much school-education, but who has been constantly at sea from his youth; and though, with the assistance of a few good friends, he has passed through all the stations belonging to a seaman, from an apprentice-boy in the coal trade to a post-captain in the Royal Navy, he has had no opportunity of cultivating letters. After this account of myself, the public must not expect from me *the elegance of a fine writer*, or *the plausibility of a professed bookmaker*, but will, I hope, consider me as a plain man, zealously exerting himself in the service of his country, and determined to give the best account he is able of his proceedings."

Nov. 2.

* * * * * *

We have had a charming paquet from Miss Allen, from Paris, containing an ample Journal of her affairs, ever since she left us, and we have since heard that she is arrived at Geneva.

[On the 21st of November, 1771, Maria was inditing a piteous and dismal letter to Fanny from Geneva, which we curtail, but give, as nearly as we can, in her own words. She conjures Fanny, by their long friendship and the love Fanny bore her, to write by the first courier, and say why she had not a line from England, although she had wrote to her mother from every town where she had stopped. She had sailed from Brighthelmstone, whence she wrote, as also from Dieppe, Rouenne (*sic*), Paris, and Lyons. She was now at Geneva, fretting away her time in forming the most cruel conjectures, and, besides her uncertainty as to whether her friends were in health, *very certain* that she had not a penny of money, and was in debt; though she *denied herself every necessary*. Only her beloved Esther had written to her, but as the letter was written only four days after she left England they might all be dead since then, and she near 700 miles away; indeed, it was too unkind, and she could not help thinking so. She had sent off a large pacquet of her journal from Paris, which Fanny and Susan must have received before now, but did not think worth answering.

She had been obliged to borrow five guineas from the best of friends, Mme. Porte, "a most sweet woman," because she had spent all the money she had for her journey—owing to the advice of "everybody" to provide herself with cloaths at Paris and Lyons as they were so much cheaper and better there. After taking so much good advice, Maria found herself without a single penny on arriving at Geneva. Mme. Porte had offered to lend her money, but shame withheld her for some days from borrowing, until necessity compelled her to write a little note. [N.B.—Mme. Porte seems to have known her in England, or elsewhere, previously.] Then Maria fires, and desires to know from Fanny if her lack of money be owing to any *impertinance* (*sic*) on the part of her uncles Allen (of Lynn)? She had written to inform them that she was leaving England—had mama sent her letters? Were they so enraged at her quitting England that they refused sending her any supplies? If so, she would take measures accordingly, and either take up money, which she could have very easily, as she should soon be of age, or sell her diamonds, which she was very glad she had with her. After this spirited burst, which is not unworthy of a young *heir*, Maria proceeds to new plans for spending money. She writes of music lessons which she may take when her "tiney forte" comes and desires Fanny to go to Griffardière's,[1] and wear them both out to look for some conveyance for her instrument and music—and Fanny is to send her "*fordyce's*" *sermons* with it. Then the penniless one proposes that Hetty shall buy her any trifles which she wants from England, keeping an account of their cost, and she repay Hetty by sending anything which Hetty may fancy from Geneva, at once, or else bringing it on her return. "My first commission is a very elegant tea cadet, very like that I bought my mother, and at the same shop, which is in Piccadilly—on the same side as the haymarket—7 or eight doors farther you will see all sorts of things of inlaid work stand out at the window, buy me a little black ebony inkstand with silver plaited tops to the bottles—and a handle like one to a basket of the same metal—They were new last winter, and then cost 18s. and the cadet not more than 12s. These two things and a very pretty naked wax doll with blue eyes, the half crown sort—I fancy at the wax-work in fleet street will be the place—Susey knows the size—Bessy and Charlotte had two ugly ones bought at the mart—and do it up that it will not be broke with cotton all over it and 100 papers. I fancy they will all come in the piano forte case." If Hetty does not want things from Geneva, Maria will send her "a bill on somebody in London," as soon as she receives any money—If Fanny and Susey do not answer this letter immediately upon receiving it (she has *exactly* calculated the time when

---

[1] Maria Allen never spelt this name correctly. She always puts an *r* into the name, and often an *o*; it is also to be found elsewhere as Gueyffardière and Gaiffardière. Fanny merely copied her errors. In her Court days Fanny was to see much more than she liked either of this man, or of some very close kinsman of his, whom she wrote of as "Mr. Turbulent." He had become French "teacher to the elder princesses, and occasionally, to the Queen herself," and was at first sight (in 1786) described by her as "well-bred and sensible." Fanny does not seem to have recognized him until he told her that he and his wife had been acquainted with Maria Allen at Geneva; and (adds Fanny to Susan) "I have some idea that both you and I once saw him. Do you remember our hearing a younger sister of his wife sing a fine French air, with all true French cadenzas?" When Croker, in 1842, abused the Diaries of Mme. D'Arblay, just as he had done the Memoirs of her father about ten years before, he blamed their editor for publishing Fanny's scenes with "Mr. Turbulent," but himself first printed his true name, in the "Quarterly Review." Macaulay describes him as "a half-witted French Protestant minister, who talked oddly about conjugal infidelity." Croker says that he was the Rev. Charles de Guiffardière (called Giffardière), prebendary of Salisbury, vicar of Newington, and rector of Berkhampstead. If so, he got on remarkably well, if he be the same whom we find here, in Wells Street as a kind of agent for his wife's mother's boarding-house at Geneva; who is, with his wife, to be teased into hurrying off Maria Allen's piano, wax dolls, and tea "cadets" to Geneva.

they will do so) they shall have neither journal nor letter more during her stay at Geneva, were it to last three years. As it did not last quite six calendar months from the date of this letter, one wonders whether the pianoforte went wandering to Geneva, laden with presents for the natives. Maria sends a chill duty to mama, and "let her know all my inquietudes"; but to Dr. Burney Fanny is "not to forget my duty and gratitude, and everything your own heart would dictate to your dear father." Molly Stancliffe, (her maid and *sub-confidante*) stands by Maria as she writes, "with her hair dress'd" [turned up over a cushion, like a lady's] "and powder'd, in a very elegant dishabille à la Genevoise"; natheless she disdains not to ask to be "remembered" to Dr. Burney's Betty. This letter is addressed by Maria, in her best writing, to "Miss Fanny Burney, at Dr. Burney's, Queen Square, Bloomsbury, London, *Angleterre*," and bears the stamp of "Geneve," with "pp" (for *par Paris*), an English post-mark of $\frac{De}{2}$ and a London "five o'clock" mark.]

* * * * * *

Nov. 4.

Returning this morning from Madame Griffardières, I went through Poland Street, a place I cannot but love, from remembring (*sic*) the happiness I have known there. I passed with great regret by Mrs. Pringle's windows, but looking at the door saw the name of [Rishman?] on it. I have too much regard for Mrs. Pringle to be indifferent to what is become of her. A woman was at the door. I asked her if she knew where Mrs. Pringle was gone? She did not, but my curiosity was excited, and I waited till a servant came to open the door. I made the same question. Without answering, the servant went and rapt at the parlour door. I was in some confusion, lest Mrs Pringle might be there, and pondered upon what possible excuse I could make for my long absence, and even felt a sort of guilt in having

* * * * * *

Nov. 6.

I have just heard by chance that Mrs. Pringle is gone to the East Indies. O that I had known her intention! Nothing should have prevented my seeing her if I had had the least idea of her quitting England. I imagine she is gone to her son Andrew. . . . . I would often have given the world to have met her *by chance*, though I had not dared to *seek* her. . . . . And thus I suppose will close for ever all acquaintance with this agreeable woman and our family. On my side how unwillingly! for I cannot join in the bad opinion mama and Mr. Crisp have so strangely, so causelessly conceived of her. Her kindness and friendship to *us* she could have no interest in, it would be ingratitude not to regard her for [it]. Independent of these more serious reasons for regret at her departure, I must also own that since we have droped her acquaintance, we have never made any half so lively and agreeable. But what principally concerns me, is that she has left the kingdom with an idea of our ingratitude. Dear, wise, and good Mr. Crisp has surely been too severe in his judgment. What a misfortune I should deem it to think so ill of mankind as he, the wisest of his race, tries to make me think!

My dear Susette has been very ill, but, thank God, is recovered. She is the most engaging creature living, and has a fund of sense and feeling almost incomparable.

November.

Susette and myself are extremely engaged at present in studying a book lately published under M. Diderot's direction, which he sent to papa, upon Music. It promises to teach us Harmony and the Theory of Music. M. Diderot's daughter was taught by the method made use of in it.[1] . . . . I am reading—I blush to say for the first time,—Pope's Works. He is a darling pet of our family. It is with exquisite delight I make myself acquainted with him; and, in serious truth, I am glad he is new to me.

I have before mentioned that Miss Barsanti had intentions to go on the stage. According to them, she applied to my father to speak to Mr. Colman concerning her. My father,

---

[1] In his first musical tour Dr. Burney makes high mention of the well-known daughter of Diderot as being a good musician.

to oblige her, consented, though unwittingly, having a superiour regard for Mr. Garrick, but Drury Lane Theatre has actresses already in Barsanti's style. Mr. Colman professed great regard for my father's recommendation, but deferred till another time settling when to see her.

December 8th.

Mr. and Mrs. Young have been in town a few days. They are in a situation that quite afflicts me, how brought on I know not, but I fear by extravagance. Be that as it may, they are at present reduced to a most distressful state. They seem to have almost ruined themselves, and to be quite ignorant in what manner to retrieve their affairs. Mr. Young, whose study and dependence is agriculture, has half undone himself by *experiments*. His writings upon this subject have been amazingly well received by the public, and in his tours through England he has been caressed and assisted almost universally. Indeed his conversation and appearance must ever secure him welcome and admiration. But, of late, some of his *facts* have been disputed, and though I believe it to be only by envious and malignant people, yet reports of that kind are fatal to an author, whose sole credit must subsist on his veracity. In short, by slow but sure degrees, his fame has been sported with, and his fortune destroyed. I grieve for him inexpressibly; he truly merits a better fate. Too successful in his early life, he expected a constancy in fortune, that has cruelly disappointed him. His children happily have their mother's jointure settled upon them. He has some thoughts of going abroad; but his wife is averse to it. He is an enterprising genius, and I sincerely hope will be able to struggle effectually with his bad fortune; but how I know not.

They went with us one night to Mr. Colman's box; but poor Mr. Young has only forced spirits. Those he does indeed exert in an uncommon manner. She, too, supports herself with more resolution and better temper than I thought her equal to.

* * * * * *

But now that I am in a scribbling vein, I cannot forbear

mentioning that the reading of Pope's Letters has made me quite melancholy. He laments with such generous sorrow the misfortunes of his friends that every line I read raises his character higher in my estimation. But it is not possible to find with unconcern that all his best and dearest friends die before him. O great misery of length of days, to preserve life only to know its little value! Pope had but one great end in view to render this world supportable to him. That was *Friendship, the peculiar gift of heaven.* This did he nobly deserve and obtain; but for how short a time! Jealousy deprived him of the affection he assiduously sought from Mr. Wycherly, and many others; but Death cruel Death was far more cruel. The dearest ties of his heart all yielded to his stroke. The modest Digby, the gentle virtuous Gay, the worthy Arbuthnot, the exiled Atterbury—but why should I enumerate these excellent men, when their very names deject me? But in nothing does Pope equally charm me as in his conduct to his mother: it is truly noble. He gives up all his time, thought, and attention to her ease and comfort. I dare not begin to mention his [long] friendship with the admirable Swift, because I shall not know where [to] stop, for the attachment of such eminent men to one another has [some]thing in it that almost awes me, and [at] the same time inexpressibly delights [me]. I must tear myself from this.[1] . . . .

Yes my dear journal! yes! with the more pleasure shall I

---

[1] This generous outburst brings to mind a noble passage on the "Letters of Pope and of his Friends," in Thackeray's "English Humourists." "I do not know in the range of our literature, volumes more delightful. You live in them in the finest company in the world—in the expression of their thoughts, their various views and natures, there is something generous, and cheering, and enobling. You are in the society of men who have filled the greatest parts in the world's story. You are with St. John, the statesman; Peterborough, the conqueror; Swift, the greatest wit of all times; Gay, the kindliest laugher,—it is a privilege to sit in that company. . . . . He who reads these noble records of a past age, salutes and reverences the great spirits who adorn it. . . . . I know nothing in any story more gallant and cheering than the love and friendship which this company of famous men bore towards one another—there never has been a society of men more friendly, as there never was one more brilliant."

regard thee thou faithful preserver and repository of my thoughts and actions. Yet I cannot forbear thinking of some lines of my dear Pope's upon a birthday applicable to my poor dear journal,—

> "With added years if life bring nothing [new,]
> But, like a sieve, let every pleasure[1] [thro',]
> * * * * * *
> And all we gain, one[2] sad reflection more;
> Is this a birthday? 'tis, alas! too clear,
> 'Tis but the fun'ral of a[3] former year."

[1,2,3] In the edition of Elwin and Courthope, Pope's words are "blessing," "some," and "the," but we are informed that Fanny's words are correct according to an early text of Pope. The verses quoted are from a poem to Mrs. Martha Blount on her birthday.

1772.

[So much of this year's journal has been cut away, that the following table of its original contents is given. The names absent from Fanny's pages for 1772, of course, indicate what we have lost.

Dr. Burney.
Miss Barsanti.
Mr. Colman—the elder.
Arthur Young.
Dr. King.
Richard Burney.
Mr. Garrick.
Mrs., après Lady Strange.
Miss Strange.
Mr. après Sir Robt. Strange.
Miss Pascals.
Mr. Pogenpohl.
Miss Susan Burney.
Miss Charlotte Burney.
Miss Eliza Allen, Mrs., Meeke.
Mr. Lattice,—the Revd.
Honable. Daines Barrington.
Mr. Hudson.
James Burney, après Admiral.
Mrs. Dr. Burney.
Martin Folks, après Sir.
Miss Eliz. Burney.
Mr. Sloper.
Capt. Cooke.
Mrs. Burney, senr.
Mr. Rishton.
Dr. Hunter.
Charles, after Dr. Chas. Burney.
Mynhere Bohmen.
Lady Ann Lindsay.
Lady Margaret Fordyce.
Mr. Scot.
Dr. Armstrong.
Mr. Charles Burney.
Mr. Burney, senr., Worcester.
Richard Burney of Worcester.

Miss Anne Burney, Mrs. Hawkins.
Miss Ann Burney.
Mrs. Charles Burney.
Signor Celestini.
Miss Rebecca Burney.
Mr. Beckford.
Revd. Mr. Pugh.
Duke of Dorset.
Mr. Hanbury.
Miss Allen.
Lady Dalston.
Mrs. Garrick.
Mrs. Forbes.
Miss Forbes.
Miss — Forbes.
Mr. Crisp.
Dr. Hawkesworth.
Mr. Barretti.
Sir William Hamilton.
Mr. Tacet.
The Abbé Morellet.
Sir William Brown.
Mrs. Lidderdale.
Miss Lidderdale.
Miss Ford, after Mrs. Wilkinson.
Mr. Edwards.
Rev. Stephen Allen.
Miss Sukey Sharpen.
Mrs. Young.
Mr. Barthelemon.
Mynhere Spandau.
Mr. Pawles.
Mr. Bremner.
Mrs. Barthelemon.
Mr. Parsons.
Mr. Daines Barrington.

Mr. Mathias.
Mr. Hudson.
Mr. Breydone.
Mr. George Garrick.
Mrs. Arne.
Mr. Hayes.
Anna Maria Burney (Bourdois).
Mr. Stanley.
Sir John Turner.
Mrs. Stanley.
Miss Arland.
Mr. Fitzgerald.
Miss Fitzgerald.
Mr. Nollikens.
Made. Le Chantre.
Mdlle. Le Chantre.]

* * * * * *

[3rd January.]

Mr. Young called here lately; I saw him with sorrow. He is not well, and appears almost overcome with the horrors of his situation. In fact he is almost destitute. I fancy he is himself undetermined yet what plan to persue. This is a dreadful trial for him; yet I am persuaded he will still find some means of extricating himself from his distresses: at least, if genius, spirit, and enterprize can avail. In defiance of the gloom his misfortunes have cast over him, some starts of his former, his native vivacity break out. Dr. King has lately published a book, entitled, "The Rites, &c. of the Greek Church." Mr. Young took it up, and opening at the Preface— " So, so; what's here ?" cried he, and read aloud that he had undertaken this work to relieve his mind from ' a most severe affliction occasioned by the loss of a virtuous and affectionate ——— But it would be impertinent to obtrude my private misfortunes on the public.'"

" He means his wife," said I.

" It would serve as well for his mistress," answered he.

" For my own part," added I (very good-naturedly) "it appears ridiculous ostentation to me, as I am almost certain he had very little regard for her, and he was never in his life more gay than since her death; for I have heard well-authenticated particulars of her marriage; and therefore it seems mere———"

" Well!" cried he, "I honour a man who dares to be singular; I like to see a man's oddities in his works."

"But, I think," said I, you are no friend to *affectation;* which to us who know him, this appears.—Are *you* affected ?"

"Affected!" exclaimed he with all his wonted impetuosity, "I had rather be a murderer!"[1]

January 26th.

Mr. Garrick is this moment gone. Unfortunately my father was out, and mama not come downstairs; yet to my great satisfaction he came in. Dick ran to him, as the door was opened,—we were all seated at breakfast. "What, my bright-eyed beauty!" cried he; and then flinging himself back in a theatrical posture, "and here ye all are—one—two—three—four—beauties all." He then with a great deal of humour played with Dick. How many pities that he has no children; for he is extremely, nay passionately fond of them. "Well, but, Madam, so your father is out. Why I can never see him. He calls upon me—I call upon him, but we never meet. Can he come to dine with me to-day? can he?" I could not possibly tell. "Well don't let him send or make any fuss—if he can come he shall find beef and pudding: but I must have him on Tuesday. Some of his friends are to be with me: and I *must* have him then." I could not venture to promise.... "I have not had a moment to myself till this morning, I can't tell when."

---

[1] Arthur Young rallied, and was seldom deserted by what Miss Burney, in 1792, calls his "old spirit and impetuosity." Between 1767 and 1815 he wrote, or edited, 150 volumes. He was for long "Secretary to the Board of Agriculture," and was accused, by the "New Whigs," of making his reports bear against the revolutionary changes in France, which, like other able men, he had at first favoured. "His agricultural tours in France and Italy I consider the only works that give an intelligible account of those countries. His tour in Ireland has given me the idea that his views of Ireland were nearer the truth than any other work.... Mr. Parker tells me that his accuracy and correctness as to all statements of prices and of all things of his day are respected and considered as matters of fact by all the leading agriculturists.... His 'Farmer's Calendar,' which is for the management [of a farm], advising what to do each month by month, is the standard book of all farmers at present, and has gone through many editions.... He was spoilt by the success of his early works, and became a book-maker.... He obtained an immediate gain, but his general reputation ceased."—Lord Lonsdale to John Wilson Croker, Sept. 4, 1849.

February 3rd.

It is amazing to me how such a man as Dr. King can have ingratiated himself into the good graces and acquaintance of the first men of the nation, which he really has done. It would be curious to discover by what methods he has so raised himself above his possible expectations; at least, above what his friends could conceive he formed! When he left Lynn, about nine years since, he knew—nobody, I was going to say; and now he is acquainted with all the men of letters in England! He is chaplain to the British factory at St. Petersburg, and perhaps he owes his happy connections to having being abroad, though at least in my opinion he has not much the appearance of a *travelled gentleman*.

He appointed to bring a Russian gentleman and an English clergyman, both fond of music, to my father yesterday, for a *conversazione;* but unfortunately my father was obliged by a sudden summons to attend a committee for the purpose of settling a benefit for decayed musicians.[1] Mamma was too indifferent[2] to quit her room; and they found only Susanna, Charlotte, Bessy, Dick, and myself to receive them. Dr. King with an attempted politeness introduced them, "Mr. Pogenpohl, *justement arrivé de Russia,*"[3] and Mr. Lattice, who I found was just returned from Denmark. Never was an introduction less requisite than to the first. With the well-bred address of an elegant man of the world he made his own

---

[1] In the words of Dr. Burney, "a subscription was set on foot" in April, 1738, for establishing a fund for the support of decayed Musicians, or their families; the subscribers forming themselves into a Society, called "the Society of Musicians." They began with an annual payment of "at least half-a-crown a quarter," and in 1766, raised it to twenty shillings. The Governors met the first Sunday in every month at the Cardigan-Head Tavern, near Charing Cross. Handel left the charity one thousand pounds. Six thousand were given to it from the profits of the Handel Commemoration in 1784, and Dr. Burney himself munificently presented the fund with the profits of his handsome quarto volume containing an account of that Commemoration with a sketch of the Life of Handel.

[2] This, in our present language, is equivalent to being *indisposed*.

[3] In all cases where foreign words are found in the text the editor leaves them exactly as found.

compliments in French. I did not dare return mine in the same language; but I found he extremely well understood English, and spoke it, for a foreigner, amazingly; though as he found I perfectly understood him in French, he rather chose the whole evening to speak it, while poor *Fanny Bull*, as my father calls me, always answered in English.

I never saw a Russian before. Contrary to all my former ideas, I shall ever, in future, annex politeness and good breeding to the thought of one. This gentleman appears about twenty-two, genteel in his person, and agreeable in his face. His manners are polished, his conversation is lively, entertaining, and sensible. I made my father's apologies as well as I could, and acquainted them that I expected him home soon. Mr. Lattice looked a good sort of half-stupid man enough. The Russian seated himself next to me, and immediately entered into conversation. It is amazing with what ease and facility foreigners in general converse with strangers. Poor Mr. Lattice was in the room near half an hour, before he ventured to utter a word.

Dr. King, *by way of joke*, said he was very *sorry* to hear mama was so *shabby*. "So *shabby!*" said the Russian with a smile, . . . "I had always understood that word in a very mean sense!" "Why," cried the Dr., "I don't know whether Mrs. Burney taught *me* that word, or I her." Presently after, some other such word being used, the Russian drolly said, "*cela vaut autant que* shabby !" They extremely admired the beautiful Dick, whom I called *Malcheek*—I suppose I spell the word terribly,—it is Russ for boy, as Dr. King had told me. M. Pogenpohl laughed heartily at my speaking it. I told him I was too proud of knowing a Russ word, not to publish it. "But did Dr. King," cried he, "teach you only *that* word?— O fie!—that can give you no idea of the softness of our language." "M. Pogenpohl," said the Dr., "will teach you much better than I can,—but did not I tell you some other word?" "No indeed." The Russian then ran on most fluently, repeating Russ expressions and words of soft sounds, —and, if I may trust his manner, soft meaning! I observed Dr. King laughed, so I did not dare repeat them after him, though he stop'ed for that purpose, and said *sallimani* or *some such* word, several times over, and appealed seriously to me to judge if it was not a more pleasing word than Malcheek? "O," cried I, "I shall never remember so much at once. I have not a head for so much." "*Mais si mademoiselle veut bien me donner l'honneur de repeter mes leçons.*"—Dr. King, by way of wit, I suppose, then amused himself with saying some Russ too;—what it meant, I know not; but M. Pogenpohl exclaimed "O fie!"—which at the same time raised my good opinion of *him*, and lessened it of the Doctor, who was inexcusable if he said any thing reprehensible, even in an unknown language. The Russian [was too well bred][1] though I must confess, there was so much archness in his look that I did not chuse to ask the meaning of what he said. He told me he had been five months in England. "But when I first came," said he, "I learnt nothing: I spoke only French with my sisters;—afterwards, Lord Morris, (I believe you would call him)——"

[Here four lines have been cut out. Fanny is next found speaking.]

"though," said I, "they may talk so much as to save you the trouble of speaking, if you only desire to learn the language, indeed, the ladies may be very proper."

When tea was over, I began to be uneasy at my father's not returning. Dr King I saw looked displeased; but the politeness and liveliness of the Russian, who was too civil to appear dissatisfied, soon dissipated my anxiety. He never once seemed to have any thing wanting or any end unanswered in his visit: while Dr. King looked at his watch, listened attentively to every rap of the knocker, started whenever the parlour-door opened, and was in visible concern the whole evening. Music was now proposed, Mr. Pogenpohl had often heard Bach, of Berlin,[2] and by his conversation showed so fine

---

[1] Here the author has effaced some words, and added the four in brackets, which confuse the sentence.

[2] Karl Philipp Emanuel Bach, a composer of music, and musician, was in the service of Frederick the Great between 1740 and 1767. He was called "Bach of Berlin" to distinguish him from Wilhelm Bach of Halle, Johann Christian Bach of London, and the best known of them all, Johann Sebastian Bach.

a taste and so good a judgment of the art, that neither Susan nor I could be induced to touch a note. Indeed we never do, though Mr. Pogenpohl's great love of music made me more than ever regret my deficiency. We, however, persuaded Mr. Lattice to play, which he did, in a horrible old-fashioned style; insomuch that I did not dare to meet the Russian's eyes, I was so sure it must be ridiculous to him. . . . .

Dr. King and Mr. Lattice entered into a dispute with him concerning the *beaux esprits* of his and our nation, and of the arts and literature of both countries. He seems to love his own country with a patriot warmth, yet with the best grace in the world, he gave up to us Philosophy and Poetry, the former with a smile that drolly implied our too great tendency that way. Civil Law, &c. he strenuously supported his right to, and indeed his antagonists had not much to urge against him. Dr. King, who is really ill-bred in argument, and Mr. Lattice, who is a plain, common sort of man, both like true John Bulls, fought with better will than justice for Old England, giving it every virtue and every science under the sun. Dr. King was absolutely ridiculous. My father has often observed of this man, that he has a knack of talking for three hours upon any given subject, without saying anything! For my own part, I very frequently after a long argument have endeavoured to recollect what he aimed at, or even what he said,—in vain! for he has no meaning, but continually dives in the dark for one. To regard it in no other light—would any man of common civility *amuse* a foreigner with exaggerated praises of England, given at the expense of his own and of all other nations?

"Our universities, Sir," said he, "are the only schools in Europe for learning; they bring forth geniuses superior to all the world."

"Are they, then," said the Russian archly, "all geniuses, Sir?"

"They are the noblest schools in the world," said the Doctor.

"You think them superior to *all* others, Sir?" cried Mr. Pogenpohl, naming some one which I have forgot.

"Undoubtedly, Sir. What nation has brought forth such men as our's? Have we not Locke?"

"Oh, oui! and you have Newton! but then have we not

Volfe (*sic*) and Beraman (*sic*),—was not he the father of Civil Law? Whom have you, Sirs, in that class?"

"Why, as to that——" said the Doctor.

"As to that," repeated Mr. Lattice,—"I can't say."

"But, Sir," continued the Doctor with a vehemence, which, rude as it was, was only *put on*, to give himself imaginary consequence, "but, Sir, are we not superior to all the world in Astronomy? in Natural History? in Poetry? in Philosophy? in Music?"

"*La Musique!*" repeated Mr. Pogenpohl, "*la Musique!*" and flung back, as if he felt the utter impossibility of arguing with a man so imposing and so very ignorant: for neither Susan nor I could help laughing. Give *England* Music! . . .

Mr. Lattice then took up the argument. He is, however, really modest, and gave his opinion with diffidence. But his taste is terribly *fogrum* and old-fashioned.[1] He began an éloge on our English Music and performers. Dr. King, without knowing what he said, joined with him; for I am sure he does not know at all the music of one master, or even of one nation, from another.

"And pray, Sir," said the Russian, drily, "*who are* they, your English composers?"

"Who, Sir?" cried the Doctor—"why, why, we have Smith! There's a great man!"[2]

---

[1] John Lettice, (1737 or 8-1832). Fellow of Sydney-Sussex College, Cambridge, Prebendary of Chichester, &c., D.D., was author of the Seatonian Prize Poem in 1764, and of books on sundry subjects. He was tutor to the brilliant William Beckford, with whom he travelled; chaplain and secretary to Sir Robert Gunning, when ambassador to Copenhagen in 1768,—and chaplain to the Duke of Hamilton.

[2] There are three Smiths from whom to choose as composers, but one only of them wrote upon music, John Stafford Smith, who was born in 1750. He was son of Martin Smith, organist of Gloucester Cathedral, was (according to Grove,) "a student, chorister, organist, and an efficient tenor-singer up to 1773, after which he composed sacred and secular music, and much assisted Sir John Hawkins in his History of Music." He was organist of the Chapel-Royal in 1802, and "Master of the Children of the Chapel-Royal" from 1805 to 1817. "He published, at various times, five collections of glees, containing compositions which place him in the foremost rank of English glee composers," but we find no music and no book of his named as being published so early as 1772.

"But he, Sir," answered Mr. Pogenpohl, " wrote *on* Music; I only speak of music for the ear. Only tell me who are your composers."

Mr. Lattice paused. Dr. King, too *bright* to consider, named Handel—Ha! Ha! Ha![1]

"Oh, pardonnez-moi, Monsieur; Handel was not an *English* composer! But you all tell me of your excellent English Music, and yet nobody will name any composer to me."

"Why, Sir," after some hesitation said Mr. Lattice, "we have Avison, and Worgan, and Stanley." . . .[2]

After this, both Mr. Lattice and the Russian most furiously attacked me to play; but of course in vain. . . . . He then made a similar attack upon Susette, who, after a long defence,

---

As Dr. King was not very clear-headed, he may have claimed John Christopher Smith, (or Schmidt, a German pupil of Handel, who played the organ at his oratorios, and at the Foundling Hospital, composed several operas, and an oratorio, and wrote for Handel when he was blind,) as being like Handel, an *English* composer, but we do not find that he wrote upon music. The third is Isaac Smith, a composer, who was born about the middle of the eighteenth century.

[1] When Fanny ends her sentences with Ha! Ha! Ha! she appears to be thinking of the directions for stage-laughter, common in printed plays of that time.

[2] Charles Avison, musician, composer of, and writer upon music.

"Not too conspicuous on the list
Of worthies who by help of pipe or wire
Expressed in sound rough rage or soft desire,
Thou whileom of Newcastle organist!"

Thus Mr. Browning "*parleys*" with Avison, in his day "*a person of importance*" enough to have had a little controversy with Dr. William Hayes, Music Professor at Oxford. Avison's Work on "Musical Expression" was published in 1753—Hayes' "Remarks" upon it, and Avison's "Reply" followed in the same year. The date of Avison's birth seems uncertain, but he died at Newcastle-on-Tyne in 1770. A march of his suddenly remembered by Mr. Browning inspired one of the finest poems in his latest volume.

John Worgan, born 1724, organist and composer at Vauxhall, 1751-1774, Mus. Doc. Cambridge, 1775, was a well-known church-organist likewise, and the composer of several oratorios, many anthems, &c.

Stanley was the blind musician and composer of music, of whom we shall read more by and by.

sat down. . . . Susette had just finished her first movement when Dr. King hastily and eagerly made his bow. He had sat upon thorns some time; and when I made all the speeches I could for my father's absence he told me *he was a macaroni*;[1] *invited company to his house and then went out!* And, indeed, but for the Russian's peculiar address and politeness I should have been in an exceeding disagreeable situation, for they came between six and seven and it was half-past nine before they offered to go, and yet no Dr. Burney appeared! . . . .

My dear father returned home soon after they went. He had been detained greatly against his will at the committee. He was extremely vexed, and much the more on hearing from

---

[1] As the word "Maccaroni" occurs every now and then in these pages, it may be well to state generally that the term represents a period of affectation between that of the "*beaux*" of the first half of the eighteenth century, and the "dandies," "bucks," or "bloods" of the time of the Prince of Wales (George IV.). It lasted long enough to pass through changes in its own fashions, but the word is always applied to something superfine, and rather unmanly. In Mrs. Brooke's novel of "Julia Mandeville" there is a maccaroni, "Lord Viscount Fondville," who arrives ("fresh from Paris") at a country-seat in a "*papier-mâché*" carriage "highly gilded," painted with "loves and doves," and drawn by "four long-tailed grey Arabians." From this he "descends" (humming an opera-tune), "dressed in a suit of light-coloured silk, embroidered with silver;" under his arm, he carries a hat with a black feather; in his button-hole is a large bouquet of *artificial flowers*, and "all Arabia breathes from his scented handkerchief." He receives some sort of "poetical justice" at the end of the story, by being married to "a detestable cit"; however, she has a large fortune to make up for her forward vulgarity—and to maintain his equipage. We next quote Garrick's "Irish Widow." *Mrs. Brady* (in man's clothes, under the name of Lieutenant O'Neale), says: "Your *Macaroons*—whipper-snappers who look so much more like girls than those I see in petticoats, that *fait* and *trot* it is a pity to hurt 'em. The fair sex in London here seem the most masculine of the two." There were "bucks," also; that is, slovenly men of fashion, contemporaneous with the "*Maccaronies*," but not so many of them as later on. As a matter of fact, the affectation of young Englishmen (in the last century) oscillated between noisy, rough, and even violent ways of trying to distinguish themselves, with slovenly disregard of dress, and much neglect of soap and water; and strained "elegance," studied frivolity, and the newest *modes* from Paris, with that *dash*, or "*soupçon*" of Italy, which converted the "*beau*" of George II. into the "Macaroni" of George III.

us what he had lost in missing the Russian, whose taste in music alone was enough to excite in my father a good opinion of him, and we spoke so much in his praise, that he declared he *must* see him. He called on Dr. King the next day, and made his apologies and peace, and settled to have the same party, if the Doctor's friends were disengaged, the following day. Mr. Burney and my sister came to meet them; also Mr. Daines Barrington[1] and Mr. Hudson and some others.

* * * * * *

Speaking of the death of the Princess Dowager of Wales, which happened two days before,—" This is a very dull week for strangers," said the Russian; " no diversions! no any thing! all shut up! very dull! is it not so, Mlle.?" to little Charlotte, who, blushing, retreated. " *Qu'en pensez-vous, Mlle.?* " to Bessy, who, smiling, advanced. " I don't know, Sir." " She is not, I think, *very* much regretted by the nation? but I—I—regret her *very much!* she is *great loss* to me."[2] He then began a comic mock flirtation with little Bessy. I could gather by what he said, though all *en badinage*, with what ridicule, perhaps contempt, he had remarked the prejudicial opinions our nation in general entertain of the Russians; the drolly absurd account he gave her of his country, could have no other meaning. " Will you not go to Russia with

---

[1] Daines, one of the sons of the first Viscount Barrington, was a " Welsh judge, and second justice of Chester." He was also a well-known " *virtuoso,*" who would write and print a paper upon *anything*— from the Polar passage, to " the sudden decay of certain trees in St. James's Park, within a year of the filling up of ' Rosamond's Pond ' "; on a newly-found bat, or a fossil; on " Mozart, a Remarkable Young Musician "; and on " the Grey Wethers," which he supposed to have been blown into Berkshire, out of some volcano, somewhere.

[2] Augusta, Princess-Dowager of Wales (mother of George III.), died on the 8th of February, 1772, after a widowhood of twenty years. She was the most unpopular woman in England on account of her supposed favour for Lord Bute. She died of a most painful malady, borne with the greatest firmness, at the very time when her daughter, the Queen of Denmark, was in prison, and in danger of her life. There seems no reason to believe the gross suppositions of the rabble, who drove her by their insults from going to a London theatre, " sang songs about her in every alley," and " scrawled the grossest ribaldry against her on every wall."

me?" said he. "Oh! you will admire it beyond expression!" "No," cried Bessy, "I should not, I am sure, I should not like your country." "No?—Why? Oh, yes; you would like it vastly! you should always be with a tiger or a lion or a wolf or some such fine beast." "No, no; I won't go." "Oh! yes; very agreeable! and you should live on high mountains covered with snow, and sit upon ice, and you should eat trees, and sometimes hay, and you should have grass and briers for sauce." "O! no; I should not like it at all." "Oh! yes; very good! very excellent! and you should have the sea always before you, and the waves should dash against you, and you should dress in tigers' skins." "O, no; indeed, Sir, I won't go." "O, very agreeable! you will much like my country."[1]

* * * * * *[2]

March 6th.

Mama is gone to Lynn; and Susanna and I keep house for my father. We are so happy! for he is so kind! ....

---

[1] There has been much more about M. Pogenpohl. That he had "an elegant address," and was "a fine gentleman without any foppery, or pretension," may still be read. It seems to have been indeed a pleasure to Fanny to meet a Russian, and find him the reverse of what the foreign singers who came to Dr. Burney's house called "*a barbar.*" Though a Russian, it looks as if he was in the service of George III. at the time, probably as an officer of those Hessian soldiers who were employed by George III., as well as by his grandfather. M. Pogenpohl came to Dr. Burney's tea and music in his uniform. He had "gold shoulder-knots," instead of *silver*, such as were worn, (he told little Bessy Allen,) by English officers, he had a scarf round his arm as a sign of mourning for the Princess of Hesse (aunt of George III.), and he explained to the child that "every officer wear it, and it will soon be for the Princess of Wales." The editor is told that M. Pogenpohl was not strictly exact in saying that English officers wore "silver shoulder-knots" only. Some regiments wore gold, others, silver.

[2] Perhaps some of the matter cut out here included an account of Captain Cook's visit to Dr. Burney in February of this year. Cook's name figures in Mme. D'Arblay's contents table, and in her "Memoirs" of her father, vol. i., p. 270, she gives the latter's account of the visit.

April 1st.

A new month, to my great regret is begun. How fast, how imperceptibly does time fly, where the mind is at ease!
I drank tea last Saturday with Mrs. Strange. I am very glad to find her journey to Paris deferred till June.[1] An old gentleman was sitting next to he[r] when I went in, whom I thought I had [met] before, but remembered very imperfectly, and [as] he did not speak to me I imagined myself mistaken. But at tea-time Dr. Smyth[2] came in. He addressed me by my

---

[1] If this journey took place in June, Mrs. Strange had been earlier in Paris than is known to her husband's biographer, Mr. Dennistoun.

[2] James Carmichael Smyth (born 1742, died 1821), M.D., F.R.S., was physician-extraordinary to George III. He twice received the thanks of the House of Commons for his public services. His eldest son commanded the Royal Engineers at the battle of Waterloo, and was created a baronet. His second, a gallant soldier, became the second husband of Thackeray's mother. We read in the "Church Times" of the 17th of February, 1888, that a brass has been placed in the new church of the Holy Trinity, Ayr, (of which a portion was opened on Quinquagesima Sunday, 1888), by Mrs. Ritchie (Miss Thackeray), with the following epitaph to the memory of her father's stepfather, the original of Colonel Newcome :—

"Sacred to the memory of Major Henry William Carmichael Smyth, of the Bengal Engineers, who departed this life at Ayr, 9th September, 1861, aged eighty-one years.

"ADSUM

"And lo, he whose heart was as that of a little child, had answered to his name, and stood in the Presence of The Master."—" Newcomes." Vol. iii., Ch. 26.

"On the rebuilding of the church, his grave was brought within the walls. He was laid to rest immediately beneath this place by his stepson, William Makepeace Thackeray. This memorial was put up in 1887 by some members of the family."

Dr. Smyth was a friend of the Stranges, as well as their physician. He attended Sir Robert Strange in his last illness. A note, without a date, exists, showing that he was called to Dr. Burney in some illness, through Mrs. Strange. She writes to Miss Burney—perhaps Fanny—after Hetty's marriage : " I was sorry I miss'd my Sweet Girl. . . . Be assur'd that the Gentleman who I recommended is a most regular bred physician as ever came out of any Collage of physicians in Europ." She is ready to send for him without delay, "as the Dr. will not be so easily got at after 8 for he goes to the Club of Drs. in St. Paul's Church Yard, than [then ?] Mr. Strange goes with Him. The sooner Dr. Burney Has help the better. His name is Dr. James Carmichel Smyth. For Shortness

name, and asked after my father. "God bless me!" cried this gentleman, "why, is this a daughter of Dr. Burney?" "Yes," cried Mrs. Strange. "My dear Miss Burney," cried he, rising and embracing me with great cordiality, "How glad I am to see you!—but why do you wear this great thing over your face? (turning up my hat) why it prevented my knowing you."[1] Quite unable to recollect who he was, I told him I fancied he was mistaken, and meant my sister. "Oh, no," cried he—" I know your sister too, I know your [mar]ried sister, and your sister Charlotte." I still could not help doubting, though he assured me I was his old acquaintance. "I knew you," said he, "in Poland Street, but I wonder you should forget *me*, I thought I was too big to be forgotten!" Seeing me still perplexed he asked my Christian name. When I told him, "O, aye," cried he, "Miss Fanny! why I knew Miss Fanny very well. I used to meet you at Mrs. Pringle's, and with very particular pleasure." Then in a moment I recollected Mr. Scot![2] I was both

---

Dr. Smith, Newport Street. He is one of the Collage Here." By the way, Foote (in "The Devil upon Two Sticks") does not overlook the Doctor's Club:—

Devil: "Do you know the public-house where they meet?"

Johnny Macpherson: "Yes, yes; unco weel, Sir; it is at the south side of Paul's Kirk."

[1] This fashion was continued for a long time. In 1774 Horace Walpole writes that Lady Mary Somerset wore a hat over her nose, so that I only fell in love with her chin." In 1777, Mrs. Delany hints to her niece that propriety "will never suffer you to wear your hat with *one edge to touch your nose*, and the other edge perpendicularly in the air"; and after 1780, Susan Burney was "*not sorry she had a hat on*," when some one alluded to her approaching marriage.

[2] "When Dr. Johnson read his own satire, in which the life of a scholar is painted, with the various obstructions thrown in his way to fortune and fame, he burst into a passion of tears one day. The [Thrale] family and Mr. Scott only were present, who, in a jocose way, clapped him on the back, and said, 'What's all this, my dear Sir? Why you, and I, and *Hercules*, you know, were all troubled with *melancholy*.' As there are many gentlemen of the same name, I should say, perhaps, that it was a Mr. Scott who married Miss Robinson, and that I think I have heard Mr. Thrale call him George Lewis, or George Augustus, I have forgot which. He was a very large man, however, and made out the triumvirate with Johnson and Hercules comically

ashamed and surprised at having forgot him. But he is much altered. I was extremely glad of the opportunity of enquiring after my old friends. He told me that Mrs. Pringle was not gone to the East Indies, but to the Isle of Wight to try whether sea bathing would be of service to her youngest boy, who, poor thing, is an absolute ideot. And that Captain Pringle was gone to Newfoundland as engineer under Captain Debieg, who was gone as commanding officer. . . . I then asked after Mr. Seton. He told me that he had been extremely ill, that he was not gone with his brother-in-law, but that *something*, he understood, *was in* agitation for him. This Mr. Scot was sub-preceptor to the King.

We are still without mama. We live in the most serene comfort possible. We have hardly a wish. My dear Susette is a companion so much to the taste of my heart, she will spoil me for any other.

April 2nd.

Dr. Armstrong called here on Sunday morning. My father was engaged. He was in very good spirits, and very droll. He is a most amazing old man,—[the oldest I know.][1] I told him I had the honour, at the Haberdashers' Hall, of seeing the Lord Mayor, for the first time I had seen one. "And how did you like him?" "Oh! very well." "Why, I think," said he, very gravely, "he is somewhat of the human species; there is some resemblance to mankind in him." . . . .

But the day after we were happy indeed, for we saw Gar-

---

enough. The Doctor was so delighted at his odd sally, that he suddenly embraced him, and the subject was immediately changed. I never saw Mr. Scott but that once in my life."—Mrs. Piozzi's *Anecdotes of Dr. Johnson*, 1786.

[1] The words in brackets have been added by the author, at a later time. If she be correct, the date of Dr. Armstrong's birth commonly given in books must be wrong. For instance, you find in the "Encyclopædia of Chronology" (Woodward and Cates) "Armstrong, John, *poet, physician*, born at Castleton, Roxburghshire, *about* 1709." Now Daddy Crisp, who is never treated as an old man in these pages, was born in 1706, or 1707. Perhaps Armstrong looked older than he was from having been physician to the army in the West Indies before 1746, and to the army in Germany in 1760.

rick, the inimitable Garrick, in Bayes! O, he was great beyond measure! Betsy and James, Sue, my aunt and I made up [the party]. I was almost in convulsions [with excess] of laughter, which he kept me in from the moment he entered to the end of the play—never in my life did I see any thing so entertaining, so ridiculous,—so humourous,—so absurd! and I have talked of nothing else—and we have laughed almost as much at the recollection as at the representation.[1] Mr. Young dined with Sue and me to-day. Fortune, I hope, smiles on him again, for he again smiles on the world.

* * * * * *

[Here may be given a fragment of a letter to Fanny Burney from Maria Allen, who was still abroad. It is numbered 13—Nos. 11 and 12 are wanting. They, and parts of Maria's journal about that time, must have contained perilous stuff indeed, as we find her here in secret correspondence with Mr. Rishton, and imploring Fanny to burn, as soon as she has read it, a copy of a letter from him, as "I don't think I act perfectly right to Rishton in going so far—As for Hetty's seeing it I own it would give me pain as she then must be acquainted with so great a weakness in favour of a Man whom she is *prejudiced* against. And As I have hitherto Concealed it from her—I should be loth now [to] incur her *Contempt* or her *Raillery*—I know I deliver him into the

---

[1] The character of Bayes, in the admirable play of the "Rehearsal," was peculiarly associated with Garrick's history. When Garrick acted in "Goodman's Fields," he gained the permission of his manager, Giffard, to imitate, not merely the chief actors of the greater theatres, but Giffard himself. He did it *too well*. Giffard challenged him, and Garrick was wounded. Again, in 1743, after his quarrel with Macklin, Garrick, as Bayes, was pelted with eggs and apples, and not allowed a hearing, by the upholders of Macklin, until "Mr. Windham, of Norfolk" (Dr. Johnson's Windham,—Windham the politician), four days later, chose thirty prize-fighters to keep the middle of the pit. They soon drove out the Macklin gang. The story of Giffard's challenge was told by Garrick to Dr. Burney, and written down by Dr. Charles Burney. Yet Horace Walpole says Cibber gave the character of Bayes better than Garrick. "Old Cibber preserved the solemn coxcomb; and was the caricature of a great poet" [Dryden], "as the part was meant to be"—not what Garrick made Bayes—"a garretteer-bard." In 1746 Gilbert Walmsley wrote from Bath to Garrick to tell him that Lord Chesterfield particularly objected to his way of "playing Bayes, which he says is *a serious, solemn character, &c.*, and that you mistake it."

hands of his Enemies in Sending you his letter. I hope Susey will remember a little of her former good opinion—but my dear *dear Girls* Spare *me* when you write—think that you speak of him on whom all my happiness in this Life depends and in whom I *wish* to see no faults. you will call me *infatuated* I know—I [1] [am not] happy at the figure I make in your Eyes—but don't [O!] don't mistake me. I don't wish you to disguise a sin[gle] sentiment of your hearts on the Contents of the letter. you would ill-merit the faith I put in you if you was Capable of flattering me at the expense of your sincerity—I only wish you would not be guided by prejudice—put yourselves a few minutes in my place—you know my heart has never once Ceased to *Beat* in his favor even when I *thought* him most unworthy—that the fear of seeing him had a great Share in my leaving England—you will not wonder that left to myself—my whole soul pleading for him that I perhaps too easily forgave him—but indeed I was so happy at his return—that had I followed the dictates of my own heart I should have wrote him a very different Answer from what I did. I Wrote 3 letters before I coud pen one *severe* and *indifferent* enough but at last Compleated a Master peace if you was to see the 2nd letter he wrote me you woud see it did not make him vain—but you must excuse my transcribing any more of Our letters—when I return you shall see them—I write to Susey the same Post therefore you will *suppress* this letter, as hers will be a suite to the present Time. *If* ever I am his Wife I will inform Hetty of what has past—but wish at present she may be kept in Ignorance. I am quite of your opinion about Crisp—don't let a hint transpire you may let him see all the Journal I send except the last *Cahier* where I mention our Affairs—I will finish this with transcribing A paragraph in his second letter—in answer to what I mentioned About the letter I wrote him—' you tell me the remembrance of the first letter you sent me to Heacham [2] has embitter'd many hours of your Life & Cost you many tears.—I grant you—such a step might have disagreeable Reflections —But pray! what reason had you for such Uneasiness? did my Character ever give you room to Imagine I shoud expose you because you Loved me? Tis thoroughly unnatural—I defy the world to bring an Instance of my behaving unworthy the Character of a Gentleman— (unless *you* Accuse me) your letter was immediately destroyed—& had I vainly boasted of such honours who would have believed me. Men of that stamp never gain Credit, but on the Contrary universal contempt—you cou'd not have Chosen a Man more unlikely to do you a *Wilfull* Injury than myself—on every Account, nor was you ignorant of my Character and Disposition when you wrote—or if *I know you* you had saved yourself the pain.' I think those the sentiments of a Man of honour and such I hope to find him. Don't be surprised at the

---

[1] Some words have been cut away with the seal.

[2] Heacham was the residence of Edmund Rolfe, Esq., who had married Dorothy Folkes, a first cousin of Mr. Rishton's mother.

beginning & call out before Mama do you remember the Memoirs of Mrs. Williams."[1] This fragment of a letter bears a London postmark of 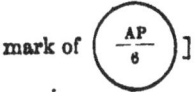]

Monday.

We—Susan and I—had a long visit to-day from the Genius, as he is called, of the elder branch of the Burney race,— Richard Burney of Worcester, Junior, a young man of very uncommon talents and parts, and of the utmost sweetness of disposition. But, unluckily for his fortitude of mind or modesty of character, he is so handsome, and so lively and amusing, from never-failing spirits, that he is quite spoiled, and seems at times to be made up of self-admiration ; yet, at others, he laughs at his own foppery as cordially as his most sarcastic censurers ; and then he will take himself off in his high airs as drolly and gaily, as he takes off, with incomparable mimicry, the airs of his neighbours. He gave us a very entertaining account of his life in the country, and suffered us to laugh at his affectation with the utmost good-nature, and flung out occasions for it as frequently as possible, even joining in our mirth, and seeming happy to be smoaked.[2] What a strange character! But I will recollect some of his conversation :

[Here there is a gap, and when Richard is found speaking, it is of some person to whose name we have no clue.]

"Such ease!—his bow was so extremely genteel!—and

---

[1] This may be an allusion to an incident in some novel. We are kindly informed that Watt (Bibliotheca Britannica), has the title of a novel called "Memoirs of Miss Williams, a History founded on facts" 2 vols., 12mo., 5s., but that the British Museum has no copy of it. The Museum possesses, however, "Authentic Memoirs of Mrs. Williams, a Domestic and Pathetic Tale," London, 1823, 24mo. This, very likely is the book, as it seems to be a reprint of an earlier edition

[2] It shows the changes of fashion in "slang" that Fanny has, (fifty years or more afterwards,) translated this (then obsolete) word "smoaked," as "quizzed," for nineteenth century readers, not that the word "quiz" did not exist in the eighteenth century, but it was chiefly used as a substantive, and applied to the object or victim, of "quizzing," —the "quiz," or "quoz." They "smoaked" a "quiz" and then they "roasted," or teased, or tormented, him.

then—nothing disturbs him;—if the whole is in confusion, he is as calm and careless as ever." " O! he's a fine fellow!" (Then he rose and took him off with inimitable humour, still pretending to admire him—though, in fact, he must be a mere copy of himself.) " Then his tooth-picks," continued he, "are in the most exact order:—he has three different sizes, for different times—and he amuses himself with picking his teeth half the day——" " I should be afraid it would be catching." (By the way, *he* does it almost continually.) "Then his tradesmen!—such wretches! O, insupportable! —here's a shoe!—and then what a coat! why that man has not three ideas in a week. Then we do so loll in a chaise! —for when I go my rounds, I always take a chaise and four —and we are *so* much at our ease!—I go from Barborne on my own horse—and so the good folks there think I ride her all the way—Ha—Ha—Ha!—but the first inn I come to—I leave the poor jade behind me, order a chaise and four—and as I return stop at the same inn—and go back to Barborne on my horse!" " This, I own, I much admire—it is so considerate for the poor horse—to let her rest;—that is really humane!" " O—meerly for the horse!—and I always feed it with corn—the creature grows so fat and plump! In truth I believe riding saves my life—otherwise, my late hours—Do you know, it stands me in a hundred a year for chaises;—the time I spend at inns—which is very little—and there I can only get Port and Madeira—for people, hang 'em, wont sell anything better." .... " But I would advise you to set up a few inns of your own—that may accommodate you better." " Then again, I subscribe to every thing—they always bring me all subscription papers—' Come—you know, you'll give us your name—I know you are a young man that encourage these sort of things.'" " O, I dare say, any arts and sciences." " And then—Ha! ha!—God so—I often sign them without reading!—and when I've wrote my name —I look over what its to!" Here he burst out a laughing, as at his own absurdity—and we cordially accompanied him. "Then they keep monstrous tables in the country—not that I care for the victuals—not in the least—only the *shew*—nay I dislike their dishes—though I always eat them

—but then the beef is always put on the side table!—so I swallow the [ragout] that is before me—though, faith, I love the [beef best] of all things!—but it would be impossible to call for it, you know." "O, utterly—that would be having such a *vulgar appetite!*" "Ha—Ha—Ha!—a *vulgar appetite!*—Then again, [I am] Master of the Ceremonies at all the Balls—and Conductor at all the Concerts." . . . .

He wished us of his party at the opera—made his bow—said it would go off with [twice] the spirit if we were there—and decamped. . . . . His foppery, airs, and affectation are dreadful, but he has at times, strong humour, great quickness, and in spight of his follies, is sensible, clever, and agreeable. And it is very obvious, that he takes much more trouble to be a coxcomb than he need to be a man of sense. . . . .

* * * * * *

About three o'clock, the rest of our company came. And from that time, was *my* comfort over, for my uncle is so . . . yet, I should not have regarded *him*, if mama had been at home, but, upon my word, appearing as *Mistress of the* house [for the first time] distressed me beyond imagination . . . . so criticizing an eye, and one that makes no allowances![1] I would not go through such another day for the world.

* * * * * *

Tuesday, April.

* * * * * *

About two my uncle came, Mr. Richard with him. The former went with my father into the study, and we had a *sequel* to the Saturday's conversation. . . . . Speaking of the clubs in and about Worces[ter] he spoke with infinite pleasure of being [Pres]ident—I found they were chiefly musical ones, and I asked him how he came to be *always* first man, which he said he was— . . . .

"O—ma'am, why I have it all my own [way] I have all power—I direct and fix every thing—nothing can be done

---

[1] Mme. D'Arblay, in 1832, describes her uncle Richard as a man of "true worth," with "a vigourous understanding," humorous, passionately fond of all the arts, and a collector of historical portraits.

without my consent. I have a casting vote—I make all the motions—in short, my power is unlimited." "And I don't doubt but you make a good use of it—and keep them all in order. And what else do you do?" "Why I put about the wine—take care they all give their toasts—First we go round with sentiments, and then ladies—" "And you take care they take but half glasses, I am sure?—or at least that they drink half water?" "O Lord no, ma'am—that is always an affront—no, a full bumper! always." "And do you give toasts?" "O yes, ma'am, every body." "And how many have you? three or [four?"] "Three or four? Lord bless me! three or four and twenty!" "And does every body drink three or four and twenty toasts?" . . . . "O, we never go beyond the [   ] but I give permission, sometimes, to some of them to mix a little water— we don't like it—but I connive at a few." "O, fie! that's terrible want of spirit! . . . . I can't imagine how you find time for all [thi]s." "O, with great difficulty, but there would be no living in the country without. All day I am fagging at business—then in the evening I begin to live. We never break-up till morning. Sometimes I go to bed at 3 or 4—and am up again at 6, and begin my rides—which keep me in health. But I am convinced that people may live upon a third part of the sleep they give themselves, if it is sound—It is all custom—[For] my part I can't bear bed—it is such a total loss of time! and then, I am commonly . . . . master of the Ceremonies, which obliges me to call all the minuets—lead out the ladies—fix on the gentlemen— O! I have such a fuss to settle disputes!—every thing is refe[rred] to me—'Sir, was not this my dance?' 'No, sir, I am sure it was my turn'—'Now p . . . .

Monday.

Richard has spent all the morning with Susette and I. I had heard his brother Charles often mention a Mrs. S., a woman of fortune and figure, who lives near Bewdley, and had taken a most violent liking to Richard, insomuch as to invite him to town with her. I enquired whether he had visited Mrs. S. since he came to town? "No; he had not had time to call." "I hear you go there very often, and are much in favour." "I am *such* a favourite, she does nothing but flatter me, and says *such* things to me, though I doubt not but she abuses me behind my back; O! I know she does, by what she says of others; but I seem to be everything there. The moment I go in, she runs up to me, '*My dear Burney;*' and leaves whoever is there to themselves. . . . . though perhaps there may be somebody of high [   ] in the room, but she flings herself on her settee, and calls me to her, and there we sit and laugh at the old codgers,—who stare so at us! ha! ha! ha! Then she'll begin to tell me the London news of the winter, and private anecdotes of Lady Sarah this, and my Lord Duke, and the Marquis,—and does so run on, and abuses everybody! And I know the moment I am gone, 'tis the same with me." "What a strange character," said I; "but how every body must wonder at her." "Oh! yes; why they'll come in, and hardly get a word from her; but she lolls at one side, and I at the other; and we have all our own talk; and we so enjoy their wonder! and, if any body comes in, she'll just turn her head and say, '*How do do? How do do?* Well; and so, Burney;'—and then run on again to me, and take no more notice of them." "Why, I think she can't be much visited." "O! she *won't*, by the country *ladies;* she won't let them come near her, and sometimes she'll be denied to people, when she's at the window! But she always lets me in, and says such things to me! before her husband!" "Her husband!" we both exclaimed, "what, is he alive? Is there a husband in the case?" "O! yes." "And what sort of a man is he?" "A very good-natured man (archly) upon my word! very good-natured!" "But how does he like this strange conduct?" "Why, I don't know; she does not mind him; he's a spruce little counsellor; but we seldom speak with him. The two Miss S——s, the mother, and I get into a party, and we leave him as much to himself, as if he was not in the room." "How old is Miss S.?" "About fifteen or sixteen,—a very fine girl." "What a strange family it must seem in the country!" "O! dear, yes; she sees *I smoak* her, and that has kept me in favour. . . . . but you'd be surprised to hear the things she says to me, such flattery, and insists on it all being true, and I laugh! O I never laugh so much anywhere else! But, she praises people in such a manner to their faces! and so many of them believe her, and then,—they are done for! She'll never see 'em again. No; it won't do! she gets rid of them as fast as possible; and so she would of me, if I had been taken in. The people of Bewdley are all so *surprised ;* they say, 'why, how does Burney manage to keep well in that house so long?'" "O! if she saw you believed her, she would soon discard you! Pray, what age is she?" "About thirty, or rather more. She has very much the look of an Italian—black eyes and hair and a sallow complexion. When she was young, what a coquet she was! She entertains me with histories of her amours[1] before her marriage, and tells me who she *really* liked, and who not, and all before her husband." "O! I think the better of her for that." "Why yes, perhaps, but its very—its odd!" "It is, indeed, that she should talk so at all." "But what does the poor man do all the while?" "Why,—he walks about the room,—as I have seen other men, at a quick rate, up and down, as if for exercise; thus—(mocking him,) and this he will do for hours. Then, he whistles,—and sometimes he'll stop, and take up my hat—and put it on,—'My dear, have you seen Burney's new hat?' Then he'll walk to the glass, and turn it about,—'Ah! these young fellows.' Then Mrs. S. calls out, 'I wish you would let the hat alone; you know nothing at all of the matter; so, pray put it down.'—'Well, my dear,—I only—' and then he walks again! Sometimes he examines my cane, or anything that is new: 'Pray, my dear, have you seen Burney's cane?'—and then she scolds, 'Mr. S., will you leave Mr. Burney's things alone?'" "But I can't help pitying the daughters."

[Here about eight lines are scored out, which seem to have contained Fanny's blame of Mrs. S. A line of Richard's defence may be read—"Why, really I do believe she is, in fact, a woman of as good principles as lives."]

"and when she is serious, extremely humane." "She is the

---

[1] Fanny adds this note, "I am sure by what I heard of her afterwards that he did not mean what in general is meant by amours."

oddest character I ever heard [of] How was you first introduced to her?" "Why, Milton" (n.b. Milton is a relation of his, and formerly assistant to his father,) went there to tune the harpsichord. O my stars! how they do laugh at Milton!—well one day when I was at Bewdley, near five years [ag]o, after my leaving London, it was settled that I should ride over there with him. We were shewn into a parlour—Mrs. S. was with company in another—so I seated myself at the harpsichord, and began playing—soon after she came in—with such an air!—and flung [her]self on a chair by the harpsichord, lent on both her elbows, and stared me full in the face! .... "Did you blush?" "O, always! I always blush! But the fact is I was a little upon the reserve at first. [Bu]t I found it would not do—no—I was [ob]liged to fling it off—And the Bewdley [peo]ple think me so different!—for one is ob[lig]ed to adapt one's self a little to the company one is with—so there I appear so serious and sedate!—and then when they see me at Mrs. S.'s—I am all airs and graces and affectat[ion] and so fine!—so much the thing!" .... "I am quite sorry for the Miss S.'s!—it is terrible to have them brought up in such a manner." "O, they enjoy it of all things." .... "Mrs. S. knows nothing at all of her family—she leans both her arms on the [tab]le, when we go to dinner, and looks about her, as if to see what there is—but she makes her husband carve—then she'll peer ab[out] 'pray what's that—in that corner?—what have you got behind that dish?—it looks nasty Burney, you sha'nt eat that.'—Then she takes great pleasure in *pumping* me, and is for ever telling me of reports she says she hears—m[ere]ly to *pump* me—so I always *assent*—I never contradict her—'do you really?'—'ay, I hear that such a one'—'do you, indeed?'—Then she'll run on about the people she wa[nts] me to see—'O, Burney, you *must* see Lady Betty! [you] will be quite in love with her—the sweetest creature—you must see Lady Betty!—Then she used to form *such* schemes for my comi[ng] to town!—and she charged me, if I did not, that I would write to her. Ha! Ha! Ha!" "Upon my word!—" "O, you can conceive nothing like it—If I am not exact to my time—when I get to Be[wdley] I am sure to find a note waiting for [me and] such enquiries sent all about Bewdley—and often [I f]ind two or three notes—read this first, wrote upon [ ]—Then such a reception![1]

* * * * * *

'My dear Burney!'....'My dear Madam!' (Here he mimicked his own foppery to admiration). Then the moment I am gone, I dare say, she calls me puppy, coxcomb, prig, and a[ll] the names she can invent—not that I ever heard she did —but she serves every b[ody] so. Then she takes great pleasure in tel[ling] us of her old favourites—'That was such a sweet fellow!—O Bet!—if you had seen Vincent!—what a sweet fellow!—O! h[ow] I loved him!—and her husband in the room all the while!—Ha! Ha! Ha!" "But what can the poor man say?" "Say!—Why he talks about the roads—whistles—'Pray, Burney, have you got that place mended in the road yet?'—Then she'll pull me by the sleeve—'Never mind *him*—'"..."so, what did he say next?"—"'I say, Burney, that is a very bad road that leads to your house—when will it be mended?' 'Why, sir——' 'Lord, don't mind *him*—well, who came—' 'Pray, Burney, have you heard who was at the [tur]npike meeting on Monday?'—Then she always pulls my sleeve, and won't let me answer him!—I just turn round to him—'Sir, I think—— O, ma'am,—there was such sport—Sir, it's next—so Mr. such-a-one—its next Tuesday, Sir,—and afterwards, Mrs. ——"

He turned from side to side with such drollness that I could almost fancy I [sa]w them, and we laughed till we were tired. "Then she'll call the youngest—girl to [her] and take off her cap, to shew me her [ha]ir, which is the finest in the world, and she even makes me feel it—'tis so soft!" "How old is she?" "About thirteen, and quite beautiful—and she says [eve]ry thing she can in her praise, and makes me say the same—and then she te[lls] me, that she is very like me!—and when I come in—'Burney, I've thought of nothing but you since you were here—and indeed I never can look at that girl without thinking of you'—though, in truth, the girl

---

[1] Nearly a page has been crossed through and through by the pen of Mme. D'Arblay after these words.

is no more like me than the moo[n]—nay, she even—you would be surprised——"

He stop'd, but we beg'd him to go on.

" Why, she took great pains to *pump* me, to know how my affections stood—and, in short—asked how I should like her B[et] for a wife?—Ha! Ha! Ha!—but I took [it] to be in jest—and I told her—that—I [was] *engaged*. But a little after, I heard of it at Bewdley—that she had said—' Why Burney must have very high views, for he refused my Bet! Who can he be p[ossi]bly engaged to?—he is very young indeed for any engagement of that sort?" " How provoking for Miss S.!—how dreadful to have such a mother! to *offer* her—what a dangerous life for young people!" " Why yes —if any body was to take *advantage* of their situation—" "But yet, I think it's ungrateful in you not to have visited them yet—" " Why, I have had no time."

* * * * * *

April 30.

Now for a little domestic business, after so much *foreign*.

Mama came home on Saturday evening, in health, spirits, and embonpoint. We have not heard lately from Geneva, but expect Miss Allen home next June.

My father continues in good health, excellent spirits, and ever in good humour. His book flourishes with praise, and we hear almost daily of new readers and admirers, and if he had time and inclination for it he might daily increase his acquaintance among the learned and the great. But his time is terribly occupied, and his inclinations lead to retirement and quiet. If his business did not draw him into the world by necessity, I believe he would live almost wholly with his family and books.

We went yesterday to make *a round of visits*, and drank tea at Lady Dalston's,[1] who is a very good sort of woman, and a very old acquaintance of both my father and mother. I shall take notice of only two of the houses we stopt at.

---

[1] The wife of Sir William Dalston, Bart.

And secondly we were so happy as to be let in at Mr. Garrick's, and saw his new house in the Adelphi Buildings, a sweet situation.[1] The house is large and most elegantly fitted up. Mrs. Garrick received us with a politeness and sweetness of manners inseparable from her. I explained to Mr. Garrick why no reply had been sent to his card of invitation, for I told him my father said it *required no answer* as he had given it one himself, by saying at the bottom that *no excuse would be taken*.

" Why, ay "—said he—" I could not take an excuse—*but* —if he had neither come *or* sent me a card ! ! "—he looked drolly defying to combat—

" O, he certainly would have done one or the other—"

" *If* he had not—why then we two must have fought ! I think you have pretty convenient fields near your house ?"

* * * * * *

May.

My design upon the correspondence of Mr. Crisp has succeeded to my wish. He has sent me the kindest and most flattering answer, which encourages me to write again. He says more in three lines than I shall in a hundred, while I live.

[May 4th.]

Dr. Hawkesworth called here lately. He has been, and still is, extremely engaged in writing this *Voyage round the World*, which I doubt not will be a very charming book. He

---

[1] The Adam brothers appear to have been under the patronage of Lord (Chief Justice) Mansfield, who was somewhat given to speculation. There was a kind of lottery to dispose of the Adelphi Buildings. Mr. Cradock tells us in his Memoirs that " the houses on the terrace, from the beauty of their prospects, were selected for particular friends. The centre was allotted to Mr. Garrick, but none of them were quite suited to him, as his health was then declining, and the bleak situation was ill contrasted with his own warm and sheltered situation in Southampton Street, but he was tempted at last to make the experiment, and acceded to the proposal. Thus Garrick returned to the same spot where he had begun life as a wine merchant in Durham Yard.

is very pressing in inviting my father and family to Bromley where he lives. I should extremely like such a jaunt.

I have had the honour, also, of seeing Mr. Baretti, author of the Journey to Spain, and many other books. He is a very good-looking man; which is all I can say, as I have not exchanged more than half a dozen words with him. But I have a most prodigious enthusiasm for authors, and wish to see all of all sorts; and I believe they find it out; for they all look at me with benevolence; though perhaps it is the nature of literary pursuits and meditations to soften the manners and the countenance. What would I not go through to see Dr. Johnson! Mr. Bewley accepted as a present or relic, a tuft of his hearth-broom, which my father secretly cut off, and sent to him in a frank. He thinks it more precious than pearls.[1]

May 5th.

If my father was disposed *to cultivate* with the world, what a delightful acquaintance he might have! We had yesterday another noble concert, at which we had again

---

[1] In 1760 Dr. Burney made his first visit to Dr. Johnson. He was left a short while alone, and looking about, to fulfil his promise to Mr. Bewley to secure him something which had belonged to Dr. Johnson, as he could see not so much as the cover of a letter, a wafer, or a split pen, he cut some bristles from an old hearth-broom in the chimney-corner, slipped them into his pocket-book, wrapped them in silver-paper, and enclosed them in a letter to Horace Walpole's nephew, Lord Orford, in Norfolk, who gave these treasures to Mr. Bewley. He kept them all his life. Dr. Johnson was told this. When he published "The Lives of the Poets," he sent a copy of the volumes which came out first to Mr. Bewley, through the Burneys, addressed, with his compliments, "For the Broom Gentleman." He afterwards wrote Fanny this note, which has not been printed, at the same time sending the later volumes of the "Lives":—

"To Miss Burney.

"Dear Madam,—Pray let these books be sent after the former to the gentleman whose name I do not know.—I am,
"Madam,
"Your most humble servant,
"July 9, 1781.   "SAM: JOHNSON"

Celestini, who led the band, and charmed us all with a solo.[1] We had Tacet also, who gave us a solo on the flute.[2]

Sir William Hamilton, whom my father knew at Naples, where he was Ambassador, honoured us *with his assistance*. He is mentioned with gratitude, in my father's book, for his very great attention to him when abroad; as is his Lady for her fine playing. They were then Mr. and Mrs. Hamilton; but he has since been created Knight of the Bath. He played out of Celestini's book, and I believe very well.[3]

Mr. Beckford brought his flute with him, and played under Tacet. He has won all our hearts by the extreme openness, good-humour, and friendly fervency of his manners.[4]

---

[1] " Rome, September 21 [1770].—The day after my arrival, at his Grace the Duke of Dorset's, I heard Signor Celestini, the principal violin here. . . . [He] played, among other things, one of his own solos, which was very pleasing, though extremely difficult, with great brilliancy, taste, and precision."—*Dr. Burney's First Tour.*

[2] Tacet was an excellent player on the flute.

[3] We find in Dr. Burney's first Musical Tour:—"October, 1770.—The Honourable Mr. Hamilton . . . . whose taste and zeal for the Arts, and whose patronage of artists are well known throughout Europe, being out of town when I came to Naples, did me the honour as soon as he heard of my arrival to invite me to his country-house, called *Villa Angelica*, at the foot of Mount Vesuvius. . . . . I was received by him and his lady, not only with politeness, but even kindness." Music, also, was not wanting, as Hamilton had two pages, one of whom was an excellent player upon the violin, the other upon the violoncello. When Hamilton went back to Naples, he gave a great concert, at which Dr. Burney heard all the chief performers of Naples, all of whom were surpassed upon the harpsichord by Lady Hamilton. She was a Welsh lady, of the name of Barlow, "a good fortune in land." She must not be confounded with the notorious Emma Hart, or Lyon, or Cadogan, whom Sir William unfortunately made his second wife in 1791. Horace Walpole, who saw Hamilton in 1776, wrote that "Vesuvius had burnt him to a cinder." He was minister at Naples from 1764 to 1800. He published a splendid book upon Greek, Etruscan, and Roman antiquities. In 1772 he sold his collection of vases to the British Museum for £8,400. The so-called Portland Vase was also his. This he parted with to Fanny's admirer, the Duchess of Portland, in 1784. His fine Correggio, of "Cupid deprived of his Bow," is now in the National Gallery. He was one of the most versatile of men. In his youth he had been in battles, and, at seventy, hunted and shot with the King of Naples.

[4] " Saturday, Sep. 22, 1770.—This evening Mr. Beckford, to whose

Mr. Price, whom I have mentioned formerly, and who is one of the macaronis of the age, came with Sir William.[1] Mr. Fitzgerald, a very sensible *old* acquaintance of the family's was another hearer,[2] as was Mr. Bagnall, a yet more sensible *new* acquaintance. He is indeed a sweet man; his manners are all gentleness; his countenance, the picture of benevolence. I hear from my father, that he is learned, fond of the polite arts, and himself well versed in them. His son and daughter came with him; the son has just purchased

---

zeal for the business in which I am embarked I have infinite obligations, made a concert for me, consisting of twelve or fourteen of the best performers in Rome; these were led by Signor Celestini."— *Dr. Burney.* William Beckford, of Somerly, in Suffolk, was, like his better-known namesakes, the Lord Mayor, and the Lord Mayor's son (the author of "Vathek"), descended from Colonel Peter Beckford, Lieutenant-Governor and Commissioner-in-Chief of Jamaica.

[1] We fancy that we have found Mr. Price in a copy of verses of the year 1771, called "A Party to Richmond." He is placed among people who (as Garrick says in one of his farces) were all "*Macaroons*, or *Savoury Vivers*" (*i.e.*, of the Savoir-vivre Club).

"To Richmond the folks of the very first mode
In coaches and chaises and cabriolets rode;
There was Bouverie and Meynell, and Greville and Crewe,
With Molyneux, Melbourn, and husbands a few;
And Fitzpatrick, and Charles—"

"Charles" was Charles James Fox. There were, besides, Sir Ralph Payne, Mr. Conway, Mr. Boothby, Mr. Price, and Horace Walpole's M. de Guignes, or Guisnes, the French ambassador. It is but poor stuff. Mr. Price opes his mouth once only, to utter this sorry couplet:—

"I shall into the kitchen and see *what's to eat*,
For methinks with discourse we should mingle some meat."

Sir Ralph concurs in this—

"The banquet convivial, dear Price, be *your* care,
Whilst I the choice fruits and cool bev'rage prepare."

All ends by Mr. Crewe saying—

"What a *terrible boar* it has been all this day!"

He may also be the same of whom Gilly Williams wrote to George Selwyn, from White's, one Saturday evening: "Your friend, Charles Price, had such a tumble last night that the whole Macaroni" [Club?] "rings with it." Probably this was a great loss at the gaming-table.

[2] This appears to have been Mr. Fitzgerald of Cookham, in Berkshire.

a commission in the Guards; he is too insignificant to deserve further mention. Miss Bagnall, too, though modest and obliging, does not appear to deserve a father of such shining and winning merit, as Mr. Bagnall. Dr. King completes my list.

Mr. Burney was again the King of the evening. His performance will never, I believe, cease to be wonderful, even to such frequent hearers. When the concert was over, my father talked over with Sir William Hamilton his Italian expedition. Sir William is a very curious[1] man, a very great naturalist, and antiquary. He took a house, or for aught I know built it, within a short distance of Mount Vesuvius, on purpose to observe its eruptions, and ran daily the utmost risque of his life, to satisfy his curiosity. He spoke with great pleasure of the *fine eruptions* he had seen, and told us that Mount Ætna was now *playing the devil*.[2] He has written several accounts of both these mountains to the Royal Society, which he said he was now correcting and collecting to print in one volume. He is to return in June to Naples, unless there is an Installation, which will detain him, as he has yet received no Star, only the Garter.[3] He said he should pass through Germany. "Shall you?" cried my father, "why, I believe *I* shall go to Germany this summer." "Well," cried Sir William, "if you'll go with me, I'll give you a cook and a bed." I verily believe, though this was said *en passant*, that

---

[1] "*Curious*" is here used in its old sense of praise. Sir William was to be admired as a persevering seeker of objects worth possessing, and as an inquirer into things worth knowing.

[2] Thirteen years later, Horace Walpole speaks of Hamilton as "*probing* Vesuvius."

[3] This is a mistake. The Order of the Bath has a badge, or cognisance, pendant from a red riband, and a star "embroidered on the left side of the upper garment." Debrett says that "no knight elect can wear either the collar or the star before his installation." Probably Sir William's *collar*, which Fanny calls a garter, was sent to him at Naples, but he waited to be installed before wearing it, or, at any rate, to receive a dispensation from the sovereign, which was in later days, if not then, always granted to knights on foreign service. There was a grand installation of fifteen new Knights of the Bath on the 15th of June, 1772, after which those new knights gave a costly entertainment.

my father will reflect upon it, for he has an insatiable rage of adding to the materials for his History, and could not go in better company. Sir William has, in a striking degree, a look that is sensible, penetrating, and even piercing; his singularly curious and enterprising turn seems marked strongly in his countenance.

To this select party had Mr. Crisp and Miss Allen been added, we should scarce have wished another.

* * * * * *

Sunday, May 10th.

* * * * * *

Monsieur L'Abbé Morellet[1] spent this evening with my father. He is a French writer of fame; his subject, *Commerce* and *Agriculture*. He is a man of science and learning, and has lately written a book on Music, which has been very much approved. He is come to England for a few months, and we hope to have the favour of seeing him often.[2]

---

[1] In 1759 "the Abbé Morellet published a small pamphlet on '*Musical Expression and Imitation*,' which is full of ingenious ideas, and written with elegance."—*Dr. Burney*. This was only an episode in the writings and doings of Morellet, who was not only an Academician and a member of the Institute, but even (in 1807) of the French Legislature, when, (in the words of Dr. Burney,) "with a collar encircled with wreaths of laurel, he girded on his sword for the first time in his life, at seventy-nine, ... and suffered it to get between his legs, and trip up his heels!" Morellet was uncle of the wife of Marmontel. He appears in Miss Edgeworth's "Ormond." She had met him in Paris, where, about 1802, Mme. D'Arblay renewed her early acquaintance with him. In 1810 she wrote to Dr. Burney: "You are always remembered here, and named with pleasure by M. Suard and M. L'Abbé Morellet, both of whom we meet chez Madame de Tessé." He had sung her a song of his own making upon completing his eightieth year. In 1811 she speaks of Morellet as "now 85 or 86," but walking about Paris like a young man, preserving "his spirits, memory, and pleasure in existence," and having "a *bookery* in such elegant order that people beg to go to see it." These were affectionate hints that Dr. Burney, who was of about the same age, was to do likewise, live on, and perhaps, also, to put his "Chaos" into better order.

[2] Morellet spent some time in the house of Lord Shelburne, afterwards the first Marquis of Lansdowne.

Thursday, May 21st.

Miss Allen,—for the last time I shall so call her,—came home on Monday last. Her *novel* is not yet over; nevertheless, she—was married last Saturday!

Good Heaven! what a romantic life has this beloved friend lived! I dare not commit particulars to paper. . . . .

[After writing came meeting. These young folks, Maria Allen and Mr. Rishton, met somewhere abroad, and were married at Ipres,[1] on the 16th of May, 1772, Mrs. Maria reaching England, if not her "Governor," on the 18th. Fanny and Susan were told the secret of the marriage, but all three were afraid to disclose it to the proper people, Maria's own mother and kindred. It was most likely Fanny's suggestion that it should be broken to, and by, Mr. Crisp. Mrs. Maria went, as Miss Allen, to see Garrick in Richard III. upon the 30th of May, and, in fact, masqueraded as a single woman until the 7th of June. She then took Susan to Chesington, where a scene of confession to Mr. Crisp was arranged, which is thus described in a joint letter from the two young ladies to Fanny; who had probably designed it as an artist. Maria begins: " My dear Fan—all's over—Crisp knows I am Maria Rishton . . . . To begin in a concise *pleasing* manner—He took me aside the first night after I had by hints hums and ha's told him Rishy and I were to be one—and shewd him the dogs picture—well the old devil grew so scurrilous—he almost made me mad—if he had been a Mahoon[2] he could not have merited what Crisp said.—So I sent him a message by Kate " [Cooke]—" who, with her thick skull guessed the whole *affair from* the beginning—that Mrs. Rishton sent compts. and hoped to see him at Stanhoe[3] this summer." Here Susan thus begins : " Sue—he came into the room to us. Maria fell on her knees instantly and hid her face on the bed—Why what is all this? sd he. Kate claw'd hold of her left hand, and shew'd him the Ring." Whereupon Mr. Crisp used some expressions which, among cultivated gentlemen like himself, were rather obsolete even in 1772, but were not *oaths*.[4] They signified that Maria had worked too

---

[1] Maria's pen at first slips, and she writes " St. Ypres "; the second time she drops the *St.*

[2] Perhaps a corruption of " Mahoun " or " Mahound "—*i.e.*, a *Turk*, according to mediæval views of Turks as fierce, nay, ferocious followers of Mahomet. The word is a survival of the time when the Turks besieged Vienna, but it was late in the day for it to be used in 1772.

[3] Stanhoe is a village in Norfolk, near the little town of Docking, where Mr. Rishton afterwards lived. It was not far from Lynn.

[4] The language of Mr. Crisp, as reported in the Diaries of Fanny and Susan, and as sometimes crossed out or altered for softer synonyms in his letters to Fanny by her tender hand, was of the strength of

much upon his feelings, when "all the while she knew he cou'd do her no good—" "He then came to me"—" Susettikin," sd he, "You know all this affair—is it so?"—" I had had my cue before—"yes Sir—Indeed"—" She is really married," sd he, arching his eyebrows with such a stare of astonishment—" She is upon my honour"—[MARIA:] "No—No—No—Indeed—Nothing—Nothing at all—its all the lyes of that impudent little toad"—[meaning *me*.]" "However poor Maria still kept hiding her face in agonies—which *confirmed* what I had before said—We shewed him the 2 letters which she has received" [from Mr. Rishton] "since she has been in England." Soon Mr. Crisp was convinced, and laughed. After this, in his capacity of Daddy to them all, "he enquired particularly where she was married—by whom—who were the witnesses, &c., &c." Susan writes again: "Maria, as you will perhaps guess, told a hundred lyes in a moment," but Mr. Crisp made out from Susan, as well as from herself, enough to show him that it was "a well-witnessed" and valid marriage, although they could not give him any very satisfactory answers to several of his questions. "He took" (Maria away from Susan and Kitty Cooke) "into his own room." Next "M. Rishton" seizes the pen, and tells how (after making her give a minute account) Mr. Crisp at once (like the man of the world, which he once had been) "changed his tone about my *sposo*," and even "said, in the room before Sue," etc., "You may see he is a man of sence and a gentleman—and he had before call'd him all the designing worthless dogs he coud think of—he wont hear of our being married again as he says that woud be putting odd thoughts into people's heads—and nothing was wanting if he had the certificate and my relations might write to Ypres if they (*sic*) but he insisted on the affair being immediately known and declared in a publick-way—and grew almost angry on my remonstrating—all the objections I coud make were like dirt in his eyes—what did we want with a house—while we had money in our pockets we might find a place any where—besides he woud have us go directly into Norfolk together and settle our affairs on the spot. he has, wrote to Mama to tell her the whole affair and insists upon my going back to Queen Square *Mrs. Rishton* and writing immediately to Martin to come over.

Queen Anne's days, which saw his birth; quite distinct from the milder expletives or metaphors which these girls were used to hear under George III. For instance, when Mr. Crisp learnt that Fanny had made him hear "Evelina," read, without telling him that she had written it, he called her "a young Devil," "a young Hell-fire," for drawing him in to read and praise it unawares. The "Hell-fire" was an allusion to a terrific club of that name, believed to have existed in his youth, on purpose to talk and act "horrid impieties." Mrs. Delany said that "the club consisted of about a dozen persons of fashion of both sexes, some of them females unmarried," and one, a maid of honour to Queen Caroline.

Maria is to write to my Uncles about this affair—and in short I am no longer to conceal my name. I told him what Rishton had said that people woud attribute to indifference his being absent from me now—' not in the least—things are exactly as they shoud be '—that I must go to my *Lord* and *Master* the instant he arrived in London if Mama would not give him house room for a day or two till we went into Norfolk—in short I fear there will be a terrible bustle—Write me word how Mama takes it—and in what manner. I hope she will send me an answer on Tuesday as I am losing my time at Chesington which is now quite precious to me. if you are asked about it tell all you know—and speak a good word for us—tell Hetty the same—and bid Molly " [Stancliffe] "not fright herself but answer clearly all the questions asked her and let her go to Mrs. Searle's" [a milliner, or dressmaker] "to get some of my things ready to be tried on on Thursday morning—and to get on with the handkerchiefs—. . . . I shan't come until I hear something from my Mother. if she is *civil to you* do press her to write directly that I may come up immediately on the receipt of her letter. Speak to that poor toad Molly directly—and write the return of the post yourself—Adieu my own Fan." This letter is numbered 14, is addressed to Fanny in Queen's Square, and has a London post-mark of (8 / IV) and an illegible country-mark.

What a kind "Daddy Crisp" he was to be a father to all these girls! He let Maria off very lightly—telling her only, "What a pretty piece of work she *might* have made of it!" and uttering a few reflections upon "the thousand difficulties in which young people involved themselves before they were aware, by concealing things from their relations"; but even at more than a hundred years distance, we cannot help pitying Fanny, who was involved in the secret of one who had no drop of her blood, and was obliged to front the culprit's mother, who was also her own stepmother. Nor was Fanny the bearer of a word of penitence or of apology. She was only told to look to the progress of Maria's "things"—that is, of her *trousseau.* " What scenes we shall have!" writes Fanny, then draws her pen through the words. We also have had *scenes* out of it, for the situation of "Evelina," disowned by her father, who had been "a very profligate young man," and had married that "ill-advised" young lady, her mother, privately in Paris, then "infamously burnt the certificate of their marriage, and denied that they had ever been united," might well have been suggested by some of the words and warnings which fell from Mr. Crisp on that night in June, 1772. Mainly for this have we dwelt upon Mr. Rishton and Maria Allen. How did Mrs. Burney take it? Very warmly, as well she might! We know not what she said to Fanny, but thenceforth she put obstacles in the way of her visiting Maria. She *did* receive the couple, sooner or later; but spoke her mind with vigour; upon one occasion giving Mr. Rishton (as poor Maria complains) an account of " every vice, fault, or foible I had ever been guilty of since my birth." The wrath of Mrs. Burney was, most likely, not so "*implacable*" as Maria describes it to have been ; but although Maria nobly announces that she forgets all her mother has ever made her suffer when Miss Allen now that they are parted; as *Mrs. Rishton*, she resented Mrs. Burney's resentment at her marriage, for long-and-long. No mention of a second marriage has, so far, been found. The Rishtons pass from our view until the beginning of 1773. The wild "Allen" is being tamed during these next months. She has married "*a Bashaw*" (as she was told by his sister, Mrs. Edgell)—a very affectionate Bashaw, but still a Bashaw; although not "a Mahoon," as Mr. Crisp had almost made him out to be, but just an only son, inclined to show and extravagance, sensitive as to what appearance was made by the careless Maria, touchy towards his kindred and hers, with many dislikes of people, which she fell into, but a loving husband when he was humoured, as he always seems to have been during the years of their married life of which we have cognizance through the letters of his wife to Fanny.]

[May.]

I have just left the famous Sir William Browne in the parlour, a most extraordinary old man, who lives in the Square,[1] and is here on a visit. He has been a very renowned physician; whether for saving or killing, I cannot say. He is near eighty, and enjoys prodigious health and spirits, and is gallant to the ladies to a most ridiculous degree. He never comes without repeating some of his verses. I can now recollect a stanza he has just told me, occasioned by some little flirtation with a lady's fan :—

> No wonder that this Fan should prove
> A vehicle to carry love ;
> But to return it I desire,
> Lest it too much should fan the fire.

I think the lines *worth preserving;* so flew out of the room to write them.[2]

---

[1] Queen Square.
[2] Sir William Browne, M.D. (1692-1774), was an M.A. of Cambridge, and wrote the well-known epigram, "The King to Oxford sent a troop of horse," etc. He has kept his name alive by founding prizes of three gold medals to be given yearly at Cambridge for the best Greek ode, the best Latin ode, and the three best Latin and Greek epigrams. He also founded a scholarship at Cambridge. He settled at Lynn about

I have had a very clever letter from my dear Daddy Crisp; I am charmed at entering into a correspondence with him.

My dear father intends going to Germany this summer, to see if he can gather any materials for his History of Music. If the most indefatigable pains and industry will render his work worthy of approbation, it will meet with the greatest.

May 30th.

Maria, Susan, and myself had the happiness to see Garrick, last night, in Richard the Third. We had always longed to see him in all his great characters, though least in this which is so shocking, though not the least, of the praise of his acting. (*sic*) .... Garrick was sublimely horrible! Good Heavens —how he made me shudder whenever he appeared! It is inconceivable how terribly great he is in this character! I will never see him so disfigured again; he seemed so truly the monster he performed, that I felt myself glow with indig-

---

1716. There he was, like Dr. Burney, under the patronage of the reigning family of Turner. In 1740 he went to London, and became, in the end, President of the College of Physicians. Bishop Warburton describes him as a little, round, well-fed gentleman, with a large muff in one hand, and a small Horace, open, in the other (1769). See a previous note, p. 52. He had been in frequent conflict with the aldermen of Lynn, as he was with the licentiates of medicine in London, but seems to have been as shrewd as he was singular. Nichols has printed his elaborate will, in which he desires that on his coffin, "when in the grave, may be deposited *in its leather case or coffin*, my pocket Elzevir Horace, ' comes viæ vitæque dulcis et utilis,' '*worn out with, and by me.*'" He also appointed himself, not only a monument with that of his late "Lady" in Hillington Church (Norfolk), but a marble monument in Westminster Abbey, to be placed "as near that of my Master, Dr. Mead (*Medicorum facilè Principis*) as any vacant arch may admit, or otherwise, in the Poets' Corner, over against that of Mr. Prior." He ordained by this will that his descendants, through his only child, Mary (who married William, brother of Martin Folkes, President of the Royal Society), should forfeit his property to the University of Cambridge if ever they dropped the name of Browne before that of Folkes. The forfeiture has so far been avoided by the baronets who have represented him. Martin Folkes Rishton was first cousin of Martin Browne Folkes, Sir W. Browne's grandson and future heir.

nation every time I saw him. The applause he met with, exceeds all belief of the absent. I thought at the end they would have torn the house down: our seats shook under us.[1]

[It may be remarked that what remains of this year's Diary is prior to Dr. Burney's departure on his German Tour, in July, 1772. Fanny fills the gap in her Memoir of her father, and gives an account of his severe illness on his return, in the very stormy weather of December, 1772; and of the droll, but dismal, incident, that he was so much exhausted by sea-sickness, that when he was told that the sailing-vessel had reached Dover, he begged to be left to rest before landing, fell asleep, was forgotten, and woke, in mid-channel, to find himself on his way back to Calais, with another stormy passage to Dover before him. He had a most severe illness on reaching Queen's Square, was sent to Chesington on recovery, and forbidden writing books for some time. The affectionate outburst in praise of Dr. Burney, written in the beginning of the Diary for January, 1773, may have been a tribute from Fanny to his patience and cheerfulness in illness.]

---

[1] Mr. Cradock writes that:—" When Garrick was about to leave the stage, he said to a party of us, ' I gained my fame by Richard, and I mean to end with it.' " When Garrick said this he was mindful of a great time when he had played Richard at an illicit theatre in Goodman's Fields, and when the whole line of streets from Temple Bar to Whitechapel was thronged by carriages of noble and gentlemen going to hear him. One night, as he began to speak, he saw a gentleman dressed in black sitting in a side box. This he knew to be the famous Mr. Pope, whose eyes, he said, shot like lightning through him, so that for joy and fear he could hardly go on, but he soon saw Mr. Pope clap his hands, and was told afterwards that Pope had said to Lord Ossory, who was sitting with him, " That young man never had his equal as an actor, and he will never have a rival."

1773.

[To give an account of the condition of this year's journal would be to repeat much of what has been said of others. One point of difference is to be noted, this is much more bulky; partly because Fanny's pleasure in writing grew with her age, partly because it consists of two journals; one of them private, to which another has been attached, which is addressed to her sister Susan. This latter describes a delightful visit to Devonshire. The following extract from a letter of Maria Rishton's to Fanny, is a piece of playful rhodomontade about what was, perhaps, one of those bursts of authorship which Fanny no longer tried to restrain. It is convenient to place it here, although it was written after the Teignmouth visit.

"And so by way of return to the very Curious Manuscript I received I have named the first Cow I ever was Mistress of Fanny. How can I thank you enough my friend for the Invaluable Treasure you have sent me. My workmen are now employed in turning an Arched Vault where it is to be deposited in An Iron Chest to preserve it from the Ravages of Times *(sic)* and hand down this Valuable piece of Antiquity to future Ages yet unborn—I intend leaving it as An Inheritance to one of my Sons who shall be instructed Early in All the Hidden misteries of Science that he may understand this great production— but as I am Afraid I am not Worthy of being Mother to such A Son I must select some favorite of the Muses to intrust this Treasure with— How came you in possession of this precious pearl ?—and how is it possible your Friend ship coud Transport you so far to let you part with it—Happy Britain ! to live to see the days when thy Children are Capable of Such Astonishing Actions—but my gratitude transports me so far I am unable to pursue the Theme, and heartily *(sic)* I coud with propriety begin your Tambour Apron At this Time—and so you wish *(sic)* all how and About us—upon *(sic)* my head is so filled with household affairs And my life at Stanhoe is so different from the Serenity of Tingmouth I can *(sic)* bring my ideas into order enough to Attempt anything in the Narritive Style "——]

January 16th, Queen's Square.

I shall begin this year without any preamble, having nothing new to say. I am in the situation of the Poet-Laureat,[1] and with him may exclaim :

---

[1] Whitehead.

"For on a subject so to tatters tore;
What can be said, that ha'nt been said before?"

This is my fifth or sixth Journal-book; yet will not, I am persuaded, be my last, but it would require very superior talents to write an annual Exordium. I must therefore content myself with plainly and concisely proceeding with my life and opinions—addressed to Myself.

And, first, it is my opinion, that the world is very ill used in being called a bad one. If people did but know how to enjoy the blessings they meet, they would learn that our share of misfortunes very often serves but to enhance their value.

. . . .

Exceptions, Fordyce says, do only confirm a general rule. For my own part, how well should I think of myself, if my deserts equalled my happiness! My father has ever been more deserving than fortunate. This saying could not be reversed in him. The longer I live, and the more I see of the world, the more am I both astonished and delighted at the goodness, the merit, and the sweetness of that best of men. All that is *amiable*, added to all that is *agreeable;* every thing that is *striking* joined to every thing that is *pleasing;* learning, taste, judgment, wit, and humour,—candour, temperance, patience, benevolence, every virtue under the sun is his!

But now to events, which will otherwise crowd so fast upon me, that I shall not be able to recollect them : what a loss would that be! to my dear—Nobody!

* * * * * *

Tuesday.

Mr. and Mrs. Rishton are in town. Yesterday they made me spend the day with them, to accompany them to Covent Garden Theatre. . . . . Mrs Bettenson and Sir Richard Bettenson,[1] uncle and aunt of Mr. Rishton, are to make our party at the play. The Baronet has a fortune of £5000 per

---

[1] Sir Richard Betenson, or Bettenson, was the widower of Mr. Rishton's aunt, [Lucretia Folkes;] Mrs. Bettenson was probably his spinster sister.

annum, and Mr. Rishton is his *presumtive heir*. Though not a *declared* one, yet he is the nearest relation. They live in our Square, and we went to take them up early, as the *Prelude* was to be done.[1] .... The servant begged us to alight, as his mistress was not ready. The moment the coach stopped Mr. Rishton said to me, "Now, take no notice, but you will see presently one of the oddest women you ever yet have seen—off the stage!" Mrs. Rishton, who was extremely eager not to miss Barsanti, having never yet seen her on the stage, was very much vexed at this delay. Her husband, more impetuous, exclaimed against such ill-breeding.—"How truly vulgar! to make people wait!" But he would not get out. "Let's sit still," cried he, "it will save both time and compliments." In about five minutes Mrs. Bettenson appeared in the passage. She is a fat, squab, ugly, vulgar woman, yet, I am told, extremely fond of her family. However, she was this evening all *condescension*.

"Won't you come in, Mrs. Rishton?—why, Lord, I have been ready this good while;—we only wait for my brother. But he says he can't go five in a coach."

This was a delicate speech for me! I began to say I was sorry, &c., but Mrs. Rishton whispered me "Remember *they* are the intruders, we made our party first." Mr. Rishton was now obliged to get out, and after a decent quantity of speeches and compliments, the Baronet and his amiable sister at last came in.

We had an upper box. Barsanti acted extremely well, and was much admired.[2] "And how do *you* like this Prelude,

---

[1] "An occasional Prelude" was written by George Colman, the elder, for Miss Barsanti's first appearance as an actress on the 21st of September, 1772. It was contrived so that she might mimic the Italian and English singers of the day.

[2] Miss Barsanti first appeared at Covent Garden Theatre on the 21st of September, 1772. She gave the happy occasion for Miss L. M. Hawkins's going, to what she looked upon as her first *real play*. It is true that she had before seen "The Alchemist," but she did not like that, and "Cato," but it was only acted by schoolboys at an academy, just as Fanny saw young gentlemen play "Tamerlane" in 1768. The rigid Sir John, and the strict Lady Hawkins, upheld Jenny Barsanti, who was "religious, discreet, and made all that she wore," even to her

madam?" asked Sir Richard, little thinking that I have seen it near a dozen times. I am glad to find it so long lived. The play was again "Elfrida,"[1] with a new entertainment called "Cross Purposes,"[2] in which is introduced a macaroni's footman who had on exactly the undress livery of Mr: Rishton's servants. Mrs. Rishton could not forbear laughing as well as myself. *She* looked up to Mr. Rishton: I did not venture.

---

stage-dresses. Miss Hawkins tells us that Jenny first appeared in "The Funeral," by Sir Richard Steele. It was a sore struggle for her to act at all that night, as her father had had a paralytic stroke that very day while at dinner. George Colman, the younger, says she "was by far the most distinguished of the actresses of her time" in talent. She was the first Lydia Languish, playing that part on the nights of January the 17th and 18th, 1775, when "The Rivals" is said by some to have failed through Lee's bad acting as Sir Lucius O'Trigger, by others, owing to its tedious length before revision. Miss Barsanti afterwards played Lydia both in London and the country during its great success. She married a Mr. Lester, or Lister, in 1777 —and Mr. Daly, manager of the Dublin Theatre, afterwards. She seems to have had tact, as she pleased both the Hawkinses and the Burneys. When acting in Dublin, she wore nothing but very rich Irish manufactures. Ladies were then wearing very full petticoats in Dublin, but Jenny made hers scantier, and turned the tide of fashion in favour of what were called "Barsanti petticoats."

[1] Mason's "Elfrida" was published in 1752, but never acted until the 21st of November, 1772. On the 26th, Walpole wrote to congratulate Mason on its "pleasing exceedingly." This Walpole learnt from "the papers, his only company at present," as he was slowly recovering from a severe fit of the gout. Mason replied, "in the spleen," (real or affected):— "do you not think it somewhat cavalier in Mr. Colman," (the manager of the theatre,) "to do what he has done without any previous intimation to me? I should have known nothing about the matter if my bookseller had not heard of it, and demanded the property of the chorus books then printing off. One of these he has sent me in which the odes are so lopped and mangled, that they are worse than the productions of Handel's poet, Dr. Morell." Dr. Arne, who composed the music for "Elfrida," is also a subject of complaint, and the only thing "that pleases me" (Mason) "in the whole business, is that Garrick is in a fidget," that "little Colman," not he himself, brought "Elfrida" upon the stage—which he would have done, had he thought it would have been agreeable to Mr. Mason. "This would almost lead me to forgive Colman, was such a man worth one's forgiveness."

[2] "Cross Purposes," a comedy in two acts, by Obrien, an actor, was first played on the 8th of December, 1772.

After all, his foible is certainly dress, and love of being *distinguished* from *the vulgar crew*. I had the pleasure to see Prior's celebrated fair "Kitty, beautiful and young," now called Kitty, *beautiful and old*, in the stage box, *i.e.*, the Duchess of Queensberry.[1]

In going back to the coach, Sir Richard and his sister gave a polite invitation to supper. I desired to be set down at home, but they all joined in asking me, and I was too happy to be anywhere with the Rishtons to refuse.

Mr. Rishton was in high spirits, and prodigiously agreeable. Mrs. Bettenson, among her other amiable qualities, has to an uncommon degree that of thriftiness, of which her brother, though not so apparently, participates. I had been told before, by Mr. Rishton, that whenever she had company she was always so unlucky as to have *just parted with her cook*,— so that I had the utmost difficulty to keep my countenance, when, upon my apologizing for my visit, she said—"O dear, ma'am, you do me a great deal of honour,—I am only sorry

---

[1] Catherine Hyde, second daughter of Henry Hyde, Earl of Clarendon and Rochester, a kinsman of Queen Anne, married the third Duke of Queensberry in 1720. Prior made her famous by his poem called "The Female Phaeton." In it, she wrings from her mother permission to go out in the chariot, and "sets the world on fire." Prior's first line is often quoted,—

"Thus Kitty, beautiful and young,"

but not so the second, which was quite as true,—

"And wild as colt untamed."

She must have been very beautiful to judge from even a poor portrait of her, but she was rather flighty than witty.—When the French Lady Bolingbroke spoke of her as "*Sa Singularité*," Mrs. Montagu tells us that the Duchess was silly enough to be "in raptures with the" (sarcastic) "appellation." She courted the Tory wits. Gay almost lived with the Duke, and she tried hard to bring Swift from Ireland to join him. She lived to 1777. Horace Walpole wrote on the 26th of June, 1773—"I saw the Duchess of Queensberry last night; she was in a new pink lute-string, and looked more blooming than the Maccaronesses. One should sooner take her for a young beauty of an old-fashioned century than for an antiquated goddess of this age. I mean by twilight." When Fanny saw her it was fifty-two years after the death of her poet, Prior.

you will not have better fare—but, indeed, my cook—and an excellent one she was,—went away yesterday."

In considering the partial dispensation of riches, I think the poor should ever have in remembrance this query :

> ——— " which is worse,
> Want—with a full—or with an empty purse ? "

The table was covered with half, or less than half, filled dishes. I should not, however, have mentioned this, but to speak of Mr. Rishton, whose behaviour was unmerciful. It is a general custom with him to eat little or no supper— but he affected a voracious appetite, and eat as if he had fasted three days. I own I had malice enough to enjoy this, as I have no pity for *grand penury*. Riches and Pride without Liberality—how odious ! I touched nothing but an orange; which was not remarked.

Mr. Rishton raised my admiration by his behaviour to this pair, from whom he has reason to expect so much. Far from flattering, he even *trims* them for their foibles ; and whenever they seem to exact any deference, he treats them most cavalierly. He declares to his wife, that he would not descend to cringe and court them for the surety of all his uncle's estate. If he humbled himself to them, he is convinced they would trample on him. Such is the insolence of Wealth.

At twelve o'clock Mr. Rishton ordered his carriage—and turning to me, with a very wicked smile, said—" The play will be over late to-night, Miss Burney ! " However, I know that my offence was given in *going ;* my *staying* did not much signify.[1]

* * * * * *

---

[1] This seems to refer to the difficulty Fanny had in obtaining the permission of Mrs. Burney to go to the theatre with those offenders against propriety, Mr. and Mrs. Rishton. A page, at the least, has been erased before the passage beginning, "Mr. and Mrs. Rishton are in town." At the top of it may just be read, "Leave, however, I obtained, though a dry one."

January 25th.

We had yesterday the most heavenly evening! Millico,[1] the divine Millico was here, and with him Sig[r]. Sacchini,[2] and Sig[r]. Celestini, that sweet violinist, whom I have often mentioned. We had no further party, which I greatly rejoiced at, as we were at full liberty to devote every instant to these. Sig[r]. Sacchini is a very elegant man and extremely handsome. Millico is of a large or rather an immense figure, and not handsome *at all, at all;* but his countenance is strongly expressive of sweetness of disposition, and his conversation is exceedingly sensible. He was very much surprised at the size of our family. My father has so young a look, that all strangers are astonished to find him such a *Patriarch.* Millico's conversation was partly Italian and partly French, and Sacchini's almost all Italian; but they neither of them speak three words of English.

Hetty being called upon to open the concert, began a rondeau in the overture to Sacchini's new opera, which has been performed but twice; but she had been to three rehearsals, and has gotten almost half the opera by ear. Sacchini almost started; he looked at first in the utmost perplexity, as if doubting his own ears, as the music of *Il Cid* has never been published.[3] Millico clapped his hands, and

---

[1] Millico came to England in the spring of 1772. Dr. Burney writes that he was a "judicious performer, and worthy man, who was not an Adonis in person, and whose voice had received its greatest beauties from art." Horace Walpole tells us that Millico sang for the first time in England on the 21st of April, 1772.

[2] Antonio Sacchini, of Naples, arrived in England in 1772, after having composed for all the great theatres in Italy and Germany, with increasing success. "In the year 1770, when I saw Sacchini at Venice, he told me that he had composed near forty serious and ten comic operas; and in 1778, enquiring of him to what number his dramatic works then amounted, he said to seventy-eight, of which he had forgotten even the names of two." .... "This graceful, elegant, and judicious composer died at Paris in September, 1786, where he was honoured with a public funeral."—Dr. Burney. It may be added that Sacchini composed the music of "a dramatic piece," adapted from Fanny's novel, "Evelina."

[3] "Il Cid" was the first opera by Sacchini ever brought upon the English stage. Millico was the chief singer in it.

laughed—"Ah! brava! brava!" Sacchini then bowed, and my father explained the manner of her having got this rondeau; at which he seemed much pleased. When she had finished her lesson, my father applied to Millico, who readily complied, and with the utmost good-nature sang his most favourite air in the new opera, only accompanied by Sacchini on the harpsichord. I have no words to express the delight which his singing gave me, more far away than I have ever received, even at the Opera; for his voice is so sweet, that it wants no instruments to cover it. He was not, however, satisfied with himself; he complained of his cold; but seeing us all charmed,—with a sweetness that enchanted me in so great a performer, he said, "Eh bien, encore une fois; la voix commence à venir"; and sang it again. Oh! how divinely! I am sure he must then satisfy *himself*, and he will never find any other person equally difficult. For my own part, the mere recollection fills me with *rapture;* my terms are strong, and yet they but weakly express my feelings.

After this, he made Sacchini himself sing (though not without difficulty), saying, "il a une petite voix; mais il chante très bien." Sacchini with the utmost merit has the truest modesty; when he found he could not excuse himself, he complied with the most graceful diffidence imaginable. He has very little voice, but great taste. Millico led the applause that was given him. This composer and singer appear to be most affectionate friends. They do indeed seem born to make each other's merit conspicuous. Millico has read in my father's countenance, I suppose, the excellence of his heart, for though their acquaintance is of short date, he reposes great confidence in him, insomuch as that he has given him some manuscript music of his own composition, which he intends for his Benefit. This MS. is for an Ode which he has had written, expressing his gratitude for his reception in England. The verses are pretty, and he has set them with great propriety. He sat down himself to the harpsichord, and played and sung his part through,—as the words are English, he desired that we would all try, whether we could understand them, which, to say the truth, was not very easy. He made my father correct the pronunciation.

When they moved from the harpsichord, to draw them back, Hetty began another air of Millico's in "Il Cid"; this had the desired effect. Millico, all good-nature, was prevailed upon to sing it; which he did—

"in notes so sweet and clear,
The sound still vibrates on my ravished ear."

Admiration can be no new tribute to the merit of this divine singer; yet he two or three times observed our delight to my father, and repeated that we had "l'alma harmonica" (*sic*); and, on Sacchini's singing an air which was quite new to us, but which we were highly pleased with, he said, "Elles connaissent la bonne musique; cela les touche à l'instant."

I again repeat, the evening was *heavenly!* If any thing on *earth* can be so, 'tis surely perfection of vocal music. Nothing is more charming than to see great talents without affectation. My father says, that there are hardly in all Italy three such modest men as Millico, Sacchini, and Celestini. They did whatever was asked of them with the most unaffected good-humour. They are wholly free from vanity, yet seemed as much to enjoy giving pleasure, as we did receiving it.

In taking leave, Millico turned to Hetty, Susan, and me, and bowing, said, " Je viendrai une autre fois, et nous passerons la soirée *comme il faut*."

February 13th.

On the above assurance have I lived ever since. The voice of Millico seems continually sounding in my ear, and harmonizing my soul. Never have I known pleasure so exquisite, so heartfelt, so *divinely penetrating*, as this sweet singer has given me. He is ever present in my imagination; his singing and his songs are the constant companions of my recollection.

My father dined last week with this Orfeo; he has invited himself to favour us again soon, and promised to bring his harp, on which he sometimes accompanies himself. But our affection to Millico has occasioned our meeting with a very disagreeable accident. Last Saturday evening mama suddenly proposed going to the Opera, *Il Cid*, the fame of which had excited our curiosity. Susy and myself joyfully skipt at the proposal, and the coach was instantly ordered. The opera is the sweetest I ever heard, and Millico sang like an angel. We stayed very late to avoid the crowd. When we went down, we got with difficulty to our coach; but, after the usual perils and dangers, we were driven out of the Haymarket and into Suffolk Street. Here we concluded we were safe; but, as we afterwards found, there had been left a load of gravel in the street, which the shade (being moonlight) hid from the coachman. We found ourselves suddenly mounted on one side. Mama, who is soon alarmed, cried out, "We are going, we are going!" I sat quite quiet, thinking it a false alarm; but presently the coach was entirely overturned, and we came sideways to the ground. Stupefied between surprise and fright, I fell without moving a finger, and lay quite silent. The glass at my side was fortunately down, and the blind up, which saved my temples from the pavement; but the glass above me broke, and the pieces fell on my face. Mama and Susan both imagined me to be most in danger, from being undermost, and my tender Susan called out to me repeatedly, "Fanny, are you hurt? are you very much hurt, Fanny? my dear Fanny?"

It was some time, from an unaccountable effect of fear, before I could answer; but the falling of the glass roused me. Some people immediately gathered about the carriage, and opened the door, which was now at the top of the coach. Mama called out, "Here's nobody hurt!" but desired them to assist me. With some difficulty I made a shift to stand up, and a gentleman lifted me out of the carriage. He had no hat on, being come out of a neighbouring house. He begged me to go with him to his sisters, who were close by, that I might get out of the mob, and promised to take care of me; but I was now terrified for mama and Susan, and could not leave the place, as we were all separated by different assistants, I heard the former call out that her arm was broken! I quite wrung my hands with horror. This gentleman took hold of me, and almost used violence to make me come away. I remember I called out to him, as he forced me on, that he would drive me distracted! He assured me that the other ladies would be safe; but, as if he had not had trouble enough with me, I answered all his civilities with, "But, go! why can't you go and help them?" However, he would not leave me, for which I believe I am very much obliged to him, as I was surrounded by a mob, and as there were assistants enough about the coach. When mama and Susan were taken out, we accepted this gentleman's offer, and went into his house, where we were very hospitably received by some ladies. My poor mother had her arm dreadfully hurt; Susan had only sprained two fingers, to save herself from falling on us; my face was very bloody from two small cuts I had received on my nose. We stayed here near a quarter of an hour, and met with the utmost kindness and civility.

Mamma declared she would walk home; my deliverer insisted on accompanying us; but John assured us that the coach was not further injured than by the glasses being broken, and that we might very safely go home in it; which we accordingly did, though in much terror. Mamma has been confined ever since. Mr. Bromfield has examined her arm; but it is so much swelled, that it can only be poulticed at present, and he has not said whether it has received any further injury than a most violent sprain.[1] I fear it will be a very tedious affair. Susan, thank God! is very well; and so am I.

Sunday, February.

Dr. Hawkesworth and his lady by appointment dined and spent the evening here. I like the Doctor more and more every time I have the pleasure of seeing him; that stiffness and something resembling pedantry, which formerly struck me in him, upon further acquaintance and more intimacy

---

[1] About that time there were several surgeons of the name of Bromfield. This may have been William Bromfield, Esq.; who, in 1776, appears as surgeon to the royal household, "with £150," and senior surgeon to St. George's Hospital.

either wear off or disappear. He was extremely natural and agreeable. His wife is a very well-bred, obliging, and sweet-tempered woman.

* * * * * *

We were all of opinion that it was necessary immediately to wait on the family in Suffolk Street, to return them thanks for their assistance; but mama was obliged to keep her room, —Susan was engaged, and therefore on Monday I went, John knowing the way to the house. They appear to be an agreeable family, consisting of a brother and three sisters. I felt very awkward, when I got into the street, lest I should be forgot. However, I determined to venture rather than omit paying thanks so well deserved; but they all immediately recollected me, and seemed very glad to hear of our safety. Their names are Miland.

* * * * * *

February 19th.

My father's German Tour is now in the press, and he is hurried and fatigued beyond expression, for this is a time of year when his business is at its height.

We had yesterday,—I know not whether to say *pain* or *pleasure*,—of seeing Mr. Garrick in the part of Lear.[1] He was exquisitely great; every idea which I had formed of his talents, although I have ever idolized him, was exceeded. I am sorry that this play is acted with Cibber's alterations, as every line of his, is immediately to be distinguished from Shakespeare; who, with all his imperfections, is too superior to any other dramatic writer, for them to bear so near a comparison; and to my ears every line of Cibber's is feeble and paltry.

---

[1] Lœtitia Hawkins says that her very unpleasant father, Sir John, threatened to punish her, and her brothers, when they took her part, in what he pompously called, a "Triple Alliance;" by *taking them all to see* "*King Lear.*" Was it as a warning against filial disobedience?— or to give them "*a good fright*"? Miss Hawkins says that Lear made her ill, from nerve-distress. Another threat Sir John once used when she had been naughty, was,—"Miss—I intend to take you to Dr. Johnson's this evening."

Thursday, February 25th.

Mr. Adam and his brother, two gentlemen whom my sister and self formerly met with at Captain Debieg's, had this day exposed to public sale a large and valuable collection of busts, statues, bas-reliefs, pictures, &c., which they purchased many years since in Italy. These gentlemen, with another of their brothers, have, since our acquaintance with Mrs. Debieg has dropt, built the Adelphi,—so called from the three *brothers* being engaged in it. The undertaking was, I believe, too great for them, and they have suffered much in their fortunes. I cannot but wonder, that so noble and elegant a plan should fail of encouragement. I went yesterday morning with my sister to the view of these things. I could not but greatly pity the collector, who is I fear obliged to part with them. As I have neither knowledge or judgment in these matters, I venture at no further opinion than that to me the sight was a great regale.[1] We saw many of our old friends of the Scotch party, but were not known to any, probably not seen, as we sate very backward, Hetty wishing to avoid them. I often suspect that Mr. Seton was thunderstruck by Hetty's marriage.

[There is a great gap in Mrs. Rishton's letters between June, 1772, and the 22nd of February, 1773, on which day she writes to Fanny, regretting her mother's injury, and the alarm of all who were in the coach accident. She writes from "Alfred's Buildings," Bath, where she seems to have spent the autumn and winter for the sake of drinking the waters. She had been ill, indeed she was not so robust as her high spirits might make us suppose. As a girl, she had bad health. She says that she is much alone, although Mr. Rishton was so kind that "there is not a sun that rises that does not make [her] more thankful for being his wife."

The Rishtons were looking forward to living at Stanhoe House, which belonged to "Mrs. 'Mun[2] Allen" (the wife of one of Maria's family), and Fanny is desired to "put no spokes in the wheel of her own Norfolk journey," as Maria hopes to see *her* at Stanhoe. "I hope not to see Bath of many years. I am surprised what a change Matrimony has made in me—and you may remember how we used to wonder at Hetty's being so *wifish*.—I woud not be condemned to

---

[1] Robert and James Adam had lived eight years in Italy, France, and Holland, [1754-1762]. They had a three days' sale of their pictures in February, 1773, but bought in the greater part of the 218.

[2] An East-country shortening of Edmund.

settle here if any one coud give me a house ready furnished." In the next letter she has suffered from servants, having been obliged to send away a butler whom they had hired in London, as he "proved so dirty, stupid, and unqualified in every respect." Maria has even a passing fit of jealousy; thinks her husband cooled towards her, and prays Fanny's pity for what she must suffer, assuring her that she may depend upon her letters being burned directly. "So be free. I have been vastly disappointed in not going to Fischer's concert to-night. I suppose all Bath will be there, for it is the last time the eldest Linley sings at Bath, she is engaged for the oratorios[1]—but Rishton who is rather more exact about dress than I am, can't think of my appearing. R .... wanted me to buy a suit of mignionet linnen fringed for second mourning[2]—but my economy prevaild over that, and as he was unwilling I should appear else, I gave up the dear Fischer—see what a cruel thing to have a sposo who is rather a p—p—y in those sort of things. Now don't you think this little anecdote put into proper hands might make a dismal tale, such as 'Ah, poor girl, she has reason enough to repent—denied going into company, left all alone, husband flirting with every Miss in his way,' &c. tho' I am afraid I am not enough in favor to be an object of pity—well all for the best. Rishton is gone" [to the concert] "fischer's hautboy has the same merit with him the Bagpipes or Jews' trump might."[3]]

---

[1] The Oratorios at Covent Garden Theatre in Lent.

[2] The delicate little garden-plant (a woad,) which in England is called "mignonette," is, in France, named "*réséda*," but our name must have come to us through France, as a synonym for daintiness in miniature. In 1721, Lady Mary Wortley Montagu asks her sister to buy "some narrow *minunet*," (a guinea's worth,) for the use of the future Lady Bute, "who grows a little woman." This appears to have been what ladies used to call "*edging*," a fine, narrow lace for trimming children's caps and tuckers. The word "*mignon*," and (its diminutive of comparison,) "*mignonnette*," serve as many purposes in France, as the much-abused word "nice" in England. A book is "*mignon*" if it has "*finesse d'esprit*," a child, if it is good. A fine kind of net, and of lace was "*mignonnette*." So was a kind of stuff made of wool and silk, and a tiny sort of pear; even a kind of pepper finely ground. In French typography there are both "*mignonne*" and "*mignonnette*" founts of type. The suit of linen, which was too expensive for Maria, was certainly very fine, as well as *fringed*. The fringe showed that it was "mourning." "Fringed, or plain linen," has but lately been left out of orders in the Gazette for court-mourning. The fringe was a substitute for lace-ruffles and "jabots" on gentlemen's shirts.

[3] For John Christian Fischer, the hautbois player, see note 1, p. 109.

[From MR. CRISP to FRANCES BURNEY.[1]]

Dear Fanny,
    Though the weak knotty joints of my knuckles are somewhat tired with writing to your Mamma by this post, I cannot forbear forcing them to pay you this short tribute of acknowledgment for your kind and entertaining letter. You are an exceeding good child, and I shall cherish you accordingly. You have good and grateful sentiments about you; in short, you have good things in you, and I wish it was in my power to bring about,—but stop, my pen! you are going beyond your line; but there are many valuable people in this wide world of ours, that for want of rightly understanding one another, do not do what Nature seems to have intended they should do; I mean draw close together by mutual attraction. 'Tis pity; for the really valuable do not over-abound. The esteem you express for sincerity, shows the world has not infected you with its contagion; but beware of too liberal a use of it, my dear Fanny; 'tis a dangerous weapon to carry about one; it is a sword that is very apt to eat into the scabbard and wound its owner. At my hour of life 'tis not worth while to change one's old habits; but, if I were to begin the world again, I should certainly carry it very much muffled up. You have drawn a very good picture of two brothers, and strikingly like I believe; I am sure one is so; and as sure all I have seen of the other is so. You with reason set a just value on your lot. . . . . .

As for sincerity, Fanny, such a young untainted, unhackneyed mind as your own may naturally enough be struck with the bright side of it; but take the word of an old sufferer; it ten times hurts the owner for once it does any

---

[1] The date of this letter is uncertain, but as it gives in a little space a very clear notion of Mr. Crisp's estimate of Fanny, and of his way of thinking, it is not much out of the place where we found it arranged among these papers, "as it gives the note" to his other letters. Mr. Crisp uses the term "*sincerity*" (as many others have done, and do), without precision, as if it were the reverse of discretion in speech. It is against too great *openness* that he is warning Fanny, as the last sentence proves.

good to the hearer; whom you are to thank and be highly obliged to, if he does not from that moment become your enemy. Whenever, therefore, you have heated your imagination with these glowing, generous, great sentiments, let me recommend to you by way of a cooler, to reflect on the following lines in the mouth of a more wary character—

"What! shall I wear my heart upon my sleeve
For daws to peck at?"[1]

* * * * * *

March.

My father's German Tour will be published next week; Heaven grant it as favourable a reception as the Italian one; he is extremely anxious and diffident beyond any author that ever, I believe, existed. He has shut himself up entirely from all who know him, but his own family. Dr. Armstrong, among others, has called fifty times unsuccessfully, though he has always the gallantry to say, *that he wants nobody, when he sees us.* I had the pleasure of a long tête à tête with him last Monday. He asked me what I conjectured to be the *prime cost* of the most capital picture in Mr. Strange's last sale? It is a landscape by Nicholas Poussin, and was purchased by Sir Watkin Wynn, at the sum of six hundred and fifty pounds. I told him that I could not possibly guess; but I supposed it to be much less than was then given for it. "But I can tell you exactly," said he, "for I have it from a gentleman, who was well acquainted with the transaction: the prime cost was seven pounds, odd shillings! and for that sum Poussin sold it! What Mr. Strange might purchase it for at Paris, I cannot say." How very hard that the man by whose labour and talents this fine landscape was produced should have worked so much for the advantage of others, and so little for his own![2]

---

[1] "'Tis not long after
But I will wear my heart upon my sleeve
For daws to peck at."—Othello, i., sc. 1.

[2] Horace Walpole sneers at this picture as having been dearly bought, but hear Mr. Dennistoun:—"Sir Robert Strange has long enjoyed an

Dr. Armstrong told me of some particulars in the will of the famous Lord Chesterfield, who is just dead. "He has given," said he, "some very excellent advice to Mr. Stanhope, his heir, admonishing him never to indulge himself in the pernicious practice of gaming, and he has taken some pretty effectual measures towards securing his advice from being forgot, as he has added a clause to it that, if ever he loses £100 by gaming, he is to forfeit £5,000. In another article he has represented the ill consequences of horse-racing, earnestly begging him not to give in to that diversion; and to this salutary counsel he has annexed a small clause that, if ever Mr. Stanhope is seen upon Newmarket Heath, he is immediately to forfeit 5,000 pounds! and these forfeited sums are all to be given in charity by the Dean and Chapter of Canterbury." I fancy it would be of great service if this will should prove a model for future ones.[1] It was but last week that this nobleman purchased two of the capital pictures of Mr. Strange's collection, though he was then so much confined, that he was obliged to have them carried to his own

---

European reputation; yet the excellence of his works is no adequate index of his merit. . . . From his native Orkney to the Land's End, his engravings brought within reach of all men the best works of great painters. . . . These engravings, offered at the same price as the trash which preceded them in the market, gradually obtained a large circulation, and became the first important step towards a general amelioration of the English taste in the fine Arts. . . . He boldly ventured the moderate capital at his disposal in importing a superior class of pictures for the home-market; and, by descriptive catalogues of these and his own works, he did much to instruct the public."

[1] This is inexact. As given by Lord Mahon, the will runs thus :— "In case my godson, Philip Stanhope, shall at any time hereinafter keep, or be concerned in the keeping, of any race-horses or pack of hounds, or reside one night at Newmarket, that infamous seminary of iniquity and ill-manners, during the course of the races there; or shall resort to the said races, or shall lose in any one day, at any game or bet whatsoever, the sum of £500; then, in any of the cases aforesaid, it is my express wish that he, my said godson, shall forfeit and pay out of my estate the sum of £5,000, to and for the use of the Dean and Chapter of Westminster." The sting is at the end. Lord Chesterfield thought that the Chapter of Westminster had made him pay very highly for the site of Chesterfield House, so he said that he would make the fine payable to a body which would be sure to exact it.

room, to examine: an evident proof that he retained not only his senses, but his love of the arts, to his last moments.[1]

I have likewise had the honour of two (short) conversations with Mr. Baretti; he called with a letter from Dr. Marsili, a physician of Padua, who desired him to send my father's Italian Tour to him, which he was very impatient to see, as he was my father's Ciceroni at Padua.[2] Mr. Baretti appears to be very *facetious;* he amused himself very much with Charlotte, whom he calls *Churlotte*, and kisses whether she will or no, always calmly saying, "Kiss à me, *Churlotte.*" He asked if she had read "Robinson Crusoe"? Charlotte coloured and said, "Yes, sir." "And pray, how many years *vas* he on *de* uninhabited island?" "Oh, sir; I can't tell that!" "*Vat!* don't you remember *vat* you read? *den*, my pretty Churlotte, you might spare your eye-sight. But can you remember *vat* was *de* name of Robinson Crusoe's island?" "Oh! sir, no, that I can't, indeed!" "And could you read all *dat* book, and not find out, *dat* it has no name at all?" He enquired of me very particularly how my sister "[Hetty]" did, whom he had seen as a child.[3]

---

[1] Horace Walpole writes to the Countess of Ossory on March the 11th, 1773:—" My Lord Chesterfield bought a 'Claude' the other day for four hundred guineas, and a 'Madame de la Vallière' four." And again to Sir Horace Mann on the 12th of March, 1773:—" You tell me how dear you pay at your theatres. I will tell you how cheap we buy pictures. Sir Watkin Williams Wynn gave six hundred and fifty pounds last week for a landscape of Nicolo Poussin; and Lord Chesterfield four hundred guineas for another, which somebody was so good as to paint a few months ago for Claude Lorraine. Books, prints, coins, do not lose their rank in proportion. I am every day tempted to make an auction." Lord Chesterfield died on the 24th of March, 1773.

[2] "Dr. Marsili, the worthy professor of botany in the University of Padua, to whose friendly offices, during my stay at Padua, I have innumerable obligations."—*Dr. Burney's First Tour.* Dr. Marsili had been in England in 1757, when Dr. Johnson gave him letters to Dr. Huddesford and to Thomas Warton, Professor of Poetry at Oxford, describing him as "a learned gentleman, and good Latin poet," whom he should be glad to have shown anything in Oxford. Marsili was also a friend of Garrick.

[3] This "kiss-a-me" was remembered. Charlotte is found in the Burney Papers as "*Chŭrlot*," and as "*Mrs. Baretti.*" She was, also, Garrick's own "*Reynold's Comedy*," (compare Goldsmith's "*Little*

Dr. Hawkesworth supped with us very lately, and was extremely sociable and agreeable; yet he always seems rather to be *reading* than *speaking;* his language is so remarkably elegant and flowing. I could not but imagine, that he was reciting one of his own " Adventurers," in an account he gave of a school-boy's holiday. I will endeavour to recollect it: " His sleep," said he, " the night before is broken and disturbed; his anticipation of pleasure is too lively to let him rest; yet he wakes, delighted that the happy day is come. If it is in his power, he lies in bed, till he is ashamed of leaving

---

Comedy's Face,") and his own *" Piety in Pattens."* Her " cherubinical face" and her liveliness lasted long. When she was sixty, Fanny describes her as " looking quite young and pretty." An amusing letter is also extant in which Hetty rallies Charlotte upon being the reigning toast of Brighton at a time when Charlotte had been twice a widow, and was a grandmother. This we are kindly told by one of Charlotte's descendants. Guiseppe Baretti, a native of Turin, had been brought to England by Lord Charlemont. in 1753. He wrote vigorous English, and was an able man, with a bad temper. He kept the best company in London, that of Johnson, Burke, Reynolds, and Goldsmith. He boasted that he had friends, both in town and country, with whom he could, at any time, spend a month. Off and on, he lived some years with the Thrales. Yet he quarrelled with almost all his friends, even with Dr. Johnson, who had known him from 1754. He sparred with Mrs. Thrale, while giving lessons in her house, and was thus excused by Johnson,—" Poor Baretti, do not quarrel with him, . . . he means only to be frank, manly, and independent. . . . To be frank, he thinks is to be cynical, and to be independent, is to be rude. Forgive him, dearest lady, the rather, because of his misbehaviour, I am afraid, he learned part from me." When Mrs. Thrale married Piozzi, Baretti reviled her in the " European Magazine." Her marriage seems to have provoked him the more as he had ridiculed the notice taken of Italian singers in England in his answer to Mr. Sharp. Boswell and he so detested each other that when Baretti met Boswell at the Thrales, Boswell did not rise on seeing Baretti; and when Baretti descried Boswell, he " grinned a perturbed glance." The Irish Dr. Campbell makes him " grin this glance," and was told by Mrs. Thrale, and by Arthur Murphy, that Boswell had wished Baretti might be hanged for that stab in the Hay-Market. Baretti once so provoked a beautiful and lively American, Mrs. Paradise, that she turned the boiling-water of her tea-urn upon him. He returned to Italy, but found that he could not enjoy it after the nearly thirty years of absence, and came back to London to be among the friends he had made,—some of whom he kept until death.

it, and at last rises ashamed of being ashamed. The remaining part of the morning he passes in considering what to do; but every plan that occurs, appears unworthy employing so precious a day. At length, evening comes, and his recollection then tells him a thousand things which he might have done; he spends the rest of the night in regretting that he wasted the day; and at last goes to bed disgusted, wearied, and disappointed." This description, however, belongs rather to young men than to boys, whose childish or boisterous amusements present themselves with the light.

* * * * * *

[April.]

We went, Susan and I, to a very fine concert lately for Mr. Fischar's (the celebrated Hautbois) benefit.[1] But can I speak of music, and not mention Miss Linley? The town has rung of no other name this month.

Miss Linley is daughter to a musician of Bath, a very sour, ill-bred, severe, and selfish man.[2] She is believed to be very

---

[1] John Christian Fischer was born at Friburg. He came to London, and married a daughter of our great painter, Gainsborough. He was a celebrated player on the haut-bois. In his "History of Music," Dr. Burney writes of the "admirable" Fischer, that "he composed for himself, and in a style so new and fanciful, that in point of invention, as well as tone, taste, expression, and neatness of execution, his piece was always regarded as one of the highest treats of the night." He was much in favour with George III., to whom he bequeathed his music. He died in 1800, being seized with a fit while playing before Queen Charlotte.

[2] Dr. Burney says of Linley, his brother doctor of music, that "he was a studious man, equally versed in theory and practice. Having a large family, he pointed his studies to singing, and became the first master of his day. He was a masterly player on the harpsichord, and a good composer." His children were "a nest of nightingales." He had to feed so many, as well as to train their voices, that he made them all sing in public, "even to the seven year olds." Linley had refused the offers of both Garrick and Colman to engage his daughter Eliza as a singer. "I think" (he wrote) "as she has acquired a reputation, I ought to have the advantage of her first performing in London myself. . . . . I do not relish giving the prime of my daughter's performances to support the schemes of others. . . . . Still, I would take two hundred guineas and a clear benefit, with choice of oratorios. . . . . I shall never lay myself at the mercy of my children, especially when their power of being of service to me depends so entirely upon chance."

romantic; she has long been very celebrated for her singing, though never, till within this month, has she been in London. She has met with a great variety of adventures, and has had more lovers and admirers than any nymph of these times. She has been addressed by men of all ranks. I dare not pretend to say, *honourably*, which is doubtful; but what is certain is, that whatever were their designs, she has rejected them all. She has long been attached to a Mr. Sheridan, a young man of great talents, and very well spoken of, whom it is expected she will speedily marry.[1] She has performed this

---

When she was only fourteen, Linley was blamed for making Eliza sing too much and too often. He bound her to himself as an apprentice, and insisted upon her working out her time. He knew no better, and was heart-broken when he found himself outlive five of his grown-up-children.

Miss Linley's charms must have been very great. J. T. Smith tells us of the miniature painter, Ozias Humphry (born 1742), that "having a wish to try his fortune at Bath, he went thither in 1762, and took lodgings with Linley, the musician, whose lovely daughter, Eliza Anne, ... was then in her ninth year. She knew all the songs in 'Thomas and Sally,' 'The Beggar's Opera,' 'The Chaplet,' and 'Love in a Village'; and these she would sing so sweetly, that many a day, at the young painter's solicitation, she chanted them, seated at the foot of his easel, looking up to him, unconscious of her heavenly features: with such features and such looks, as prevailed on the motley visitors of Bath, when she so gracefully held up her little basket, with her father's benefit-tickets, at the door, as they passed in and out of the Pump-Room."

[1] This beautiful girl had, it is said, been married to "a Mr. Sheridan" about a year before Fanny saw her; but without the knowledge of his father, or her own. At the end of March, 1772, Sheridan escorted her to France, to withdraw her from the disgraceful attentions of a married man, with whom Sheridan, in the end, fought two duels, and very nearly three. She had persuaded herself that she was going to take shelter in a nunnery from admirers, many of whom were more honourable than Captain Matthews, and none less so. Sheridan induced her to marry him by the way, somewhere near Calais, quite in Maria Allen's style. Her father pursued her to Lille, and took her home to fulfil the musical engagements which he had made for her. In fact, she was a runaway apprentice. Though he found Sheridan at Lille, he does not seem to have suspected the marriage of a youth just of age, and a girl under it by two years at least, if not three. He took Sheridan back in the same chaise with his daughter, but forbade them afterwards to meet. Still Sheridan contrived to see her by sometimes disguising himself as a hackney-coachman, and driving her

Lent at the Oratorio of Drury Lane, under Mr. Stanley's direction. The applause and admiration she has met with, can only be compared to what is given Mr. Garrick. The whole town seems distracted about her. Every other diversion is forsaken. Miss Linley alone engrosses all eyes, ears,

home from the theatre. This is T. Moore's account, given him by Sheridan's family. It is very improbable, and there is great doubt whether there was anything more than a flight from Bath until the 13th of April, 1773, (according to Sylvanus Urban,) " Mr. Sheridan of the Middle Temple," (which he had only entered three weeks before as a law-student,) was married publicly to " the celebrated Miss Linley," after which she never again sang for pay, and sometimes not even to give pleasure. There is a story that Sheridan refused to let her sing to the Prince of Wales. Sheridan's " triumph," says Moore, " was the first that *even rivals* knew of his love." Even his own brother, even his best friend, Halhed, who had loved Miss Linley before Sheridan seems to have seen her, and who confided in him, were kept in the dark. Halhed, who had been his school-friend at Harrow, sailed to India on hearing of his success. She was more than musical and lovely. She was his right hand, and perhaps worked harder for him than she had done for her father. As manager of a theatre she helped him by keeping the account of the weekly receipts, by reading the plays sent to him, suggesting changes in them, and in fact acting as a copying clerk. She was his secretary when he was a member of the House of Commons. She set his verses to music, and sang them to her harp. She herself wrote good, unaffected letters, and very fair verses. Yet he wore out all this love. Susan Burney has left an amusing account in her unpublished journal, which belongs to a later period than these diaries, of how Sheridan provoked the delightful singer Pacchierotti by his facile excuses, and broken appointments, and above all by not paying his salary, to write him a grotesque letter to tell him that " Pacchierotti was very displeas'd to be obliged to call him *rascal*." The letter ended with a sketch of Sheridan dangling from a gallows. Susan stopped its being sent. As Susan Burney was, in the words of Pacchierrotti, " *capable de juger en professeur*," we give, from her diary, a few lines of comparison between the singing of Miss Harrop and of Mrs. Sheridan, written some years later than this diary :—" Miss Harrop's manner *some times* [was] very good—much more Italian than Mrs. Sheridan's ever was when I heard her. But every now and then things escaped her that were really *vulgar*, in her recitative particularly, and a howl and bad manner of taking her notes, which Mrs. S. was always free from. *She* was never *vulgar*, tho' without the soul or refinements of a great Italian singer "

Miss Linley's sister Mary, whom Fanny saw with her, married Richard Tickell, a wit, who was a grandson of Addison's friend, Tickell. The late J. A. Roebuck, M.P., was grandson of Richard and Mary Tickell.

hearts. At Mrs. Stanley's invitation, mama, Susan, and myself sat in her box at Alexander Balus, to see and hear this Syren.[1] Her voice is soft, sweet, clear, and affecting. She sings with good expression, and has great fancy and even taste in her cadences, though perhaps a finished singer would give less way to the former, and prefer few and select notes. She has an exceeding good shake, and the best and most critical judges, all pronounce her to be infinitely superior to *all* other English singers. The Town in general give her the preference to any other. To me her singing was extremely pleasing. Perhaps, except the divine Millico, I would rather hear her (if I also saw her!) than any other.

As Mrs. Stanley's box is very high, and I am very near-sighted, I could only perceive that Miss Linley's *figure* was extremely genteel, and the form of her face very elegant. I had heard from Miss Kinnaird, who is acquainted with Mrs. Stanley, that she always went into the green-room after the oratorio, and I determined to make interest for the same favour, as it had been granted to Miss Kinnaird.[2] I had immediate success. As soon as the performance was over, we all went into that famous apartment, which I was surprised to see, was lined with *red!* There was not a creature there; but at my request Miss Arland, Mrs. Stanley's sister,[3] went

---

[1] Alexander Balus, an oratorio by Handel, 1748.

[2] Fanny writes to Susan, in June, 1779:—"I find by the papers that Miss Kinnaird is married to a Mr. Wiggan." [Miss Kinnaird was a daughter of the sixth Baron Kinnaird. Her husband's name is given in peerages as Wiggins, or Wiggens.] "I hope, therefore, she is settled in England, and that I may see her again. I quite long to know if she has met with a man at all deserving of her. I never had so much affection for a short acquaintance in my life as for this sweet girl. Ah, how does the word *affection* joined to *sweet girl*, remind me of our dear Barsanti! I hope you sent my letter, and if you wished it, added some lines of your own. I am not sorry now that I never saw Mr. Lister, since I could see him no more, but pray, my dear love, if any answer comes from *poor* Jenny, let it be instantly sent me." This passage, (hitherto unpublished,) shows that Fanny, then in full fame, had a heart very retentive of old friends. Jenny Barsanti had just lost her first husband, whom George Colman the younger calls Lesley.

[3] John Stanley, who was born in 1713, and lost his sight at two years of age, was at eleven, organist of All Hallows, Bread Street; at

into another room, and asked Miss Linley and her sister to favour us with her company. The rest of the family, viz.: father, mother, and brother were already in the red green room.

Had I been for my sins born of the male race, I should certainly have added one more to Miss Linley's train. She is really beautiful; her complexion a clear, lovely, animated brown, with a blooming colour on her cheeks; her nose, that most elegant of shapes, Grecian; fine luxurious, easy-sitting hair, a charming forehead, pretty mouth, and most bewitching eyes. With all this her carriage is modest and unassuming, and her countenance indicates diffidence, and a strong desire of pleasing,—a desire in which she can never be disappointed. I most sincerely and earnestly wish her well, safely, and happily settled. I think that so young a woman, gifted with such enchanting talents, and surrounded by so many admirers, who can preserve herself unconscious of her charms and diffident of her powers, has merit that entitles her to the strongest approbation, and I hope, to the greatest happiness :—a union from affection with a man who deserves her!

[In No. 38, which is dated "Tingmouth, April y* 25th," Maria tells Fanny that she never made so pleasant a journey in her life as in the

---

thirteen, chosen out of nearly twenty candidates to be organist of St. Andrew's, Holborn. This, with an appointment as one of the organists of the Inner Temple, he kept until his death—in 1786. He played the first violin, was a composer of music, an excellent whist-player, and a most pleasant companion. In 1779, he succeeded Dr. Boyce as master of the King's Band. He married a Miss Arland, or Arlond. Her sister, who is here named by Fanny, had refused to marry Sir John Hawkins. The Stanleys are (among many others), ill-spoken of by Miss Hawkins, who, although she complains a little of her father, was dutiful enough to continue, as well as to chronicle most of his resentments. Dr. Burney says that "about 1730, whenever there was a charity sermon, or a new organ to be opened, the young blind Stanley seems to have been preferred" (as organist) "to all others." The divine, who is known to readers of Mr. Napier's Boswell's Johnson, as "the Irish Dr. Campbell," met Stanley in 1775, and says that he was comely for a blind man. He sat down to cards after tea, and played with as much ease and quickness as any man I ever saw." The cards were pricked for him with a pin, by his wife's sister ; but so well were they done, that Dr. Campbell "could not make out the key whereby he marked them." If Miss Arland once played an oratorio through to him, he was able to conduct it in public.

three days spent in going from Froome to Exeter, driving with her husband in the "whiskey," her maid and the baggage being in the chaise. "Tingmouth" (a spelling of the name which Fanny copied from Maria and always retained) "surpasses everything her imagination had formed of the most beautiful;" she goes on to say that:—

"You see nothing here but women in the summer—their husbands all go out to the Newfoundland fishery for 8 or 9 months in the [year] so the women do all the laborious business such as *rowing* and *towing* the boats and go out a fishing yet I never saw cleaner Cottages nor healthier finer Children—the Women are in general Handsome none plain tho' tall and *Strapping* owing their robust work—Their husbands come home about november or december—consequently the winter is their time for Mirth and Jollity. They are very poor, yet no signs of poverty appear, nor have I seen a beggar since I came—I will now litterally describe our dwelling—the owner is a captain of a ship, such as Molly[1] Stancliffe's father, not at all in a higher style—they have one of the very neatest *Thatchd* Cottages you ever saw—we have it almost all that is a little parlour not much bigger than the 3rd Room in Queen's Square—the furniture a very elegant set *Beaufet* painted blue—and Open—filled with Curious odd bits of China glass *flowers* etc. that the Captain has pick'd up during his Voyages—a very fine *picture* of our Saviour on the Cross—supposed to be a Raphael—and a Magdalen by Corregio—with a vast many curious prints cut out of Common Prayer-book and I am afraid the old Family Bible is a Loser —the window with very pretty flower in pots—and a Most delightful Mirtle hedge as thick as any common one in a very little Spot of Garden before the house—we have behind our parlour a Scullery converted into a Kitchen over this is two very neat Bedchambers with nice Clean Linen Beds—in short this Cottage woud make a very great figure in Miss *Minifies*'[2] hands and very much resembles the retreat of some heroine—the front of our house looks on a fine green not a quarter of a Mile from the Ocean we have a fine view of a Cliff that resembles that Shakespear describes at dover—We don't know half the beauties of the place yet we have rode out once—thro' such Lanes that open every now and then to the Sea. There is delightful fishing here for Whiting Mackerel young Salmon etc.—we shall often go out and take our dinners with us—the people are so Simple and happy—I am quite Charmed with them, here is one of the finest beaches for Bathing you ever saw. We have a brace of beautiful Spaniels and a remarkable fine pomeranian dog R gave a great deal of money for at Bath to please me—we have great diversion with them they all take the water and are our Constant Companions—we intend getting a very large Newfoundland dog before we leave this place."

---

[1] Molly was Mrs. Rishton's maid.

[2] The Misses Minifie, of Fairwater, Somersetshire, were novel writers of that day. One of them married General Gunning, brother of the beauties, Lady Coventry and the Duchess of Hamilton.

What is given of this letter is *literally* transcribed, with Maria's characteristic omission of little words, and her little dashes to make up for the absence of stops. After her signature Maria writes her address: "at Capt. Whitbourne's, Tingmouth, near Exon, Devon."]

Sunday, May 3rd.

I have a thousand things to write, too many to observe method, and therefore I shall commit them as they occur.

Premierement,—We have had from the Cape of Good Hope the welcome news of my brother's promotion, Lieutenant Shanks, a young man who was on board the *Adventure*, one of the three sloops under Captain Cooke, was so ill, that he was obliged to leave the ship, and return to England, "in whose place," says the Captain's letter to Lord Sandwich, "I have appointed Mr. Burney, whom I have found very deserving." This is most comfortable intelligence and rejoices us unspeakably; he will be a lieutenant of three years' standing by his return. He has written to us in very good spirits, and assures us that the Cape of Good Hope is a very agreeable place! . . . . .

Mr. and Mrs. Rishton are turned absolute hermits for this summer, they have left Bath, and are gone to Tingmouth in Devonshire where they have taken a *cottage* rather than a house. The country she says is beautiful. They are however only to remain there till Stanhoe House which they have taken for 7 years is ready for them—I hear very often from Mrs. Rishton, whose friendship, affection, and confidence, will, I believe, end only with our lives.

My father's German tour has been published this week; in it are inserted proposals for publishing by subscription his History of Music. If he has not 500 subscribers by next Christmas, he declares he will not publish it at all.[1] I will at least

---

[1] A gentleman, who did not wish his name to be made known to Dr. Burney, proposed to him, through two eminent city merchants, that he should not drop his work in case the 500 copies were not subscribed for by Christmas, but go on under his guarantee to take every copy that was left on hand. Dr. Burney thanked him heartily, but preferred letting things take their natural course. He proved right, as the subscription-list was quickly and freely filled; but the generous offer of a man whose name he never knew, kept alive in him his warm

hope, that the German tour will not disgrace its brother of Italy. Mr. Garrick writes that "nothing can be more pleasing to his friends or more agreeable to the public; and that it is clear, interesting, instructive, and delightful." My father has made a prodigious quantity of presents of this book, viz.; to Messrs. Garrick, Colman, Woïde,[1] Baretti, Strange, Hayes, Crisp, Edwards,[2] Young; to Doctors Shepherd,[3] Hunter,[4] Armstrong, Hawkesworth; to Mr. Fischer,[5] to Lord Sandwich, and to Mr. Burney.

Captain Brydone, whom Mr. Beckford brought to one of our concerts, has just published, "A Tour to the Islands of Sicily and Malta, in letters to William Beckford, Esq., from P. Brydone, F.R.S." I have received very great entertainment from this book; it is written in an easy, natural, and lively style, and is full of anecdotes, observations, and descriptions, and in many places is very philosophical. It discovers throughout a liveliness of imagination, an insatiate curiosity after knowledge, and the most vehement desire of instruction. I very much wish, that the author may continue his acquaintance with my father; for I am sure he must be very agreeable.[6] . . . . .

---

love for the City of London, in which, from boyhood, he had been shown great kindness.

[1] The learned Dr. Woïde, of the British Museum, reader and chaplain at the Dutch Chapel in the Savoy.

[2] This may have been Dr. Johnson's friend, Dr. Edwards, of Jesus College, Oxford, "my convivial friend," whose loss Johnson laments in 1784. Although Dr. Johnson does not appear to have given Dr. Burney a letter asking the help of Dr. Edwards for the Welsh part of the History of Music until 1778, Dr. Burney may have met Dr. Edwards at Oxford when he took his musical degree in 1769.

[3] Dr. Anthony Shepherd, Fellow and tutor of Christ's College, and Plumian Professor in the University of Cambridge.

[4] There were several doctors of the name of Hunter living in London at that time. One of them had attended Dr. Burney's first wife in her sudden and fatal illness. As the famous anatomist, John Hunter, is commonly called Dr. Hunter in books of that time, it may have been himself; if not, it was probably Dr. William Hunter, a man of some distinction.

[5] John Christian Fischer, who is before named.

[6] Patrick Brydone, a Berwickshire gentleman, published this very lively book in 1773.

Dr. Goldsmith has just brought on the stage a new comedy, called, "She stoops to Conquer." We went to it with Mr. and Mrs. Young; it is very laughable and comic; but I know not how it is, almost all diversions are insipid at present to me, except the opera......

Miss Linley is married to Mr. Sheridan. She has entirely given up singing in public, and I am very glad to find that the Queen has taken her under her protection, as private singer to Her Majesty, and allows to her a salary of £600 per ann.[1] I hope this *double* settlement will ensure her peace for life, though heaven knows how many hearts it may break!

My father came home between four and five, all kindness and indulgence, he asked if we should like to go to the Opera? Mama declined it; but Susan and I were quite in rapture. To the pleasure of hearing such sweet music,—it was Tamerlano, —was added the interest we took in its success on account of the composer. We called upon my sister, who was delighted at joining us.

Mr. Harris of Salisbury, famous for his Treatises on Music, Happiness, &c., sat just before us at the Opera, and was introduced by Mr. Batt, a gentleman with him, to my father. I found he was an enthusiast for Sacchini, whose music my father and himself seemed endeavouring which should praise most. "Such ingenious accompaniments, so much taste, such an inexhaustible variety, &c.". Mr. Harris also mentioned that he was acquainted and consequently charmed with the man as well as the musician. . . . . I have not heard any Opera that has given me equal pleasure, except *Il Cid*.[2]

---

[1] This seems to have been what Dr. Johnson called "a wandering lie;" or, speaking more politely, a mere idle rumour.

[2] James Harris, of Salisbury, nephew of that Earl of Shaftesbury who wrote "the Characteristics," and father of the first Lord Malmesbury, is ranked as a writer upon music in a list given by Dr. Burney in his "History of Music." He published the book referred to "On Art, Music, and Happiness," 1744. Mr. Harris was, also, a composer of music. At Gloucester-music-meeting in 1776, "the pastoral of Daphnis and Amaryllis, written by the learned James Harris, Esquire, and first produced at Drury Lane in 1762, for the purpose of bringing his *protégé*, young Norris, on the stage," was performed. "The airs were admirably adapted by its author, who was a great proficient in

Now for our Concert,—Sacchini and Millico came early. Sacchini was in apparent high spirits, and had an animation in his countenance, that I had thought was foreign to it, as he has hitherto appeared too mild and gentle to be even lively, which however could merely have been owing to his bad health, or else his inquietude about his operas; for this evening he was all spirit. He was seated next to mama,— who, when he found it in vain to address in French or Italian, he said in a very droll voice, "Eh bien!—I *most* speak *Engelise;*" then bowing to her, "How do you do, Madam? very well?" This little attempt included, I believe, almost all his English learning.

My father then told Sacchini how much he had been charmed with *Tamerlano*,[1] which he had heard the night before. Signor Sacchini receives compliments with the graceful modesty of a man by nature diffident, yet by custom inured to them. Millico pursued the conversation concerning the opera, and very drolly going to the harpsichord, played a passage in one of the choruses, and mimicked a most terrible man, who in spite of all the instruction he has had, always ruins it. This chorus is exceeding spirited, and though very indifferently performed, has a very fine effect, and is very much admired. "It shows the composer," said my father, in Italian; "notwithstanding his mildness and sweetness, he breaks out, now and then, with all the Neapolitan fire: he is a *Vesuvius* at times!"

Mrs. and the Miss Ellerkers now entered;[2] the mother is a

---

that science, to the music of Pergolesi, Handel, Jomelli, &c." "Master Norris" had been a chorister of Salisbury Cathedral. He sang in Doctor Burney's exercise for his musical degrees at Oxford in 1769. Mr. Batt was a "Commissioner of Bankrupts."

[1] Tamerlano, an opera by Sacchini, was brought out in May, 1773, with Millico as chief singer.

[2] Eaton Mainwaring Ellerker, Esq., of Risby Park, in Yorkshire, left three co-heiresses. These young ladies were, the eldest, Arabella, who married the second Earl Onslow, and the second daughter, Charlotte, who married George Ferrars Townshend (in right of his deceased mother, Baron de Ferrars of Chartley and Baron Compton); he was afterwards the second Marquis Townshend. On the 4th of November, 1782, Fanny, "with all our house," (that is, with the Thrales and Dr. Johnson) "met Lady de Ferrars, whom you" (her sister

slow, dawdling, sleepy kind of dame; the daughters are accomplished, and anxious for distinction, and good and well-principled; but very stiff and affected. I like them, nevertheless, for their real enthusiasm for Millico and Sacchini. There is always soul with enthusiasm, though not always sense. .... Miss Ellerker now led the way to the study. Millico, like another Orpheus, was embracing his harp. We all flocked about him, but he would not sing a note till we were all seated. Oh! how he did sing then! His voice with the harp, how infinitely sweet! the delicacy of his piano so affectingly soft! smooth, *melting* I may say,—the forte clear, well-toned, exactly and nicely in tune. The harp alone is proper to accompany such a voice. He sang to airs, all of his own composition and expressly made for the harp; they are very pretty, but serve as mere outlines for him to fill up. He has lately published them. He told my father, that it was not to *get*, but simply to *save* money, that he printed them; for that, wherever he played them, he found so many ladies requested them of him, that he should have been ruined in paying copyists. ....

In the midst of this performance, two beaux entered; Mr. Grimston, eldest son of Lord Grimston, and his brother.[1] He is just returned from making the grand tour. .... When we had breathed, which we scarcely allowed ourselves to do while Millico sung, Mr. Burney was requested to play: he was animated, and never performed better. It is impossible to express the delight which his performance gave to Millico. His amazing execution really excited in Millico the most hearty laughs. The Italians cultivate harpsichord-playing so little, giving all their time to the voice, that execution such as Mr. Burney's appeared miraculous, and when Millico saw him make a fine and long shake with his fourth and

---

Susan) "may remember as Charlotte Ellerker, and her lord and sisters," at Brighton, "by mutual appointment"—"Lord de Ferrars is very ugly, but extremely well-bred. .... His lady is much improved since we knew her in former days, and seems good-humoured, lively, and rather agreeable. Miss Ellerker is nothing altered."

[1] James Bucknall Grimston, afterwards third Viscount Grimston, in the peerage of Ireland, and first Baron Verulam in that of England.

little fingers, and then change from finger to finger, while his left hand kept on the subject, he was really almost convulsed. And when it was over, rising from his seat, he clapped his hands and cried with emphasis and in a very droll accent, "It is terrible, I really tink."

* * * * * *

Miss Barsanti's Benefit was the 10th. She however did the Prelude, and acted Sophy in the "Musical Lady."[1] I think she acquitted herself extremely well ; . . . . with spirit and propriety. She had a very great house. . . . . I am much pleased that this evening has proved at once so creditable and so profitable to her.

I do not know whether I have ever mentioned the *breach* that happened some years since between my father and Mr. Greville, occasioned by some dispute, in which the latter conducted himself with so much arrogance that, notwithstanding the very long friendship and intercourse between them, they broke off all acquaintance; and have not met since. But this last week my father received the following curious note: Query ?——N. B.—I have quite forgot what the query was; but this followed :—

"Lord March[2] and Mr. Greville have a small bet upon this, and have both agreed to refer the matter to Dr. Burney's decision. They will, therefore, be much obliged to him, if he will send his answer to Almack's." My father accordingly did; but we have heard no more of it, save only a note of thanks from Mr. Greville. I am always concerned at the breaking of old friends. I am sure that Mr. Greville loves my father, and I doubt not wishes much to renew his intimacy; but he is

---

[1] In Mr. Genest's "History of the Stage," Miss Barsanti's benefit is stated to have been on the 10th of May, 1773. "The Musical Lady," which was then played by her for the "first time," was a part of Colman's play of "The Jealous Wife," which Garrick had cut out when he produced that comedy in 1761. In December, 1762, "The Musical Lady" was acted separately, as a farce.

[2] The disgraceful "old Q." In 1778, the betting and bad Lord March succeeded to the Dukedom of Queensberry. In 1771, a bet of his as to which of two men would die first, was actually brought before Lord Chief Justice Mansfield, and settled by the verdict of a jury.

a haughty man, and must be too sensible that he has acted ill, to be able to make a graceful reparation.[1]

My father's friend, Mr. Beckford, is just married; we have not seen him since, though he has called. I should like to be acquainted with his bride, who I think *must* be amiable.

* * * * * *

[May].

Mama is gone to Lynn already for the summer; Bessy and the sweet Dick are gone with her; and I am once more here *en maîtresse*; but, thank Heaven! my dear father is *en maître*; I am never half so happy as with him.

---

[1] This was only one of a series of reconciliations, the last of which (upon record) was in 1778. Mme. D'Arblay admits that Garrick showed her father some slight degree of his well-known fickleness. It may be that in Garrick this was little worse than *mobility*, without which he would not have been the Garrick that he was, but Mr. Greville's friendship had acute intermissions. He was of an arrogant temper. He had paid Dr. Arne to cancel Burney's articles of apprenticeship, that he might take him into his own household. All his life, he acted as if he had a lien upon Dr. Burney. Greville's demands upon Burney's time were inconsistent with the doctor's maintaining half-a-dozen children by his profession; even setting aside the composition of music, and of books. In a letter written to Hetty, in November, 1820, Mme. D'Arblay relates how in the year 1812 she went with her father " through the letters of Mr. Greville, from the commencement of that early intercourse " (in 1744 or 5), "all of which were clever, but many" (so) "disputative, quarrelsome, and highly disagreeable," that Dr. Burney "did not preserve above three or four." These Mme. D'Arblay meant to have printed, with those of Garrick, and others to her father, in three volumes of "Correspondence," which never appeared.

To show the intermittent character of the friendship, Mme. D'Arblay, in 1781, says that she had not seen her godmother, Mrs. Greville, for many years. When Mr. Greville died, Fanny says it was "rather a shock than a loss." She adds that he had "highly irritable nerves;" yet, whatever may have disturbed, nothing seems to have shortened his existence, since, though nearly alienated from his family, estranged from his connexions, and "at war with the world, he lived until over ninety," dying about the same time that Dr. Burney lost a group of more reasonable friends, Lord Macartney, the accomplished and excellent Mr. Twining, the learned Mrs. Elizabeth Carter, and Dolly Young, who is mentioned in the History of Lynn, by Mr. Richards, among the intellectual people of Lynn.

We were at the Fund-Play last year. Garrick did King Lear—but too well! He has alarmed us extremely by hinting at a design of leaving the stage next year. I hope he will be prevailed upon to change his resolution. He has been here twice lately,—in most excellent spirits. One morning he called at eight o'clock, and, unfortunately, Susette and I were not come down stairs. We hurried in vain; for he discovered our laziness and made us monstrously ashamed by his raillery. "I shall tell Mrs. Garrick," said he, "that I found the Doctor reading Petrarch, in flannel, like a *young man*—but where, says I, where were the young ladies? where do you think were *my* favourites? why *in bed!*"

When he went away, he caught Charlotte in his arms, and ran with her down the steps, and to the corner of the square, protesting he intended taking her off, as his own *Reynolds's Comedy*, which she looks as if she had sat for, he says—[1]

Mr. Baretti called here last Sunday. He told my father that Dr. Johnson will be very glad to see him; that he has read both his Tours with great pleasure, and has pronounced him to be *one of the first writers of the age* for travels! Such praise from Dr. Johnson, whom my father reveres above all authors living or dead, has given him the highest delight.

[Here follow six lines, which may be read as saying that F. has had a most earnest and pressing invitation from the Rishton's to pass the summer with them at Teignmouth. "My father, however, does not wish to part with his *Librarian* at present—but when he goes into Norfolk I fancy and hope I shall make a trip into Devonshire."

In a letter written from Teignmouth on the 23rd of May, which was given to a man going to Exeter to be posted there, but which was quite forgotten by him until the 28th, Maria urges Fanny not to go to Lynn, but to spend the summer with her at Teignmouth. It is but sixty miles farther; if Dr. Burney can spare Fanny to go to Lynn, he can spare her to go to Teignmouth. She can come in a chaise in twenty-six hours, or if she does not "like the fatigue of that," there is

---

[1] The allusion is to the picture by Sir Joshua Reynolds, of Garrick between Tragedy and Comedy. George Colman wrote to Garrick from Paris, in 1766, "There hang out here in every street pirated prints from Reynolds's picture of you, which are underwritten '*L'homme entre le Vice et la Vertu.*'" It is probable that the "little Comedy's face" of Goldsmith was also a comparison of the younger Miss Horneck with this picture.

a " regular machine comes in two days to Exeter, where we woud meet you at the Oxford Inn." She is to stay till September, when Maria will take her up to town, and thence to Lynn in her own chaise.

Fanny need not lay out a penny for Teignmouth, as she must for the visitings at Lynn. Maria herself wears nothing at Teignmouth but "a common linnen gown," and has not had her hair once dressed since she came there. She writes at the suggestion of Mr. Rishton, who would fain " go out oftner a fishing and shooting," had his wife any companion. Maria can ask none but Fanny, as her rooms are " so littered with dogs and poultry," and she can only offer Fanny the room in which her own trunks are kept.]

Sunday, June 13th.

This day, time was!—gave me birth; but no bells have rung, no guns have fired: I am strangely neglected! . . . .

Susan and I are extremely comfortable together; and my father who is all kindness, makes us truly happy. . . . . We are both studying Italian. We are reading some of the best French works together, not regularly, but only such parts as are adapted either to our capacity or inclination. We have just finished the *Henriade*. I am not absolutely in raptures with it; I think Voltaire has made much too free with religion in giving words to the Almighty. I doat on poetry; but cannot allow of even poetical licence giving language human to the Divine Power. For which reason I am more attached to poetry concerning fabulous times; for Jove, Juno, Minerva, Venus,—may talk as much as they please. I am never hurt even at their quarrelling. But a man pretending to believe in revealed Religion, to presume to dictate sentiments to his maker,—I cannot think it right. Nay more, he actually makes his God so very a human creature, as to give up His intended proceedings, upon the prayers of Lewis! It is very well for a Jove or any other fabulous God, to be softened, or enraged, and mutable; but an all-seeing Eye—can it leave anything for another to represent? an all-wise, all-good Power,—can it have any design which is better to be laid aside? But M. Voltaire, I understand, is not a man of very *rigid principles*, at least not in religion. . . . . .

Sacchini told my father that, when he first came to England, he dined with a person of distinction, along with Seignior Giardini (who loves mischief better than any man alive); and Giardini gave him a lesson that, when he wanted wine and water to drink, he must ask for it in English, by saying, "*How do do?*" Accordingly, when he was thirsty, he turned to a servant, and said very civilly, "*How do do?*" the man made a very low bow, and seemed very much confused; but brought him no wine and water! He was obliged to be patient; but took the first opportunity of saying to another of the men, "*How do do?*" the man grinned, and bowed; but still, no wine and water! he found himself extremely dry, and very much surprised, and perhaps thought he spoke ill; but yet again repeated his demand to a third servant. Upon which *il Padrone della casa* called out to him, "Mr. Sacchini, you are very civil to my people; how came you to know them all?" "*Moi!*" cried he, "*j'ai seulement demandè à boire?*" "*Et que dites-vous pour cela?*"—"*How do do.*" Giardini's lesson was then betrayed; the laugh, I doubt not, was very hearty.

* * * * * *

[FROM MRS. RISHTON TO MISS BURNEY.]

[In No. 42, which is dated, June y⁵ 6th, Mrs. Rishton complains that there has been no answer to the foregoing letter or to one to Dr. Burney enclosed in the same frank, a fortnight previously. She repeats the substance of these letters. She begs Fanny to buy Mr. Rishton, "Two Cricket Batts, made by Pett of 7 Oaks—you will get them at any of the great Toy shops, the makers name always stamp'd upon them—ask for the very best sort, which costs 4s. or 4s. 6d. each —let them weigh 4 oz. and a qu' or 4 oz. and ¹/₂ each, send them by the Exeter post coach. This is followed by a letter of the 13th of June, which claims "the clause in the latter part" of Dr. Burney's reply, which Maria has just received, "as an absolute promise, for it is impossible you can be A person of such immense consequence that you can be able to work during your Father's Absence at Lynn without his guiding—unless you are to be the Authoress of the History of Musick—only intend following the plan of Marmontel's Connoisseur —that is out of great generosity allow the Dr. the merit of it—and let it pass in his Name—I own that will be Noble.[1] . . . . . their is one of his scruples which I must endeavour to Answer—as you seem to say it is the principal—that is his fear of your travelling alone—Now really my dear Fanny—I must say with a deep sigh—we don't Live in

---

[1] We give this as there is no reference in Fanny's Diaries to her incessant labour for her dear father, although many are the allusions made to it in Maria's letters. Fanny took it as a joy, although she

an Age for Adventures—Nor have we the men spirit enough to be knight errants—really to my sorrow I say it—I never met with an Adventure in my life—I have travelled from 16 (a critical Age Fanny—) till I married without meeting with a single occurrence in my travels worth publishing.[1] I have been from London to York and from York to London—to *Bath, Lynn,* Brighthelmstone with a long &c., and I am afraid was ever *Unnoticed* from *the Vulgar Crew*

'Full many a flower is born to *Blush unseen*
'And waste its sweetness in the desert air.'

Exactly my Case—Fanny—Grey certainly thought of me when he composed those Lines—I own I am fond of them for that reason—but Joking apart I really believe take it in general the Company in a Stage Coach Consists chiefly—of perhaps reputable tradesmen their wives or daughters—or perhaps a mantua Maker or Milliner—but really they are generally good Harmless civil kind of people—who if you can bear with their Nonsense will treat you very well.—It is not the Conveyance for *Bucks* or *Mackeronies*. . . . . . I wonder the Dr. has never thought of your travelling to Exeter on a Cow—and feeding on her Milk I have long'd to go a journey that way ever since I read his journel. . . . . . That I hope your Absence for a Month or six Weeks will not much retard his Book—as you coud not have workd much in the dog-days." Describing in this letter her enjoyment of the lovely Devonshire scenery, as viewed with Mr. Rishton, she adds, "though if we had set out to visit a pig stye or Braudon Sands I shoud have been happy and delighted in his Company or must have been the most ungrateful Creature breathing."[2] . . . .

Fanny is given a commission.—" Mr. Rishton begs you wou'd open a bill for him at *Nounes*[3]—or to make use of his Elegant Expression *spring a Tick* with him at that Booksellers—let him know the lad is no sharper and send him down—Hawksworth's Journal—and at the same time—Veneronis Grammar—which tho' he likes Antoninis very much yet he is told may be useful to him in some respects—but Noune knows the youth is no Sharper—let them be sent as soon as possible—by the Exeter Waggon, if the Work is not Published Mr. R. would be glad to be a Subscriber—Write a long letter with the Books."]

often had not time to make her diary complete, and carried "Evelina" about in her head, long before she could write it down in patches, on scraps of paper, which she at last copied by slow degrees.

[1] What, by the way, about getting married at Ipres?
[2] Brandon Sands are where Norfolk joins Suffolk, about seven miles from Thetford, the "little Ouse," or Brandon river, runs between the two counties. The late Lord Lytton has given the name of Brandon to the chief characters in his unequal, but charming romance of "Paul Clifford."
[3] This name is probably meant for *Nourse,* John Nourse being at that time bookseller to the king.

[June.]

I have now to mention a visit from *Roscius;* he came again last Wednesday before eight o'Clock. I had fortunately been up above an hour. When I went into the study, he was playing with Charlotte. I had, as it is pretty usual with me on seeing him, something of a *grin* upon my face. " Oh here she comes! " cried he, "and resolved to look as handsome as she can. I shall run away with *her* next." My father read to him an article he had been drawing up for a new Dictionary of Arts and Sciences, a sort of English Encyclopedia. Dr. Goldsmith is the Editor, and is to be assisted by many of the best writers. Among others, Dr. Johnson is to take ethics; Sir Joshua Reynolds, painting, and Mr. Garrick, acting. It was Mr. Garrick, who mentioned it to my father some time since, and told him he wished to have his name in the list for the article, *music;* he wrote to Dr. Goldsmith concerning it, whose answer I will copy by memory:

" To David Garrick, Esq.
" Dear Sir,
" To be thought of by you, obliges me ; to be served, still more ; I am very happy that Dr. Burney thinks my plan of a Dictionary useful ; still more, that he will be so kind, as to adorn it with any thing of his own. I beg you will also accept my gratitude for procuring me so valuable an acquisition. I am, Dear sir,
" Your most affect^e. serv^t.
Oliver Goldsmith."

This very civil note Mr. Garrick enclosed in a short one from himself:

" My dear Doctor,
" I have just received the enclosed. Dr. Goldsmith will be proud to have your name in the list of the chosen. You shall have the books very soon.
" Yours ever, D. G."
" My love to your fair ones."

My father cannot do much in this work, without robbing his History; but he has written the article *Musician*, which he read to Mr. Garrick, who was pleased to admire it very much.[1] He also read to him an Answer, which he is preparing to some complaints made by French writers, concerning his censure of their Music. When Susette came down, and he had spoken to her, he said to my father, "And so you have these young creatures all about you in a morning?"

"Oh yes!"

"And so they prattle,—and you rest your understanding?" This was monstrous!

"Quite the contrary," cried I, "my father *exerts* his understanding to keep pace with us!"—He understood me, and getting up in a violent hurry, he came to the table where I was making tea; and with a thousand whimsical gestures, he cried, "Oh! you quite mistake me;—I meant to make you the greatest compliment in the world! I could not make you a greater!—what I meant was—to say that—that when you were all about him, he could then most delightfully"——

"Repose?" cried Susette. "Aye," cried he, "repose, and —and—most delightfully—do this, and that, and the other."

"Excellent, Mr. Bayes!" cried my father; and indeed he made it as *clear* as Mr. Bayes could possibly have done,— and with the most affected earnestness, he declaring repeatedly that he meant to pay us an amazing compliment.

* * * * * *[2]

[Mr. Rishton is said by Fanny to have had "a husky voice." There is also something husky in his pen-strokes; his being the final note that ends this letter-writing.

"Mr. and Mrs. Rishton hope Miss Burney will excuse not having

---

[1] The reader will find in the most complete edition of Goldsmith's Works (that of Mr. Gibbs, in Bohn's Library,) that this Dictionary never went beyond a happily-written prospectus, which was found among poor Goldsmith's papers, after his untimely death. The prospectus has disappeared, and it is not known whether or not any one of "the Club" wrote his promised paper. If Dr. Burney did so, he probably restored his facts and opinions to their proper place in his "History of Music."

[2] Of the erasures here only a date, June 30th, as heading, can be made out.

it in their power to fetch her, as they did not receive her favour until this moment, have sent the whisky, and will make proper apologies on her arrival at Tiugmouth.

"Leave y' things to the care of Mrs. Tucker at the Oxford Inn, and they will come by the carrier to-morrow."]

TINGMOUTH JOURNAL.

Editor's Preface to the "Tingmouth Journal."

The Teignmouth journal was, originally, no part of this year's Diary. It was, what Mme. D'Arblay herself called a "*Journal Letter*," addressed to that sister, Susan, who, in return, sent her records so full and frank of all that passed in the house of Dr. Burney, that the greater part of them were destroyed by Mme. D'Arblay, on account of their "confidential openness." This Teignmouth journal may be called Fanny's first book, privately circulated. It was handed to Mr. Crisp, who loved to dwell long on the writing of these girls. He even had "Allen's" Geneva journal (1771-2) as well as this, still in his keeping in 1775. We find Maria, in October, 1774, in distress, and even alarm; wishing that her journal had never been out of her own hands. Yet Fanny had kept back from Mr. Crisp what there was in it of "perilous stuff." Mr. Crisp was so charmed with Fanny's letter on Omai in December, 1774, that, after reading it to those about him who were able to value it, he sent it to his two sisters, a widow (Mrs. Gast), and a spinster, who were living at Burford, in Oxfordshire. Mrs. Gast was a woman of education and refinement. She was delighted with her brother's "delectable Fanny," and, in an effusive letter, thanked Mr. Crisp for it, telling him that she had, like himself, "entertained others with it, who had any taste for *cleverility*"—[a word which we hope that we may never find anywhere again.] Now it happened, that in the beginning of the Omai letter, Fanny had implored Mr. Crisp to return her Teignmouth journal, as "papers which *can* only furnish entertainment, if any, from the first perusal; but to *me*, who know all the people, and things mentioned, they may possibly give some pleasure, by rubbing up my memory, when I am a very tabby, before when I shall not think of looking into them. But the return was the condition, so give me my bond." She also begged that he would return Maria's journal. Mr. Crisp audaciously replied, that in sending his sisters the letter, " in order to make them understand what those papers were which you reclaim'd with such fury," he had been obliged to explain that they were " your journal and the Allen's,"—that his sister, (whose letter he copies in part), has, with much warmth, entreated that she may have a sight of his "charming Fanny's" journal,—and why should she *not?*—and why not of Allen's, too ; *her* name being concealed ? Thereupon, follows Fanny's positive denial in the case of her friend, and an expression of great reluctance in her own. "Ever since her marriage," Maria, "had a thousand, nay a million of times, both by letters, and by word of mouth, conjured Fanny to get her papers from Mr. Crisp, and destroy them at once." Fanny adds that she had only preserved that part of the journal which Mr. Crisp had never seen, in order that she might give Mrs. Rishton the satisfaction of seeing it burnt before her face,—together with that part which she begs him to send to her. He answers that Mrs. Rishton's journal shall be given up to Fanny, when he can find some safe way of sending it. This he has not found in July, 1775, although by March he has restored the Teignmouth journal to its writer; but merely in order that she may read it before he sends it to his sisters. She reviews it *critically;* and "feels a thousand times more repugnance" than before, to letting Mr. Crisp's sisters see " such folly," but yields, rather than contest the point with him; yet stipulates that he shall write a line or two to tell them that it was at his desire that they receive her journal; not through her own vanity. She asks him to return the letters which she has written to him, but this he not merely refuses to do, but apparently sends all of them which do not touch upon family affairs to Mrs. Gast, whom Fanny has, so far, never met. The love of Fanny's letters grows upon Mr. Crisp, and his demands for them increase. He even shows a little jealousy of her spending time in writing to Mr. Hutton, and to Mrs. Brooke, the novelist, when she might have been writing more letters to *him.* Later on, Fanny meets Mrs. Gast at Chesington, loves her, and is loved by her. There is no more withholding of papers from her. Mr. Crisp even copies with his own feeble fingers, Fanny's journals, which, after 1776, are mainly addressed to Susan, then passed on to him, and he sends them, (at least in part) to Mrs. Gast, who is to read them to no one but "Molly Lenthal," her great friend. Dr. Johnson is shown a letter from Mrs. Gast to Fanny, that he may admire, as he does admire, her elegant handwriting. On the death of Mr. Crisp in 1783, Mrs. Gast, as his executrix, became possessor of Fanny's letters to him. Her cousin, and executrix, Mrs. Frodsham, restored them afterwards to Madame D'Arblay; a fact which is gratefully recorded in the Memoirs of Dr. Burney.

Two leaves, at least, are missing, so that this journal begins abruptly, thus—

[July.]

. . . . some repair, and I therefore, was very late before I came in sight of Tingmouth, half a mile from which Mr. and Mrs. Rishton walked to meet me.

I was received with the most cordial welcome by my dear Maria, who had been quite uneasy, lest any accident had happened to me. I was very glad to find their company were all gone.

Tingmouth is situated the most beautifully of any town I ever saw, or perhaps in England, ever can see. Mr. Rishton's house is on the *Den*, which is the *Mall* here. It is a small, neat, thatched and white-washed cottage, neither more nor less. We are not a hundred yards from the sea, in which Mrs. Rishton bathes every morning. There is no end to the variety of delightful walks and rides which this sweet spot affords.

The morning after I came they insisted on my accompanying them to the Races, and I had a very civil invitation from Mrs. Phipps, in whose chaise and company Mrs. Rishton and myself went. Mr. Rishton drove Mr. Phipps in his *whiskey*. The Phipps' are newly married, and in great favour with Mr. Rishton and Maria.

We got a very good place in the stand, where there was a very great deal of company, and the races, being quite new to me, really afforded me a great deal of entertainment. But I must not omit mentioning that Mrs. R. announced to me that the first person for agreeability, cultivation, pleasantry, and good breeding of their acquaintance was a half name-sake of my dear Daddy Crisp,—*i.e.* a Mr. Crispen.

Mr. Rishton is still more in love with retirement than his wife, if that is possible ; there are but two families he approves keeping up acquaintance with : though I find there is at present a great deal of company at Tingmouth, as this is the *season* for sea-bathing, and as the rural beauties of the place become every year more known, in so much that the price of all provisions, &c., is actually doubled within these three years. The two families honoured with Mr. Rishton's preference are those of the Phips and the Hurrels, which latter consists of Mr. Hurrel, a clergyman of [£]1500 per ann. his wife and her sister, Miss Davy, who are daughters of Sir John Davy.

In returning from Mrs. Phips we were met by Mr. Crispen. It seems he has interested himself very much in my father's musical plan. He is on the wrong side of an elderly man, but seems to have good health and spirits. He has spent many years abroad, and is perfect master of French and Italian. He is at Tingmouth for the summer season, but I believe Bath is his usual place of residence.

I was also introduced the same morning to Miss Bowdler, a young woman, who according to Mr. Rishton, bears a rather singular character. She is very sensible and clever, and possesses a great share of wit and poignancy, which spares, he says, neither friend or foe. She reckons herself superior, he also adds, to the opinion of the world and to all common forms and customs, and therefore lives exactly as she pleases, guarding herself from all real evil, but wholly regardless and indifferent of appearances. She is about six and twenty; a rather pretty little figure, but not at all handsome, though her countenance is very spirited and expressive. She has father, mother, and sisters alive; but yet is come to Tingmouth alone; though for the moment indeed, she is with a Miss Lockwood, a rich old maid; but she will very soon be entirely *at liberty*. She and her family are old acquaintances of Mrs. Rishton, and of mama; she is therefore frequently here; but Mr. Rishton, who gave me most of this account of her, cannot endure even the sight of her, a woman, he says, who despises the customs and manners of the country she lives in, must, consequently, conduct herself with impropriety. For *my* part I own myself of the same sentiment, but, nevertheless, we have not any one of us the most distant shadow of doubt of Miss Bowdler's being equally innocent with those who have more worldly prudence, at the same time, that her conduct appears to me highly improper: for she finds that the company of gentlemen is more entertaining than that of ladies, and therefore, without any scruples or punctilio, indulges her fancy. She is perpetually at Mr. Crispen's, notwithstanding a very young man, Mr. Green, lives in the same house; not contented with a *call*, she very frequently sups with them; and though she does this in the fair face of day, and speaks of it as openly and commonly as I should of visiting my sister, yet I can by no means approve so great a contempt of public opinion. As to Mr. Rishton he almost *detests* her; but his wife is really attached to her, which is an unfortunate circumstance. I heartily [wish] that she was not here, as she always drives Mr. Rishton away when she appears; for he is delicate, or rather scrupulous, to an uncommon degree in his choice of acquaintance for his wife. Nevertheless, when she offers to entirely give Miss Bowdler up, he does not consent to it, because he knows it would be much against her will, and because if it was not, he would not risque her character to the *lash* of Miss Bowdler's tongue.

"After the Races," said Miss Bowdler, in taking leave, " I shall do myself the honour to wait on Miss Burney."

"Ay," cried Mr. Rishton, when she was gone, "they will soon make this as errant a public place as Bristol Hotwells or any other place."

Thursday we again went to the Races, with Mrs. Phips, &c.

Friday morning Mr. Crispen called, and said that he should sooner *have paid his respects* to me but that [he] understood I had been engaged at the Races.

But before I talk any more of other people, let me, my dear Susette, more particularly mention my home. And, first, our dear friend *Maria*, is just the same I ever knew her, save that she is become more gentle in her manners in general, and less indulges herself in that disposition for *whim*, which Nature so lavishly gave her; but this *restraint* is more in actions than words; for her conversation, except in company very formal and old, is as flighty, as ridiculous, as uncommon, lively, comical, and truly entertaining as ever we knew it; and her heart generous, frank, undisguised, admits of no alteration. We are most excessively comfortable together, and have nothing to repine at, but the impossibility of wholly avoiding visits and visitings, though she has almost all her former carelessness of what she does in this particular, to save herself the torment of seeing people she does not care for.

Her adored Rishton improves daily in my opinion, because I think I daily observe in him an encrease of real affection and tenderness for his wife. They are, indeed, most unaffectedly happy in each other; even I who live in the house with them, should find it at present difficult to determine which of them is more affectionately, I might say, *passionately* attached to the other. Mrs. Rishton's love has long admitted of no addition, though her happiness certainly has, as time makes her know how peculiarly fortunate her choice has been. There is a remarkable similarity in their humours; for he is as whimsical and odd as herself; but he is so very difficult in his opinion of proper companions and acquaintance for his wife, that he is really miserable whenever she speaks to any but the select few of his option. Though this exceeding *scrupulosity*, and some other things of this nature, have perhaps their rise from pride, yet he evidently proves that all his thoughts and attentions are directed towards her, and seeking to do her honour. There is a kind of generous impetuosity in his disposition, which often hurries him beyond the bounds which his own cooler judgment would approve; and here again he resembles his wife—that he cannot at all disguise any thing that he feels.

I find myself very happy here. I am treated with the most unbounded confidence by Mr. Rishton himself as well as by his wife, and I am most comfortable in finding that every thing in the family goes on just the same as if I was away, and that I am no restraint either in their affairs or conversation.

The rest of our family consists of four dogs who are prodigious favourites. Two of them are spaniels, Vigo and Trump; the third is a Newfoundland dog, excellent for diving, who always goes with Mr. Rishton to swim or bathe: he is named Tingmouth; the fourth is most particularly for Mrs. Rishton, it is called Romeo and is a very faithful old dog, it is a brown Pomeranian.

Mr. Rishton having some business in London on Saturday, Mrs. R. and myself accompanied him as far as Exeter in his way. But I should mention that before we went Mr. Crispen paid us another visit, in the course of which he was pleased to offer himself for the most devoted of *my slaves !* but, he said, it was in all humility, and only till I met here with a *younger:* and *then* he would resign his pretensions.

He asked Mr. Rishton how long his stay here would be. "It is quite uncertain," answered he, "according to what news I hear from Stanhoe.[1] Perhaps I may be kept till Christmas:—if we could but keep Miss Burney."

---

[1] Stanhoe House, near Docking, in Norfolk, where Mr. and Mrs. Rishton lived shortly afterwards, was near Hillington Hall, the seat of his mother's cousin, Martin William Browne Folkes, who was created a baronet in 1774.

"O," cried Mr. Crispen, "if *Miss Burney* stays, *I do!* though I intended to go in five or six weeks. She has accepted me for an old lover, though indeed I was in love with her before I saw her by what I heard from *the Lamb* (a name he has given to Mrs. R), and now—" &c., &c. We agreed to go again to Exeter on Thursday, which day Mr. R. had fixed upon for his return, and on Sunday evening Mrs. R. and myself called in at Mr. Crispen's to borrow the poem of the Minstrel.

This Mr. Crispen seems attached to the fair sex in the style of the old courtiers. I am told that he has Dulcineas without number, though I am the reigning sovereign at present. Miss Bowdler, who is on the list, and who I take for a very formidable rival, was sitting with him. He insisted on Mrs. Rishton's coming in, but demanded instantly "have you brought my little flame with you?" We stayed but a few minutes, and in that time Mr. Green entered. Mr. Crispen introduced me to him, and added "you must say every thing that is *civil*—but nothing that is *fond* to this young lady—for yesterday I poured forth the effusions of *my* heart to her."

"I will with a great deal of pleasure," answered Mr. Green, "both say and do every thing that is civil that is in my power."

"Miss Bowdler, do you allow of all this?" cried Mrs. Rishton. "O, I am obliged to it," replied she—"for I am but an old wife!" She made no scruple of being left with the two gentlemen, when we came away.

Mr. Crispen and Mr. Green were to set out the next morning on a trip to Plymouth and Mount Edgecombe, with a family who are here for the season, of the name of Colbourn, consisting of Mr. Colbourn, who was a Bath apothecary, but has had an immense fortune left him, and is now enjoying it, his wife and daughter. They were to return on Thursday.

Monday and Tuesday Mrs. R. and myself spent in the most comfortable manner possible,—but for Wednesday I must be more particular.

Mr. Hurrel[1] has an exceeding pretty boat of his own here,

---

[1] This name is properly "*Hurrell*"; some memory of it is obvious

with which he makes frequent excursions on the river Ting, and sometimes on the sea. His wife called here on Tuesday evening, to invite us to be of their party on Wednesday, when they intended sailing to Torbay, to see a Fleet under Admiral Spry, which was just come from Portsmouth. We very gladly accepted the offer, and set off the next morning about seven o'clock, our company consisting of Mr. and Mrs. Hurrel, Mr. Phips, a boatswain, another sailor, Mr. Hurrel's servant, and ourselves.

Mr. Hurrel is quite a poet's priest; he is fat as Falstaff, unable to use exercise and eke unwilling; his love of ease is surpassed by nothing, but his love of good living, which equals whatever detraction has hitherto devised for a parson's gluttony. Mrs. Hurrel is an obliging, civil, tiresome woman.

Our plan was to see the fleet, and if possible, a man o' war's *inside*, and then to land on one of the safest and pleasantest rocks, to dine, as Mr. Hurrel had taken especial care of this particular. But when he came near the ships, the sea grew rough, and having no invitation, we were obliged to give up the thought of entering any of them. There were seven men of war in the bay, and we sailed round them. They are most noble vessels. I had reason to think myself very fortunate that I was not sea-sick, though I never before was on the ocean. We *put in* at Brixham, a most excellent fishing-town, but very dirty and disagreeable. We made but a short stay, and set sail again. Brixham is about ten miles from Tingmouth by sea.[1]

The wind was against us, and we were hardly out of the harbour, before we found the sea terribly rough. I own I

---

in the "Harrels" of "Cecilia." It is remarkable how names strike the fancy of authors. The editor saw "Donnithorne" (the "Donnithorne" of "Adam Bede") over a shop in Penzance long before she knew that George Elliot had stayed in Penzance; and the name of "Inglesant" was seen some time ago over a paltry shop in a shabby street, yet no name could have been better, quainter, and more mysterious than that for the book which brightened it. But these things (according to Balzac) are pre-ordained, and novelists do but "*take the good the gods provide*" them.

[1] In 1779 the churchyard of the old church at Brighton reminded Fanny of Brixham, "where the houses are built by the sides of hills."

was not very easy, as our boat, though a large one for the Thames, was very small for the sea; but still I considered myself as the person of the least consequence, whatever our danger. However, it was no sport to me to be danced up and down, and to find the waves higher and rougher every instant, especially when I saw Mr. Hurrel who had hitherto guided us, quit the helm to the Boatswain, and exclaim, "We shall run foul of these rocks!"

The waves foamed in little white mountains rising above the green surface of the sea; they dashed against the rocks off the coast of Brixham with monstrous fury; and really to own the truth, I felt no inclination to be boat-wrecked, however pathetic and moving a Tale our adventure might have made. Mrs. H. grasped my hand, and looked very much frightened; her agreeable husband repeated several times his most comfortable exclamation of, "We shall run foul of the rocks!" There followed a most terrible confusion. I don't remember or understand sea-phrases; but the hurrying, loud, violent manner in which they gave orders to one another, was really frightful. "Is there any danger," cried Mrs. Hurrel; pray, Boatswain, tell me, is there any danger?" "No; I don't think there is Ma'am."

This was the most alarming sound I had heard yet—I don't *think there is!* However, I found we were all in equal danger; for the two sailors assured us their swimming would be totally useless, as the fury of the waves would presently swallow them up. Mrs. Hurrel grasped my hand harder than ever. Her husband forgot his cloth, and began to swear, but always adding, "God forgive me!"—At length, after being tosst up and down in a most terrible manner for about a quarter of an hour, the Boatswain said we should not reach Tingmouth before midnight; and just then the waves seemed to redouble their violence, and the boat scooped one fairly over us.

I gave up the ghost; Mrs. Hurrel burst into tears, and cried vehemently, "For mercy's sake! Mr. Hurrel, pray let us go back to Brixham,—pray do,—we shall be all drowned! Oh! pray don't let me be drowned! Set me down! set me down!" . . . .

"But where are we to *dine?*" cried he.

"Oh! any where, Mr. Hurrel, any where, so as we do but get a-shore! I don't mind, I assure-*ee* !"

"Oh! that's pretty talking," answered the priest, "but that won't serve for a meal."

However, I believe he also had no objection to prolong his days; for when the boatswain said that it blew fresher higher up, he immediately ordered, that we should *tack about;* and so we returned to Brixham.

When we landed, I was so very giddy, that I could hardly stand, and was obliged to go into the first house for a glass of water; but I am only amazed that I was not dreadfully seasick. How to get home, was the next consideration. Mrs. Rishton had promised to meet Mr. R. at Exeter the next day, and was determined rather to walk than disappoint him; but it is sixteen miles from Tingmouth by land; there was no post-chaise to be had; nor could we hear even of any horses. We went into the best inn of the place, and Mr. Hurrel ordered dinner. After a thousand enquiries, *pro's* and *con's* &c. we were settled thus: Mrs. R. procured a horse, Mr. Phipps another, on which he accompanied her back to Teignmouth; and Mr. Hurrel, his wife and myself, to my great regret, were obliged to stay all night at Brixham.

But I forgot to mention that a sloop filled with *Tingmothians*, was obliged to put in at Brixham as well as us, they were a very gay party, who had come out with the same view as ourselves, among them were Miss Lockwood and Miss Bowdler. I was sorry to see the latter in such company, for they behaved in a most ridiculous and improper manner dancing about the town and diverting themselves in a very unmannerly *easy* and careless style, and though Miss Bowdler herself behaved with propriety yet her party reflected some thing on her [1] and has much added to Mr. Rishton's aversion to her. But to be brief. We passed a weary evening, and the next morning at three o'clock we got up and set sail for Tingmouth, intending to breakfast in the boat. But, Oh grief of griefs! the awkward boatswain managed to destroy all the matches; and we were obliged to give our breakfast up, to Mr. Hurrel's very great anger and sorrow.

[1] A word illegible—it *may* be "sense."

I will mention nothing more of our perils, though they were not inconsiderable in my opinion. But however we landed at last, safe and sound, about nine o'clock. The Hurrel's insisted on my going to breakfast with them; after which I came home, and went to bed for a couple of hours, not having undressed myself at Brixham. But I caught a *very* bad cold, and know not when I shall part with it.

Mr. and Mrs. Rishton returned from Exeter to dinner, and in the evening Mr. Crispen called, just arrived from Plymouth. He protested he could not rest till he came; that this was his first visit; and that where the *thoughts* were, there the *person* must wish itself!—&c.—all addressed to little me!

"But I think," added he, "that *my love* expressed no great joy at seeing me?—*My* heart went *pit-a-pat* all the way I came."

He said he had rode the whole way from Plymouth on horseback, having given the Colbourns *the slip:* he pronounced a very high character of the daughter both for accomplishments and propriety of conduct. He declared that he found himself so little fatigued with his journey that he was ready to shew his prowess by going on the beach and declaring the *Bright Burney, the best of her sex!*

"Except," said Mr. Rishton," "Miss Colbourn!"

"Without *any* exception! I have a very great esteem for Miss Colbourn; and admire her greatly; but here———"

"But then, Miss Bowdler? what do you do with her," returned Mr. Rishton.

"For the little Bowdler I have indeed a most particular regard; but still—still Miss Burney!———"

Mr. Rishton mentioned some more fair Dulcineas, to all which he answered, "O, these are but my diversion!—but Burney is my Home!" Then, turning to me "your little hand . . *I love you!*—I was prepared to love you before I saw you; —but now I find in you a strong resemblance to a sister who was very dear to me, that I must love you more for her sake."

The next morning Miss Bowdler called. She seemed in a very angry humour with her old friend Mr. Crispen. I fancy she wishes to be more *unique* with him than she finds it is in her power to be.

"He is returned quite a young man," said Mrs. Rishton, "and not at all fatigued."

"Yes," answered she, "but he droops this morning! he must take another journey to Plymouth to recruit. He tells me that Miss Colbourne was all perfection. I only laughed: to *me* she appears the most affected, conceited thing I ever saw: however, I am glad Perfection is so easily attained!"

"We shall hear Fanny's opinion of her to-night," said Mrs. Rishton, "for she drinks tea here."

"Well, much good may it do you!—they extol her painting too—but I'd lay my life all the landscapes she has taken this journey are from Green:[1]—however, Crispen can afford to lavish away a multitude of compliments without feeling their loss: but novelty is all in all for him."

She said much more to the same purpose, and made me very angry with her, as Mr. Crispen deserves more consideration from her, and seems her first-rate favourite. In the evening the Colbourns came. The father is a worthy kind of man, but full of that parade and bluster which constitute that sort of man whom we call *purse-proud*. The mother is an insipid, good sort of woman. The daughter is a very smart girl, somewhat affected and not *too* diffident of her accomplishments; but extremely civil and obliging, and very well behaved.

I don't know when I shall come to the present time; but *Patienza!*

Saturday morning Mrs. Rishton and I walked out [to] avoid a very disagreeable scene; for the day before Mr. Rishton came home in great haste and pertubation, (*sic*) and calling his

---

[1] There were, about that time, four brothers Green, two of whom were engravers, and two painters. This might be Amos Green, a flower and landscape-painter; or his brother Benjamin, who was teacher of drawing at Christ's Hospital. Crispen is not a name in the index to Mrs. Delany's Correspondence, but, although our reference is lost, a memory remains that we saw in one of those six ponderous volumes that a Mr. Crispen was very polite in showing Mrs. Delany pictures at an exhibition of either the "Society of Arts," which was founded in 1755, or of the "Society of Artists of Great Britain," which was a few years its junior.

wife told her that he had broke Romeo's leg! This was occasioned by the poor dog's running after sheep, for which he has often been, in vain, very severely beat; but now he and one of the spaniels got a poor sheep quite down and began to tear her to pieces. Mr. R. rode up to them, and catching Romeo at first by the leg, to prevent his biting, began to flog him violently, till he found that by the twist, he had broke his leg short off! He was beyond measure concerned, and gave a man a crown to carry him home gently in his arms; and the next morning had a surgeon to set the poor animal's leg,—which not chusing to see we sauntered before the door till it was done: in which time Mr. Crispen went by on horseback. "Are these my ladies?" cried he,—"and how does my love? I did not see her all yesterday—the day was heavy! I felt something wanting!—and how fares it with the Lamb?"

"I wish you would come and hear me read Italian," cried she, now do, Mr. Crispen, I want help extremely."

"And does my little Burney speak it? or learn it?"

"O yes," answered Mrs. R.

"*Then* I'll come!—the sound of her voice—"

"Well," returned she I never heard anything so genteel! upon my word, Mr. Crispen, there's no bearing all this—"

"Nay—you know I always loved the sound of yours," cried he, as he rode off.

In the evening, however, he came; but as Mr. Rishton was at home, we had no Italian: for he is too far advanced in that language to profit by such lessons as we want. Mr. Crispen brought with him some drawings on cards of Mr. Green's performance. Two of them were views of Tingmouth, and he made a great fuss about them, asking me how I would bribe him for a sight? I told him that I had nothing at all to offer.—

"Why, now" said he, "methinks two drawings deserve two kisses—and—if—"

"No, no, no," cried I, "not that!" much surprised at his modest request. But he only spoke in sport I am sure.

He brought one view for Mrs. Rishton which Mr. Green had sent her as a present; saying "I wish it was for my little Burney!"

The drawings were extremely pretty. One of them I was admiring very much—it was a night piece—for its *coolness*— "O," cried Mr. Crispen, "that is it! you would like a *cool* lover, then? I am too *passionate* for you?"

When we had examined these cards, "Come," said Mr. Rishton, " won't you sit down, Mr. Crispen—there's a chair by Miss Burney!"

"That is where I mean to sit," answered he. Poor Romeo's misfortune then *came on the carpet*, and Mr. Crispen gave Mr. R. some very good and very free advice, on restraining his passions, and keeping them more under command;—and Mr. R. who is quite afflicted for the dog, took it very candidly [1] and sensibly; indeed, they both did themselves honour. But, however, nothing could engage the old gentleman long from his gallantry to me. He turned towards me with a mournful air: "I don't know how it is but my little Burney and I don't hit it off well together! I take all possible pains,—but I cannot please her!—Well, I can't help it!—I can only say, you would not have used me thus forty years ago!"

Thank God I *could* not, thought I. But, really, I scarce knew what to say, and indeed have seldom made any other answer than laughing; but I took the first opportunity of his being engaged in conversation with Mr. Rishton to move off and seat myself in the window. He perceived it immediately, and with a reproachful voice, called out, "Now is this *decent*, Miss Burney? are you afraid of only *sitting* by me?" Then rising and getting his hat, "Well, I shall go to my little Colbourn—*she* will not use me thus!"

However, he altered his mind, and brought a chair and placed himself before me; and the subject was changed to Miss Bowdler and the Brixham party.

Miss Bowdler might have blushed to have heard the benevolence with which he spoke of her. He lamented in very affectionate terms that she had been unfortunately mixed with so giddy and imprudent a party, and recommended it very strongly to Mrs. Rishton to make it known as much as she

---

[1] "Candidly" is here used in its old sense, and is equivalent to *mildly, with gentleness, without impatience or ill-temper.*

could, that Miss Bowdler was an exception to the general set, when the company was named. He regretted her being alone here and hoped Mrs. Rishton would extend her friendship to protect her, and be as much with her as possible, after Miss Lockwood's departure. He spoke of her in very high terms and said he owed her so much regard and respect that he would himself be always with her, but that he knew the people here would only sneer about it. It seems, in a bad illness which Mr. Crispen had, she was his constant nurse.

Mr. Rishton very openly blamed her for mixing with the Brixham party. Mr. Crispen could hardly justify her. "I would not," said he, "have had a daughter of mine there—or my little Burney, for the whole world!"

Then again he renewed his discourse to me, and begged me to remember an old proverb—that

"Love burns slowest in old veins—
But when once entered, long remains."

"Indeed," said I, "I did not come to Tingmouth at all prepared for such fine speeches!"

"*Fine speeches!*" exclaimed he—"ah! that is always the way you answer old bachelors!"

Now, to tell you my private opinion, my dear Susy, I am inclined to think that this gallantry is the effect of the man's taking me for a fool;—because I have been so much surprised at it that I have hardly ever had a word of answer ready. You, who know how *wise* I am, must allow the injustice of such an inference! But I cannot write or recollect half the fine things he says. But don't let all this make you think *him* a fool. He is much of a gentlemen, has an easy and polite address, is very sensible and agreeable in conversation, and remarkably mild, candid, and benevolent in his opinions and judgments: but he has lived so long abroad that I suppose he thinks it necessary to talk nonsense to we fair sex.

Monday, Aug.

We are just going to Tingmouth Races, which, indeed, are to be held in sight of our house. We hope for very good sport,—a great deal of company are arrived on the Den.

Aug. 19th.

I have not had a moment for writing this age—I never had less, as Mrs. R. and myself are almost inseparable. The Races, however, must by no means pass unrecorded.

Miss Lockwood and Miss Bowdler invited themselves to accompany us to the Race ground: Mr. Crispen also called in and joined us. Mr. Rishton was not at all pleased, and the half hour which we spent before we set out, he sat almost totally silent. Mr. Crispen addressed himself to me with his usual particularity, which really put me quite out of countenance, as I dreaded Miss Bowdler's opinion, and feared she would rank me with Miss Colbourne. I seated myself quietly at a distance, but Mr. Crispen, determined to torment me, drew his chair quite close to mine, and in so particular a manner that I could not keep my place but got up and seated myself next to Mrs. R. on the window.

I then wished that I had not, for every body (except Mr. R.) laughed: I felt my face on fire. "Do you run away from me," cried Mr. Crispen, "to take shelter under the Lamb?" But it was in vain, for he immediately moved after me, and continued, in the same style, to complain of me. I endeavoured to change the subject, and made some enquiries concerning the Races; but nothing would do. "Ah!" cried he, "would that your heart was to be run for! What an effort would I make!" "Yes," cried Miss Bowdler (not very delicately), "you would break your wind on the occasion, I doubt not." "What will they do," said I, "with the poor pig after the Races?" (one was to be run for).

"O that my heart," cried Mr. Crispen, "could be as easily cured!"

"Never fear," said Miss Bowdler, "it has stood a good many shocks!"

"Were it now to be opened," answered he, "you would find Burney engraved on it in large characters."

"O yes," cried she, "and you would find a great many pretty misses there besides!"

"Ay," said Mrs. R., "there would be Miss Colbourne."

"But Burney," cried he emphatically, "is my sum total. I own, I avow it publicly, I make no secret of it!"

"Yes, yes," returned Miss Bowdler, "the *Present* is always best!"

I just then recollected a little dispute which we had had with Mr. Rishton, on the pronunciation of some Italian words, and giving a grammar to Mr. Crispen, beg'd him to decide it.

"Look another way, my dear little Burney," cried he, "look another way—I must take out my reading glass!— You have a natural antipathy to me, but don't strengthen it by looking at me now!"

I was very glad when this conversation was concluded, by our being all obliged to march. We found a great deal of company, and a great deal of diversion. The sport began by an Ass Race. There were sixteen of the long eared tribe; some of them really ran extremely well; others were indeed truly ridiculous; but all of them diverting. Next followed a Pig Race. This was certainly cruel, for the poor animal had his tail cut to within the length of an inch, and then that inch was soaped. It was then let loose and made run. It was to be the property of the man who could catch it by the tail; which after many ridiculous attempts was found to be impossible, it was so very slippery. Therefore the candidates concluded this day's sport by running for it themselves. The great *Sweep Stakes* of the asses were half-a-guinea; the second prize a crown, and the third half-a-crown. However, the whole of it was truly laughable.

The next Race day was not till Friday, which day was also destined to a grand Cricket Match. Mr. Rishton is a very good player; and there is an excellent ground on the Den. Two gentlemen who were to be of the match breakfasted here in the morning. They are sons of Dr. Milles, Dean of Exeter. . . . . . The cricket players dined on the green, where they had a boothe erected, and a dinner from the Globe, the best Inn here,[1] to which Mrs. Rishton added a *hash*,

---

[1] It is the editor's impression that the roomy lodging-house in which she first stayed at Teignmouth, five-and-twenty years ago, was, in 1773, "The Globe Inn." On the first floor, a large ball-room had been turned into bed-rooms (with never a chimney), by wooden partitions, so slight that each movement, or speech, could be heard in the chambers adjoining. The Editor finally saw it pulled down; and a modern high house,

which Mr. T. Mills assured her was most excellent, for Mr. Hurrel himself eat three times of it! and that, he remarked, indisputably proved its goodness.[1]

The Cricket Match was hardly over before the Tingmouth games began. All that was [to] be done this second day was Wrestling, a most barbarous diversion, and which I could not look on, and would not have gone to if I had not feared being thought affected. A ring was formed for the combattants by a rope railing, from which we stood to see the sport!! The wrestler was to conquer twice, one opponent immediately after another, to entitle himself to the prize. A strong labouring man came off victorious in the first battles; but while his shins were yet bleeding, he was obliged to attack another. The hat (their gauntlet) was thrown by a servant of Mr. Colbourn's. He was reckoned by the judges an admirable-

---

looking due west to the red cliff (which Maria Allen likened to Shakespeare's cliff at Dover), was reared high, in place of the long, low building.

In August, races (less grotesque) are still run on the Den, or Dene, at Teignmouth (a sandy grass-grown stretch of some acres between the sea and the irregular line of houses which front it), and reviews of militia, or yeomanry, are held on it; the Den being three fourths of a mile long. There is still a good Newfoundland trade, and excellent home-fishing. The beauty of the colouring of the sea, and of the vivid red sandstone cliffs, capped with bright green to their edge, no words can describe.

[1] It must not be supposed that Mrs. Rishton gave, or Mr. Hurrell approved, what a naïve cook of the last century calls "*a harsh;*" that word is still too often a just description of cold meat, sliced and warmed. This was most likely a lordly dish, such as Mrs. Glasse tells us how to make, in the sixteenth edition of her "Art of Cookery," 1786, pages 28-9—"To hash a calf's head," or to hash it "white." It was more than a. "*ragoo;*" strong gravy, eggs and butter, red wine, or white, truffles, morels, mushrooms pickled, or not, eschalots, lemons, and sweet herbs, forced-meat balls, fried oysters, and toasted bacon, cream, artichoke-bottoms, and asparagus, float before the astonished eye upon these pages. The fried oysters, (twenty in number), were indispensable. There is nothing of a hash about it, except that the calf's-head is *scored* with a hashing-knife while *whole*, and hot from the pan, before it is browned. It is a "*hâchis,*" not a *hash*—and such an one we give Mrs. Rishton credit for offering to her friends. In 1765, we find Voltaire writing that he cannot eat a "*hâchis*" of turkey, hare, and rabbit, which his friends try to persuade him is composed of one viand only.

wrestler, and he very fairly beat his adversary. A sailor directly flung his hat: he was sworn friend of the defeated labourer. He entered the lists in a passion, and attacked the servant, as all the gentlemen said, very unfairly, and, while a short truce was declared for the man to have his shoe unbuckled, he very dishonourably hit him a violent blow. Upon this they both prepared for a boxing match, and were upon the point of engaging (though the whole Ring cried out "shame" upon the sailor), when Mr. Rishton inflamed with generous rage at this foul play, rushed precipitately into the Ring, and getting between the combattants, collared the sailor, declaring he should be turned out of the lists.

I am really amazed that he escaped being ill-treated; but, at the very instant, two of the young Mills ran into the Ring and catching hold of Mr. Rishton insisted on his not venturing himself against the brutality of the enraged sailor. However, he would not retire till the sailor was voted out of the lists as a foul player. Mr. Rishton then returned to us between the Mr. Mills. Every body seemed in admiration of the spirit which he exerted on this occasion.

The Tingmouth Games concluded the day after with a Rowing Match between the women of Shaldon, a fishing town on the other side of the Ting, and the fair ones of this place. For all the men are at Newfoundland every summer, and all laborious work is done by the women, who have a strength and hardiness which I have never seen before in our race.

The following morning, while Mrs. R. and myself were dressing, we received a very civil message from Mrs. and Miss Colbourne to invite us to see the rowing in their carriage. Mrs. R. sent word that we would come to them on the Den; but afterwards we recollected that we were engaged to tea at Mrs. Phips. This put us in a dilemma; but as Mrs. Phips's was the prior engagement, we were obliged to march to Mr. Colbourne's coach on the Den to make our apologies. The first object I saw was Mr. Crispen. He expressed himself prodigiously charmed at seeing us. I said we were obliged [to go. He] said he had heard of our not being well—" I could ill bear," he added, " to hear of the Lamb's illness—but when they told me that *you* was not well!—I should not have been so long without seeing you, but from having had a violent cold and fever myself—[and I] thought in my confinement that one half hour's conversation with you would completely recover me."

"If I had known," said I, " my miraculous power—"

" O," cried he, taking my hand, " it is not yet too late ! If you are mercifully disposed."—I skipt off.

We made our apologies as well as we could, and they insisted on setting us down at Mr. Phips', Mrs. Colbourn and Mr. Crispen on one side and we three lasses on the other. All the way we went Mr. Crispen amused himself with holding the same kind of language to me, notwithstanding the presence of Miss Colbourne.

The women rowed with astonishing dexterity and quickness. There were five boats of them. The prizes which they won were, shifts with pink ribbands. Games such as these, Mr. Crispen says, ought to make future events be dated as universally from Tingmothiads as former ones were from Olympiads.

I must now miss a whole week, having no time to recollect any thing which passed. Last Sunday Mr.[1] and Mrs. Western arrived here, to make a week's visit. Mrs. Western[2] is cousin to Mr. Rishton, being sister to Mr. Martin Folkes. She is infinitely the most agreeable of her family, good-tempered, lively, well-bred, and obliging. Mr. Western is a very sensible man ; but has an oddity in him, which I know not how to characterize. He has a good deal of drollery ; but I fancy makes a very uncomfortable companion. I think he has the *remains* of a very agreeable man, as strongly marked in his looks and manners, as I have ever seen the *remains* of a celebrated beauty visible in a countenance. He is still a young man, but has such very indifferent health, that it embitters every moment of his life. Mrs. Western was most violently in love with him when they married, though their fortunes on each side were too considerable to make either of

---

[1] Maximilian Western, Esq., of Cokethorpe, near Witney, in Oxfordshire.

[2] Elizabeth, fourth daughter of William Folkes, Esq., by his first marriage, was cousin to Mr. Rishton's *mother*, and *half*-sister to Martin Browne Folkes.

them be styled *romantic*. But I think at present she seems to have the most perfect, the coldest indifference towards him that ever wife had. Mr. Western is still reckoned a very *gay* man, in no very *constant* sense of that word. He may, therefore, have trifled away her affection, while his own for her appears still continued. O, what bad policy in men, to accustom their wives to their fickleness till even their love becomes a matter of indifferency! Indeed I am sorry for them both, as each of them seem formed for [a degree] of happiness to which they really seem to deny each other. Mrs. Western has, in the politest manner, invited me to accompany Mr. and Mrs. R. to Oxfordshire when they return this visit. As to Mr. Western, he and I are particularly good friends, indeed Mrs. R. and myself are as free from restraint or ceremony as before they came, for, fortunately, they neither of them have the least grain of it in their composition.

We all went on Monday evening to the sea-shore, to see the *scene* drawn; this is a most curious work, all done by women.[1] They have a very long net, so considerable as to cost them thirteen or sixteen pounds. This they first draw into a boat, which they go off the shore in, and row in a kind of semicircle, till they land at some distance. All the way they spread this net, one side of which is kept above water by corks. Then they land and divide forces; half of them return to the beginning of the net, and half remain at the end; and then with amazing strength both divisions at the same time pull the net in by the two ends. Whatever fish they catch, are always encircled in the middle of the net, which comes out of the water the last; and, as they draw towards each other, they all join in getting their prey. When once they perceive that there is fish in their nets, they set up a loud shout, and make an almost unintelligible noise in expressing their joy and in disputing at the same time upon their shares, and on what fish escaped them. They are all robust and well-made, and have remarkably beautiful teeth, and some of

---

[1] This drawing of the *seine* is no longer done by the Teignmouth women, who are now very much like the fisherwomen at other sea-side places, and seem to have lost their beauty with their savagery.

them are really very fine women. Their dress is barbarous; they have stays half-laced, and something by way of handkerchiefs about their necks; they wear a single coloured flannel, or stuff petticoat; no shoes or stockings, notwithstanding the hard pebbles and stones all along the beach; and their coat is pinned up in the shape of a pair of trousers, leaving them wholly naked to the knee.[1] Mr. Western declares he could not have imagined such a race of females existed in a civilized country; and had he come hither by sea, he should have almost fancied he had been cast on a newly discovered coast. They caught this evening at one time nine large salmon, a john dory, and a gurnet. On Tuesday evening we went again, and saw them catch four dozen of mackerel at a haul.

After this was over, we crosst the Ting in a ferry-boat to Shaldon, and took a most delightful walk up a high hill, from whence the prospects both by sea and land are inconceivably beautiful. We had the three dogs with us: poor Romeo is still confined, and, as he is an old dog, I fear will never recover.[2] We returned by the same boat. The dogs have always swum across, and they jump'd into the water as usual; but the tide was very high, and we were obliged to go a quarter of a mile about before we could land. Mr. Rishton hallowed to the dogs, and whistled all the way to encourage them, however, the current was so strong at the point where we landed that they could not stem it. Mrs. Western, R., and myself walked home and left the gentlemen to watch the dogs. Tingmouth, the Newfoundland dog, after a hard struggle, by his excellent swimming, at length got safe on shore. Trump, who is a very cunning brute, found out a shorter cut, and arrived safe. His fellow spaniel, Vigo, they could see nothing of. Mr. Rishton went after him, but he did not appear all night—and the next morning we found that he was drowned! This has been a great concern to us all. The drowned spaniel cost Mr. Rishton [ ] guineas.

---

[1] "Coat" used to mean the upper skirt of a woman's clothing. The editor has heard the word used in country villages after 1840.

[2] Some may be glad to know that Romeo recovered and enjoyed his after life in Norfolk, with "Tingmouth."

Yesterday was settled for a grand cricket match, but it proved so miserable a day that the gentlemen relinquished it. We went out of curiosity to the beach; the sea was extremely rough, and the waves uncommonly high: as we stood looking at it, a wave came suddenly, with such amazing force, that though we all ran away full speed, Mrs. Western and Mrs. Rishton were wetted all over. I had happened to be not so near. We hurried home, and they were obliged to new dress themselves.

In the evening the Mr. Mills called to settle on to day for Cricket. They brought with them two gentlemen (who were on a visit at the Dean's, on purpose to be of the party) Captain Saltern and Mr. Gibbs, the latter of them is esteemed one of the most learned young men alive, having won the [ ]¹ Prize at Cambridge. Our little parlour was quite filled.

Mr. T. Mills begged me to remark the beauties of our chimney piece, on each side of which are placed, just opposite to each other, a dog and a cat. "I am sorry," said he, "to see these animals here, for I fancy they are meant as an emblem of husband and wife. Now no two creatures disagree so much as dog and cat"—" And husband and wife?" cried I. "O, no, I beg your pardon, ma'am," cried he, "I am only sorry *these people* have ill judged them so!"

To day has been but very so-so—nevertheless the Cricket match could be no longer defer'd. Mrs. Western, M. R., and I went on the Green at noon. Mr. T. Mills, not being then engaged in play, met us, and got three chairs out of their booth, for us to sit without danger of the ball. But it was too cold. Capt. Saltern and Mr. Gibbs walked round with us. Mr. Gibbs came on my side pretending to screen me from the wind, and entered into small talk with a facility

---

¹ Fanny left a blank for the name of the prize, but never filled it. It was one of the Craven Scholarships that was taken, in 1772, by Mr. Gibbs, afterwards Sir Vicary Gibbs, Lord Chief Baron of the Exchequer and Lord Chief Justice of the Common Pleas. He was born at Exeter. Towards the end of 1818, H. Crabb Robinson writes: " Kaye the Solicitor told Gurney once that he had, that day, carried the Attorney-General," [Gibbs] "100 general retainers. . . . . These were on the Baltic captures, and insurance cases."

that would not have led me to supposing how high his character stood at the university. Mrs. Rishton was in one of her provoking humours. She came behind me every now and then and whispered "Fie, child!" and then shaking her head and walking off "Upon my word, the girls of this age! there is no more respect for a married woman than if—well, I'd rather be whip'd than be married, I declare! Really, Mrs. Western, we matrons are no more regarded by these chits than so many pepper-corns." Mr. Gibbs stared, but continued his talk. Then in a few minutes she returned to me again, "Really, Miss Fanny Burney, I don't know what you mean by this behaviour! O girls! girls! girls!"

When the wind grew more violent we went into the booth for shelter. Soon after Captain Saltern called out—"Take care ladies all!" and then hurried me suddenly out, for the cricket ball came over the booth. Mrs. Rishton, with one of her droll looks of sternness, came behind me and in a half whisper cried, "Very well, Miss Fanny Burney, very well! I shall write to Dr. Burney to-morrow morning."

They have all diverted themselves with me, not a little, ever since, except Mr. Rishton, who does not approve of these sort of pleasantries. However, his wife sufficed for *two*, at least! She and Mrs. Western have talked of the *Captain* ever since. And Mr. Western has been very *dry* about the Mr. Mills.—"They are very agreeable young men," said he, "but I think he that sat by Miss Burney (Mr. G.) is much the most agreeable. What do *you* think Miss Burney?" "O yes," answered I. Then again at supper yesterday, he said—"A very agreeable evening, upon my word,—don't you think so, Miss Burney?" And to-day, after dinner, he said he was going to the cricket ground, to see how they went on—"I shall acquaint the gentlemen," said he, "how industrious you all are (we were picking sea-weeds), and that tea will be made in the same corner it was yesterday—hey, Miss Burney?" 'Tis quite enough *to be younj*, my dear Susey, to be an object for gallant raillery.

Friday, Aug*.

We have been taking a most delightful walk on the top of the rocks and cliffs by the sea shore. Mrs. Western is so charmed with this country that she endeavours to prevail with her husband to buy an estate and reside here: indeed it is a most tempting spot.

Sunday, Aug.

Yesterday morning we went to Ugbrook the seat of Lord Clifford,[1] about five miles from here, the gentlemen on horseback, and we three in Mr. Western's chaise.

What is most remarkable in the House is a bed of exquisite workmanship, done under the direction of the Duchess of Norfolk. It is on a beautiful pink ground, and worked in birds and natural flowers with such glowing colours, and so exact a resemblance to nature, that it is reckoned the most finished piece of work in the kingdom. The House is situated in a most delightful Park filled with deer. We went five miles round his lordship's grounds, and took a view of the rocks at Chudleigh, which are the most romantic and beautiful imaginable.

This morning Mr. and Mrs. Western left us, which we are all sorry for,—we passed a very gay week with them, being all of us perfectly intimate and easy. Mr. Western is really a very agreeable man, and his wife is a charming woman. Mr. Rishton is quite melancholy at their departure, as they are prodigious favourites with him. Indeed this has been the dullest day we have spent yet. Mrs. Western has very particularly repeated her invitation to me, which I fancy, as Mrs. Rishton is extremely earnest with me for it, I shall accept—with il caro Padrés permission.

We seem to have quite dropt Mr. Crispen. He cannot but have perceived Mr. Rishton's coldness, as he never calls. Mr. Rishton has an uncommon aversion to every thing that leads towards flirtation, and Mr. Crispen from being much regarded by him, as the first man here, is become almost odious. I

---

[1] This is Ugborough in boo: s; but the peasants say something like " Ugbrook."

fancy that his friendship for Miss Bowdler has much contributed to make Mr. Rishton dislike him. However, whenever I meet him he assures me of the constancy of his passion, though I really endeavour to shun him, to avoid Mr. Rishton's disapprobation.

It is not possible for a man to make a better husband than Mr. Rishton does. He spends almost every moment of his time with his wife, and is all attention and kindness to her. He is reading Spencer's (*sic*) " Fairy Queen " to us, in which he is extremely delicate, omitting whatever, to the poet's great disgrace, has crept in that is improper for a woman's ear. I receive very great pleasure from this poem, in which there is an endless fund of invention and fancy, ingenuity and poetry.

Mrs. R. and I study Italian together, though very slowly. Indeed we go out so much, either walking or in the whiskey, that we have hardly any time.

There are not above three houses here that have not thatched roofs. One of the three is Sir John Davy's, which we have been to see. It is delightfully situated on the river Ting. . . . . .

Mr. T. Mills has told Mr. Rishton that he was in the same College with my father when he was at Oxford, at the Installation, and that no man has been received with so much honour there as Dr. Burney since it was a University. Hearing Mr. Rishton name him, "Pray," said the Dean, "are you talking of *the* Dr. Burney?"

Wednesday, Aug[st].

On Monday the three brothers dined here. They are really very agreeable and amiable young men. I add the latter clause presuming upon the harmony and affection which seems to reign among them ; and they appear to regard their father only as an elder brother, to whom they owe more respect but not less openness.[1]

After dinner Mrs. R. and I took a walk, and the gentlemen

---

[1] Dr. Milles married Edith, daughter of Archbishop Potter. His sons, Jeremiah (whom Fanny, in her notes, calls "James,") and Thomas, both became barristers. The youngest, Richard, was afterwards a Prebendary of Exeter.

went on the Den to play at quoits. We returned first, and were just seated, when we heard a rap at the parlour door. "Come in," cried I, "whoever you are." The door opened and Mr. Crispen entered. "Whose sweet voice bid me come in?" cried he, "May I hope that my love welcomes me?" He came immediately and drew a chair before me, as I sat on the window, and began to relate his sufferings from his long absence. I told him that I thought it rather an affront that he was alive. He complained very much of my usage of him, which he said was extremely ungenerous, as I took advantage of his fondness to treat him with cruelty. To say the truth he has of late grown rather more gallantly courteous to me than I wish, having taken it into his head to pay me many compliments of too ridiculous a nature to bear writing; besides he is somewhat troublesome in taking, or rather making, perpetual opportunities of taking my hand. I was very glad that his attention was just called off, to look at a particular kind of cane, which he moved away from me to examine, as the gentlemen returned. Mr. Rishton made him a very cold bow, and the eldest Mr. Mills came and seated himself in the chair which he had left vacant, and entered into conversation with me. Mr. Crispen was obliged to seat himself at some distance. The first *interval* he could catch he said to me— "I observe that my sweet friend is not without ambition, for I have taken notice that she always seats herself as high as possible." "It is only," answered I, "because I require some assistance to my heighth." Tea and coffee were now brought in—Mr. Crispen presented my cup, and then hastily made his exit. I fancy that his reception was such as will by no means speed another visit from him. Miss Bowdler, too, was with us all the morning, and if she is not determined to be blind, *must* perceive Mr. Rishton's coldness to her.

* * * * * *

Friday, Aug[st].

To-day, for the first time, I bathed. Ever since I went to Torbay 1 have been tormented with a dreadful cold, till within this day or two, and Mr. Rishton very much advised me to sea bathing in order to *harden* me. The women here are so poor, and this place till lately was so obscure and retired, that they wheel the bathing machine into the sea themselves, and have never heard of [   ]. I was terribly frightened, and really thought I should never have recovered from the plunge. I had not breath enough to speak for a minute or two, the shock was beyond expression great; but, after I got back to the machine, I presently felt myself in a glow that was delightful—it is the finest feeling in the world, and will induce me to bathe as often as will be safe.

Saturday, Aug^t.

* * * * * *

Sunday, August.

This morning *all the world* was at church, as the Dean of Exeter preached. He gave us an excellent discourse,[1] which he delivered extremely well. We met all the family as we came out, and Mr. T. Mills joined our party. The morning was lovely, and we took a very pleasant walk. Mr. Rishton proposes going to Ivy Bridge or Staverton in a short time, for a few days, in order to fish. Mr. T. Mills invited himself to be of our party. We had again the pleasure to hear the Dean in the afternoon, who gave us a most admirable sermon on *Moral Duties*. The singing here is the most extraordinary I ever heard; there is no instrument, but the people attempt to sing in parts,—with such voices! such expression! and such composition! They to-day, in honour I presume of the Dean, performed an Anthem; it was really too much to be borne decently; it was set by a weaver, and so very unlike anything that was ever before imagined, so truly barbarous,

---

[1] Dr. Jeremiah Milles, Dean of Exeter (1762), F.R.S., and President of the Society of Antiquaries, seems to have been a very worthy man, and a very frequent contributor to the "Archæologia." He took the wrong side about "Rowley's Poems," against such experts as Warton and Percy. He is the object of many sneers in Walpole's letters, not merely because of Rowley, but for daring to doubt Walpole's own "Historic Doubts," as to the character and person of Richard III. and to say so in print.

that with the addition of the singers trilling and squalling,—no comedy could have afforded more diversion. Mrs. Rishton and I laughed ourselves sick, though we very much endeavoured to be grave. Mr. Rishton was quite offended, and told his wife, that the eyes of the whole congregation were on her; but nothing could restrain us, till the Dean began his prayer; and there is a something *commanding* in his voice, that immediately gained all our attention.

Monday, Augst. 30.

This morning, Mr. Rishton being out, his wife and I were studying Italian, when we received a visit from Mr. Crispen.

He was scarce seated, when, turning to me—"Now, did not I behave very well t'other day?" said he, "when the Mills's were here?—I told you that when a *young* lover offered, I would retire, and, really, the eldest Mills took to my little Burney just as—indeed he is a very pretty young man—and I think—" I interrupted him with very warm expostulations—letting him know, as well as I could, that this discourse was quite too ridiculous. Mrs. Rishton got the Peruvienne Letters,[1] and beg'd him to hear her read—which when he had done, he insisted on giving *me* a lesson. I was extremely shy of receiving one, but he would take no denial. "Don't mind *me*," said he, "what am I? if it was Mr. Mills, indeed—"

To silence him, I then began. He paid me prodigious compliments, and concluded with modestly saying—"Yes, I will follow you to London, and give you a lesson a day, for three kisses entrance, and two kisses a lesson."

Really I believe the man is mad, or thinks me a fool, for he has perpetually proposed this payment to himself for different things. I was very grave with him, but he was only the more provoking.[2]

---

[1] "Lettres Péruviennes," by Madame de Graffigny, published in 1747.

[2] Mr. Crisp gives the best explanation of Mr. Crispen, in writing later on (of Dr. Fothergill), to Fanny:—"I find he has taken to you, and I observe we old fellows are inclinable to be very fond of you. You'll say, what care I for old fellows? Give me a young one! Well, we

"Why, now," said he, "you think this is a high price for *me*—but it would be nothing for Mr. Mills!—"

In short, I believe he has determined to say any and every thing to me that occurs to him.

When he was going he turned to me *pathetically*—"This was a most imprudent visit!—I feel it *here* stronger than ever—I must tear myself away!" Seating himself, however, again, the conversation, I know not by what means, between Mrs. R. and him turned on ill-proportioned marriages, on which he talked very sensibly, but concluded with saying— "Had I come into the world thirty-five years later, here I had been fixed," taking my hand, and then he went on in a strain of complimenting till he took his leave.

As soon as he was gone, we went to pay a visit to Miss Bowdler; and here again we found Mr. Crispen.

We both remarked that she was most excessively cold in her reception and behaviour. Perhaps Mr. Rishton has infected her; and perhaps Mr. Crispen's unexpected perseverance in his devoirs to me offends her, for she would be his Eloïse—a character she, beyond all others, admires—at least her behaviour has that appearance.

Mr. Crispen said I looked like a picture he had seen of Ione. I never saw it, and could therefore make no speeches. I told him I had never before been compared to any picture but that of the Goddess of Dullness in the "Dunciad." His usual strain was renewed.[1] Mrs. Rishton observed that he

---

don't hinder you of young ones; and we judge more coolly and disinterestedly than they do; so, don't turn up your nose even at our approbation." In 1779, Mrs. Streatfield called Fanny "the dove," just as Mr. Crispen had done. "For what reason" (writes Fanny), "I cannot guess, except it be that the dove has a greenish grey eye, something like mine; be that as it may, she called me nothing else while I stayed at Tunbridge."

[1] "In clouded Majesty here Dulness shone,
Four guardian virtues, round, support her throne."

Well, after all, the four guardians might have supported Fanny, in no ironic sense, such as was meant by Pope. Fortitude, Temperance, Prudence, and Justice, were fitting upholders of "Madame Minerve," or "the Old Lady," or "Flora, Goddess of Wisdom." See "The Dunciad," book i., lines 45 to 54.

must make love to *me.* "Ay," cried Miss Bowdler, " or to any body!"

"No, no," cried he, "if I had but been born thirty-five years later—I had certainly fixed here for life!"

"Or else with Miss Colbourne," cried Mrs. Rishton.

"Never did Miss Colbourne hear such a declaration," said he, "no, never!"

"Ay, but the little Bowdler!" returned Mrs. R.

"No, nor the little Bowdler neither," answered he.

"O," cried she, "I am quite out of the question *now.*"

"And *always,*" said he, "in regard to *love, always* out of the question!—"

"Why, yes," replied Miss Bowdler, colouring,—" to give him his due, he never talked that nonsense to me."

Tuesday, Aug. 31st.

We dined at Mr. Hurrel's, and met there Mr. and Mrs. Onslow. The latter is a sister of Mr. Phips. They are the handsomest couple I ever saw. Mrs. Onslow has suffered very much from illness, but must have been quite beautiful. They are well bred and sensible.[1]

I cannot imagine what whim has induced Mr. Rishton, so lively, so entertaining as he is himself, to take a fancy to the Hurrels, who are, Mrs. R. and I both think, most truly stupid and tiresome. Miss Davy, the sister, is a well-bred and conversible old maid, and I much prefer her.

Wednesday, Sept. 1st.

I was never before at the house of a sportsman on this most critical day, and really it is not bad diversion. Mr. Onslow and Mr. T. Mills agreed to be of Mr. Rishton's company this morning, in shooting. At four o'clock the commotion in the house awoke me. I heard a thousand different noises; the horses prancing, the dogs called, the gentlemen hallooing.

---

[1] Arthur, third son of General Onslow, Lieutenant-Governor of Plymouth, married Frances, daughter of Constantine Phipps, Esq. He became Archdeacon of Berkshire, and Dean of Worcester.

Messrs. Onslow and Mills were here before Mr. Rishton was up: the house was in an uproar, and it was by no means light though they were so eager for sport.

* * * * * *

Friday, Sept. 3rd.

* * * * * *

Nothing is now talked or thought of but shooting and game. Mr. R. is just now set off with Mr. T. Mills; dressed such figures! really sportsmen have no regard to even common appearances.

They complain very much of poachers here; for my part, I have no great compassion for their injuries. Mr. H. who is too fat and too lazy to shoot, is also too great a *gourmand* to deny himself game, and is therefore suspected to be a very great encourager of poachers. They live but next door to us, and came out this morning, as well as Mrs. R. and me, to see the sportsmen set off. Mr. T. Mills very slyly began to entertain them with discoursing on the injuries they received from poachers, and added, "it is not for the birds; we sportsmen do not much value them, but for the pleasure of *finding* them, that we quarrel with poachers"—and (turning to me) "I am sorry to say, for the pleasure of *killing* them."

"I had some intention," said I, "of sending an 'Ode, on the 31st of August, with the Partridges' Complaint,' to every sportsman in the county."

"I am sure I should have been very happy," cried he, bowing *with an air*, "to have received it from you, and to have given it"—— Here he stopped, checked, I presume, by conscience from giving any promissory professions.

* * * * * *

Sunday, September.

This morning we heard Mr. Onslow preach. He says he always travels with a brace of sermons, that he may be ready to give occasional assistance to his brother clergymen when requested. I did not at all admire him, as he seems to be conceited; and indeed the Dean has at present made me difficult. After service the two youngest Mills and Mr. Onslow called in, to settle their next shooting party with Mr. Rishton. It is amazing what a laborious business this is : they go out before breakfast; after two or three hours' shooting they get what they can at any farm-house; then toil till three or four o'clock, when sometimes they return home ; but, if they have any prospect of more sport, they take *pot-luck* at any cottage, and stay out till eight or nine o'clock. The weather makes no alteration in their pursuits; a sportsman defies wind, rain, and all inclemencies of either heat or cold. As to Mr. Rishton, he seems bent on being proof against everything ; he seeks all kinds of manly exercises, and grows sun-burnt, strong, and hardy.

We went to dinner at Star-Cross, a little town about eight miles off; Mrs. Rishton, as usual, driving me in the whiskey, and Mr. Rishton and the man on horseback. We dined at an Inn in a room which overlooked the river Ex. We were very unfortunate in the evening, and were overtaken by rain, wind and darkness ; and, as these roads are very narrow, very steep, and very craggy, we should really have been in a very dangerous situation after it grew too dark for Mrs. R. to see to drive, had not her husband made the man lead his horse, while in the midst of the wet and dirt, he led the whiskey himself by hand. On these occasions he is very uncommonly good-natured and attentive to female fears and cowardice.

Thursday, September.

* * * * * *

Mr. Tom Mills breakfasted with us this morning at 6 o'clock, and then set out with Mr. Rishton on a shooting party. Mrs. R. and I went in the whiskey to Dawlish a mighty pretty village on the sea coast. We had the Hurrels with us in the evening. That stupid couple, to whom Mr. Rishton has taken a most unaccountable liking, *ennui* both his wife and me to death. Her good nature is so tiresome and officious that I would prefer even a bad temper, with a little portion of understanding.

We have seen Mrs. Phips but seldom since her sister-in-law Mrs. Onslow has been here. She is a sweet woman and has pretty blue eyes, like my dear Susan's.

Sept^r.

I must give you this last week all in a lump, for I have no time for daily dottings.

We have been to Staverton. . . . It was a very agreeable excursion. We slept at Ashburnham, and went in the whiskey many miles round. The county of Devonshire is inexhaustible in the variety of its rural beauties. Hills, vallies, rivers, plains, woods, lanes, meadows — everything beyond all description, romantic and beautiful. The river Dart, which is the boundary of the Staverton manor, is the most rapid clear and delightful one I ever saw. There are walks along the banks that are delicious. The whole manor belongs to the Miss Folkes and their married sisters.[1] The richness of the land is astonishing, plenty and abundance reign *partout*— but I have neither time or talents to describe this most charming country. There are places about Tingmouth which do altogether exceed every other, as all the prospects have some view of the sea, which is so noble an object that it enlivens and beautifies all others.[2]

Thursday, Septr. 16th.

We leave Tingmouth to-morrow.

It will not be without regret that I shall quit this incomparable county. . . . .

Mr. Crispen went yesterday. We have seen very little of

---

[1] These ladies appear to have been the cousins of Mr. Rishton's mother. We have already met on these pages Mrs. Rolfe and Mr. Western, the second and the youngest daughters of William Folkes, Esq. Ursula, his eldest, and Mary, his third daughter, were probably the ladies of Staverton. Ursula afterwards married Admiral John Macbride, and Mary, John Balchen West, Esq.

[2] This most genuine and just feeling Fanny expressed to Sir Joshua Reynolds, and in spite of villa-building, it is still true. We copy an unpublished paragraph in her Diary for 1778:—" We had a good deal of talk about Devonshire, Sir Joshua's native county:—and we agreed perfectly in praise of Tingmouth and its environs, indeed, he said, he was *sure* I must admire it, for no person of taste could do otherwise,— so, you see, we had a little touch of gallantry as well as of *virtù*."

him lately; Mr. Rishton's extreme coldness has been too visible to be unnoticed. We were not returned from Staverton when he went, and so took no leave of him; by which means I dare say I lost an abundance of fine speeches: though I believe he thought himself laughed at by Mrs. Rishton as well as slighted by her husband,—for of late he has contented himself with insisting on my never marrying, *without his consent*, and on my letting him give me away—this he has been vehement about .... And he earnestly and very seriously solicited me to write to him, that he might prepare himself for his office, &c. [Honestly, my dear Susan, I have never been able to quite understand him; but when he lets alone his gallantry he is full of information and very agreeable.]

Miss Bowdler, who goes to Bath to-day, called this morning. We have all parted upon very civil terms, though I am sure her penetration is too great to have suffered Mr. Rishton's dislike to escape her. ....

We spent yesterday between packing and leave-taking. We only found time to go down to the beach, to take a last view of the sea. Mr. Rishton was in monstrous spirits all day. I am afraid he was grown somewhat tired of Tingmouth, where he has been six months. I wish it may happen, that I may ever see Mrs. Phipps again, [and the very clever Miss Bowdler.][1]

---

[1] The wish to see Mrs. Phipps again, originally ended this sentence, and the Teignmouth Diary. The words, "and the very clever Miss Bowdler," were added much later, and are of the nature of a palinode. In 1818, Mme. D'Arblay wrote of "My oldest friend, to my knowledge, Mrs. Frances Bowdler," making a point of seeing her about seven weeks after the death of General D'Arblay, and staying two hours, when Mme. D'Arblay scarcely saw any friends. These two, who were young ladies in 1773, may have met again at Bath, where Miss Burney was, either in 1776, of which we have no journal, or in 1777, of which there is but an imperfect Diary—at any rate, they did meet again at Bath in 1780. Seven years had made one Fanny famous, and "Bowdlerized" the manners of the other, so that Mr. Crispen could be named (as he was) without exciting pique or petulance. In 1780, Fanny found Miss Frances Bowdler "more agreeable than formerly .... very sensible, and uncommonly cultivated," .... "so that her conversation and company were well worth seeking." The Bowdler family were in high, and more than local, esteem, within the memory of the living. Worthy people

" Mrs. R. and I went to sit with the Hurrels and Miss Davy in the evening. Lady Davy, who is a great fright in every sense of that word, was there. They took a very affectionate leave of us. We then went to Mrs. Phips.

[No account remains of the journey eastward. The Rishtons took Fanny to London, and left her, and Romeo, (whom she was to nurse,) in Queen's Square. The further movements, and something of the after-life of Maria and her husband will be told at the end of this year's diary.]

Queen Square, October.

Mr. Garrick, to my great confusion, has again surprised the house, before we were up; but really my father keeps such late hours at night, that I have not resolution to rise before eight in the morning. My father himself was only on the stairs, when this early, industrious, active, charming man came. I dressed myself immediately; but found he was going, as I entered the study. He stopped short, and with his accustomed drollery, exclaimed, " Why now, why are *you* come down, now, to keep me? But this will never do! (looking at his watch) upon my word, young ladies, this will

---

revered them as a family of moral and religious authors. Their mother wrote theological works, a brother was the cause of a new English verb, to " Bowdlerize." He immortalized himself by such vigorous excisions from Shakespeare's plays, to make them fit for "family reading," that we have been told by a strict governess of the old school that when she held the true Shakespeare, and set her pupils to read to her from the Bowdler, she discovered that Dr. Bowdler had seen evil where none was, and pruned without heed or need. He afterwards treated Gibbon's " Decline and Fall of the Roman Empire " in like manner. He was a Tunbridge Wells physician, and F.R.S. The youngest daughter, Mrs. Harriet, wrote poems, essays, a novel or more, and sermons (without her name), which were taken for those of a divine, and preached by real divines. In 1780, Miss Bowdler (Jane) had totally lost her voice for the three previous years after a severe cold. She wrote, for her own consolation, essays and verses, which were published by her family after her death, and ran through sixteen editions between 1787 and 1830. The high opinion of her family, and the fact that the profits were to be given to the Bath hospital account for this, as, taken away her sad condition and the pity of it, there is nothing in the volume. Frances was the second daughter, and seems to have kept *her* pen quiet, preferring the use of her tongue. In a family numbering seven authors this was no small distinction.

never do!" He invited my father in Lord Shelbourne's name to go with him to dine at his lordship's, as he has a fine statue lately come from Italy, which has a musical instrument, and which he wishes to show my father.[1]

My father asked him for his box for us at night, to see the Mask of Alfred, which is revived.[2] But he insisted upon our going to the front-boxes. "You shall have my box," said he, "any other time that you please; but you will see nothing of the new scenes up there. Now, you shall have my box to see me, or the *old new* play that is coming out, with all my heart."

"O! dont say that," cried I; "dont say to see *you;* you don't know what you promise." He laughed; but I determined not to let such an offer be made with *impunity*.

He took much notice, as usual, of Charlotte; he seems indeed to love all that belong to my father, of whom he is really very fond. Nay, as he went out, he said, with a very comical face to me, "I like you! I like you all! I like your looks! I like your manner!" And then, opening his

---

[1] William, second Earl of Shelburne, and first Marquis of Lansdowne, the well-known minister of George III. Dr. Burney was always on the search for ancient, or even savage, musical instruments. Banks and Solander brought him from Iceland a "long spiel," played with a bow, so obsolete that only one Icelander could be found to play on it, and Bruce supplied him with a beautiful drawing of an Abyssinian lyre.

[2] James Thomson and David Mallet wrote the "Masque of Alfred," by command of Frederick, Prince of Wales, for the birthday of his eldest daughter, "the Lady Augusta." It was acted in the gardens of Cliveden, upon the 1st of August, 1740, and repeated. The decorations, dresses, and scenery were the finest that had then been seen, nor were there wanting "triumphal arches, dances of furies, and incantatations." It was revived in 1750, with music partly composed by Dr. Burney. Thomson died in 1748. Mallet made changes in the Masque that Garrick might have more of a part to play as Alfred. Mallet was much blamed for mangling the work of Thomson, "retaining" (says Arthur Murphy) "only three or four of Thomson's speeches and part of one song"—the famous "'Rule Britannia,' which he altered for the worse"—but this may have been a mere political criticism, as Bolingbroke, Mallet's patron, wrote some stanzas of "Rule Britannia," with intentional reference to politics, and to his favourite idea of a "Patriot King."

arms with an air of heroics, he cried, "I am tempted to run away with you all, one after another." We all longed to say, *Pray, do!* . . . . . .

Dr. Hawkesworth dined here the same day; his wife and Miss Kinnaird were to have accompanied him; but were disappointed. I was very sorry at not seeing Miss Kinnaird, who is a sweet girl. I find that she is sister to Lord Kinnaird, a young Scotch nobleman, just come of age. Dr. Hawkesworth looks very ill; he has had very bad health lately. Indeed I believe that the abuse so illiberally cast on him, since he obtained £6,000 by writing the Voyages round the World, has really affected his health, by preying upon his mind. It is a terrible alternative, that an author must either starve and be esteemed, or be vilified and get money.

Seeing in the papers on Thursday "Abel Drugger by Mr. Garrick," I prevailed with my dear father to write him a note, which he did very drolly, claiming his promise, but begging for only two places. He sent immediately this answer:

"My dear Dr.,
"I would rather have your family in my box, than all the Lords and Commons.
"Your's Ever,
"D. G."

* * * * * *

Never could I have imagined such a metamorphose as I saw; the extreme meanness, the vulgarity, the low wit, the vacancy of countenance, the appearance of *unlicked nature* in all his motions. In short, never was character so well entered into, yet so opposite to his own.[1]

We have had a visit from Miss Ford and her companion

---

[1] Abel Drugger is a character in Ben Jonson's play of "The Alchemist," which was altered by Colman, and played at Drury Lane. Drugger is an uncouth and dull tobacco-vendor, who consults the Alchemist as to success in his trade. Garrick had the art of making himself look so stupid and insignificant in this part, that someone who had been favoured with a letter of introduction to him, after seeing him as Abel Drugger, said that "now he had seen what a mean-looking creature Garrick was, he should not present his letter."

Miss Mills. She lent us her box yesterday to see Miss Barsanti in the part of Charlotte Rusport in the *West Indian*. She did it with great ease, sprightliness, and propriety, and looked exceedingly well.[1] I am very glad, that she has succeeded in so genteel a part. But how unfortunate the loss of voice that drove her from a concert-singer to the stage!

* * * * * *

Novr. 9th, 3 in the morning.

My poor mother is extremely ill of a bilious fever. This is the third night that I have sate up with her; but I hope to Heaven, that she is now in a way to recover. She has been most exceeding kind to us, since her return to town; which makes me the more sensibly feel her illness. She is now sleeping, so is her nurse, and I write to avoid the contagion.

* * * * * *

Dr. Fothergill, the celebrated Quaker, is mama's physician.[2] I doubt not his being a man of great skill; but his manners are stiff, set, and unpleasant. His conversation consists of sentences spoken with the utmost solemnity, conciseness, and importance. He is an upright, stern, formal-looking old man. He enters the room, and makes his address with his hat always on, and lest that mark of his sect should pass unnoticed, the hat which he wears, is of the most enormous size I ever beheld. Nevertheless, this old prig sometimes affects something bordering upon gallantry. The first time he came, after he had been with Mrs. Allen[3] to the bed-side, and spoken to mama,—and then written her prescription;

---

[1] "The West Indian," Cumberland's best comedy, was first acted, at Drury Lane, in 1771.

[2] John Fothergill, M.D. (1712-1780), left £80,000. He made £7,000 a year when in full practice. He founded the Quaker school at Ackworth, in Yorkshire. His medical writings were four times published, by three different editors, between 1781 and 1784. There is a notice of him and a very Quakerish portrait in Nichols's "Literary Anecdotes." He was Dr. Melchisedech Broadbrim in Foote's "Devil upon Two Sticks."

[3] The mother of the second Mrs. Burney.

—he stalked up to me, and endeavouring to arrange his rigid features to something which resembled a smile; "And what," cried he, "must we do for this young lady's cough?" Then he insisted on feeling my pulse, and with a kind of dry pleasantry, said, "Well, we will wait till to-morrow; we wont lose any blood to-night."

November 24th, 2 in the morning.

Though it is now a fortnight since I wrote last, I take up my pen exactly in the same situation and with the same view, as I then did,—save that mama is exceedingly recovered, and thank God! nearly well. Since I wrote last, I have myself been ill with a sore throat, which I believe was the effect of over-rating my strength. Dr. Fothergill has been my very good friend, and that, whether I would or not. He immediately perceived when I was taken ill, and after seeing mama, said to me, "I am afraid thee art not well thyself?" On examining my throat, he advised me to be very careful; for that it was catching, the sort which I had, which was the putrid, though in a slight degree. He told me what to take &c., and was most exceeding attentive to me the whole time; and really, for him, has been amazingly civil and polite to me. But yesterday, after complaining of his fatigue and great business, he turned suddenly to me, and taking my hand, cried, "My dear, never marry a physician. If he has but little to do, he may be distressed; if he has much, it is a very uncomfortable life for his companion."

He came here several times, before he saw my father, who, when at home, is always shut up in his study; but one evening, when mama was very ill, being anxious to hear the Doctor's opinion, he came up stairs. He addressed himself, like a man of the world, to the Doctor, who rose, and with great solemnity said, "I suppose it is Dr. Burney that I see?" My father bowed, and said he was happy in being known to him. "I never," answered he, "had the satisfaction of seeing Dr. Burney before!" "No, Sir;" said my father, "I have always been so unfortunate as to be out, when you have been here." "*Most commonly*," answered the old Quaker, with a dryness that seemed not to give implicit faith to the assertion. But since this, they have had many conversations, and are very good friends. And really with all his stiffness and solemnity he appears to be as humane as he is skilful.

Mama has so good a night, that I fancy this will be the last of my nocturnal communications. While she was ill, she desired me to write for Miss Young, who is now here. I had not seen her some years; she is exactly the same she was,—sensible, intelligent, bashful, shy, awkward, affectionate, feeling, and truly worthy. I love her much, and hope we shall keep her some time. Mama is almost recovered. Dr. Fothergill makes his visits very seldom. He says he always knows when his patients are really recovering by these signs: if men, he finds their beds covered with newspapers; if women, he sees them with new top-knots, or hears them exclaim, "Dear me! what a figure I am!"

* * * * * *

I have now entered into a very particular correspondence with Mr. Crisp. I write really a Journal to him, and in answer he sends me most delightful long, and incomparably clever, letters, animadverting upon all the facts &c., which I acquaint him with, and dealing with the utmost sincerity in stating his opinion and giving his advice. I am infinitely charmed with this correspondance—*ant* I mean—which is not more agreeable than it may prove instructive.

[From Mr. Crisp.]

[1773.]

My Dear Fanny,

In consequence of our agreement, I shall now begin with an instance of the most pure and genuine sincerity, when I declare to you that I was delighted with your letter throughout,—a proof of which (that perhaps you would have excus'd) is this immediate answer with a demand for *more*— The horseleech hath two daughters, saith the wise man, saying, "Give! Give!"—I find myself nearly related to them on this occasion. I profess there is not a single word or expression or thought in your whole letter, that I do not relish,—not that in our Correspondence I shall set up for a Critic or Schoolmaster or observer of composition—the deuce take them all! I hate them. If once you set about framing studied letters, that are to be correct, nicely grammatical, and run in smooth periods, I shall mind them no otherwise than as newspapers of intelligence. I make this preface, because you have needlessly enjoined me to deal sincerely, and to tell you of your faults; and so let this declaration serve [to tell you] once for all, that there is no fault in an epistolary correspondence like stiffness and study. Dash away whatever comes uppermost; the sudden sallies of imagination, clap'd down on paper, just as they arise, are worth folios, and have all the warmth and merit of that sort of nonsense that is eloquent in love. Never think of being correct when you write to me. So I conclude this topic, and proceed to be sorry and glad that you and your Mammy have been ill and are better. Your Dr. Fothergill I am well acquainted with by character, and pronounce you a very able portrait painter. I find he has taken to you, and I observe we old fellows are inclinable to be very fond of you. You'll say, "What care I for old fellows? give me a young one!" Well; we don't hinder you of young ones; and we judge more coolly and disinterestedly than they do; so don't turn up your nose even at our approbation.

Now, Fanny, I do by no means allow of your re-consideration and revocation of your Tingmouth Journal; on the contrary, I demand it, and claim your promise, and confirm my own, viz.; to return it safe to Charly Burney's, well and carefully sealed up, and the contents lodged in my own snowy bosom.[1] Your pleas, frivolous ones they are; and I reject them all. . . . .

As to that rogue your father, if I did not know him to be incorrigible, I should say something of that regular course of

---

[1] These girls seem to have thought that "the Governor" considered their papers lawfully subject to her control, and inspection. Maria took very little pains to deprive "the higher powers," (as she writes) of chance of reading *her* journal, which was apt to be "lying somewhere about the house"—although she demanded great caution on the part of Fanny and Susy.

irregularity he persists in—two, three, four, five o'clock in the morning, sups at twelve!—is it impossible for him to get the better of his constitution? has he forgot the condition he was in the winter after his first return to England? perhaps he is like a seasoned old drinker, whose inside is so lined with a coat of tartar, that his brandy only goes in [. . .] like a worm in a still, without affecting the vessel it passes through. Certain it is, that he uses his thin carcass most abominably, and if it takes it at his [hands,] it is the most passive, submissive slave [of a carcass] in Europe.

I am greatly pleased with the growing reputation of his Tours; of which I never had the least doubt; and no less so, with those marks of favour and esteem for the Great and the Eminent, and only wish him to make that worldly use of them, which he ought; in which particular he has hitherto been so deficient; and I desire you will transmit to him the enclosed quotation, which I have lately read in a Letter from his friend Petrarch to Mainard Accurse:—

Now, if Petrarch (for whom all the Princes and Geniuses of Europe were contending for fifty years together) could find out this severe and mortifying truth, surely 'tis a lesson to all future candidates for fame and favour, to make that *bienveillance* (which at bottom is all self and vanity) turn to some account, and make hay while the sun shines.

* * * * * *

I am quite comforted to hear he is so full [of business, which] if it does not improve and increase, 'tis his own fault—On my blessing I charge him, not for any consideration, to neglect *that*, and which at last, and at the long run, will prove his surest, firmest, best, perhaps his *only* Friend—mark that—while he preserves that, it will prove his best security for holding fast other friends—I cannot too much inculcate, beat, drive, hammer, this saving Doctrine into him which makes me dwell so long on this Article. . . . .

[MR. CRISP TO FANNY BURNEY.]

[Although this fragment of a letter from Mr. Crisp to Fanny is not of the same date as that which precedes it, we place it here, as it dwells on the same subject, Dr. Burney's bent towards working more than was good for his health. At its head are these words written by Mme. D'Arblay.—" Written at the time when my dear indefatigable father was working at night at his History."]

I'll tell you what, Fanny.—I yesterday received a letter from Hettina, wherein she gives such an account of your papa that, when I come to town (which I believe will not be very distant) I shall without ceremony send for Dr. Monro,[1] have a strait waistcoat immediately put on him, debar him the use of pen, ink, and paper and books, to which (if he is mutinous) shall be added a dark room—what does he mean? if he has no consideration for himself, has he no regard for his relatives? I am out of all patience with him,—I have lately had just the same pain in my side he has; but 'tis of no consequence; it comes and goes, and the booby has nothing to do, but to allow some repose to his thin carcase, to get well again.—I call him *booby;* but that is not half bad enough for him; 'tis downright idiotism; how true is it, that he that increaseth knowledge, increaseth sorrow! I had rather be a frog, an oyster, an onion, than a Sçavant at such a rate! Adieu!

I sadly want to know about Mr. Greville and his motions; . . . . have you seen him lately? send me all about him and your absurd Father particularly, and that immediately. Adieu!

* * * * * *

I am glad that my father has recovered an old friend, with whom he had a breach; he is, at length, entirely and most cordially reconciled to Mr. Greville, who has been here two or three times, in his old way, without fuss or ceremony. . . . .

I have had, lately, a very long, and a very strange conversation with Mr. Young. We happened to be alone in the

---

[1] John Monro, M.D., was chief physician to Bridewell, and to Bethlehem Hospital, vulgarly known as Bedlam.—

"Close to those walls where Folly holds her throne,
And laughs to think Monroe would take her down.
. . . .
One cell there is concealed from vulgar eye,
The cave of Poverty and Poetry."—*The Dunciad.*

parlour, and either from confidence in my prudence or from an entire and unaccountable carelessness of consequences, he told me "that he was the most miserable fellow breathing," and almost *directly* said that his *connections* made him so, and most vehemently added, that if he was to begin the world again, no earthly thing should ever prevail with him to marry! that now he was never easy, but when he was litterally in a plow cart; but that happy he never could be! [I a]m sorry for him—but cannot wonder . . . .

I am truly concerned, as we all are, at the untimely death of Dr. Hawkesworth.[1] He had not strength to support the abuse he has most unjustly been loaded with. I cannot help attributing his death to the uneasiness of his mind, which brought on a slow fever, that proved mortal. When he was last here, he told us his plan of defence, which he was then preparing for the press, as soon as a lawsuit, then depending, was decided. I am doubly sorry that he left this plan unaccomplished and his fame and reputation at the mercy of his enemies; who have, however, been wholly silent since his death. The world has lost one of its best ornaments,—a man of letters who was worthy and honest. Poor Mrs. Hawkesworth is in great affliction.

* * * * * *

REMNANT OF AN OLD LETTER TO MR. CRISP.[2] [1773].

* * * * * *

The death of poor Dr. Hawkesworth is most sincerely lamented by us all, the more so as we do really attribute it to the abuse he has of late met with from the newspapers. His book was dearly purchased at the price of his character, and peace, and those envious and malignant Witlings who persecuted him, from his gaining money, are now satisfied and silent. You may perhaps doubt of this, but indeed if you had known him more, you would not. He dined with us about a month before he died, and we all agreed we never saw a man

---

[1] Dr. Hawkesworth died, Nov. 17, 1773.
[2] This heading is in the writing of Madame D'Arblay.

more altered, thin, livid, harassed! He conversed very freely upon the affair of his book and abuse: my father told him there was hardly a man in the kingdom who had ever had a pen in his hand, who did not think that he could have done it with more propriety,[1] and that his enemies were all occasioned by his success, for if he had failed, every voice would have said "poor man 'tis an ingenious, well written book, he deserved more encouragement." Dr. Hawkesworth said that he had not yet made any answer to the torrent poured upon him,[2] except to Dalrymple who had attacked him by name. He added he was extremely sorry when any of his friends had vindicated him in print, for that a lawsuit was then depending upon Parkinson's publication, and that he would take no methods of influencing justice, but as soon as it was decided, he should publish at once a full and general answer to the invidious, calumniating and most unjust aspersions which had been so cruelly and wantonly cast on him. He has not lived to accomplish his plan! He told my father that he had earned every thing he

---

[1] 'Propriety' is not used here in its present sense. What is meant is, that every hack or scribbler, who was envious of the high pay received by Hawkesworth, thought *he* could have done the work better, was, in fact, more fit, or *proper* for it.

[2] "Mr. Cradock of Leicestershire," whom Boswell describes as "a very pleasing gentleman," says in his "Memoirs":—"All Lord Sandwich's other friends were severely assailed on account of a passage relative to a particular providence in the preface to Hawkesworth's book, and it was maliciously urged that, "till Dr. Hawkesworth had been connected with the India House and the Admiralty, he had always written on the side of morality and religion." Mr. Cradock adds, "I constantly met Dr. Hawkesworth at Lord Sandwich's table at the Admiralty about the time of his publishing 'Cook's Voyages.' He was a most agreeable companion; but he became careless and luxurious; hurt his constitution by high living; and was consequently very unhappy. His excellent and intelligent wife was always discreet; and had the management of his great work, 'The Voyages,' been left *entirely* with her, nothing either immoral or offensive would ever have appeared before the public. I never knew, till lately, how much merit, in former publications, was due to her. She was an unassuming woman, of very superior talent. The Doctor never 'sinned but against himself.' He was quite finical in his dress, by which he sometimes subjected himself to ridicule, though a favourite with all." In 1799 Dr. Burney writes of the Abbé Delille, "His person is not very unlike little Hawkesworth's, but *più brutto.*"

possessed by dint of labour and industry, except the last
£6000—that he had had no education or advantage but what
he had given himself: but that he had preserved an un-
blemished character and reputation till this last year; since
when, I believe he has had reason to detest the fortune which
only preceded detraction and defamation. He died of a lingering fever which had begun to prey upon him when we last saw
him. My father read to him a great deal of his history,[1] with
which he appeared much pleased, and only objected to one
word all the way. He candidly declared it was all new to
him, and that though he had never studied or cared for music,
he found it easy to understand, and very entertaining. He
expressed much curiosity about the remainder, and made my
father explain his design and intentions. . . . .

[When their pleasant sojourn at Teignmouth was ended, the
Rishtons, after leaving Fanny in London, went to visit Mr. and Mrs.
Western at Cokethorpe, in Oxfordshire. Maria wrote from Tetsworth, the very next day after a parting so tender that she threatened
Fanny with a quarrel when next they met for "making the first
fifteen miles of her journey very uncomfortable." Indeed her distress confused Mr. Rishton, who lost his way, and, instead of taking
the Oxford Road, (now Oxford Street,) drove up the Tottenham
[Court] Road in order to go to "the Crown and Cushion," at Ux-
bridge, where they were to sleep. They next ran over "Tingmouth,"
"who was travelling under the body of the whiskey,[2] but though the

---

[1] "The History of Music," published 1776 to 1789.

[2] In 1773, Mr. Rishton felt that he could not drive through London
in a "*buggey*," although he might in a *whiskey*. In 1824, Sir Walter
Scott describes the whiskey of Mrs. Margaret Dods, of the Cleikum
Inn, St. Ronan's, as being "a vehicle, which, had it appeared in
Piccadilly, would have furnished . . . . laughter for a week. . . . . It was
a two-wheeled vehicle, sturdily and safely low upon its little old-
fashioned wheels." About 1830, the buggy had its revenge, by becoming the fashion in Paris. "*Le boguey*" is among the sterile
pleasures, the empty amusements, in which M. P. G. Viennet, a French
poet, in his Epistle to a "désœuvré," (or unoccupied young fellow,)
upon the charms of Study, entreats his "cher Raymond" no longer to
consume his leisure, and squander his youth. Earnestly does he
ask him,

"Mais les bals, les concerts, les festins où tu cours
Ton boguey, tes chevaux, tes frivoles amours,
Les spectacles, les jeux, remplissent-ils ta Vie?"

As for Martin Rishton's "phaeton and four bays," when an under-wheel went clean over her body, after giving herself two or 3 hearty shakes and *wriggles* she began romping with Trump ... and pursued her journey on foot." Maria " begs an account of the governour's health." In her next, of " Oct. y• 2nd, 1773, she hopes Fanny and herself will soon meet and forget over a chearfull bottle all past sorrows." She dwells on the beauty of the road from High Wycombe to Tetsworth, lying chiefly through Lord Le de Spencer's woods. As she is "not gifted with a descriptive talent," she will defer " these beauties " until they meet; but she pauses to tell of his stables, &c., which he has made so " ornamental as they appear like temples." They arrive at Oxford on a showery morning, and " R. did not seem sorry, as I believe he much dreaded trailing about Oxford to shew me the colleges—it was almost as bad as driving thro' London in a buggey—*vous m'entendez* —how coud we bear to be seen in Oxford, where we had once shone forth the gay, the extravagant Martin Rishton—whose only carriage was a phaeton and four bays—metaphorsed (*sic*), into the attentive kind husband, who I believe prefers a *dot-and-go-one* with his wife to the fiery coursers without, as I saw how matters stood, I put of seeing anything and begd it might be left to another opportunity, on which I was exceedingly press'd, but I was obdurate." She had her hair dressed by the worst *friseur* she had seen for many years—"took a snap-dinner," and then set off. Next they ran over another of their dogs, " Judge," and hurt "Tingmouth," as well as a dog called " Swinger;" the dogs being "crazy." From Witney to Cokethorpe the road was almost impassable. The mud hindered them from more than walking the horse at the slowest pace. Cokethorpe they gained at half-past six. " The park and house very melancholly ... as we drove up there seemed a deadlike silence. ... The shutters were shut in the front. ... We drove into the stable-yard; still no appearance of any living creature ... but Rishton attributed all this to the order and method of Mr. Western. Thomas dismounted and hallowd (*sic*). No one answerd. ... Still R. said, ' Ah, you see what order and regularity reigns in this family—the servants are all employed.' I own my thoughts were full of the sleeping beauty in the wood, which I dared not communicate. After straining our voices the old shepherd appeared, who told us Maister and Madam was not at home, but he woud call Maister Thomas, who coud tell us more about it." This was a servant, who said that Mr. and Mrs. Western were gone into Buckinghamshire, and had written to prevent the Rishtons coming there until Wednesday. *He* pressed them to stay, but they braved the bad road and slept at Witney; returning next day to meet their kinsfolk. " Whisker" (the horse) is knocked up, Swinger is better, Tingmouth has had the distemper, " been blooded," and " takes regularly" the powders

---

graduate, that would indeed be a sight to amaze all Oxford in our time, for in nothing is that University more changed than in the very small proportion of undergraduates who keep a horse at all—to the great number who did so fifty years ago.

"of Dr. James" (which are said to have been fatal to Oliver Goldsmith), and "is walked out gently for exercise," led by Maria in a string; "it is thought that Tingmouth must *ride* all the way to town."

After a few days, they again passed through London, on their way to an old house, at Stanhoe, infested by rats, and much out of repair, which belonged to the wife of one of Maria's Allen kinsmen. A letter is extant in which Maria first says that she will send Fanny a plan of the house, next adds, that Fanny would not understand it if she did; then begins a description of it, but breaks off with, "but hang descriptions—I never understood one in my life till I had seen the premises, so will give you some account of our manner of life. We have hardly seen a soul since our arrival except Mrs. Mun Allen who comes *prying* about pretending to look after her workmen—she has given us a *ten* years lease on the condition we go half the expence of new sashing the house—which we agreed to do readily as we have *at present* nothing to look forward to that need make us mind a hundred pounds, for look and convenience; it is a monstrous good bargain for her, as the frames of the windows are so rotten they woud not have hung together two years longer and then she must have done them at her own expence—we are making vast out door improvements. We found every thing in the most ruinous condition we are new planting the garden—cleaning and cutting out new walks in the wood—indeed it is a sweet spot I every day find new beauties in it and am determined to think it my own and not look too much into futurity ten years will make a great break in our lives and I hope we are comfortably settled for the best ten years of it. I own when I first came for a day or two I let the foul fiend get so much the better of me as to think within myself what signifies making this place agreeable to me or laying out money on Other people's estates, tis ours to day and theirs to morrow—but I hope I chased such narrow minded ideas from my heart and that I shall be as happy to see the fruit trees I plant flourish the last year of my lease as I shoud the first—you may remember while at Tingmouth I dreaded engaging in the cares of so large a family but am now convinced there are pleasures for every station and employment for I now woud not give up my bustling mornings for the loitering life I led in Devonshire—that might have tired this cannot as I hope I am acting properly what shoud I do—As I have no children, to fill up my mornings with—sometimes Rishton is out from breakfast till dinner—I then dedicate an hour or two to the kitchen..... Mr. R. has spared me a very pretty yard and house for my poultry and I have several friends who have promised to supply me with some—we have got one cow and are to have others and have one of the prettiest neatest dairys you can imagine. I *potter* after Rishton everywhere."—Then comes a list of the dogs, old and new; the last being "a Portugal pointer from the banks of the Dowrow—from whence he takes his name." For awhile, Maria wrote of her house and manner of living with a sense of enjoyment—so that she has little time to write to Fanny, whom she is always begging to visit her. There is even a very daring statement that she "does not envy Fanny Lord Stanley's *fête-*

champêtre.[1] I think the entertainment of my chicken and poultry-yard and dog-kennel, far exceeds it." But her spirits rose and fell. At another time, it was a cry of "How I regret the calm life I led at Tingmouth."—" Ah, Fanny, Tingmouth, Tingmouth! What a difference between a man and a maid, and nine servants!"—" I am not formd to manage a set of caballing insolent servants."—" The more there are, the more insolent, and if R. was of my mind, I woud give up one half of those we have." Her Lynn connexions visit her and pity her for living away from " that seat of the muses, that meridian of taste, the second Athens for learning, the favourite retreat of the gods where the golden age flourishes again, where simplicity, virtue, benevolence, candour, have taken their abode—Lynn. . . . . . I will endeavour to prevail on my soaring gineus (*sic*) to drop his fluttering pinions and descend to a vulgar style suited to your grovling ideas," &c.

Again, " Not even my kitchen is sacred from the Lynn Managers." Her Lynn visitors follow her into it, and she is " still so awkward and bashfull, (a favorite expression of Martin,) that she cannot order a dinner before them." She breeds turkeys and poultry, and toils with Martin over ploughed fields to look at his barley. She is often "in a *Moil* " (as they still say in Norfolk), but " Rishton, Who I believe is the Most Active Creature Alive is never easy to see me *Stupyfying* myself with domestic employments—if I sit down to the Tambour for half an hour—' Come Maria you must go with me and see how charmingly Damon (the new pointer, the reigning Favorite) hunts and what good command I have him under—I know of a pheasants Nest about two Miles of you Shall go and see it,' then away we trail broiling over Corn-fields—and When we come to the pit some Unlucky Boy has Stole the Eggs as was the Case the other [day,] then I spend Whole Mornings seeing him Shoot Rooks—grub up trees—and at night for we never come in now till Nine o'Clock—When tea is over and I have settled my Accounts or done some company business—bed-time Comes."

There is no certain sign that Fanny was ever again in Norfolk until after she left the Queen, but her brother James visited the Rishtons when he chanced to be on dry land. We find them interested in Dr. Burney's " History of Music," and for Jem's sake, in Captain Cook. Mr. Rishton gives Jem two choice puppies, which some less favoured connexion covets, so that Jem had better not speak of the gift. At a later time, Captain Burney names his only son, (the " Martin Burney " of Charles and Mary Lamb,) after the Norfolk squire Martin Rishton. We find Mr. Rishton in company with Mr. Windham, in the diary of the latter.

The doctor and Fanny were high in Mr. Rishton's good graces, but he thought his mother-in-law " very tolerable, and not to be endured."

---

[1] If Fanny went to this *fête*, she has left no description of it. Lord Stanley gave it at his villa, the Oaks, near Epsom, on the 9th of June, 1774. See the correspondence of Mrs. Delany, pp. 1-4, Vol. II. Series II.

Indeed, he was hard to please, and, it may be, that, for long, Maria humoured his fastidious fancies and proneness to cavil at his kinsfolk and her own, far beyond what loyalty demanded. He raised bars about her by being what the French call '*difficile*' in character, quick to disapprove, and prompt in expecting his wife to share his distastes. He oscillated between setting up fine equipages, and selling his coach-horses to spare expense. Things must be showy, or non-existent. Not long after her marriage, Maria writes that " Rishton has got a phaeton building in London. I dont think it quite Prudent so many Expences but I am become a much better manager and cannot think of throwing Cold Water as I have hitherto on an Amusement he has wished for ever since we married. I must endeavour to save in other Matters, you may believe me when I assure you If he w^d permit me that I woud rather go in a Linnen or Stuff gown all my Life than debar him of the vast pleasure indeed it is no merit at all of mine as you well know—Dress was never an Object with me—but one must Conform a little to the manners of the World at least he wishes I shoud."

She was childless, and often alone. By degrees her letters lose their wild gaiety—she is, (she writes,) "so entirely seperated from those I love"—"from a lovd society that I remember with the greatest pleasure notwithstanding the maney rubs we used to meet with, when browsing over my little [fire], and eating good things out of the closet by the fire side." She is always "very inquisitive to know anything about" the Burneys, "from my *Mo*, and my *Do*" [Dr. and Mrs. B,] "to the cat and Charlotte's Sparrow." To the Burneys ; above all to Fanny and to Dr. Burney,[1] she shows (throughout a correspondence with Fanny, lasting until 1821) a devotion and gratitude, which find even passionate expression, increasing as the years go by, although the time had long passed when (as she says) "our connexions and friendships were nearly the same ; " and all subjects were in common.

She has *her* Mrs. Coke of Holkham, while Fanny has, for a while, her Mrs. Thrale. Mrs. Coke entreats Fanny, whom she knows only as the author of " Evelina " and " Cecilia," to choose her a governess, whom she will take from *her*, unseen. We have dwelt upon this friendship, mainly because it is another proof of the steady warmth of Fanny's heart ; and of that constancy, which was (as she truly said to a lover of her own, later on,) her favourite virtue. Fanny survived her " beloved friend " about twenty years. Maria, who was then a widow, died in 1821.

---

[1] Maria writes in 1786, " I must be the most ungrateful of human beings coud I for a moment forget the paternal kindness I received from him while I boasted his protection." "There is an even melancholy regret—in the shape of a sincere wish that none of my family had ever quitted his sheltering roof till placed under the protection of a worthy husband." This refers not only to her own case, but to that of her younger sister, who was still more imprudent, and more unhappy in her marriage.

1774.

[The diary of this year originally contained passages concerning Dr. Burney, Mr. and Mrs. Stanley, and Mr. and Mrs. Arthur Young, before the description of the visit to Miss Reid.

The Crisp letters of the year are enclosed in a quarto sheet of paper, marked No. II, and headed "Parts of Letters of my honoured Mr. Crisp, of the year 1774." Below, is this note, addressed by Mme. D'Arblay to her son; "I have kept only one whole letter of my own this year. The rest were too trivial for a place in the *Rectory*—for which I try to select some innocent *prog*."[1]

That Fanny was writing something, beside letters, early in this year seems to be shown by the following passage, which we find in a letter dated Feb. 7:—

[MARIA RISHTON TO FANNY BURNEY.]

And so Mr. Cartwright has made Miss Burney a new riding habit—and she is riding away on her pretty nag Grub—at least one w^d imagine so by my not having receivd a single line.—" Are you sure, James, Miss Burney did not give me any letter or parcel ? " " No indeed, ma'am." " Well then she is a false perfidious girl, and so much for her."]

[FROM MR. CRISP.]

Chesington, Jan. the 1st.

A happy new year to the Fannikin ! and I think I begin it well; and as an instance of my sincerity, I own to you, I answer your letter so soon, just as your over grateful people profess their acknowledgements for benefits received—in hopes of more—your letter, when it came, was an excellent one; but you are devilish long-winded, pray mend that fault ——****'s history is something singular, and highly entertaining—you sum up the whole with this question—

" Is each man perjur'd, and each Nymph betray'd ? "

---

[1] This alludes to those hopes of her son's preferment in the church, which were never fulfilled so far as a *rectory* was concerned.

You don't state the matter right; but in the light you consider it, the plain, positive answer, is,—*Yes*.

Now, you are young, artless, open, sincere, unexperienced, *unhackney'd* in the Ways of Men; consequently you have high notions of Generosity, Fidelity, disinterestedness, Constancy and all the sublime train of Sentimental Visions, that get into girls' heads, and are so apt to turn them inside out—No wonder therefore, that you rail at men, and pull the poor devils to pieces at such a rate—Now I must endeavour to set you right, and persuade you to see things as they really are, in Truth and in Nature; then you will be more favorable, and no longer think them monsters, wretches, etc.—be assured, my Fanny, they are just what they were design'd to be—Animals of Prey[1]—all men are cats, all young girls mice—morsels—dainty bits—Now to suppose when the mouse comes from her hole, that the generous, sentimental Grimalkin will not seize her, is contrary to all Nature and Experience, and even to the design and Order of Providence—for depend on it, whatever is, is right; and however strange such a doctrine may seem, the constant, universal, and invariable, innate Disposition and Practice of all mankind from the beginning of things, and in all ages, must have been originally meant and intended; and tho' particulars, and individuals, are the sufferers, I have no doubt, but that the general order and design of Providence is carried on by these irregularities and misfortunes—Teeth and claws were given to tygers; and nimble heels, and quick ears to the roebuck, by him who gave all to all—I don't mean by this to justify particular instances of treachery, ingratitude, breach of hospitality, etc., which are ever to be detested, and their authors should be banished from society; but barely to inculcate and if possible immoveably to fix in your mind this position, that in the commerce between the two sexes, a sense of what is right and wrong is too feeble a restraint to have the least dependence on; in many cases, the incitement is so violent, and uncontroulable, that even a long-try'd virtue

---

[1] This reminds us of a speech of my Lord Ogleby's, in Garrick and Colman's "Clandestine Marriage," (1766,) "I look upon women as *feræ naturæ*, lawful game," etc. Some sentences in this letter are an enlargement of a few lines in the "Misanthrope" of Molière.

snaps in two like a thread at the first attack—such is human nature—the only Security is flight, or Bars and Bolts and Walls.[1]

* * * * * *

[MISS BURNEY TO MR. CRISP.]

7th Feb.

Did you draw me into a correspondence, my dear Daddy, with no other view than that of mortifying me by this entire breach of it? I take it for granted that you were heartily tired, and repented of your scheme. Though I allow this to be very natural, I cannot forbear noticing that it seems of necessity for men to be capricious and fickle, even about trifles. However, I acknowledge that if I had had any *head* I must have foreseen this blow, but as I *never had none* it has almost stunned me. Yet I will frankly own, that even while I received your letters they appeared to me too flattering to last long. But, if by any chance, I have been so unfortunate as to offend you,—though I can hardly suppose it—I intreat you my dear Sir, not to punish me with *silent* resentment. I would rather receive from you the severest lecture you could pen, because while I might flatter myself with even meriting your notice I should indulge hopes of regaining your kindness;—and, if you will so far favour me, I will gladly kiss the rod.

But if, after all, I have only weaned you, do not think me so weak as to wish to teaze you into writing—I could not forbear sending this remonstrance, but will not trouble you again unless you should again desire it—which I only fear you should *now* do out of compliment, or compassion. However, I will not further pester you, but only subscribe myself,

My dear Daddy,
Your ever affectionate and obliged
FRANCES BURNEY.

If you *should write*, I conjure you to let it be with frankness.

[Addressed—" Samuel Crisp, Esq⁰., at Mrs. Hamilton's, Chesington, near Kingston-upon-Thames, Surrey." Numbered 2, *i.e.*, of this year.]

---

[1] This letter is numbered as II. (of 1774), and headed by Mme. D'Arblay, "severe portrait and strictures on mankind at large."

[MISS BURNEY TO MR. CRISP.]

Queen Square,
9th Feb.

My dearest Sir,

The sight of your hand, once again directed to *me*, really made me *jump*. I am a thousand times more comfortable, too, in knowing that you wrote before my foolish scrawl could reach you, for which I now beg your pardon, though I can only now urge in my excuse that the readiness of your first answers quite spoiled me. I cannot imagine how you can contrive to laugh with so much *gravity*, as when you are pleased to speak of my letters—however, though my swallow is not quite so deep as you apprehend, yet while I can at any rate procure *answers*, I neither can or will forbear writing.

I dare not—perhaps indeed *can* not—pursue your [* * * *] Coquetry, I must acknowledge, is almost universal, and I know fewer girls exempt from *that* passion than from any other—it seems irresistible—I was going to add something of vanity and love of pleasure, but there is no sort of occasion to make concessions to *you*, who are so little inclined to over-rate our merits. I will therefore only say, that though I readily allow you a *general* superiority over us in most other particulars, yet in constancy, gratitude, and virtue, I regard you as unworthy all competition or comparison.[1] The flights and failings of women are oftener from some defect in the *head* than the *heart*, which is just reversed by you—so that where we are *weak* you are *wicked*—now which is least justifiable?[2]

*   *   *   *   *   *

February 20th.

What will become of the world, if my Annals are thus irregular? Almost two months have elapsed without my recording one anecdote! I am really shocked for posterity!

---

[1] Compare this with what Miss Austen puts into the mouth of Anne Elliot, in "Persuasion," Chapter XI., Vol. 2.
[2] This is a fragment, numbered 3, *i.e.*, of this year.

But for my pen, all the adventures of this noble family might sink to oblivion! I am amazed when I consider the greatness of my importance, the dignity of my task, and the novelty of my pursuits! I should be the Eighth Wonder of the World, if the world had not already, and too prematurely, nominated so many persons to that honour!

* * * * *

Thursday mama took us with her to Miss Reid, the celebrated paintress,[1] to meet Mrs. Brooke, the celebrated authoress of 'Lady Julia Mandeville.' Miss Reid is shrewd and clever, where she has any opportunity given her to make it known; but she is so very deaf, that it is a fatigue to attempt conversation with her. She is most exceeding ugly, and of a very melancholy, or rather discontented, humour. Mrs. Brooke is very short and fat, and squints; but has the art of showing agreeable ugliness. She is very well bred, and expresses herself with much modesty upon all subjects; which in an *authoress*, a woman of *known* understanding, is extremely pleasing.[2]

---

[1] Catherine Reid, a Scotch portrait-painter, was called " the English Rosalba"; Rosalba being a Venetian lady crayon-painter, of high note in Europe in the earlier half of the eighteenth century. Miss Reid, in 1745, painted the beautiful Isabella Lumisden, (afterwards Lady Strange,) as a maiden in a blue snood, pressing a white rose to her heart. The Editor saw this with singular pleasure among other interesting family portraits and Jacobite relics in the kindly possession of a granddaughter of Sir Robert and Lady Strange, Mrs. Edmund Ffoulkes, the wife of the Vicar of S. Mary the Virgin, in Oxford. The face is oval; there is a power in the chin and forehead which gives expression to the regular beauty of all the features. She appears as if archly looking at some one who has just spoken. The utterance may have been "*whiggish*," as she answers by the mockery of her eyes, and the closer pressure of the rose. In the same collection there is a portrait of Mr. Lumisden, brother of Mrs. Strange, by Miss Reid. He, too, is very handsome. Family-tradition tells that he was also charming, and that the paintress felt the charm even too much for her happiness.

[2] Frances Moore, daughter of a Norfolk clergyman, married the Rev. John Brooke, rector of St. Augustine's Church in Norwich, and of Colney, also in Norfolk. Mr. Brooke was, at one time, chaplain to the garrison of Quebec, which gave his wife the opportunity of describing Canadian scenery in her novel, "Emily Montague," and of drawing

The rest of the party consisted of Miss Beatson, a niece of Miss Reid's, Mr. Strange, and Dr. Shebbeare. Miss Beatson is a very young and very fine girl, not absolutely handsome, yet infinitely attractive; she is sensible, smart, quick, and comical; and has not only an understanding which seems already to be mature, but a most astonishing genius for drawing, though never taught. She groupes figures of children in the most ingenious, playful, and beautiful variety of attitudes and employments, in a manner surpassing all credibility, but what the eye itself obtains: in truth, she is a very wonderful girl.[1]

---

on herself, by praises of "the fine prospect up the river St. Lawrence," the remark from Dr. Johnson, "Come, Madam, confess that nothing ever equalled your pleasure in seeing that sight reversed, and finding yourself looking at the happy prospect down the St. Lawrence." [Just like "the high road to England." See Boswell.] Mrs. Brooke's "Lady Julia Mandeville" was esteemed a "standard novel," and is to be found as such in Mrs. Barbauld's edition of "The British Novelists." The plot of the story is absurd, and the manners are, on the whole, "imaginary," that is, when they are semi-Arcadian; but it would appear to have touched the fancy of better novelists who read it in their 'teens. There is in it a very coquettish widow (by far the best-handled character in the book), whom you expect to turn out something like the "Lady Olivia" of Miss Edgeworth and the "Lady Susan" of Miss Austen, but who stops far short of those dangerous charmers, and, after alarming you, is left the *only* happy person at the end of the novel, with the exception of a very patient colonel, whose constancy she rewards, so that the "modish" people turn out the most sensible. We suspect that a well-meaning but very tiresome novelist, Mrs. Brunton, borrowed from "Emily Montague" for her novel of "Self-Control." Mrs. Brooke was also a writer of plays, and had the usual quarrel of playwrights with Garrick, whom she put into one of her novels, but said afterwards that she regretted it. Hannah Moore took up her pen for Garrick against Mrs. Brooke. About the same time that Mr. Crisp's "Virginia" was played, Mrs. Brooke sent Garrick a play of her own upon the same subject. Garrick refused to read it until Mr. Crisp had printed his tragedy.

Mrs. Brooke appears to have been a pleasant and amiable woman. In proof whereof, although she joined Mrs. Yates, the actress, whom she had met by chance, in the management of the King's Theatre in the Haymarket, they lived in harmony until Mrs. Yates died in 1787, when "an accurate account of her life from the admired pen" of Mrs. Brooke was printed in the "Gentleman's Magazine."

[1] "Nelly" Beatson, niece of Miss Reid, was Helena, daughter of

Dr. Shebbeare, who was once put actually in the pillory for a libel, is well known for political and other writings.[1] He absolutely ruined our evening; for he is the most morose, rude, gross, and ill-mannered man I was ever in company with. He aims perpetually at wit, though he constantly stops short at rudeness. He reminded me of Swift's lines:

"Thinks raillery consists in railing,
Will tell aloud your greatest failing."

For he did, to the utmost of his power, *cut up* every body on their most favourite subject; though what most incited his spleen was *Woman*, to whom he professes a fixed aversion; and next to her his greatest disgust is against the *Scotch*; and these two subjects he wore thread-bare; though indeed they were pretty much fatigued, before he attacked them;

Robert Beatson, of Killerie in Fifeshire. In 1777 she married Charles Oakley, who held several important offices in the East India Company's service. He was made a baronet in 1790, and Governor of Madras in 1794.

[1] John Shebbeare, M.D., was fined, imprisoned, and nominally pilloried, for some trash called "Letters to the People of England" (1756-7). No. 7 of these letters was seized by the Government. Beardmore, Under-Sheriff of the City of London, happened to be an old brother-scribbler of Shebbeare's, and took such care to treat him gently, that he was himself fined and imprisoned for neglect of his duty—in fact, for making the pillory too pleasant. Afterwards Shebbeare was pensioned by another government. "I," says Boswell, "observed" [to Johnson] "that the pillory does not always disgrace; and I mentioned an instance of a gentleman who I thought was not dishonoured by it." "Ay, but he was, Sir. He could not mouth and strut about as he used to do, after having been there. People are not willing to ask a man to their tables who has stood in the pillory." Here, however, he is found "mouthing" as if he had never stood in the pillory. Some sentences which Fanny wrote down in amazement have been crossed out (seemingly by another hand) as too "gross" to be suffered to stand even in manuscript; yet, as it is, we have here a good specimen of those stupid efforts at satire which sent him to the pillory. He was a Jacobite, so Mr. Strange and Miss Reid put up with him, and Smollett writes of him in his "History of England" as "this *good man*." Yet he is said to have been "Ferret" in Smollett's novel of "Sir Lancelot Greaves." His last appearance in the pillory is in one of Macaulay's Essays.

and all the *satire* which he levelled at them, consisted of trite and hackneyed abuse. The only novelty which they owed to him was from the extraordinary coarseness of language he made use of. But I shall recollect as much of the conversation as I can, and make the parties speak for themselves. I will begin with Mr. Strange's entrance, which was soon after ours. After his compliments were paid to the *fair sex* he turned to the *Growler.*—

"Well, Dr. Shebbeare, and how do you do?"

Dr. Shebbeare.—Do? why, as you see, pestered by a parcel of women.

Mrs. Brooke.—*Women* and the *Scotch* always fare ill with Dr. Shebbeare.

Dr. Shebbeare.—Because they are the two greatest evils upon earth. The *best* woman that ever I knew is not worth the *worst* man. And as to the Scotch—there is but *one* thing in which they are clever and can excell the English, and that is they can use both hands at once to scratch themselves—the English never think of using more than one.

Miss Reid.—Ay, Dr., you only abuse us because you are sorry that you are not one of our countrymen.

Dr. Shebbeare.—What, *envy*, hey? Why its true enough that they get every thing into their own hands; and when once they come they take care never to return, no, no!

Miss Reid.—You was saying, Mrs. Brooke, that you did not not know till I told you that Dr. Burney had a wife; what do you think then of seeing these grown up daughters?

Mrs. Brooke.—Why, I don't know how, or why, but I own I was never more surprised than when I heard that Dr. Burney was married.

Dr. Shebbeare.—What, I suppose you did not take him for a fool?—All men who marry are so, but above all God help him who takes a widow!

Mr. Strange.—This is a strange man, Mrs. Burney, but nobody ever minds him.

Dr. Shebbeare.—I don't wonder that Dr. Burney went abroad!—all my amazement is at his ever coming home! unless, indeed, he left his understanding behind him, which I suppose was the case.

Mrs. Brooke.—I am sure that does not appear from his Tour. I never received more pleasure than from reading his account of what he saw and did abroad.

Dr. Shebbeare.—I hate authors! but I suppose one wit must hate another.

Mrs. Brooke.—Those few authors that *I* know give me great reason *not* to hate them;—quite the contrary—Dr. Johnson, Dr. Armstrong, and I wont say *what* I think of Dr. Burney; but for Dr. Armstrong I have a very particular regard. I have known him more than twenty years.

Dr. Shebbeare.—What, I suppose you like him for his intrigues?

Mrs. Brooke.—Indeed, I never heard he had any.

Dr. Shebbeare.—What, I suppose you had too many yourself to keep his in your memory?

Mrs. Brooke.—O, women, you know, Dr., never have intrigues. I wish Dr. Burney was here, I am sure he would be our champion.

Dr. Shebbeare.—What, do you suppose he'd speak against himself? I know but too well what it is to be married! I think I have been yoked for one and forty years, and I have wished my wife under ground any time since.

Mama.—And if she were you'd marry in a week!

Dr. Shebbeare.—I wish I was tried.

Mr. Strange.—Why this is a sad man, Mrs. Burney, I think we must toss him in a blanket.

Dr. Shebbeare.—Ay, with all my heart. But speak for yourself (to Mrs. Brooke), do you suppose your husband was not long since tired of you?

Mrs. Brooke.—O, as to that—that is not a fair question; —I don't ask you if you're tired of *your* wife.

Dr. Shebbeare.—And if you did, I'd tell you.

Miss Beatson.—Then *I* ask you, Dr. Shebbeare, are you tired of your wife?

Dr. Shebbeare.—I did not say I'd tell *you*, Bold Face.

Mama.—I wish that Mrs. Strange was here; she'd fight our battles admirably.

Mr. Strange.—Why do you never come to see her, Doctor?

Dr. Shebbeare.—Because she has so much tongue, that I

expect she'll talk herself to death, and I don't choose to be accessary.¹

* * * * *

Mr. Strange.—What do you think of the Bookseller's Bill and the state of literary property, Doctor?²

Dr. Shebbeare.—Why, I don't think at all about it. I have done with books! I have not written a line these twenty years—though indeed I wasted a pint of ink last week.

Mama.—Then I am sure you must have *spilt it,* Dr.

Dr. Shebbeare.—I never knew a bookseller who was not a scoundrel; I was cheated plaguly about 'Lydia,'³ and the

---

¹ It *does* seem a pity that Mrs. Strange was not there; but we shall hear a little (too little) of her by-and-by. Nothing could be more characteristic of Mr. Robert Strange, than his (next to no) share in this conversation. A lady connected with his family, wrote thus of him, a little later: "I was very happy with Sir Robert Strange. I never saw so pleasant an equal-tempered agreeable man in my life, and so modest. His wife and he are the very oposite; (*sic*) for she is all fancy, fire, and flash, yet very steady to the main chance; but he admires her, and is so well amused with her fancys (*sic*) that, when silent, he starts a subject to make her shine."

² This was a bill in the interest of the booksellers, designed to give them the monopoly of reprinting their own lapsed copyright works, of which the decision at law of Beckett and others *v.* Donaldson, 1771, had deprived them, and to otherwise modify the copyright act of 8th Anne, c. 19. Burke and Alderman Harley were on the side of the booksellers, and Attorney-General Thurlow and C. J. Fox were against them. The bill passed the Commons in May, 1744, but was thrown out at the first reading in the Lords on June 2nd. See Parl. *Hist.*, 1744, Feb.-June.

³ Shebbeare's novel of "Lydia, or Filial Piety," was published in 1755, in four 12mo. volumes. The man wrote thirty-four novels. His name is fixed in the editor's memory, as, when a girl, she was sharply rebuked for reading one of them, of which she can recall neither the name, or the plot; but this conversation brings back to her its dulness. This novel was in a collection of novels from Don Quixote to Richardson and a few later writers, with the Arabian Nights and all manner of imitations of them—Tales Turkish, Persian, Tartarian, and of the Genii. She has seen but one copy of the set, which was in forty-eight volumes; a dear and delightful collection, never to be forgotten. It was printed in double columns, had full-page engravings of Robinson Crusoe and Friday, Noureddin and the Fair Persian, Sir Hargrave carrying off Harriet Byron from the masquerade, Sir Charles Grandison bowing over her grandmother's hand in the

rascal who sold the 'Marriage Act' promised to share the profits, yet though I know that there have been six editions, he always calls it the first.[1]

Miss Reid.—Pray Dr. have you seen Nelly's last drawing? She has made *me* dance a minuet!

Dr. Shebbeare.—Well said, Nelly! I'll make thee immortal for that! I'll write thy life.

Mrs. Brooke.—She'll make *herself* immortal by her works.

As to Susy and I, we never presumed to open our lips for fear of being affronted! but, when we were coming away, Dr. Shebbeare called out to us, "Here! mind what *I* say; be sure you never marry!" You are right, thought I, there could not be a greater antidote to that state, than thinking of you.

Miss Reid was, I suppose, somewhat scandalized at this man's conversation, as it happened at her house, and therefore, before we took leave, she said, "Now, I must tell you that Dr. Shebbeare has only been jesting; he thinks, as we do, all the time."

"This it is," cried he, "to have a friend to lye for one!"

What a strange fancy it was, for such a man as this to write novels! However, I am tired of writing; and so, Adieu! sweet Doctor Shebbeare. I must read "The Marriage-Act," and "Lydia," nevertheless.

March 17th.

The Spring is generally fertile in new acquaintances. My father received a note last week from Mr. Twiss, a gentleman

---

cedar-parlour, &c. It was bound in the best style of the latter half of the eighteenth century. The backs shone with gold. Mrs. Barbauld's "British Novelists" was the successor to this collection. Mrs. Barbauld left out some inferior novels, and added those of Fanny Burney and Mrs. Inchbald. Her own prefaces to the novels have great merit.

[1] The title of this novel was "The Marriage Act, a Political Novel; in which the ruin of female honour, the contempt of the clergy, the destruction of private and public liberty, with other fatal consequences, are considered in a series of interesting adventures." By John Shebbeare, M.D. The subject was not the Royal Marriage Act of 1772, but Lord Hardwick's Marriage Act of 1753, which put an end to Fleet Marriages. This act was very unpopular, as it enforced greater publicity of marriages. Goldsmith wrote two papers against it in the "Public Ledger," 1760, which are reprinted as No. lxxii. and No. cxiv. in "The Citizen of the World."

just returned from a tour in Spain; and he writes, ardently desiring to know my dear father, and converse with him on Spanish music. My father was much pleased with this note, and soon after waited upon Mr. Twiss, who presented him with many scarce Spanish national airs, and made an appointment to drink tea here on Sunday. Being at present a candidate to be a member of the Royal Society, he requested my father to sign his certificate; to which he very readily agreed.

On Sunday he came at five o'clock, and was shown into the study, where he was *cabinetted* with my father till seven, when they descended into the parlour to tea. He is very tall and thin; there is something very odd in him. I pretend not to even sketch his character, not being able to form any precise idea of it; but it would be strange, if there was *not* some peculiarity about him, when it is considered he has spent more than a third of his life in rambling about foreign countries, and that he is still a young man, and has not seen England since he was seventeen, till within a few months. He has travelled entirely at his own pleasure, and without even a tutor; he has not only been all over Europe, except the North, but over great part of Africa. He speaks Spanish, Italian, French, German, (and I suppose of course Greek and Latin) with great ease and fluency.[1]

As my father has never visited Spain or Portugal, and as Mr. Twiss has always been very curious concerning musical matters, he drew up a collection of Spanish queries relative to this subject, which I copied for this traveller. While he was drinking tea, he turned suddenly to my father, and asked him in Italian, which of us two (Susy or me) played the harpsichord so well? My father told him that the player was not here. "è maritata?" demanded Mr. Twiss. "Si, è maritata," answered my father.[2] As I know enough of Italian to under-

---

[1] In 1776 Mr. Twiss wrote: "I have now visited the greatest part of England, Scotland, Ireland, Holland, Flanders, France, Switzerland, Germany, Bohemia, Italy, Portugal and Spain, and including sea-voyages, have journeyed about 27,000 miles, which is 2,000 more than the circumference of the earth." He gives very fair reasons against travelling with companions, or tutors, and seems to have been by no means extravagant in his expenses.

[2] This was Hetty (Mrs. Burney).

stand any common and easy conversation, I could not help rather *simpering*, which I suppose he observed; for he turned again to my father, "Credo che questa signorina intende l'Italiano?" However, as my father had not denied that we played a *little* and for our own diversion, Mr. Twiss was very earnest with him to speak to us for that purpose; but, thank Heaven! in vain. Soon after, he said something to my father, which by the direction of his eyes, concerned us, in a whisper; to which he answered, "No;" and then the other said aloud, "And do both the young ladies sing likewise, Sir?"

"No, no, no!" from all quarters. He talked a great deal about Spain, which as being least known, my father was most anxious to hear of. Among other things, he said that the married ladies were very *easy of access;* but that the single who, indeed, very seldom left a convent till the day of their marriage, were kept very rigidly retired, and that it was death to touch them even by the little finger! He said that no ladies were to be seen walking, but that they appeared openly at the Theatres, where they sat, however, generally in the darkest part, but without veils; and that they had *glow-worms* strung into beautiful shapes, for ornaments to their hair, and for stomachers; which had a most striking effect. This tale made Mrs. Allen immediately his enemy; and the moment he was gone, she railed most violently at the *lies of travellers*. Mama, too, did not believe a word of it, arguing upon the short life of glow-worms, when once they were taken in the hand. For my part, I stood up Mr. Twiss's advocate, and urged the unfairness of judging of animals any more than of men, only by those of our own country and climate. All that shocked me was, the cruelty of stringing them.[1]

* * * * *

[1] Mr. Twiss tells us in his "Travels through Spain," (published in 1775) that after the plays or operas at Cadiz were ended (which was usually about half-past eleven) it was customary to walk in the Alameda, or Mall. "Here I saw,

'Donne e donzelle,
D'ogni età, d'ogni sorte, e brutte e belle.'
—Ariosto, Cant. xvii., v. 33.

Among the rest I observed several ladies who had fixed glow-worms

March 30th.

I have a most extraordinary evening to give account of. Last night we had a second visit from the Spanish traveller, Mr. Twiss. Mrs. Young drank tea with us. Her husband is infinitely better; which I much rejoice at. Dr. Shepherd also *assisted* at that *warm* collation. Mr. Twiss did not come till late, and was shown into the study. . . . .

When they had finished their private conversation, my father brought Mr. Twiss into the parlour, and invited him to stay supper, which from him in his present hurry is no small favour. The discourse till supper was entirely in parties. Mrs. Young, Mrs. Allen, and Mama talked upon fashions, which is ever an agreeable subject to Mrs. Young, and constantly introduced by her; Dr. Shepherd, Mr. Twiss, and my father conversed upon foreign countries, and Susy and I sat very *snug* together, amused either by ourselves or them, as we chose.

Dr. Shepherd is going abroad himself in a short time, as tutor to a young man of the name of Hatton. He has never yet been farther than the Netherlands, though he has *intended* to travel I believe for thirty years of the fifty he has lived; but a certain *timidity* seems to have restrained him. Giardini relates that, when he was on the continent, being obliged to wear a sword, which his cloth prevents his being burthened with here, he was so extremely awkward for want of practice, that the first day he walked out, the sword got between his legs, and fairly tript him up—over—or down—I don't know which is best to say. He is prodigiously tall and stout, and must have made a most ludicrous appearance. He enquired many particulars concerning Mr. Twiss's travels, with a kind of painful eagerness; and, whenever he related any disasters,

---

by threads to their hair, which had a luminous and pleasing effect." Thus he slightly modified the statement which had raised the wrath of Mrs. Allen the year before. He goes on to say, "I find that the Peruvian ladies likewise ornament their heads, necks, and arms with strings of shining flies, the splendor of which gives them the appearance of coronets, necklaces, and bracelets of natural lights."

the poor Doctor seemed in an agony, as if the same dangers were immediately to become his own.[1]

Mr. Twiss has certainly travelled upon a sensible plan, as he has carried with him twelve curious Questions to be asked wherever he went; and he made his stay at the towns he visited always according to the entertainment he received. He has written four quarto volumes of observations and descriptions during his peregrinations. He intends to publish his Tour through Spain and Portugal, as being the countries of which there is the least known. He is going soon to Danemark, and Russia: his curiosity seems insatiable; and I think his fortune too ought to be inexhaustible.

When supper appeared, Mr. Twiss desired to sit by the young ladies; and making me take a place next to Mrs. Allen, seated himself by me. . . . . Dr. Shepherd still kept the conversation upon travelling. Mr. Twiss spoke very highly of the Spanish ladies, whom he fully intended hereafter to visit again. He said that the bull-fights, which he much admired, were still in high vogue at Madrid. "It is curious to observe," said he, with a sly kind of seriousness, "that the *ladies* are very fond of assisting upon these festivals; and they who scream at a frog or faint at a spider, will with all imagin-

---

[1] Captain Cook says that he named "a group of small islands, 'Shepherd's Isles,' in honour of my worthy friend, Dr. Shepherd, Plumian Professor of Astronomy at Cambridge." Dr. Shepherd published, in 1772, "Tables for correcting the apparent distance of the moon and a star from the effects of refraction and parallax," which were probably used in Cook's expeditions. Dr. Shepherd was a Canon of Windsor when Fanny was at Court, and tried to please by offering to give her a concert, and by bringing the great M. Lalande to see "*cette célèbre demoiselle;*" but she never would be pleased by Dr. Shepherd, and seems always rather hard upon him. Mrs. Schwellenberg suggested that he was a suitable match for her. "A large man," said Mrs. S., had come into *her* room, and then left it, "bob-short" upon seeing *her* only. "Vell, when he comes so often he might like you. For what won't you not marry him?" Fanny said that she would not have him if he were Archbishop of Canterbury. Mrs. Schwellenberg approved her. "Vell, you been right when you don't not like him, I don't like the men neither. Not one from them!" Still, later on. Mrs. S. returned to the charge, adding that "she had been told Dr. Shepherd would marry me!"

able courtesy fling nuts upon the ground to make the Cavaliers stumble; and, whenever they are in danger, they clap their hands, and call out, 'Bravo, Torre! Bravo, Torre!'"[1] However, he did confess that there were ladies in Spain, who were never seen at the bull-fights; which for the honour of my sex I rejoiced to hear. It seems amazing to me, that this barbarous diversion should not be exploded.

When Naples was mentioned, he was pleased to make confession, that he left it in disgrace, that is, that he was obliged to *run away!* As these sort of avowals immediately imply a *love-affair*, and wear a strong air of vanity, my father, who smoaked him, putting on a look of mortification, said, "Well, I was told, that when I arrived at Naples, if I did but show myself upon the Piazza della ———[2] I should be sure to receive three or four billet-doux in a few moments. Accordingly, as soon as I got there, I dressed myself to the best advantage, and immediately went to the Piazza; but to no purpose! and though I walked there every morning I stayed, the devil a billet-doux did I ever meet with!" Every body laughed, and Mrs. Young cried out, looking full at Mr. Twiss, "Well; Dr. Burney, when you go next, you must put a mask on!"

I don't know whether Mr. Twiss felt the reproof my father meant to convey or not; but he fought off the billets-douxs, and declared that he also had not had any. "But, why should you run away then, Sir?" cried Dr. Shepherd, who is dullness itself. "O, Sir," answered Mr. Twiss, "the *ladies* are concerned! but another time, Dr. Burney, when we are alone ———" " The *ladies?*" cried Dr. Shepherd, "but how could the *ladies* drive you away? I should have supposed *they* would have kept you?" "Have a care, Dr. Shepherd," cried Mrs. Young,

---

[1] Fanny should have written "*Toro.*" Mr. Twiss gives all this in his book. He lost nothing for want of taking pains to see it. On Sunday, the 25th of July, 1773, he crossed the bay between Cadiz and Port Mary, nine miles broad, in a boat, and (for 3s. 4d.) saw ten bulls and nine horses slaughtered within two hours and a-half. After that, he went to as many more bull-fights as he could: but he "owns with pleasure," that he knew many Spanish ladies who had never seen, or meant to see, such savageries.

[2] A blank which was never filled has been left for the name of the Piazza.

who showed as much too much quickness, as the Doctor did too much dullness; "don't ask such questions!" "But, Dr. Burney," said Mr. Twiss, "was you never accosted by *una bella ragazza?*" Then turning to me, "You know what a *ragazza* is Ma'am?" "Sir?" "A *Signorina?*"

I stammered out something like neither yes or no; because the question rather frightened me, lest he should conclude that in understanding *that*, I knew much *more;* but I believe he had already drawn his conclusions, from my foolish *simpering* before, upon his first visit; for he began such an attack, in Italian, of preposterous compliments, that my head was almost turned. Yet it so happened, all he said being of the *easy style*, that I understood every word, though it is wholly out of my power to *write* in that language. Finding me silent to his astonishing panegerick, he said in English, "Why, what objection can you have to speaking to me in Italian?" "A very obvious one," answered I, "because it is not in my power." "Mais vous aurez la bonté de me parler François," cried he; but I again assured him of my inability; for I was quite ashamed of this address, as every body was looking at us, and all of them were listening. He turned then to my father, "*Questa Signorina è troppa modesta.*" My father, all kindness, had seemed to pity my embarrassment; "Poor Fanny!" cried he, "she has not had such an attack before; this is as bad as a bull-fight to *her!*"

"I hope not, Sir," cried Mr. Twiss, rather hurt, and then again turning to me, "Do you go to the Masquerade advertised for Monday the 11th of April?" "No, Sir." "Have you ever been to one?" continued he. "I was—at a private one." "And what character did you honour with supporting?" "Oh! none; I did not venture to try one." He then went on with some high-flown complimentary *guesses* at what I personated.

"Did I tell you, Dr. Burney, how horribly I was served about the *fandango?* I went to Hammersmith purposely to find a dancer and found an old woman! I was never so mad."[1] "Well;" said my father, "if I see a Spaniard at

---

[1] This must be taken as *angry*, and *snug* as *quiet;* not telling people your own affairs.

the next Masquerade, I shall know who it is!" "Why, no;" answered he, "I am not determined; sometimes I think of a Highlander." "Oh! I know you'll be *snug*," said my father, laughing. "But if you see a *fandango*, danced," cried I to my father —— "Oh! Ma'am," cried he, eagerly, will you dance it with me? and give me leave to give you lessons?" "No, Sir; I should require too many." "Oh no; Ma'am; I can easily teach you. Upon my word, the fandango, like the allemande, requires *sentiment*, to dance it well; without an agreeable partner it would be impossible; for I find myself so animated by it,—it gives me such feelings! I do declare that I could not for the universe dance the fandango with an old woman!" "No, Sir," cried old Mrs. Allen, angrily, "and I suppose that an old woman could not dance it with you?"

When supper was removed, Mr. Twiss again attacked me in Italian.—" Credo che inamoratà, perchè non mangiava."¹ "Oh! no;" answered I, truly enough, though laughing, "I am not, indeed." "È il lingua d'amore," continued he, and added that it became "*una bella bocca*." "And it had best be confined to such," answered I. After something further, which I have forgotten, he asked me in a tone of pathetic reproach—" Ma perchè," &c., " but *why* will you not answer me in Italian?" "Because I assure you I cannot." "*Ma*, but you have understood all I have said!" "Some part, by accident only." "Well, Ma'am," cried he in English, I hope that when I have the honour to be further known to you, you will speak to me in no other language! I think, Dr. Burney, that the Spanish is the noblest language in the world! I would, if it was in my power, always speak Spanish to men, and Italian to women. As to English, that is quite out of the question, you know! but for *French*, I protest I am ashamed of speaking it; it is become so very vulgar and common." "See! how it is," cried my father, archly, "the French language from being spoken at every Court in Europe, and being reckoned the politest living language, is now sunk to worse than nothing,—to vulgarity!"

"I think I never knew a foreigner," said Mr. Twiss,

---

¹ Mr. Twiss probably said, "Credo ch' è innamorata," etc.

"who spoke English so well as Baretti does; but so very slow," (in a drawling voice, turning to me) "that if he—were—to—make—love—it—would—take—him—*tree*—hours—to utter a declaration. However, I am of opinion, Dr. Burney, that the English bids fair to be the standard language at the European Courts in another century.—Have you ever seen, Ma'am, any of the great Dr. Johnson's curious hand-writing?"

He then put into my hand a letter from that awful *Colossus* of literature, as he is often called. I told him that I *had* seen his writing (which is scarce legible) in a letter to my father. However, he showed me one word; (it was *testimony*) that I could not possibly make out.

"But, Ma'am," added he, "you write so well yourself! I have the Spanish Queries you did me the honour to write; and upon my word, it is very seldom a *lady* writes so correctly." "Oh! cried I, I am particularly proud of the spelling of the Spanish words! I hope you admired that?" He had already pointed out a mistake I had made; he looked quite shocked.

Mrs. Young then began to speak of Ireland, where her husband had some thoughts of going. She asked Mr. Twiss, if he had been there? Not having well attended to what was said, he took it into his head that she was of that country, answered very civilly, "I reserved the *best* for the *last*, Ma'am. Pray, do you speak Erse, Ma'am?"

"Who? I? Sir;" cried Mrs. Young, staring, "speak Erse?"

"I did not know, Ma'am—I thought that being an *Irish* lady, perhaps you might. Well, I declare solemnly, the more I go out of my own country, the more I admire it; as to Ireland and Scotland, I mean to include them; but I have travelled from the age of seventeen, and return with double satisfaction to England. And of all the countries I have seen, upon my honour I would not take a *wife* out of my own for the universe; for, though I may prefer a foreign lady to dance or sing with, and though they have a certain *agrément* that is charming in the vivacity with which they make acquaintance with strangers; yet in the English women there is a reserve, a modesty, and something so sensible; they are *too* sensible indeed, to be intimate with strangers; yet I admire them for it; though I own the Spanish ladies charmed me much, and the Portuguese—Oh! Ma'am; (to me) if you are fond of hair-clubs, you should see the Portuguese ladies' hair!—they have them thus broad,[1] and they wear no caps, only a few jewels or flowers,—or—"

"What?" interrupted Mrs. Allen, with a sneer, "and I suppose some of those pretty shining things—those *glow-worms* that you mentioned?"

"Glow-worms are caught in great plenty in Spain," said he to me, taking no notice of Mrs. Allen's palpable sneer, "and they have an exceeding pretty effect in the ladies' hair; but then, if *you* wear them, *you* must shut your eyes, or they won't shine!"

"There's for you, my dear!" cried Mrs. Allen.

"Nay, Ma'am," said mama, "it was not said to *you!*"

The conversation soon after turned upon dancing. Mr. Twiss spoke of it in very warm terms, "I love dancing most exceedingly. I prefer it to anything." "I blush for you," cried my father, laughing,—" is this you who pretend to love Music?" "Aye," said Dr. Shepherd, "what becomes of music?" "Oh, dancing beats all music! I should prefer a country-dance, with *you*, Ma'am, to all the music in the world! But this is only for *your* ear, Ma'am. You must not hear this, Doctor. Do'nt you love dancing, Ma'am?" whispering quite languishingly. "Me, Sir?" said I, "Oh, I seldom dance —I don't know." "What Assemblies do you frequent, Ma'am?" "Me, Sir? I hardly ever dance; I go to none!" "To none? bless me! but—pray, Ma'am—will you do me the honour to accept any tickets for Mrs. Cornely's?" "Sir, I am obliged to you; but I never—" "No, Sir;" said my father, gravely; "she does nothing of that sort."

He seemed extremely surprised, but continued, "I danced last Thursday till past two o'clock; but I was so unlucky, as to

---

[1] Mr. Twiss meant that they wore their hair like the men, "*clubbed*," or in "*queues*"; that is, in one thick plait, hanging at the back of the neck.

fix upon a very stupid partner, from whom I hardly could get a word, all the evening. I chose her, because she was a pretty girl,—Miss Ladbroke." "How could a pretty girl be stupid?" cried Dr. Shepherd. " Aye;" said my father; "her eyes should have sufficed to make her eloquent; but English girls are often shy." "Shall you go to the Lock Hospital Oratorio, ma'am?" "No, Sir;" answered I. "To that at the Foundling? O! I hope it!" "No, Sir; I seldom go out." This was followed by an Italian moaning, at my retiring spirit. "Well! my dear," cried Mrs. Allen, "you have it all! poor Susy is nothing to-night."

She said these kind of speeches, though in a sort of whisper, so often, during his almost heroics of compliments, that I was exceedingly frightened lest Mr. Twiss should hear her; and Mrs. Young fixed her eyes with such curious observation! My father, too, began to grow very grave; so that altogether I was in a very embarrassing situation, which I believe was pretty obvious; for they all endeavoured to turn Mr. Twiss away from me, and my father made several attempts at changing the conversation, though the florid traveller was too flighty to regard them. However, at length, he attacked Susy, and talked a little French with her; but, as I was more conveniently situated for him, he returned again soon to me.

"Have you read Miss Aiken's Poems? Dr. Burney, they have been much admired. There is one poem in them, '*Come here, fond youth*,' that describes the symptoms of love, which all the ladies I meet with have by heart. Have not *you*, Ma'am?" "Me? no, Sir."[1]

---

[1] Anna Lætitia Aikin was the daughter, sister, and aunt of authors, of whom she was the best. In this year, 1774, she married Mr. Barbauld. We are told by H. C. Robinson that "It was after her death that Lucy Aikin" (her niece) "published Mrs. Barbauld's collected works, of which I gave a copy to Miss Wordsworth. Among the poems is a stanza on Life, written in extreme old age. Long after, Wordsworth said; 'Repeat me that stanza by Mrs. Barbauld.' I did so. He made me repeat it again, and so he learned it by heart. He was at the time walking in his sitting-room at Rydal, with his hands behind him; and I heard him mutter to himself, 'I am not in the habit of grudging people their good things, but I wish I had written those lines.'" In 1845, Robinson says, "Rogers spoke highly of Mrs. Barbauld, and

"But, Dr. Burney, of all the books upon this subject, none was ever equal to Rousseau's *Eloise!* what feeling! what language! what fire! have you read it, Ma'am?" "No, Sir." "Oh, it's a book that is *alone!*" "And *ought* to be *alone*," said my father, still more gravely.

Mr. Twiss perceived that he was now angry, and with great eagerness he cried, "Why, I assure you I gave it to my sister, who is but seventeen, and just going to be married." "Well," returned my father, "I hope she read the Preface, and then flung it away." "No, upon my honour; she read the Preface first, and then the book. But pray, Doctor, did you ever meet with a little book upon this subject called the Dictionary of Love? It is a most elegant work. I am surprised you have not seen it. But it is difficult to procure, being out of print. It is but a duodecimo, but I gave half-a-guinea for it. Indeed Davies[1] had a commission from me to get it for five guineas, but it took him three years. I have it now binding in gold, for a present to a lady. But first I shall do myself the honour to show it to you, Ma'am, though you cannot want it—you have it all ready—it is only for such bunglers as me." I made no answer. He spoke this rather in a low voice, and I hoped that nobody heard him, for I was quite ashamed of receiving such an offer, and did not seem even to hear him myself.

His next attempt was for music. He began a most urgent

---

related that Madame D'Arblay said she repeated every night Mrs. B.'s famous stanza." We give the lines which Fanny repeated nightly, and Wordsworth wished that he had written:—

"Life! we have been long together,
Through pleasant, and through cloudy, weather:
'Tis hard to part when friends are dear;
Perhaps 'twill cost a sigh, a tear:
Then steal away; give little warning;
Choose thine own time;
Say not good-night; but, in some brighter clime,
Bid me good-morning."

[1] Mr. Twiss seems to have been solemnly in earnest about his little book. Two years later, in a note to his "Tour in Ireland," we find him urging the ladies to read this "small duodecimo," as it was well fitted to give them sage counsel.

and violent entreaty to me to play—"I will kneel to you,—for a quarter of an hour!" I answered very seriously, that I could not possibly comply: he would not be rebuffed. "To whom must I apply for assistance, Dr. Burney? pray, speak for me!" "Sir," said my father, half jesting, half earnest, "the young women in this house, like those in Spain, do nothing, before they are married."

He was silent a few moments; and then turning to mama, with a supplicating tone said, "Will you use *your* influence, Ma'am? I will kneel to YOU to obtain it." "Sir," said she rather sharply, "I am not a Duenna!" "Duenn*ia*, Ma'am," said he, "is the true pronunciation. What shall I say? *One* air before I go,—only one air will make my sleep so delightful!" "If you would go to sleep *first*, Sir," said I, "perhaps ——." "Why, aye, Fanny!" said my father, "*do* play him to sleep!" "No, no, Dr. Burney, not to sleep; but my dream after it will be so fine——" "Well!" cried Mrs. Young, "here's a lady who can play, if she will," turning to Susan. He immediately arose, and went and flung himself on his knees to Susy. She refused his request, and changed her place; he followed her, and again prostrated himself. "Well, however," cried Mrs. Allen, "I am glad he is gone a little to Susy at last." This scene lasted but a short time; finding he sued in vain, he was obliged to rise; and Dr. Shepherd, who had been quite out of his element all the evening, rose to depart, and proposed to take Mr. Twiss with him. This was agreed to; and Mr. Twiss giving me three times most obsequiously his lowest bow, was forced to quit the field.

I think this was the most extraordinary evening I ever passed. Mr. Twiss is such a man as I never saw before, or scarcely any one whose character even *resembled* his. He piques himself upon having travelled many years, and, when very young, without a tutor; but I am apt to attribute greatly to this very circumstance, the extravagant strangeness of his manners. Always his own master, he has scampered from place to place, met with new customs and new men every month, without any sensible or experienced friend to point out the good or evil that he saw. He is really a creature of

his own forming; for he seems to have seen every thing and copied nothing. Nothing could be more improper, more injudicious than the conversation which he chose to enter into. Indeed, I often wondered where he would stop. It is, however, evident that he *meant* no offence or impertinence, by his prating at such a rate, before my father and mother. Yet what a novice should we conclude any man, who could imagine that any father would approve of such sort of a conversation! and more especially, that any man of letters would be entertained by so much frivolous gallantry and forwardness; for I have not written half his fine speeches, no, nor a quarter. But perhaps he is of that number of men, who conclude that all females take nonsense for politeness, and that it is necessary to banish sense and reason, in order to be understood. . . . .
He has really put our house into a commotion; his behaviour was so extraordinary, that he has been the sole topic of discourse since his curious visit; and even my gentle and candid father says that *he has quite mistaken the thing*, and that he shall never see a *table-cloth* in his house again, or be invited evermore to the tea-table.[1]

---

[1] Mr. Twiss crosses these pages once more, but there is no sign that he ever again saw Dr. Burney's table-cloth. In 1775 he published his travels in Portugal and Spain, and Dr. Johnson advised Mrs. Thrale to read the book. In it, he was rather more discreet in speaking of the "*donne e donzelle*," but, here and there, we find the same want of delicate perception of *fitness* which perplexed Fanny, and displeased her father. He was quite in earnest about the Fandango. He employed his master, Giardini, the first violin-player of the time, to set him a bass for "El Fandango." A page of his goodly quarto is filled by an engraving of the notes. Mr. Twiss speculates (in handsome print), as to whether the Spaniards did not learn the dance from their Indian subjects, and teach it to their old subjects in the Netherlands. There he had seen veils like those of Spanish ladies, and also "*plugge dansen*" which were much like the Fandango. He compares the modulation of the Fandango, with that of Corelli's air, "*La Follia di Spagnia.*" He compares "the fury and ardour" with which Spaniards are possessed on hearing the music of the Fandango, with the impatience of the racehorses at a Roman Carnival, as restrained by a rope breast-high, across the street, they wait its removal to run riderless. Next came his "Irish Tour," in which Twiss maddened a whole nation by writing that Irish women were not slender about their ankles. Great was the inkshedding thereupon; Irish newspaper-scribblers and versifiers reviled

April.

In one of Mr. Twiss' late letters to my father concerning Spanish music he says.—"Inclosed is the form of folding Italian billet-doux which I promised to the young ladies."

As to *promised*, which is a strange word, and which only this strange man would use, all that passed concerning the billets was that he asked me if my father had ever shown me the Italian method of folding them? I answered no. "Then pray ask the Doctor," said he,—"*I* dare not!" I begged to be excused, and neither said or thought more upon the subject. And this he calls a *promise!*

---

him in a truly Irish style. Mr. Douce has preserved an Irish newspaper article on Twiss, in his own copy of the "Irish Tour," which is now in the Bodleian Library. He has also written, on a fly-leaf, a short account of Twiss, which is nearly as incorrect as the article, though not so abusive. Mr. Douce makes him out to be the Twiss who married (as he says, "off the stage,") the beautiful Miss Kemble, sister of Sarah Siddons. One would not wonder if he had; but it was his brother Francis, a clergyman, who was much reviled by Dissenters for making a complete index to every edition of Shakespeare then in print. Francis was the father of Horace Twiss. Our Richard was very ingenious in many ways, being a good player on the violin, a skilful chess-player, and the author of a clever book on that game. He injured his fortune by setting up mills to make paper out of what accounts of him call "straw." We suspect it to have been Esparto-grass, from Spain, which is now much in use. He unfortunately began his mills before the supply of rags had lessened, and was, perhaps the first inventor of methods now prospering in England. It has not been by any means a dull part of the Editor's work to read some of the books of "Traveller Twiss." He had seen much, read much, and closely compared several countries and their customs, with other customs and other countries. His comparisons are always ready, and often apt. He was "a coxcomb, but a *satisfactory coxcomb*." We part with Mr. Twiss in the words used to his namesake, Sir Travers Twiss, in the Sheldonian Theatre, where he had eulogized those presented for honorary degrees with so many words ending in "issimus," that it was thought that all the superlatives of praise in the Latin Dictionary must be exhausted, so one of his hearers added aloud, "*et Travers-Twissimus*." Our Mr. Twiss was certainly *Richard-Twissimus*, but such as he was, Dr. Johnson gave him letters of introduction to Ireland. He was to be found with Garrick, and even with Hannah More, to whom he gave,—well, *not* "the Dictionary of Love," or "La Nouvelle Héloïse," but a curious edition of Horace.

The billet is folded in form of a heart; and very prettily. It is sealed with a very fine impression of the Emperor. The direction was—

Alla più bella.

Susette and I both refused to open it. Perhaps the gentleman fancied we should pull caps upon the occasion! However, my father himself saved us that trouble. Within were these words, written in an elegant hand.—

Di questa parte, i cicesbei Italiani scrivono loro lettere gallanti ed amorosi alle loro dame essendo la figura di questa carta forma.

I shall now go from an odd *young* to an odd *old* man, both new acquaintance to us.

Soon after the publication of the German Tour, my father received a letter from a stranger, who called himself *Mr. Hutton of Lindsey-House, Chelsea,* and a friend of Dr. Hawkesworth. It contained some criticisms on the German anecdotes concerning the poverty and wretchedness of that country. He said that he had frequently travelled there, but had always met with *white bread,* and vindicated several other particulars which seemed to bear hard upon Germany, concluding with supposing that my father's servant or other people must have misinformed him; and signed himself his real well-wisher and a great admirer of all *other parts* of his *charming book.*

My father wrote an immediate and angry answer to this letter, acquainting Mr. Hutton, that his veracity, which had never before been disputed, was what he should most carefully and invariably defend and adhere to; that the accounts he had given of the miserable state of the German Empire, were from his *observations* made with his *own* eyes, and not the result of *any* information; that if Mr. Hutton had found that country more reasonable, fertile, and flourishing, he was sure he must have travelled before the last war, when the most terrible ravages were committed by the King of Prussia;[1] and that whatever reasons he might have for defending Germany, they could not be more powerful than those which would ever

---

[1] The Seven Years' War.

impel himself to defend his own honour. Then, after answering particularly to his several remarks, he added that, if he desired any further satisfaction or had any remaining doubts, he would at any time receive him, and endeavour to convince him in Queen Square.

Soon after this, poor Dr. Hawkesworth brought a letter from Mr. Hutton, filled with apologies and concessions, and allowing that he *had* travelled before the last war. He protested that his letter was extremely well-meant, and expressed the greatest concern and contrition that he had given offence. With this letter, Dr. Hawkesworth gave a character of Mr. Hutton, the most amiable that could be drawn. He said that he was his old and intimate friend; that a more worthy being did not exist; but that he was singular and wholly ignorant of the world; that he was a man who was a true lover of mankind, and made quite miserable with the idea of hurting or displeasing any living creature. In short, he made his portrait so full of benevolence and simplicity, that my father whose heart is replete with all "the milk of human kindness" wrote to him immediately a letter of reconciliation, apologizing in his turn for his own hasty answer to his first epistle, and begging the continuance of his esteem and friendship.

The much-regretted death of Dr. Hawkesworth, which happened soon after, did not put an end to this strangely begun correspondence. Mr. Hutton wrote letters that were truly *his own*, being unlike any, either printed or manuscript, which we ever before saw. They contained a good deal of humour, very oddly worded, and the strongest expressions of kindness.[1]

---

[1] Up to this point, all said about Mr. Hutton is retrospective, and refers to the year 1773. It may have happened just after Fanny's return from Teignmouth, as Dr. Hawkesworth is named in her Diary as calling on Dr. Burney about a month before his death on the 17th of November, 1773. There was not much in James Hutton, but his name is often found in books; notably, in that set of letters which, by some odd chance, came into the hands of Dr. Priestley, who published them to vex the Methodists. From them Southey drew a sketch of Hutton (for his "Life of Wesley") but omitted to state that he was the son of a former Fellow of King's College, Cambridge, who had given up the Berkshire living of Stanford in the vale of White

About three months ago he called here. I heard him parleying in the passage, and delivering his name; which induced me (having only Susy at home) to ask him into the parlour. He looks about sixty, good-humoured, clever, and kindhearted. He came up to me, and said, "Is your father at home? for I am deaf." He had not heard the man's answer. He stayed a little while with us, and desired his respects and love to my father. "Tell him, said he, that I know him very well, though I never saw him." Last Good Friday he called again, and then had the good fortune to meet with my father. He was also introduced to mama and all the family. He came with open arms, and my father was very soon extremely intimate with him. He enquired concerning us all, and whether one daughter was not married? "Yes," "And pray," said he, "are you a grandfather, young Gentleman?" My father has indeed a remarkably young look. He said

---

Horse, rather than take the oaths to King George I. James Hutton was (according to his mother, who was second a cousin of Sir Isaac Newton,) "good-humoured, very undesigning, and sincerely honest, but of weak judgement." She had expected that "his weak brain would have been quite turned" (after a fever) by so many Moravians coming about him. John Wesley was his first Pope; afterwards he obeyed Count Zinzendorf. He was a bookseller, who left his shop to others, or preached in it; and roamed about in England and on the Continent, pushing himself, whenever he could, among persons and into things beyond and above him. Hence his letters to, and calls on Dr. Burney. In many cases his good-nature and oddity bore him through; but when he tried Voltaire, on the ground that he was a relation of Sir Isaac Newton, Voltaire found himself ill in bed; and, silly as he was, Hutton suspected Warburton, for he writes, "the Bishop of Gloucester *was said to be out when I called upon him.*" In 1778, Hannah More writes from London, that she has been to a party— "incongruous, heterogeneous,—Lords and ladies, with the whole *corps diplomatique*, some learned foreigners, Marchesi, the famous new opera-man, General Paoli, Hutton the Moravian, and Mrs. Abington, the actress."

The very silliest thing he ever did was attempting to settle the American war by interviews, in 1775, between himself and Dr. Franklin, with whom he had got acquainted over the printing of Whitefield's Journals. He told Franklin that he had access to King George, etc. It all ended like the famous visit of the three Quakers to the Czar Nicholas. Some of his philanthropic ramblings may have given hints for the character of Abany in "Cecilia."

many other humorous things, and left us all in high good humour with him.

The next day I received a letter in a hand that I was unacquainted with; and to my great surprise saw the name of Hutton at the bottom. The letter is so extraordinary, considering the manner of his being known to us, that I will copy it, though I hate the "*Dear Miss*," at the beginning; the rest of the letter is worth preserving. There was in it one enclosed to my father.

[MR. JAMES HUTTON TO MISS BURNEY.]

Lindsey House, Chelsea.[1]
April 2, Thursday in the evening.

Dear Miss,

I have wrote here a longish kind of Letter to your dear Papa, whom I saw with infinite pleasure you love so tenderly.

---

[1] Lindsey House, Chelsea, a very large house, with a terrace, and gardens to the river, and a history, had fallen from its high estate, when, in 1750, Sir Hans Sloane gave Count Zinzendorf a lease of it for 999 years to make it into a Congregation House for the "Unitas Fratrum," commonly called the Moravians. After that, it had, or was meant to have, a meeting-house and a burial-ground. Hutton and his wife were put into it as part of the household in 1752 or 1753. He was to act as Secretary to the Society: The house was called the "Disciple House," Count Zinzendorf being "*The Disciple*." He was always addressed as "Papa," in the sense of *father*, but it might just as well have been in that of *Pope*, since from 1747 "all" (Moravian) "Bishops and elders submitted to him . . . and as 'The Disciple' he became, as it were, the visible representative of the Invisible Head." These are the words of Mr. Benham, the hagiographer of James Hutton, whose book the editor received in 1886 from the uncongenial shelves of the Bodleian Library, where it had stood uncut since 1856, when it was published. Yet there are delightful passages in it, as when Mr. Benham describes Hutton's father (who gave up his living because he would not take an oath to King George) on this wise—"*although* he had *conscientiously* declined performing the official parts of his clerical function, he was a devout and pious man." Mr. Benham also states that he was "of a genteel family." Count Zinzendorf died in 1760, and in 1764 the government of the Moravians was entirely removed from England, and the archives transferred to Germany. As for Lindsey House and the lease of 999 years, by 1824 we find it divided into many small dwellings.

As you love him therefore so much, I shall recommend to you to give him this Letter, when he is in some degree at leisure for the babble of a friend of his, perhaps after dinner on Monday or some such time : or you may leave the disposal of it to your mama, if you should be going out. He is just as well off in one of you as in the other. How well does he deserve you both? I mentioned to him the use of the steam of coffee for his eyes so well employed for himself, his family, and for all who have taste in the world. You and your Mamma together will know how to surprise him into the use of it, as I express in the enclosed, for, if you consult much with him, he may perhaps, as most other studious men do, till it be too late, desire to be excused, but if he should be averse to it after the first surprise, do not teaze him for the world : for you will teaze him I know in nothing else, and I should be sorry if I should be a means of his being teazed.

I will tell you something else, Miss, if my skill in physiognomy has not totally deceived me, he is happy in his lady and children, and you in him. This gives me a high pleasure, as domestic happiness is all harmony and melody, capable of being expressed with a thousand graces, the irregular and new, as well as the old grave of forty years ago; the thousand small attentions accompanying the solid fundamental Melody, charm beyond expression.

May ye all, all of you be blessed together! Happy will that man be, that shall be blessed with *your* hand, or I am totally out. How do I wish my young friend, as I call your Father, may have nothing but blessings in his Children and Grand-children. Pray where does your brother-in-law live that I may run and take a peep at him and your sister? and what is his name? You will always be married *sat citò, si sat bene*. But, how shall we find a man who will deserve a daughter, who loves her parents as you do? Your Father is the proper person to explain that Latin phrase to you. If I live till next Good Friday, I may perhaps meet with your Father again at home, or on some Sunday afternoon when his book is finished ; though then I shall rob all of you of part of the pleasure his leisure gives you, which at present you can have but little of. An old man as I am, is garrulous, and deaf people often are so : Now, I am both old and deaf. Discretion bids me finish. I hope you believe that I am, with the greatest esteem,

Your obedient humble Servant,

JAMES HUTTON.

[P.S.]—I was married 34 years ago, by recommendation of friends, as our Princes used to be; and have had nothing to make me repent. If I had chosen for myself, I fancy I might not have been so well off;[1] for I have had domestic happiness in the highest degree, and have still as much esteem and tender friendship and love,—and it is reciprocal,—as in the first month. Am not I happy? I believe this little anecdote may give pleasure in Queen Square, and therefore I mention it; else I know it is not fashionable for a man to talk of his domestic happiness.

Perhaps Mr. Hutton thought the intelligence of his marriage was necessary, after so civil a letter, to prevent any *mistakes* on my part! However, he is an exceedingly good man, and I like him very much; nevertheless, his letter was so odd, that I could not attempt to answer it.

Some time after, my mother met this gentleman, and he sent me a reproach for not writing; which I therefore was then obliged to do, excusing myself as well as I could. The very day after, he called here again. He came up to me, and shook my hand—" Thank you for your letter; you thought I

---

[1] In 1740, Count Zinzendorf desired Hutton to marry Louise Brandt (a French-speaking Swiss, who had joined the brethren the year before), on the ground that she would be useful among the Moravians in London. Zinzendorf himself married them. The poor woman was very uneasy at first. She found, she said, that she had got a husband "who could not sit still for a quarter of an hour, and was of a very warm and impatient temper." She was also fearful of the displeasure of Mr. and Mrs. Hutton. They, however, treated her as if they had been consulted in the matter, and made her welcome as a daughter.

wanted a *performance;* but I only wanted the *heart;* but I have got *that,* and a performance too ! "

It seems he had been speaking very highly of my father to the King, who he was accidentally admitted to the speech of, by being one morning in the apartments of M. de Salgas, who is sub-preceptor of The Prince of Wales, when the King came in, who entered into conversation with great complacency and condescension.[1] He had given an account of this to my mother. She told him now, that my father was much pleased to have had so good a friend speak of him before the King. "Madam," cried he, "I will speak of him before *God*, and that is doing much more !"

Since this, I have received another letter from him, much in the style of the former, very much desiring me to write to him; which I yesterday did; though I think few young persons have entered into a more singular correspondence.

[MR. JAMES HUTTON TO MISS BURNEY.]

Lindsey House, Chelsea,

April 24, Thursday [1774].

Dear Mad^m

My little visit at your house on Saturday can by no means dispense with my thanking you in writing for your kind and charming answer to my former letter. I hope by this time you have courage to write to one who is no critic, but an admirer of all the Burneys, and if I *was* a critic you need not with a heart and expression like yours be afraid of the nicest eye, any more than any of the most exquisite singers your father heard were of his ears.

I was again so pleased at Queen's Square that I have just now mentioned in a L^r, which *perhaps* the King and Queen may see, that I supposed the domestic happiness of your father was one of the causes of the charming spirit one finds in his writings, the good humour this must put a heart in that is like

---

[1] The King called De Salgas, or Solgas, "Hutton's son." Hutton acted as father, by going to de Salgas' wedding in Holland, in 1778.

his, is a kind of inspiration; but I do not forget that the good humour originated where it should, in the parents.

If my little short occasional visits can give pleasure in Queen's Square how delightful will it be to me to give pleasure in return for so much I am sure of receiving? I would add to your father's time if I could instead of taking it from him, pray tell him then, at some not greatly employed moment, that I am not so unreasonable as to wish him to write to me; and if you will now and then snatch a moment to tell me half a word from him I shall get more than I have any pretence to.

I loved your father long before I saw him, and the sight of him did not disappoint me, and your fondness for him and his ease and yours together was the finest of all exhibitions, but whoever could do that? the arts are but imitations of nature. Have you learnt to paint? If you have I wish I could get a small profile of your father, to send to a learned man abroad who is making a collection of Heads in order to establish his system of Physiognomy.[1] If *you* can do it there will be expression in it, which no painter who does not feel for the object will ever be able to hit. If you can not, I should be glad, by-and-by, if there be any good picture drawn of him, that satisfies you or your mama tolerably well at least, to get a profile taken of it, for that great work I mentioned above. If you can draw a likeness yourself you can do it from memory, for he has no time to sit for any such work.

If *I* could paint I would paint his benevolent look at me and you, feeling for something in his pockets on the chair and looking pleased at a stranger that you saw loved your father; but I should never be able to express my satisfaction and the happiness of that moment. At another time I would paint the joy of your father last Saturday with four of his daughters round him, and the friendly looks of that kind groupe. I am glad too that I saw your married sister, to whom now I wish, with increase of good will, every sort of happiness.

Can you find a minute to ask your father his Taste of

---

[1] As Hutton had travelled in Switzerland, (after marrying a Swiss in Germany,) it is probable that this was Lavater who published his famous book in 1776.

Pere's[1] his compositions? Mr. Sulgar, who just drank coffee with me, desired me to enquire. He is a Swiss who subscribes for the "History of Music"; is vastly fond of the "Musical Tour," and believes all I say of the Burneys.[2] Mrs. Hutton loves you too, was vastly pleased with that letter of yours I was so proud of, and takes my word for all I tell her of you. She does indeed bestow happiness on me, and will do as long as we live. I only wish to keep pace with her in that best employment, where friendship and esteem and love are all blended. Will you present my love to your own family? They have it indeed, and I am with truth and a warm heart

Your obedient and very humble servant,
JAMES HUTTON.

You will perhaps recollect that the first page at least of this is in answer to several parts of your letter, which I have before me, though it was so impressed upon my mind as that I could answer without looking at it again. Whenever you write from the *heart* be assured that every correspondent of taste will have reason to be satisfied and pleased, and never let letter writing cause you any study. Dip your pen *there* and you must succeed. Nothing ever disgusted me so much as many laboured printed letters I have seen, which were rather Performances than Letters, and therefore painful, stiff, far-fetched, unnatural stuff. Such are all Bussi Rabutin's almost. Madame de Sevigne's are infinitely more to the taste of the discerning, while Rabutin's vex and teaze my heart and disappoint it and are nauseous to my very soul, considered as letters: after I had thus tasted them I found that many others were of my taste with regard to those Letters. Affectation spoils every thing in writing, singing, speaking, looks, gesture, gait, in short, every thing and every where. I have

---

[1] Probably David Perez, Spanish-Italian composer, 1711-1778, of whom Dr. Burney gives an account in his History.

[2] Johannn Georg Salzer, a native of Zürich, Professor of Mathematics at Berlin, was author of a book on the "Universal Theory of the Fine Arts," published 1771-4—but his name does not appear among Dr. Burney's subscribers.

found much pleasure in Madame de Maintenon's Letters (except in Theologicals and Spirituals), they are often most cordial, free, easy, unaffected and therefore vastly clever. But why should I not leave off?

[FROM MR. CRISP.]

[April, 1774.]

My dear Fanny,

I tell you what—you are a Jew,—an Ebrew Jew—of the line of Shylock, and I shall henceforth call you, Jessica; because you, an over-grown rich Jew, can give me an entertainment of a hundred dishes, do you expect the like from such a poor, forked, unbeleiving Christian, as I am?—You riot in provisions of all sorts, and have nothing to do, but to choose, or reject; and your Cookery is at your fingers' ends, and to do you justice has the true relish, and is highly season'd; all this I give you credit for; I devour the feast you give me, finish the dessert, lick up the jellies and ic'd creams to the last drop, and am thankful—but all this wont do it seems. The Mosaic Law says—"*An eye for an eye, and a tooth for a tooth;*" and if I have neither, *then I must have your pound of flesh, says Jessica*. The truth is, Chesington produces nothing but Bacon and Greens, with a new laid egg, or so, and the week round the meats are pretty near the same; so that I can give you no better than I have Fanny. You say, because I don't like your new young acquaintance, Mr. Twiss, I am so short —here you are mistaken—I like your *picture* of him, just as in Raphael's School of Athens at the Vatican, I like his picture of the Pope's frightful Dwarf, which for fun and spite he lugg'd by head and shoulders into that fine composition.[1] I wont pretend to say, like that beast Shebbeare, I will make you immortal for your pictures; but I shall make a choice Cabinet Collection of them, and review them often for my own entertainment.

As to your young, travelled, dying lover, Twiss, I own it is matter of surprize to me, that one who has seen and known so

---

[1] As Socrates, lying on the steps, between the illustrious groups above and below. If this is not in books, Mr. Crisp perhaps repeats a tradition which he had heard in Italy.

much, and who you say has drollery in him, &c., &c., should at the same time, in other things be so thorough a puppy—has your Daddy had any further intercourse with him, or seen any of his Collections?—Tell me all about the progress of the History, the new Subscribers, new acquaintance, Garrick, Charles, Hetty; .... likewise about Mr. Beckford, and above all, about your new acquaintance, whom you threaten me with,—Mr. Hutton—I believe I should like him greatly. What did King George say about Daddy's book? or had he read it? I want somebody that has weight and power to push his interest home. As for that scrub Lord Hertford, I devote him to everlasting contempt;[1] but I should think Lord Sandwich, Lord March, Lord Shelburne, or some of these chaps might and should exert themselves. But when I recollect what the world is my surprise at their neglect ceases.

Send a minute Journal of every thing, and never mind their being trifles,—trifles well-dressed, are excellent food, and your cookery is with me of established reputation.

[April or May.]

My father has bought a House in St. Martin's Street, Leiceister Fields,—an odious street—but well situated, and nearly in the centre of the town; and the house is a large and good one. It was built by Sir Isaac Newton! and, when he constructed it, it stood in Leicester *Fields*,—not *Square*, that he might have his observatory unannoyed by neighbouring houses, and his observatory is my favorite sitting place, where I can retire to read or write any of my private fancies or vagaries. I burnt all up to my fifteenth year—thinking I grew too old for scribbling nonsense (*sic*), but as I am less young, I grow, I fear, less wise, for I cannot any longer resist what I find to be irresistible, the pleasure of popping down my thoughts from time to time upon paper.

---

[1] Mme. D'Arblay states that when her father was in Paris (in 1764), Lord Hertford promised him the Mastership of the King's Band when it should become vacant, but broke his word next year, on being solicited by the Duke of York (the King's brother) in favour of another musician. This appointment seems to have been a perquisite of the Lord Chamberlain, but there must be some error as to dates, since Lord Hertford did not become Lord Chamberlain until 1766.

My good old new friend, Mr. Hutton, made me two visits while my mother was at Chesington. We had a good deal of conversation upon Lord Chesterfield's Letters, which I have just read. I had the satisfaction to find, that our opinions exactly coincided; that they were extremely well written, contained some excellent *hints* for education; but were written with a tendency to make his son a man wholly unprincipled; inculcating immorality, countenancing all *gentleman-like* vices, *advising* deceit and *exhorting to* inconstancy. "It pleased me much," said Mr. Hutton, "in speaking to the King about these Letters, to hear him say, *"For my part, I like more straight-forward work."'*

* * * * * *

I have had the honour, not long since, of being in company with Mr. Keate, author of an account of Geneva, Ferney, and some other things, chiefly poetical. He is an author, *comme il faut*; for he is in affluent circumstances, and writes at his leisure and for his amusement. It was at the house of six old maids, all sisters, and all above sixty, that I met Mr. Keate.[1] These votaries of Diana are exceedingly worthy

---

[1] George Keate, F.R.S. and F.S.A., is described by George Colman the Younger, as "a worthy gentleman of independent fortune, of good connexions, and good family;" who was therefore fittingly said (in the "Biographia Dramatica"), to have "*obliged the world* with several poems of *distinguish'd* elegance and reputation," with his own portrait attached to them. He "*obliged the world*" with a poem in thin 4to. yearly, from 1760 to 1769, and also with some in after years. His best book is in prose, being a compilation from the Journals of Captain Henry Wilson, called "An Account of the Pellew Islands (1778), wherein our grandparents read the touching story of "Prince Lee Boo." George Colman wonders how Keate came to sit for his portrait, "for his countenance was more grotesquely ugly than the generality of human faces." Keate told the elder Colman a story which permits us to think that he had humour, and was not unaware of his own strange looks. He said that he had been in a side box of one of the London theatres, when there was a cry of "Fire." He was so much alarmed, that when he got safely home, he found that his *eyebrows and eyelashes had dropt off* through fright—"and they have never,—as you may perceive, Sir,—grown again!" Some verses on Shakespeare in his poem of "Ferney" caused Keate to be made free of Stratford-on-Avon, at the same time with Garrick, in the "Jubilee-year," 1769.

women of the name of Blake; and I heartily wish that I, who mean to devote myself to the same goddess, should I be as ancient, may be as good.

Mr. Keate did not appear to me to be very brilliant; his powers of conversation are not of a shining cast; and one disadvantage to his speeches is, his delivery of them; for he speaks in a slow and *sluggish* voice. But what principally banished him from my good graces was, the conceited manner in which he introduced a discourse upon his own writings.

"Do you know, Mrs. Blake," (addressing himself to the senior virgin) "I have at last ventured upon building, in spite of my resolution, and in spite of my Ode?"

Mrs. Blake fell into his plot, without being sensible that he had laid one. "Oh! Mrs. Burney" (cried she to mama), that Ode was the prettiest thing! I wish you could see it!"

"Why I had determined, and indeed promised," said he, "that when I went into my new house, I would either give a Ball or write an Ode;—and so I found the Ode was the more easy to me; but I protested in the poem, that I would never undertake to *build*." All the sisters then poured forth the incense of praise upon this Ode, to which he listened with the utmost *nonchalance*, reclining his person upon the back of his chair, and kicking his foot now over, and now under, a gold-headed cane.

When these effusions of civility were vented, the good old ladies began another subject; but, upon the first cessation of speech, Mr. Keate broke the silence he had kept, and said to mama, "But the worst thing to me was, that I was obliged to hang a carpenter in the course of my poem."

"Oh dear, aye;" cried Mrs. Blake; "that part was vastly pretty! I wish I could remember it. Dear Mrs. Burney, I wish you could see it! Mr. Keate, it's a pity it should not be seen—"

"Why surely" (cried he, affectedly), "you would not have me *publish* it?"

"Oh! as to that,—I don't know," answered with the utmost simplicity, Mrs. Blake, "*you* are the best judge of that. But I *do* wish you could see it, Mrs. Burney."

"No; faith!" added he, "I think that, if I *was* to collect my other brats, I should not, I believe, put this among them."

"If we may judge," said mama, "of the family *unseen* by those in the world, we must certainly wish for the pleasure of knowing them all."

Having now set the conversation upon this favourite topic again, he resumed his posture and his silence, which he did not again break, till he had again the trouble of renewing himself the theme, to which his ear delighted to listen; else he only

"Sat attentive to his own applause."

My father, who, thank Heaven! is an author of a different stamp, pursues his work at all the leisure moments he can snatch from business or from sleep.

Sunday night, June 26th.

Mama with Bessy and Dick are gone for a few days to Bradfield, on a visit to Mrs. Young. A message came this evening, while my father and I were *tête à tête* in the study, from Mr. Coney of Lynn, with compliments, and that he was coming to pay a visit here with an intimate friend of my father's. Not conjecturing who this might be, and knowing that Mr. Coney did not merit the sacrifice of an evening, word was sent that my father was not at home; but they had left home before the messenger returned, and were therefore told the same tale at this door. However, they came in to see me, Mr. Coney first, and then Mr. Bewley! my father's very learned and philosophical friend, who is come to town only for this one evening! I protest I was quite confounded at the sight of him. I well knew that my father would as earnestly desire to see Mr. Bewley, as he had *not* to see Mr. Coney. I was upon the point of saying, *tout de bon*, at sight of him,—"Mr. Bewley, my father is at home"; but the recollection of the third of a second told me what a gross affront that would be to Mr. Coney, whose name had already been sent, and without success. I therefore restrained myself, and to my great concern, after about a quarter of an hour spent in chatting, I was obliged to suffer Mr. Bewley to march off in the same ignorance with his companion. My father has since sent half the town over in search of Mr. Bewley; but in vain; for I could not procure from him any satisfactory account of his place of abode; which indeed he did not seem to know himself. He was so extremely *distrait* during the visit, that I believe he was uncertain whether he was in Queen Square in reality or in a vision.

Mr. Coney, who piques himself upon having the address of a man of the world, and who is very conceited, gave himself the air of being diverted at Mr. Bewley for his absence, and ignorance of the town, &c. He protested he had done nothing but laugh since they arrived. Ah! thought I, my merry gentleman, however you may presume upon your external acquirements, that quiet unassuming man, who makes your diversion, may also from *you* receive his own![1]

* * * * * *

I have been interrupted by a visit from Dr. Armstrong. He must be very old, and looks very much broken; but he still retains his wit and his gallantry. When I regretted my father's being out, and thanked him for coming in to see *me;* " To *you,*" repeated he, shaking my hands, " do you think there

---

[1] Although William Bewley was a poor and hard-worked surgeon in an almost unknown country-town, he was in correspondence with the chief anatomists and writers on chemistry and electricity of his time, and for twenty years wrote articles on science and foreign literature for "The Monthly Review." He had never done more than pass through London on business until 1783, when illness took him thither to consult for himself John Hunter and Mr. Potts, Dr. Warren, and Dr. Jebb, to whom he had often written on the maladies of others. He travelled from Norfolk to London by Birmingham, where he paid Priestley a visit which had long been promised. Under Dr. Burney's roof he revived, seeing London with the zest of a boy, and having the delight of being presented to Johnson as the proud owner of the tuft of bristles from the doctor's old hearth-broom. He next visited Griffiths, the Editor of "The Monthly Review," at Turnham Green. There his illness became severe, and he returned abruptly to the house of Dr. Burney, who was summoned (by express,) from Chesington. The sick man's wife was with him, but nursing and doctors could avail nothing. He died of an incurable internal tumour in September, 1783, in the house of Dr. Burney, and was buried in the neighbouring church of St. Martin-in-the-Fields.

is any body I would sooner come in to see than *you?*" Speaking of physicians, I said that it appeared to me to be the most melancholy of all professions, though the most useful to the world. He shook his head, and said that indeed he had never been happy till he was able to live independant of his business; for that the pain and anxiety attendant upon it, were inconceivable.

* * * * * *

But now let me come to a matter of more importance and, at the same time, pleasure : My brother is returned in health, spirits, and credit. He has made what he calls a very fine voyage; but it must have been very dangerous. Indeed, he has had several personal dangers; and in these voyages of hazard and enterprize, so, I imagine, must every individual of the ship. Captain Cooke was parted from in bad weather, accidentally, in the passage from the Society Isles to New Zealand, in the second and so fatal visit which they made to that barbarous country, where they lost ten men in the most inhuman manner. My brother, unfortunately for himself, was the witness and informer of that horrid massacre. Mr. Rowe, (the acting Lieutenant), a midshipman; and eight men were sent from the ship in a boat to shore, to get some greens. The whole ship's company had lived so long upon good terms with the New Zealanders, that there was no suspicion of treachery or ill usage. They were ordered to return at three o'clock; but upon their failure, Captain Furneaux sent a launch, with Jem to command it, in search of them. They landed at two places without seeing anything of them. They went among the people, and bought fish; and Jem says he imagined they were gone further up the country, but never supposed how *very* long a way they were gone. At the third place, it is almost too terrible to mention, they found [1]——

* * * * * *

---

[1] This requires some correction from Captain Furneaux's Narrative of his proceedings in the "Adventure," after he was separated from Captain Cook by the storm. Mr. Rowe was a Midshipman, who was sent as acting Lieutenant in the large cutter, with a crew of nine of the

[MR. CRISP TO MISS BURNEY.]

Ches. Aug. 22.

Dear Fanny,

You are a good sort of girl enough and I don't hate you violently.—You kept me in hot water about Jem tho' for a minute; which small penance (as you love mischief at your heart, and cannot help it) I can forgive since you set matters to rights in three or four lines afterwards. But I see in the papers that a Lieutenant Clarke is to go out next voyage with the command of the "Resolution"—how will Jem like that, instead of his favourite Captain Cooke? (sic)[1] Or is it all one to Jem who he goes with, so as he does but once more visit Otaheite and his dear Piece that he left behind there? But I wish him good luck with all my heart, for I have taken a great fancy to him.—I suppose that R[ogue] your father is at Buxton before now.—Have you heard from or about him? Let me know. I wish I had anything from hence, to keep up the ball of correspondence; but in short instead of offering to pay your ballance I can only send you an order for

---

best men in the ship to "gather wild greens," with orders to return the same evening. The poor lad was in such a hurry to be off, that he went an hour before the time fixed. He did not return even on the following morning, when the "Adventure" was to sail. Captain Furneaux put it down to his desire to explore (on his own account) a bay into which none in the ship had ever entered; but was sufficiently alarmed to send second-Lieutenant Burney, with a crew, and ten marines, in the launch, in search of him. Captain Furneaux writes, "Mr. Burney having returned about eleven o'clock, the same night, made his report of a horrible scene indeed, which cannot be better described than in his own words." Here (in Cook's Voyages) follows the report of Lieutenant Burney, who did *not* "witness the massacre," but found the remains of Rowe and the crew. Fanny has left the greater part of her page blank, with the intention, seemingly, of giving details; but she may have found them too "terrible." As they are both *terrible* and *horrible*, we do not give them.

[1] This was an incorrect report, but Captain Clerke, or Clarke, succeeded Cook in the "Resolution," after he was killed by the savages, and died while in command of that vessel.

more goods. To say that I, and Ham, and Kate have much missed you, and would much have you again, is, or at least ought to be no news to you—it is true however. . . . .
Adieu,
Yrs sincerely,
S. CRISP.

* * * * * *

The present *Lyon* of the times, according to the author of "the Placid Man's" term, is Omy, the native of Otaheite; and next to him, the present object is Mr. Bruce, a gentleman who has been abroad twelve years, and spent four of them in Abyssinia and other places in Africa, where no Englishman before has gained admission. His adventures are very marvellous. He is expected to publish them, and I hope he will. He is very intimate with the Stranges, and one evening called here with Miss Strange. His figure is almost gigantic! he is the tallest man I ever saw;[1] but well made, neither fat or lean in proportion to his amazing height. I cannot say I was charmed with him; for he seems rather arrogant, and to have so large a share of good opinion of himself, as to have nothing left for the rest of the world but contempt. Yet his self-approbation is not that of a *fop;* on the contrary, he is a very manly character, and looks so dauntless and intrepid, so that I believe he could never in his life know what fear meant.

* * * * * *

September 1st.

My father received a note last week from Lord Sandwich, to invite him to meet Lord Orford and the Otaheitan at Hinchinbrook, and to pass a week with him there; and also to bring with him *his son, the Lieutenant.* This has filled us with hope for some future good to my sailor-brother, who is the capital friend and favourite of Omai, or Omiah, or Omy,

---

[1] Bruce was six feet four.

or Jack, for my brother says he is called by all those names on board, but chiefly by the last appellation, *Jack!*

* * * * * *

Chesington, Saturday, Sept.

Willingly, my dearest Susy, do I comply with your request of *journalizing* to you during my stay at this place. This dear, dear place where we have all been so happy! Our dearest father is already better; our delightful Daddy is in high spirits at his arrival, and of me his reception was so kind—kind—kind—that it has beaten at my heart ever since. Mrs. Hamilton and Kitty are joyous also. Mrs. Simmons[1] as usual, vulgar and forward; her daughter struggling to be polite, and Mrs. Moore contentedly at the head of stupidity.

I have no adventures to communicate. Mlle. Rosat is just what she was, sensible, reserved, civil, and silent. Mlle. Courvoisyois, who is newly arrived at Chesington on a visit to Mlle. Rosat, seems to be good-natured and agreeable enough; but to have what may be called a merry heart and shallow head! She laughs eternally; neither her own illness nor other people's can make her grave even a moment. She speaks very good English for a French woman; for so she is as to language, though born in Switzerland.

One thing which diverts me a good deal, and which is equally at least a diversion to Mlle. Rosat, is that not a soul in the house can pronounce Mlle. Courvoisyois' name, except Mr. Crisp, and *he* never will, as he always calls her *petite méchante*. Mrs. Hamilton calls her Miss *Creussy*; Mrs. Simmons Miss *what's your name*; Mrs. Moore calls her Miss *Creusevoye*; and

---

[1] Under Captain John Simmons, of the "Cerberus," James Burney served for a time in the following year, on the North America Station. On the 12th of April, 1782, Simmons was Captain of the "Formidable," the flagship of Admiral Rodney, who that day won his famous victory over Comte de Grasse, off Dominica. Some who knew Captain Simmons thought him the original of Fanny's Captain Mirvan, nor does she quite disclaim it, as she merely says that he was not in her mind at the time when she wrote.

Kitty, to cut the matter as short as possible, and to save trouble, only says Miss *Crewe*.

Mrs. Simmons, who because she can smoak the folly of her sister Moore, who is quite silly, thinks *herself* a prodigy of wisdom; and I dare say would think herself an immediate descendant from Minerva, if she had ever happened to hear of such a person; for her conceit raises her to the utmost height of her *conceptions*. Well; this wise lady held poor Mlle. Courvoisyois more cheap than any other person in the house; and I really believe she took a dislike to her, from finding she could not pronounce her name. When she spoke of her, it was generally in this manner, "That Miss *What's her name*, there, Miss *Fid-Fad*, as I call her. There she has been laughing, till she made my head ache ready to split. Yet I gave her a good *set-too* just now. I suppose she won't like me,—who cares? Not I, I promise her! I think she's the greatest fool that ever *I see*. She should not be a tutoress to my cat."

I have almost, though very undesignedly, occasioned a *grand fracas* in the house, by a ridiculous conceit which I *sported* for the amusement of Miss Simmons and Kitty. We had been laughing at some of poor Mrs. Moore's queer phrases, and then I mentioned some of Kitty's own. Her Cousin joined in laughing violently; and as I proceeded from one absurd thing to another, I took Miss Simmons herself to task upon some speeches she had made; and in conclusion I told them I intended to write a *Treatise upon Politeness* for their edification. All this was taken as it was said, in sport, and we had much laughing in consequence of my scheme, which I accompanied by a thousand flighty speeches and *capricios*, for you know what my spirits are at Liberty Hall, Chesington. After this, upon all indecorums, real or fanciful, I referred Miss Simmons and Kitty to my book for instruction, and it became a sort of standard joke among us, to which we made every thing that passed applicable, and Miss Simmons who enjoyed hearing me *run on* as she called it, introduced the subject perpetually. Indeed, the chief amusement I have made myself when with the two cousins, has been indulging liberally in that kind of rhodomontade discourse, that it will be easy to you to recollect some instances of. . . . All this did very well among ourselves; but the day after the Simmons's left us, while we were at dinner, Kitty blundered out, "Good people, I tell you what;—*she's* going to write something about Politeness, *and that*, and it's to be for all of you, here at *Chiss*, to mend your manners."

"I'm sure," cried Mlle. Courvoisyois, "we shall be very much *oblige* to the lady."

"I'll subscribe to the book with all my heart," cried Mlle. Rosat. "I beg leave to bespeak the first copy. I am sure it will be a very useful work."

"She's to tell you all what you're to do," resumed Kitty, "and how you're to do this—and all that."

"Exceedingly well defined, Kate," said Mr. Crisp; "but pray, Fannikin, what shall you *particularly* treat of?"

"Oh, Sir," cried I, "all parts of life! it will be a very comprehensive work; and I hope you'll all have a book."

"Pray, what will it cost?" demanded Mrs. Moore, seriously.

"A guinea a volume," answered I, "and I hope to comprize it in nine volumes."

"Oh, lud!" exclaimed she, "I sha'nt give *no such money* for it."

"*I* will have two copies," said Mlle. Rosat, "let it cost what it will. I am sure it will be exceeding well executed."

"I do'nt doubt *in least*," cried Mlle. Courvoisyois, "of politeness of Miss Burney; but I should like to see the book, to see if I should *sought* the same."

"Will it be like Swift's 'Polite Conversation'?" said Mr. Crisp.

"I intend to dedicate it to Miss Notable,"[1] answered I; "it

---

[1] "Miss Notable" is the lively heroine of Swift's ironical little piece "Polite Conversation," which runs side by side with his "Directions to Servants." One has actually been taken as a minute account of the manners, "amusements, and occupations of persons of fashion in London," in Swift's own time; the other, as a bad little book, teaching the ignorant to do wrong. In fact, one is a summary of every blunder, fault, or vice, which Swift had known silly, mischievous, or wicked servants (especially *Irish* servants) capable of committing; the other, a collection of all the pert, vulgar "smart answers," "repartees, or

will contain all the *newest fashioned* regulations. In the first place, you are never again to cough."

"Not to *cough?*" exclaimed every one at once; "but how are you to help it?"

"As to *that*," answered I, "I am not very clear about it myself, as I own I am guilty sometimes of doing it; but it is as much a mark of ill breeding, as it is to *laugh*; which is a thing that Lord Chesterfield has stigmatized."

"Lud! well, for my part," said Mrs. Moore, "I think there's no fun without it."

"Not for to *laugh*," exclaimed Courvoisyois, with hands uplifted, "well, I declare I *did* not *sought* of such a *sing*."

"And pray," said Mr. Crisp, making a fine affected face, "may you *simper?*"

"You may *smile* Sir," answered I; "but to *laugh* is quite abominable; though not quite so bad as *sneezing*, or *blowing the nose*."

"Why, if you do'nt blow it," cried Kitty, taking me literally, "what *are* you to do with it?"

I pretended to be too much shocked to answer her.

"But pray, is it permitted," said Mr. Crisp, very drily, "to *breathe*."

"*That* is not yet, I believe, quite exploded," answered I; "but I shall be more exact about it in my book of which I shall send *you six* copies. I shall only tell you in general, that whatever is natural, plain, or easy, is entirely banished from polite circles."

"And all is *sentiment* and *delicacy*, hey, Fannikin?"

"No, Sir; not so," replied I with due gravity; "*sentiments* and *sensations* were the *last* fashion; they are now done with; they were *laughed* out of use, just before laughing was

---

rejoinders," which he had been able to rake together, with some details of bad manners to match the phrases. In a preface (as ironical as the rest), Swift tells us that "the flowers of wit, fancy, wisdom, humour, and politeness scattered in this volume, amount to 1,074." Compare Fanny's projected book on politeness with her sarcastic " Directions for coughing, sneezing, or moving, before the King and Queen," contained in a letter to her sister Hetty, written at Windsor, on the 17th of Dec., 1785, before she had any notion that she was for years to be subject to what she ridicules.

abolished. The present *ton* is *refinement;* nothing *is to be,* that *has been;* all things are to be *new polished* and *highly finished.* I shall explain this fully in my book."

"Well; for my part," cried Mrs. Moore, who took every word I said seriously; "I don't desire to read *no* such *tiddling* books. I'm very well as I am."

It's well you think so, thought I.

"Pray, Ma'am," said Mlle. Rosat, "is it within the rules of politeness to *pick the teeth?*"

"Provided you have a little *glass* to look in before you," answered I, and rose to go up stairs to my father.[1]

"Pray, Ma'am," cried she again, "is it polite, when a person talks, if you don't understand them, to look at another, as if you said, 'What nonsense she says.'"

"I should imagine not," answered I, moving off alarmed, as I found these questions were pointed against poor Kitty.

"Pray, is it polite, Ma'am," cried Mlle Rosat again, "to make *signs* and *to whisper?*"

"I suppose not," cried I, opening the door.

"And *pray,*" cried Kitty, colouring, "is it *pelite* to be *touchy?* and *has* people any business to suspect *and* to be suspicious?"

"Oh!" cried I, "these are things that don't come into my cognisance;"—and away I ran.

My father, however, sent me down again, to ask Mr. Crisp up stairs to play at backgammon. I found them all silent. Mr. Crisp went up immediately, and presently every body went out, but Kitty, Courvoisyois, and me. I told Kitty, who I saw was swelling with anger, that I began to be sorry she had mentioned the Book. "Oh! it does not signify," cried she, bursting into a violent fit of tears. "I don't mind, if people will be cross; it's nothing to me. I'm sure I'm as obliging as I can—and if people don't like me they must let it alone."

---

[1] This may be compared with the passage in "Sense and Sensibility," in which the Dashwoods first see the "puppy" Robert Ferrars, in a London jeweller's shop, "debating for a quarter of an hour over every tooth-pick-case . . . . deciding on all the *different horrors* of the different tooth-pick cases," etc.

We tried to pacify her; Courvoisyois gave her a glass of wine, and insisted on her drinking it. "I did not *sought*, said she, "that Miss Rosat did mean you. I am sure she always says you are very good."

"You're very obliging, Miss *Crewe*," cried Kitty, sobbing; "but I can *see* as well as other people; and I know what Miss *Rossiter* meant"—[N.B. she calls her *Rossiter*; no one knows why, not even herself.] "because the thing was, that one day my cousin and I were together, and so *Rossiter* came in, and I'm sure I did nothing more than I do at this moment; my cousin can witness for me; but she went out of the room in a huff; nobody knows for what; and then afterwards she goes and tells my Aunt Hamilton, that when she came into the room, I said '*Humph!*' Now, I purtest I never said *no such* a thing; and so my cousin would say, if she was here; for I should scorn it; and though I a'nt so *pelite* as Miss Rossiter, I'm sure I always try to be as obliging as I can, and if ever she wants any thing at any time, I'm always ready to go for her."

"I'm sure I always *hear* her say so, Miss Cooke," cried Mlle. Courvoisyois, "I *sink* you are certainly *of* a mistake."

I was very glad she spoke, as I could not; for the account of the cause of the disagreement was told so very ridiculously, that it required a painful effort to forbear laughing out; it was all I could do to be decent. However, after some time we consoled her, and made her dry up her tears, which she did, all the while protesting that "*she would not say such a thing as Humph for the world*," and that "*nobody was further from it.*"

They are now upon very good terms again. Poor Kitty has as honest and worthy a heart as any human being, and cannot bear to be thought ill of. Yet I can never cease to be astonished, that she can have lived so many years under the same roof with such a man as Mr. Crisp, and yet be so *very* unformed, [really] vulgar. I often wish it was possible to set down, as they occur, the strange speeches which she makes, as I am sure they would highly divert your own quaint fancy, though not so quaint as your humble servant's.

Thursday, Goose-Day.

How I wish you were here, my Susette! I have returned to all my old original rattling spirits, that used to divert you so much at this dear old Liberty Hall, Chesington,—our beloved Mr. Crisp, chieftain—

* * * * * *

Newton House St. Martin's Street,
Leicester Fields.
Oct. 18th.

My father, very much recovered, and myself left Chesington ten days ago. We came immediately to this house, which we propose calling *Newton House*, or *The Observatory*, or something that sounds *grand*, as Sir Isaac's identical observatory is still subsisting, and we show it, to all our visitors, as our principal Lyon. I am very much pleased with the Mansion.[1]

* * * * * *

The first opera [of the season] was performed last Tuesday. The morning before Mrs. Brooke called here, and very civilly invited my mother, Susy, and me to her box. We were very desirous to hear the new singer Rauzzini, of whom my father has said so much in his German Tour; and we agreed to wait upon Mrs. Brooke about seven. Accordingly we went. Her house in Market Lane, by means of divers turnings and windings, has a passage to the Opera House. We intended to

---

[1] When Dr. Burney entered this house (which is now marked by a tablet, set up by the Society of Arts), Newton's Observatory "overlooked all London and its environs." It was a glazed turret, that is, a mere framework of small panes; with a small fire-place and chimney, and a cupboard. On the little landing was a cupboard for coals. Dr. Burney's first act was to repair it, "at a considerable expense." Four years later, in a hurricane, the leaden roof and glazed sides were whirled away; and he all but reconstructed it, in his ardour for Newton's memory. If his name has no place on the recent tablet, the more is the pity. J. T. Smith describes the house as being No. 36, "next door to Orange Street Chapel, where I have frequently heard Mr. Toplady preach."

have sat in her box and have seen only her; but when we went, we found she was up stairs with Mrs. Yates! and she immediately asked us to go up stairs with her. This we declined; but she would not be refused, and we were obliged to follow her. We were led up a noble stair-case, that brought us to a most magnificent apartment, which is the same that belonged to the famous Heideger[1] and since his time has always been the property of the head manager of the Opera. Here we saw Mrs. Yates, seated like a stage queen, surrounded with gay courtiers and dressed with the utmost elegance and brilliancy. What most provoked me was, that though our visit was only to Mrs. Brooke, ... yet, as we entered the room, our names were announced in an *audible* voice. All I can comfort myself with is, that it was only at the Opera-House that we met, and that of *late years* Mrs. Yates has had no harm said of her. . . . .

Mrs. Yates, to a very fine figure joins a very handsome face, though not now in her *première jeunesse;* but the expression of her face is infinitely haughty and hard. With an *over done* civility, as soon as our names were spoken, she rose from her seat hastily, and rather *rushed* towards, than meerly advanced to meet us; but I doubt not it was meant as the very *pink of politeness.* As to poor Mr. Yates, he presumed not to take the liberty in his own house to act any other part than that of waiter, in which capacity he arranged the chairs. We were not absolutely seated, when the door was opened by an officer. Mrs. Yates again started from her seat, and flew to receive him, crying, "General Cholmondeley, I am happy to see

---

[1] John James Heidegger, a Swiss, was the Manager, and principal lessee of the Opera House in the Haymarket, and up to 1734 in partnership with Handel. Horace Walpole describes him as being "the caterer for public amusements" of his day; in fact, the male counter-part of Mrs. Cornelys. He was the ugliest man of the time. In "the Author's Farce," which contains a Puppet-Show, called "the Pleasures of the Town" (1729), Fielding brings him in as "Count Ugly," saying,

"I disdain
O'er the poor ragged tribe of bards to reign.
Me did my stars to happier fates prefer,
Sur-intendant des plaisirs d'Angleterre;
If *Masquerates* you have, let those be mine."

you!"[1] Then turning to her *Jerry*, "Mr. Yates, pray, get the General a chair." Mr. Yates obeyed, and then we rose to go to the Opera. We were to sit in a box by ourselves.[2]

[An account of Omai, which is given in a letter to Mr. Crisp, is so much more full than that in the Diary, that it has been thought advisable to print the letter rather than that passage; especially as it has not been published in the "Memoirs of Dr. Burney." The notice of Omai in that book (p. 28, vol. i.) is compiled from this letter, and from this Diary, with some additional details from memory. More than the first page of this letter is given to complaints that Mr. Crisp has not yet returned the "Tingmouth Journal." It was written in "St. Martin's Street on Thursday night," and received by Mr. Crisp on December 1, 1774.][3]

---

[1] The second Earl of Cholmondeley had been kind to Dr. Burney's father. This was James, his second son, who is often named by Horace Walpole, whose own sister married the third Earl of the name, brother to James.

[2] Mrs. Yates (who had before been Mrs. Graham) was the second wife of "Dick Yates," a popular actor, to whom Garrick brought her as a pupil. She had shown intelligence as an actress, but Garrick thought she had not experience enough to play the heroine in Arthur Murphy's "Orphan of China;" indeed, he had at first refused that drama. Murphy gave the discouraged actress of his discouraged play his own instructions how to act in it; finally both the tragedy and the actress gained a great success. Mrs. Yates was Romney's "Tragic Muse" in a picture, before Reynolds painted his majestic Siddons; and, it was said, that as Romney was to Reynolds, so was the Tragic Muse Yates to the Tragic Muse Siddons. Mrs. Yates was playing "sentimental heroines" when Foote very nearly produced her on his stage as "The Handsome Housemaid, or Piety in Pattens," in mimicry of her manner of acting, and of Cradock's dull "Zobéide," and Cumberland's "Fashionable Lover." Her husband, whom Fanny calls "Jerry" (see Foote's "Mayor of Garratt,") survived her until 1796, and is said to have died at the age of 89, "from getting into a violent passion." Yet, after all, if (as our Mrs. Harris says) she played well the charming Bellario in the fine play of "Philaster," she may have surpassed Sarah Siddons, who was too stately for Violas or Rosalinds—tender ladies in male attire for the nonce—to whom Beaumont and Fletcher's Bellario is a younger sister.

[3] The narrative in the diary begins thus: "What is my present inducement to resume my pen is to write an account of a visit we have received from Omai, the native of Uliteja, brought from the South Seas, &c. .... The visit of Omai was at the invitation of my brother, who has not only been his shipmate and companion, but who speaks the language, which is the same as that of Otaheite, with great ease and fluency."

[MISS BURNEY TO MR. CRISP.]

St. Martin's Street, Thursday night.

* * * * * *

I have seen Omai, and if I am, as I intend to be, very minute in my account, will you shake hands and be friends? "Yes, you little Devil you! so *to business*, and no more words." Very well, I obey. You must know, then, in the first place, that glad as I was to see this great personage, I extremely regretted not having *you* of the party, as you had half promised you would be,—and as I am sure you would have been extremely well pleased, and that the Journey would have more than answered to you: but the notice was so extremely short it was impossible. Now to facts.

My brother went last Monday to the play of Isabella at Drury Lane—He sat in one of the Upper Boxes, from whence he spied Omai and Mr. Banks—upon which he crossed * * * * over to speak to his friend. Omai received him with a hearty shake of the hand, and made room for him by his side. Jem asked Mr. Banks when he could see him to dinner? Mr. B. said that he believed he was engaged every day till the holydays, which he was to spend at Hinchinbrooke. * * * * However on Tuesday night, very late, there came a note which I will write down. It was directed to my brother.— Omai presents his Compts. to Mr. Burney, and if it is agreeable and convenient to him, he will do himself the honour of dining with Mr. Burney to-morrow, but if it is not so, Omai will wait upon Mr. Burney some other time that shall suit him better. Omai begs to have an answer, and that if he is to come, begs Mr. Burney will fetch him.

Early on Wednesday morning, Jem called at Mr. Banks, with my father's compts to him, and to Dr. Solander, and begging their company also. But they were engaged at the Royal Society.[1]

---

[1] At a dinner, "where my father himself would have been, but on account of his ill state of health."—DIARY.

Mr. Strange and Mr. Hayes, at their own motion, came to dinner to meet our guest.[1] We did not dine till four. But Omai came at two, and Mr. Banks and Dr. Solander brought him, in order to make a short visit to my father. They were all just come from the House of Lords, where they had taken Omai to hear the King make his speech from the Throne.

For my part, I had been confined up stairs for three days— however, I was much better, and obtained leave to come down, though very much wrapt up, and *quite a figure*, but I did not chuse to appear till Mr. Banks and Dr. Solander were gone. I found Omai seated on the great chair, and my brother next to him, and talking Otaheite as fast as possible. You cannot suppose how fluently and easily Jem speaks it. Mama and Susy and Charlotte were opposite. As soon as there was a *cessation* of talk, Jem introduced me, and told him I was another sister. He rose, and make a very fine bow, and then seated himself again. But when Jem went on, and told him that I was not well, he again directly rose, and muttering something of the *fire*, in a very polite *manner*, without *speech* insisting upon my taking his seat,—and he *would* not be refused. He then drew his chair next to mine, and looking at me with an expression of pity said " very well tomorrow-morrow? "—I imagine he meant *I hope* you will be very well in *two or three morrows*—and when I shook my head, he said " *no? O very bad!* " When Mr. Strange and Mr. Hayes were introduced to him, he paid his compliments with great politeness to them, which he has found a method of doing without *words*.

As he had been to Court, he was very fine. He had on a suit of Manchester velvet, lined with white satten, a *bag*, lace ruffles, and a very handsome sword which the King had given to him.[2] He is tall and very well made, much darker

---

[1] In the Diary it runs: " This *lyon* of *lyons*, for such he now is of this town."

[2] Mr. Cradock tells us that Omai soon found out that his suit was only of *English* velvet, not of velvet from Genoa, in which the gentlemen were dressed between whom he sat at the dinner given by Lord Sandwich at the Admiralty. He was very angry at the distinction of velvets made between himself, who never had a coat at all, and

than I expected to see him, but has a pleasing countenance.[1]

He makes *remarkable* good bows—not for *him*, but for *anybody*, however long under a Dancing Master's care. Indeed he seems to shame Education, for his manners are so extremely graceful, and he is so polite, attentive, and easy, that you would have thought he came from some foreign Court.[2] You others, and said so to Mr. Cradock and to Mr. Bates.—"None," (say the French) "are so dainty about their food as those who have eaten their potatoes raw before they came into service." The Diary adds "he has long left off his Otahiete garments, which were, I suppose, in every respect improper for England."

[1] "He is tall, swarthy, and young, extremely well made, and a fine figure, and though by no means *handsome*, he has a good and pleasing countenance."—DIARY.

[2] Captain Cook gives this account of Omai. "Before we quitted this island" (Huaheine), "Captain Furneaux agreed to receive on board his ship a young man named Omai, a native of Ulietea, where he had had some property, of which he had been dispossessed by the people of Bolabola. I at first rather wondered that Captain Furneaux would encumber himself with this man, who, in my opinion, was not a proper sample of the inhabitants of these happy islands, not having any advantage of birth, or acquired rank; nor being eminent in shape, figure, or complexion: for their people of the first rank are much fairer, and usually better behaved, and more intelligent, than the middling class of people, among whom Omai is to be ranked. I have, however, since my arrival in England been convinced of my error: for excepting his complexion (which is undoubtedly of a deeper hue than that of the *Earees*, or gentry, who, as in other countries, live a more luxurious life, and are less exposed to the sun), I much doubt whether any other of the natives would have given more general satisfaction by his behaviour among us. Omai has most certainly a good understanding, quick parts, and honest principles . . . . as he was very watchful into the manners and conduct of the persons of rank who honoured him with their protection, he was sober and modest. . . . . During his stay among us . . . . his principal patrons were the Earl of Sandwich, Mr. Banks, and Dr. Solander." It may be added that, although Banks and Solander had not gone with Cook on his second voyage, they at once patronised this young Otaheitan on his landing. George Colman, the younger, gives an amusing account of meeting them with Omai, when his father took him as a lad on a visit to Captain Phipps (Lord Mulgrave), in Yorkshire. Sir Joshua Reynolds painted a fine portrait of "Omiah." Ulietea is one of the six islands which Cook named "the Society Islands," because they lay near each other. According to the newspapers, the French flag has recently been set upon Omai's Huaheine.

will think that I speak in a *high* style; but I assure you there was but one opinion about him.

At dinner I had the pleasure of sitting next to him, as my cold kept me near the fire. The moment he was helped, he presented his plate to me, which, when I declined, he had not the *over-shot* politeness to offer *all round*, as I have seen some people do, but took it quietly again. He eat heartily and committed not the slightest blunder at table, neither did he do anything *awkwardly* or *ungainly*. He found by the turn of the conversation, and some wry faces, that a joint of beef was not roasted enough, and therefore when he was helped, he took great pains to assure mama that he liked it, and said two or three times—" *very dood,*—very *dood.*" It is very odd, but true, that he can pronounce the *th*, as in *thank you*, and the *w*, as in *well*, and yet cannot say *g*, which he uses a *d* for. But I now recollect, that in the beginning of a word, as *George*, he *can* pronounce it. He took a good deal of notice of Dick, yet was not quite so well pleased with him, as I had expected him to be.

During dinner, he called for some drink. The man, not understanding what he would have, brought the porter. We saw that he was wrong, however, Omai was too well bred to send it back, he took it in his hand, and the man then brought him the small beer;—he laughed, and said—" Two !" —however, he sent off the *small* beer, as the *worse* of the *two*. Another time he called for *port-wine*. And when the bread was handed, he took two bits, and laughed and said " *one*—two " He even observed *my abstinence*, which I think you would have laughed at, for he turned to me with some surprize, when dinner was almost over, and said " *no wine ?* "

Mr. Hayes asked him, through Jem, how he liked the King and his Speech. He had the politeness to try to answer in English and *to* Mr. Hayes—and said " *very well*, King George ! "

After dinner, mama gave the king for a toast. He made a bow, and said " *Thank you, madam* " and then *tost off* " *King George !* "

He told Jem that he had an engagement at six o'clock, to go with Dr. Solander to see no less than twelve ladies.—Jem translated this to us—he understands enough of English to find out when he is talked of, in general, and so he did now, and he laughed heartily, and began to count, with his fingers, in order to be understood—" 1, 2, 3, 4, 5, 6, 7, 8, 9, 10—*twelve—woman!* " said he.

When Mr. Banks and Dr. Solander went away, he said to them *Good-bye—good-bye*. He never looked at his dress, though it was on for the first time. Indeed he appears to be a perfectly rational and intelligent man, with an understanding far superior to the common race of *us cultivated gentry*. He could not else have borne so well the way of Life into which he is thrown, without some practice.

When the man brought him the *two* beers, I forgot to mention that in returning them, one hit against the other, and occasioned a little sprinkling. He was *shocked* extremely —indeed I was afraid for his fine cloaths, and would have pin'd up the wet table cloth, to prevent its hurting them— but he would not permit me; and, by his *manner* seem'd to *intreat* me not to trouble myself!—however he had thought enough to spread his handkerchief over his knee.

Before six, the coach came. Our man came in and said " Mr. Omai's servant." He heard it at once, and answered " *very well*." He kept his seat about five minutes after, and then rose and got his hat and sword. My father happening to be talking to Mr. Strange, Omai stood still, neither chusing to interrupt him, nor to make his compliments to any body else first. When he was disengaged, Omai went up to him, and made an exceeding fine bow—the same to mama—then seperately to every one in the company, and then went out with Jem to his coach.

He must certainly possess an uncommon share of observation and attention. I assure you every body was delighted with him. I only wished I could have spoke his language. Lord Sandwich has actually studied it so as to make himself understood in it. His *hands* are very much *tattooed*, but his face is not at all. He is *by no means* handsome, though I like his *countenance*.

The conversation of our house has turned ever since upon Mr. *Stanhope* and *Omai*—the first with all the advantage of

Lord Chesterfield's instructions, brought up at a great school. introduced at fifteen to a Court, taught all possible accomplishments from an infant, and having all the care, expence, labour, and benefit of the best education that any man can receive,—proved after it all a meer *pedantic booby* ;—the second with no tutor but Nature, changes, after he is grown up, his dress, his way of life, his diet, his country and his friends ;— and appears in a *new world* like a man [who] had all his life studied *the Graces*, and attended with [unre]mitting application and diligence to form his manners, and to render his appearance and behaviour *politely easy*, and thoroughly *well bred!* I think this shows how much more *nature* can do without *art*, than *art* with all her refinement unassisted by *nature*.[1]

If I have been too *prolix*, you must excuse me, because it is wholly owing to the great curiosity I have heard you express for whatever concerns Omai. My father desires his love to you, and says that if you will but come to town, as soon as Omai returns from Hinchinbrooke, he will promise you that you shall still have a meeting with him.

[This letter is endorsed by Mr. Crisp, "December 1." Fanny appears to have sat down and written this letter of more than seven quarto pages that very Thursday night.]

* * * * * *

Not having opportunity of proceeding in my *ingenious* narration, it has laid by so long, that I have now forgot all

---

[1] Boswell tells us that Dr. Johnson was in company with Omai, after he had been some time in this country. Johnson was struck with the elegance of his behaviour, and accounted for it thus : " Sir, he had passed his time, while in England, only in the best company ; so that all that he had acquired of our manners was genteel. As a proof of this, Sir, Lord Mulgrave and he dined one day at Streatham ; they sat with their backs to the light fronting me, so that I could not see distinctly ; and there was so little of the savage in Omai, that I was afraid to speak to either, lest I should mistake one for the other." This compliment to Omai must, however, be qualified with what Mrs. Thrale says of Lord Mulgrave . . . " Rough as a boatswain, and fond of coarse merriment, approaching to ill manners, one never knew what he would say next."

I intended to have added, and I cannot give myself the trouble of recollection, not being in a prosing humour. I shall therefore take an abrupt and rather cavalier leave of this adventure (*sic*); and as I am already much in arrears with some *new* ones, I shall reserve all my forces for those by way of *amende honorable*—to whom? why to myself, that is to Nobody! Heigh-ho! poor me! Are Nobody and I one and the same person?

END OF VOL. I.

COSIMO is a specialty publisher for independent authors, not-for-profit organizations, and innovative businesses, dedicated to publishing books that inspire, inform, and engage readers around the world.

Our mission is to create a smart and sustainable society by connecting people with valuable ideas. We offer authors and organizations full publishing support, while using the newest technologies to present their works in the most timely and effective way.

COSIMO BOOKS offers fine books that inspire, inform and engage readers on a variety of subjects, including personal development, socially responsible business, economics and public affairs.

COSIMO CLASSICS brings to life unique and rare classics, representing a wide range of subjects that include Business, Economics, History, Personal Development, Philosophy, Religion & Spirituality, and much more!

COSIMO REPORTS publishes reports that affect your world, from global trends to the economy, and from health to geopolitics.

COSIMO B2B offers custom editions for historical societies, museums, companies and other organizations interested in offering classic books to their audiences, customized with their own logo and message. **COSIMO B2B** also offers publishing services to organizations, such as media firms, think tanks, conference organizers and others who could benefit from having their own imprint.

FOR MORE INFORMATION CONTACT US AT
INFO@COSIMOBOOKS.COM

- if you are a book lover interested in our current list of titles
- if you represent a bookstore, book club, or anyone else interested in special discounts for bulk purchases
- if you are an author who wants to get published
- if you represent an organization or business seeking to publish books and other publications for your members, donors, or customers.

COSIMO BOOKS ARE ALWAYS
AVAILABLE AT ONLINE BOOKSTORES

VISIT COSIMOBOOKS.COM
BE INSPIRED, BE INFORMED

Milton Keynes UK
Ingram Content Group UK Ltd.
UKHW011506050524
442175UK00001B/59